Captives in Blue

Captives in Blue

The Civil War Prisons of the Confederacy

Roger Pickenpaugh

THE UNIVERSITY OF ALABAMA PRESS
Tuscaloosa

The University of Alabama Press
Tuscaloosa, Alabama 35487-0380
uapress.ua.edu

Hardcover edition published 2013.
Paperback edition published 2020.
eBook edition published 2013.

Typeface: Garamond

Cover image: *Above*, Richmond's Castle Thunder prison, courtesy National Archives, Washington, DC; *below*, Belle Isle, Richmond, Virginia, courtesy Massachusetts MOLLUS Collection, United States Army Military History Institute, Carlisle Barracks, PA
Cover design: Michele Myatt Quinn

Paperback ISBN: 978-0-8173-6006-1

A previous edition of this book has been cataloged by the Library of Congress.
ISBN: 978-0-8173-1783-6 (cloth)
E-ISBN: 978-0-8173-8651-1

To Patrick Harrison Brooks

Contents

Acknowledgments

One incurs a number of debts writing a book of this sort. As with so many other projects, my greatest debt is to my wife, Marion. Once again she spent countless hours at libraries and archives, working skillfully and tirelessly at the task she refers to as a "treasure hunt." At the other end of the process, she again got out her packs of note cards to prepare the index.

My mother, Fern Pickenpaugh, again served as a keen proofreader. More important, she instilled in me from an early age the importance of proper grammar. Mistakes the reader encounters will be there despite her efforts.

Having two lovely stepdaughters and their families strategically placed in northern Virginia makes research trips a blessing. My thanks again go out to Anya Crum, Jocelyn and Patrick Brooks, and grandchildren Parker Dianne and Patrick Harrison Brooks. More recently I have also had the pleasure of spending time with Anya's boyfriend, Mike Huie.

My sister and late brother-in-law, Jill and Gene Stuckey, offered a friendly base of operations when my research took me to Georgia. I miss Gene as an eager proofreader and even more as a friend.

Locally, members of the Noble County Authors' Guild helped with skilled proofreading and appreciated support. Thanks to Gary Williams, Mary Lou Podlasiak, Ken Williams, and Jim Leeper. Andrea VanScyoc, a gifted former student and dear friend, proofread the manuscript and assisted with the index. Further from home, Dr. James M. Gillespie, author of the excellent *Andersonvilles of the North*, read most of the manuscript and made a number of excellent suggestions.

Dr. Rick Nelson of the Ohio State University Hospitals read the entire manuscript and offered valuable suggestions concerning the health of the prisoners.

Countless librarians and archivists helped make this book possible; and in almost every case they did so with extreme courtesy. Among those providing expert assistance were Dr. Richard Sommers and Rich Baker, United States Army Military History Institute; Alan Marsh, Jay Womack, and Fred Boyles, Andersonville National Historic Site; Heather Turner, Julie Holcomb, and Rosalie Meier, Navarro College; Sean Casey, Boston Public Library; Matthew Turi, University of North Carolina; Dee Anna Grimsrud, Wisconsin Historical Society; Christie Moraza, Connecticut Historical Society; Zachary Elder and Elizabeth Dunn, Duke University; Anne Causey and Margaret Hrabe, University of Virginia; Jeff Flannery, Library of Congress; Russ Horton, Wisconsin Veterans Museum; Brigid Shields, Minnesota Historical Society; Mary Jo Fairchild, South Carolina Historical Society; Glenna Schroeder-Lein, Abraham Lincoln Presidential Library; Marie Cunningham, Bentley Historical Library; Janet R. Bloom and Barbara DeWolfe, William L. Clements Library; Marjorie Strong and Bernadette Harrington, Vermont Historical Society; Peggy Powell and Jeffrey Marshall, University of Vermont; Jill D'Andrea, National Archives; Charles Scott, State Historical Society of Iowa; Joy Dugan, Library of Virginia; Jennifer Vipperman, Virginia Tech; Charles Mutschler, Eastern Washington University; and Greg Wheeler, Delaware State Archives. To any I have omitted, I apologize.

In many communities located near Confederate prisons, library staffs are helping preserve their local Civil War heritage. Among those who assisted me are Margaret Collar, Drs. Bruce & Lee Foundation Library, Florence, South Carolina; Muriel McDowell-Jackson and Christopher Stokes, Middle Georgia Regional Library, Macon; and Kathy Petrucelli and Vanessa Sterling, Rowan Public Library, Salisbury, North Carolina.

Closer to home, I am very much indebted to the staff at Muskingum University Library in New Concord, Ohio. They handled numerous interlibrary loan requests, saving me much time and expense. Thank you, Zelda Patterson, Nicole Robinson, Jamie Berilla, and Elaine Funk. Thanks also to a dear departed friend, Mary Williams, who introduced me to this talented staff.

As always, the people at the University of Alabama Press made a difficult process much easier. Their courtesy and professionalism are greatly appreciated.

Captives in Blue

I

"We all feel deeply on their account"

Richmond Prisons, 1861

At first they came in a trickle. In June 1861, only a few weeks after the shots at Fort Sumter plunged the United States into civil war, newspapers in Richmond, Virginia, began to report the arrival of Yankee prisoners. They came from Manassas Junction, Newport News, and other places where the two armies were feeling each other out for the battles that lay ahead. Generally there were fewer than fifteen brought in at a time. On June 15 a detachment of the Confederate army arrived from Yorktown with thirteen Union prisoners actually taken in battle. They had been captured five days earlier at the battle of Big Bethel. In reality the fight had been little more than a skirmish, lasting only about an hour. It resulted in genuine prisoners of war, however, and as the captives were taken to the Richmond customs house, according to one newspaper account, "Many of our citizens evinced some curiosity to get a peep at the captured Yankees."[1]

On July 2 the *Richmond Dispatch* reported that there were "from 75 to 100 of Old Abe's disciples" in the Confederate capital. They arrived in a city unprepared to receive them and unwilling to keep them. The Confederate Congress had voted on May 11 to move the capital from Montgomery, Alabama. On the heels of the announcement, a flood of eager Southern recruits quickly arrived in Richmond. On May 29 President Jefferson Davis and some one thousand employees of the Confederate government followed. Meanwhile, like a magnet, the new capital attracted several thousand border-state refugees, office seekers, and individuals of varying characters who saw varying forms of opportunity in the newly minted capital city. All this bustle left little time or inclination to formulate a coherent policy to deal with the trickle of military prisoners. As a result the uninvited Yankees were dealt with as they arrived. This makeshift approach would prove to be the general precedent for Southern prison policy for the rest of the war.[2]

The Confederate government never intended for its capital to be a permanent site for housing Union captives. Rather, Richmond was to serve as a temporary holding place until the Yankees could either be exchanged or shipped to established depots farther south. The June arrivals, however, pushed the number of prisoners in Richmond beyond the capacity of the jail and the customs house. This forced officials to make other arrangements. On June 25 orders emanated from military headquarters in Richmond to move all prisoners confined in the city jail to "the house lately prepared for them."[3]

"The house" was Ligon's warehouse and tobacco factory, the first of many such facilities pressed into service. The three-story building was located at the corner of Main and Twenty-fifth streets. Eager Richmond citizens flocked to the site to view the captives. They would soon have hundreds more to amuse them.[4]

On July 21, 1861, a newly christened Union army commanded by Gen. Irvin McDowell met the forces of Confederate generals P. G. T. Beauregard and Joe Johnston along Bull Run near Manassas Junction, Virginia. It was a clash of untested and virtually untrained armies. This gave the Confederates, fighting on the defensive, an advantage, and by late afternoon McDowell's army was retreating toward Washington. As the Federals withdrew, Confederate forces scooped up nearly fifty officers, one thousand enlisted men, and a handful of civilians who had ridden out to watch the anticipated glorious victory. Among the latter was one Alfred Ely, a congressman from upstate New York. The trickle was now a flood, and officials in Richmond had to scramble to find housing for the Union captives headed their way.

The man most responsible for dealing with Yankee prisoners was Brig. Gen. John Henry Winder. A career soldier, the Maryland native had risen to the rank of major in the United States Army. When secession came Winder agonized over the decision of where to place his loyalty. He finally decided to cast his lot with North Carolina, where he had lived for some thirty years. At sixty-one years of age, he was too old for a field command, but with his commission came an assignment as provost marshal general of Richmond. It was a thankless post that forced him to deal with drunken soldiers, citizens suspected of disloyalty to the Confederacy, and the assorted riffraff that had flocked to the new capital. The sudden influx of a thousand prisoners of war only added to Winder's headaches.[5]

The first large detachment of prisoners reached Richmond on the evening of July 23. There were 631 officers and men on the train. All were crammed into Ligon's warehouse. The next morning Winder visited the facility and apologized to the officers and such prominent civilians as Ely for the crowded and Spartan conditions. By the end of the day Winder had moved those prisoners to the adjacent

Howard's factory. There they gained a few items of furniture, some eating utensils, and Confederate cooks. With the two classes of prisoners separated, Winder gained a little more security.[6]

As more captives reached the city in the days that followed, the provost marshal looked for places to keep them. Among the first buildings he pressed into service was Harwood's factory. As early as June 25 the facility was being "fitted up" as a prison. By July 27 it was in use. On August 2, according to two local newspapers, there were "several hundred" wounded among the Union prisoners in Richmond. All had been receiving treatment at a hospital on Second Street. The facility had been taxed to its capacity, however, and when seventy more arrived that day, they went to Ross's factory.[7]

The next wave of Union prisoners came after the Confederate victory at the battle of Ball's Bluff, fought near Leesburg, Virginia, on October 21. On the 24th the *Richmond Examiner* announced that the city must make ready for six hundred captured Yankees. "The capacious tobacco warehouse of Robt. A Mayo, on 25th between Main and Cary streets, was thereupon engaged for their reception," the paper continued. They arrived that day in two groups. Both the *Whig* and the *Dispatch* placed the number in the first detachment at 525 and in the second at 132. Neither sheet was particularly impressed with the enemy soldiers. The *Whig* noted that the enlisted men were clad in new winter uniforms, "but their apparel could not disguise their foreign nativity and rough, repulsive, personal appearance."[8]

The very presence of the prisoners in Richmond prompted more serious concerns from local editors, who cited problems and posed questions that would plague the Confederacy for the rest of the war. On August 5 the *Whig* claimed that the "Yankees . . . are not treated with that rigor which some have supposed." To support that claim the paper noted that captives observed through prison windows seemed to be "quite contented with [their] lot." On other occasions prisoners detailed to aid their wounded comrades had crossed the street from one facility to another unescorted. Five days later the *Whig* urged Southern officials to remove all prisoners except those with severe wounds from the city's general hospital to make room for Confederate soldiers. "The brave men who have periled life and limb in defense of Southern rights deserve our first care and most attentive consideration," the paper asserted.[9]

On September 20 the *Enquirer* raised a concern that was destined to become the South's preeminent problem in dealing with Union captives. The paper noted that there were some seventeen hundred prisoners "in the several tobacco warehouses selected for that purpose." Citing unnamed officials, it estimated that their care was costing the Confederacy nearly $1,500 a day. The Confederates had already removed coffee and sugar from their daily rations. Still, the *Enquirer* claimed, the prisoners admitted that their rations were "more plentiful and nutritious than that which constituted their usual fare in the Federal camps." Soon the Richmond correspondent of the *Charleston Mercury* was reporting that a number of the citizens felt the prison rations were far too generous. "Some people think we ought to feed them on fodder or mixed horse feed," he wrote, "while others say the cheapest plan would be to destroy them outright."[10]

No paper was more vociferous in its criticism than the *Richmond Examiner.* The paper was edited by Edward Pollard, the future Confederate historian. An ardent secessionist, Pollard was equally ardent in his opposition to the administration of President Jefferson Davis. He cast a wide net with his criticism, and Winder and his prison policies were soon entangled in it.

Pollard began in July, complaining editorially that Winder was pampering the prisoners in his charge as Confederates suffered from alleged barbarity in Northern prisons. In the weeks that followed the criticism intensified. Yankee surgeons, he complained, were not only paroled to attend to their wounded, they were "living in fine style at one of our city hotels." On another occasion, the editor learned, a Union captive had been permitted to visit the home of a Richmond citizen "formerly known as a 'Union' man." While there he had written a letter to be sent through the lines. Perhaps most annoying to Pollard was the report that a black Union prisoner, taken while serving as a teamster at Manassas, had visited a local market on an errand for Union officers. The *Examiner* learned that he had been the slave of a Union man in Washington, DC. One of the man's sons, a Richmond resident, had recently been discharged from the Confederate army because of poor health. "Under the circumstances," the paper asserted, "we think this young gentleman should be allowed to take and sell the negro and appropriate the proceeds." It was a proposition that would later come to haunt the issue of prisoner exchange.[11]

When not complaining of the leniency allegedly extended toward Union captives, the press of Richmond was often reporting on guards shooting at those same captives. On July 31 the *Whig* and the *Examiner* reported that a sentinel at the Harwood prison had fired at a prisoner who was talking to someone outside the prison windows. According to the *Whig*'s account, the guard had warned him to stop but "in reply received a volley of abuse, mingled with oaths." The shot missed its mark, almost hitting another prisoner. "Some of the prisoners are very saucy and 'need taking down a peg or two,'" the paper concluded. Apparently the incident failed to register with the prisoners because two days later the *Examiner* reported a similar incident. Again the paper reported that the guard fired only after the prisoner failed to heed warnings to stay away from a window. As before, the shot missed its mark. "Perhaps the third who tries the experiment may not be so fortunate," the paper predicted.[12]

The prediction proved accurate. On September 21 Cpl. N. C. Buck of the Seventy-ninth New York Volunteers was fatally wounded as he stood by a window at Ligon's prison. Recalling the incident thirty-four years later, one of his fellow prisoners claimed the man had been shaking out his blanket. According to the *Enquirer,* Buck had "approach[ed] the window in a suspicious manner, as if contemplating an escape." The paper further reported that the guard had given "repeated commands" for the prisoner to step away before he fired.[13]

The Richmond press and the memory of a former prisoner also conflicted over an incident that occurred on the night of October 8. Both the *Dispatch* and the *Enquirer* reported on November 21 that sentinel Hezekiah Robinson had been exonerated in the shooting of Pvt. Charles Tibbetts and a second prisoner. Tibbetts died several days after being shot. His comrade suffered a wound to the arm. Richmond mayor Joseph Mayo, who tried the case, concluded that Robinson's weapon had discharged accidentally as he attempted to cap it. The *Enquirer* even claimed that, before he died, Tibbetts "expressed his conviction that the shooting was entirely accidental." According to the postwar account, however, Robinson had "deliberately raised his gun and fired" at the men.[14]

The Richmond press also devoted a great deal of space to the frequent escape attempts from the makeshift prisons. September was a particularly busy month for would-be escapees. The first attempt came the night of the 4th, when two Union soldiers dashed away from an unidentified prison. The guard force responded quickly, recapturing both and shooting one in the process. Two nights later eleven Yankees made the effort. All were captured within four days. Two of them, taken at a tavern in Essex, claimed that they had made their departure by simply walking out the front door after observing lax security at the entrance. Four captives dashed for freedom on September 14. As had been the case ten days earlier, the results were tragic. Several guards pursued them, shooting and killing two and returning the others. The Yankees nevertheless remained undeterred. Either six or seven escaped from Ligon's on the 18th, and as October dawned, three more made the attempt. At least one of them was quickly retaken.[15]

Prison officials believed they knew where to place the blame for the numerous escapes. In reporting the September 6 incident to Winder, Capt. George Gibbs, who commanded the prison guard, wrote, "I can account for the escape of prisoners only by supposing that some particular sentry was drunk on post." Gibbs contended that no amount of vigilance could keep liquor away from the guards "unless the grog-shops in the neighborhood of these prisons are closed." Through a subordinate, Winder asked Mayor Mayo to have them closed. According to Maj. J. T. W. Hairston, who later succeeded Gibbs, the problem lay as much with the capabilities of the guards themselves as it did with what they might have been drinking. Recalling events three decades later, Hairston wrote, "These new recruits were generally so awkward and inefficient that I hazard little in saying there was seldom a day while I was in charge of the rebel prison, when the whole crowd of Federal prisoners . . . might not have marched out and away with impunity."[16]

The Richmond press, of course, was quite willing to offer its own views concerning the frequency of escapes. The *Whig* complained that anyone who placed "his big toe an inch over the 'line' on the sidewalk" in front of the prisons was ordered back. Meanwhile people passing out of those same prisons left virtually unquestioned. The paper suggested, "The officers in command should reform this practice . . . as it is far more important to keep strangers in than to prevent them from entering." The *Enquirer* offered a different—and surprisingly supportive—opinion. It regretted that the escapes had prompted "repeated and sweeping charges of inefficiency and official neglect against the courteous and energetic officers" in charge of the city's prisons. Those prisons, the paper pointed out, were "scattered over a large area." They housed some 2,250 prisoners, yet were guarded by only 150 Confederates "taken indiscriminately from new regiments of untrained volunteers."[17]

Although Winder did not enter into this debate, he did complain about a lack of consistency in his staff. On July 29 he addressed the issue in a message to Gen. Samuel Cooper, the Confederacy's adjutant and inspector general. In a month's time, Winder noted, six officers had been detailed to assist him, not including those at the prisons. Only one remained. "These officers do not remain long enough to acquire sufficient knowledge of the details to assist me much," he complained.[18]

Two of the prison officers who ended up under Winder's command remained with the general at least long enough to became controversial figures. One of them was David H. Todd, a half brother of U.S. First Lady Mary Todd Lincoln. He was one of three brothers to cast his lot with the South at the outbreak of the war. On July 1, 1861, he reported for duty to Gen. Winder. He was soon given general supervision of Richmond's military prisons.[19]

An alcoholic, Todd gained a reputation for cruelty. Stories told in prison memoirs had Todd perennially heaping "foul and scurrilous abuse" upon the captives, striking and stabbing them with his sword, and denying them access to the sinks so that they fouled their quarters and themselves. Prisoners contributing their accounts to William H. Jeffrey's 1895 book *Richmond Prisons, 1861–1862* were unanimous in their disdain for Todd. "Lieutenant Todd, when upon the street near our windows one day, overheard some conversation that did not suit him," one wrote. "He drew his sword and rushing upstairs, stabbed the first man he came across, wounding him so that he had to be removed to the hospital." The same man claimed that a favorite expression of Todd's was, "I would like to cut 'Old Abe's' heart out."[20]

Published prison narratives of Civil War soldiers are notoriously unreliable, although the number of former prisoners leveling charges against Todd suggests a certain credibility. Unfortunately only one prison diarist made any reference to the lieutenant. On August 30 Lt. Charles Carroll Gray, an assistant surgeon captured at Manassas, dined out with Todd. All he wrote of the evening at the time was, "An excellent dinner and considering the company a comfortable time." When he revised his diary in 1877, Gray added that Todd was "a humbug" and that he had spent the evening relating farfetched stories about his daring military exploits.[21]

On August 26 Special Orders 134 detailed Pvt. Henry Wirz to Winder's office. At the time he was serving in the Madison Infantry, a Louisiana outfit. Wirz obviously impressed Winder. He would soon earn promotion to sergeant. Within a year he would be a captain and would be put in charge of Richmond's military prisons. Eventually he would serve Winder in Andersonville, Georgia, an assignment that would lead him to a hangman's noose. Because of Wirz's ultimate fate, postwar prisoner writings about the Swiss captain are subject to question. The views expressed by Richmond prisoners released in 1861 and early 1862 are somewhat less tainted, although they too should be considered with care. One of them, Lt. William Harris, published his memoirs of prison life in 1862. The Ball's Bluff captive generally spoke well of his captors, with the exceptions of Winder and Todd. As for the "Dutch Sergeant," Harris wrote, "He was a good fellow at times, and a very bad one at others. He would show his angular smile of half-stubborn good humor to-day, and curse us in his fragmentary English to-morrow." He did not pronounce Wirz cruel, but rather termed him "the essence of authority at the prison." On January 4, 1862, the *New York Herald* reported on the arrival at Baltimore of a group of Richmond prisoners. "There is a Swiss sergeant in charge of the prisoners, whose brutality is attested by them all," the paper reported. To back up this contention, the story asserted that he would strike prisoners over the head with the butt of his musket if they were tardy for roll call.[22]

Prison diarists were much less likely to complain about their captors than they were about the facilities in which they were housed. Among them was Pvt. Willard Wheeler of the Seventh Ohio, who was captured on August 26 at a skirmish at Cross-Lanes, near Summersville, Virginia. A week of severe marches over the Appalachians followed before Wheeler and his fellow captives clambered aboard "comfortable passenger cars" for the ride to Richmond. They reached the Confederate capital on the afternoon of September 3. "Crowds of people came around to see the live Yankees," he wrote. Neither they nor their town impressed Wheeler. "Nothing is elegant and flourishing but the houses are dingy and the streets dirty," the private observed. "The people too are coarce looking and about ⅓ are negroes."[23]

Wheeler ended up in Atkinson's factory, one of about four hundred prisoners confined there. They found three rows of tobacco presses running the entire length of the cavernous building. "We went to work to clean up this morning," he wrote, "and after much sweeping and digging we made the old room look more comfortable but still it is a mere hog pen." Rations were skimpy, a half loaf of bread and some meat in the morning and the same amount of bread with a small quantity of soup in the evening.[24]

Jonathan P. Stowe of the Fifteenth Massachusetts was among those taken captive at the battle of Ball's Bluff. Although Stowe did not identify the prison in which he was held, his rations were identical to Wheeler's. His description of the facility was similar. "We are over crowded *in three rooms that are too filthy to describe.*" Stowe and his comrades slept on the hard floor for nearly a month before the Confederates issued quilts of cotton drilling and wadding. Stowe added to his comfort by purchasing an overcoat. He could do nothing, however, about the crowding in his room, and this more than anything else was a constant annoyance. "Fine day but what of it!" he wrote on October 31. "The room is so full of tobacco smoke and also noisy with confusion, and gambling with cards etc." Stowe complained frequently of the smoky conditions, although he did see one possible silver lining, observing, "It is all smoke here and the smell of tobacco, will I hope, keep off the vermin."[25]

Among the most common complaints of the captives was the tedium of prison life. "The life in this place is exceedingly monotonous," wrote Hiram Eddy, chaplain of the Second Connecticut. "A large part eat, and drink, and sleep, and play cards, and do no more." He found little solace in the company he had to keep. "A large percentage of the officers is made up of New York hards," he informed his wife in a letter. As a result, "It is one roll of profanity from morning until late night." Stowe found his situation much the same. "Spend my time in singing, writing, thinking, trying to keep clean and lounging," he wrote. "I want to get books to read." Wheeler agreed, observing, "One day comes and goes and is followed by another and brings no change of any account. The same dreary monotony." He and his fellow prisoners at Atkinson's were so bored that scraps of 1859 newspapers they found were "read with eager interest. We read them all even to the advertisements," he enthused.[26]

On one occasion Wheeler broke the monotony by washing clothes for the prison hospital. In doing so he replaced boredom with pathos. "It is truly painful to see the poor men with amputated limbs and pale faces," Wheeler wrote in his diary. "They were wounded in most every way imaginable." The prisoners' observations of their medical treatment ranged from mildly to severely negative. "The surgeon comes in every morn. and gives some medicine, but I do not take any," Stowe wrote.[27]

Elisha R. Reed of the Second Wisconsin viewed Confederate care firsthand, and he was far more critical. Wounded at First Manassas, he was among a group of eleven prisoners captured between Centreville and Fairfax during the retreat that followed. On July 26 Reed arrived in Richmond aboard a train loaded with wounded prisoners. Because his wound was the least severe of any of the prisoners in his ward, Reed was detailed to assist the Confederate surgeons in caring for his comrades. His work impressed a Rebel doctor, who requested that Reed remain as an assistant when he recovered. This kept him out of prison, but Reed was unimpressed with what he observed while working in the hospital. "The only dressing any wound got was to wash them once a day and keep them wet with cold water," he wrote. Reed was shocked when a severely wounded man was left solely in his care by the doctors. "They did nothing for [him] but left it all for me to do."[28]

Reed remained at the hospital until September 11, when a change in orders landed him in Ligon's. There he was equally critical of his captors' approach to medicine. When a friend died from diarrhea and "conjestion of the lungs," Reed complained, "[t]he Drs would do nothing for him." He added, "The Dr's pretended that his death was a mystery for his disease was not dangerous. Well I think myself it was not the disease that killed him, but pure neglect." Later, when another friend lay dying "of consumption," the doctors further annoyed Reed by not allowing him to visit the man.[29]

On August 1 Dr. Samuel P. Moore, serving as acting surgeon general of the Confederate Army, conducted an inspection of Ligon's and Howard's prisons. In a brief report he noted that the policing of both was "very bad." He also complained of overcrowding, but his concerns were not solely with the prisoners. "From the crowded state of these buildings it is feared that a pestilence may make its appearance, and if it would the city would be the sufferer," he wrote. Secretary of War Leroy P. Walker forwarded the report to Winder and urged him to "provide more ample room for the accommodation of prisoners in [the] future." This upset the sensitive Confederate general, who replied that the only reason the two prisons were crowded was that Moore had appropriated a third facility to use as a hospital. Winder had secured another building and, he concluded, "I respectfully think the complaint of the Surgeon-General was to say the least premature."[30]

Among the prisoners most directly involved with Confederate care was Lt. Todd's dinner companion Dr. Gray. Gray reached Richmond on August 2. He received a parole that allowed him to go about the city, and he stayed at the home of a War Department clerk. There was plenty for him to do. "Found lots of patients & doctors," he wrote of his first day on the job. "Worked away all day & slept but little at night being up till one." At first he spoke highly of his captors. The Confederate doctor who had charge of the hospital was "a very fair fellow" who Gray believed provided the best care he could. The other physicians, Union and Confederate, were "good fellows," although he complained of their "ridiculously vulgar stories."[31]

This changed on August 31. After visiting wounded soldiers in various locations, Gray and a fellow prisoner returned to the hospital "and found the Devil had been loose in our absence." Winder, he was told, had visited the hospital and was "furious" over the freedoms given the officers on parole. As a result all paroles had been withdrawn and all communication cut off with the North. Gray suspected the cause of their ill humor was a Confederate defeat. "At all events I believe something has occurred to sour their tempers." Actually it was the high number of escapes that had soured the Confederates' tempers, but the tighter security and frequent inspections that resulted irritated Gray. "[The] guards are mad enough to murder all & make themselves as disagreeable as possible," he wrote. This, along with deteriorating hospital conditions, served to sour the Yankee doctor's own temper. "Provisions are getting scarce and hundreds of men had no supper last night," he wrote on September 9. "Fever is getting rife and filth, impure air & scarcity [of] food will soon accomplish a good deal for the C S in an economical way."[32]

The prisoners were not in Richmond long before the Union and Confederate governments began sparring over the proper policies for dealing with military captives. Those captives quickly became pawns in this struggle. During the early months of the war, most of the problems grew out of President Abraham Lincoln's dogged insistence that nothing be done that would in any way imply an official recognition of the Confederate government. In his inaugural address the president had firmly asserted that the Union was perpetual under the Constitution, rendering secession illegal. "Resolves to that effect are legally void," Lincoln insisted.[33]

The president's views were sound in theory. Any sign of recognition, however implicit, could have provided European powers a pretext to extend formal recognition. However, the Civil War was anything but theoretical, and a series of incidents involving Confederate privateers soon put Lincoln's philosophies to the test. Only days after the guns sounded at Fort Sumter, the Davis administration initiated a policy of issuing letters of marque and reprisal. This allowed privately owned vessels to attack Northern commercial ships. On June 5 the Union captured one of those vessels, the schooner *Savannah,* along with its crew of twenty. The Lincoln administration proclaimed the crew members pirates. Since secession was illegal, they could not be considered sailors of a legitimate government. They were hauled to a New York jail and indicted on June 26. In part the indictment said that they "did . . . violently, feloniously and piratically rob, steal, seize, take and carry away" property from the brig *Joseph.*[34]

At first Jefferson Davis's response to the capture of the *Savannah* was measured. On June 19, at the president's direction, S. R. Gist, the adjutant and inspector general of South Carolina, sent a message through the lines to Capt. Samuel Mercer, commanding the U.S. blockading fleet at Charleston. He proposed that the crew members be exchanged, according to number and rank, for prisoners held by the Confederates. Mercer replied obliquely, "The prisoners to whom you refer are not on board of any vessels under my command," sidestepping an issue that he apparently realized was too hot for him to handle. Davis's next message went to a much higher level and was much less measured. On July 6, after news of the impending trial on capital charges reached Richmond, he sent a letter through the lines to Lincoln. "It is the desire of this government so to conduct the war now existing as to mitigate its horrors as far as may be possible," the Confederate president wrote. After noting that Union prisoners had been treated with "the greatest humanity and leniency consistent with public obligation," he got to the heart of the matter:

> A just regard to humanity and to the honor of this Government now requires me to state explicitly that painful as will be the necessity this Government will deal out to the prisoners held by it the same treatment and the same fate as shall be experienced by those captured in the Savannah; and if driven to the terrible necessity of retaliation by your execution of the officers or crew of the Savannah that retaliation will be extended so far as shall be requisite to secure the abandonment by you of a practice unknown to the warfare of civilized man and so barbarous as to disgrace the nation which shall be guilty of inaugurating it.[35]

The day before he sent his message to Lincoln, Davis ordered Winder to revoke the paroles of two Union officers in Richmond. Still, the prisoners were to be granted "every kindness and attention in your power compatible with their safe-keeping." On July 20 the president informed the Confederate Congress of the "savage practices" in which the Union was engaging. He included a copy of his message to Lincoln and expressed regret that he had not received a reply. Davis noted his decision to revoke the paroles of the Northern prisoners, saying the actions of the Union government "admit of repression by retaliation." Congress formally replied on August 30. By then more privateers had fallen into Union hands, and the Confederate legislature authorized the president to "select such prisoners taken from the United States and in such numbers as he may deem expedient upon the persons of whom he may inflict such retaliation in such measure and kind as may seem to him just and proper."[36]

The jury could not agree in the *Savannah* case, but in November Walter Smith, captain of the Confederate brig *Jeff Davis,* was convicted of piracy and sentenced to death following a trial in Philadelphia. On the 9th Confederate secretary of war Judah P. Benjamin, who had succeeded Walker, ordered Winder to choose by lot a hostage from among the highest-ranking Union prisoners. The officer selected was to be confined in a felon's cell. If the death sentence was carried out against Smith, this hostage would be executed. Thirteen other officer prisoners, a number equal to the Confederate privateers awaiting trial, were to be selected and confined as well.[37]

Winder carried out the order, going to Howard's factory and asking Representative Ely to select one of six slips of paper containing the names of the highest-ranking Union prisoners. The name chosen was that of Col. Michael Corcoran, flamboyant and popular commander of the Sixty-ninth New York Infantry. Corcoran had been transferred to Charleston, South Carolina, but the word spread quickly. On November 12 Dr. Gray, who had also been sent to Charleston, recorded the news in his diary. Eight days later he wrote that Corcoran was in a cell in close confinement. Four other officers confined in Charleston, among the hostages held for the safety of the other thirteen crew members, joined him. According to Gray, their treatment was not severe. They were "secluded from their comrades [but] are placed in cells opening upon a corridor of which they have the liberty." Still, Gray noted, "We all feel deeply on their account although believing that it will end in nothing." Abetted by his Confederate captors, Corcoran worked hard to make certain that it all ended in nothing. The colonel had a large following in New York's Irish and political communities. In the weeks that followed Southern officials allowed a torrent of his letters to pass through the lines. Many ended up in the *New York Times* and other influential newspapers. This resulted in another torrent, as Corcoran's supporters appealed to the Lincoln administration to do something to have the gallant colonel spared.[38]

Corcoran was not the only correspondent encouraging people back home to work on his behalf and toward a policy of prisoner exchange. George W. Kenney of the Seventy-first Pennsylvania wrote his parents on November 12, assuring them, "I have plenty to eat and drink, and a fine bed to sleep upon." Nine days later he wrote, "I hope they will not hang Smith if they do they will be sure to hang Col. Corcoran, and if they will only act rightly and liberate the 13 Savannah privateers the 13 that is here held as hostages will also be liberated." As late as December he was urging his father, "I hope you are all striking hard for a speedy exchange." Lt. Col. Paul Joseph Revere, grandson of the Revolutionary War rider, was among those selected as a hostage. In a letter to a friend, Revere explained that he had chosen not to write to his wife, "hoping to spare her the anxiety." He added, "There is I think no doubt of the determination of the [Confederate] government to carry out its expressed intention in this matter."[39]

Among the most extreme letters, bordering on Confederate propaganda, were those of James Jenkins Gillette. A member of the Seventy-first New York State Militia, Gillette was captured at Manassas. "We are in the hands of a generous people," he wrote his parents on August 8, "and if our government will exhibit the same desire for an exchange as do people here, we will soon be restored to our families and friends." He further urged, "*Dont hang the privateers* unless you are willing we should be similarly treated." Ten days later he admonished his father, "Let this matter of exchange . . . be 'talked up' untill public sentiment loudly and persistently expressed demands their exchange in terms too strong to be denied by any stubborn policy to the contrary." A majority of his fellow prisoners, Gillette contended, "entertain no very amiable feelings towards Mr. Lincoln" because of his refusal to enter into exchange negotiations with the Confederate government. These inflammatory letters did not remain private communications between Gillette and his family. They soon found their way to Manton Marble, editor of the *New York World,* a paper that was on its way to becoming a leading organ of the Democratic Party. Remarkably, they even made it back indirectly to Gillette. "The article in the 'World' upon my letter written some time since has given us great encouragement," he informed his parents. "It was copied in the Richmond Examiner and thus reached our eyes."[40]

Although the extent is difficult to gauge, the letters written by Corcoran and others clearly helped bring about a shift in public opinion away from support of Lincoln's policies. Newspapers that had editorially proclaimed the righteousness of hanging traitors suddenly urged caution. Meanwhile the lobbying of Corcoran's friends kept the ordeal of their hero on the minds of administration officials. Put in simple terms, in his first battle of wits with Jefferson Davis, Abraham Lincoln had been outflanked. Court officers in Philadelphia, all set to make arrangements for an execution, were surreptitiously advised not to go through with the hanging of Smith.[41]

In January the administration went farther, quietly offering to exchange Smith for Corcoran. By then the pressure was so great that Secretary of State William Henry Seward got personally involved. On January 13 Seward informed Gen. George McClellan, "The great anxiety of the friends of Colonel Corcoran upon the subject induces me to inquire if you have received any answer upon the subject." The Confederates obviously sensed this anxiety and held out for a better deal for their captive privateers. When Maj. Gen. Benjamin Huger finally responded to the Union proposal, he declined to exchange Corcoran until there was "an absolute, unconditional abandonment of the pretext that they are pirates." This verbal sparring went on for the next several months and was sometimes marked by confusion. On one occasion Union officials offered to exchange a Virginia colonel for Corcoran only to discover they had already exchanged that officer. Corcoran eventually returned home in August, part of a series of exchanges under a cartel that Union and Confederate officials had agreed to a few weeks earlier.[42]

That cartel meant freedom for thousands of Union prisoners, some of whom had been held nearly a year. For the Confederacy it ended the administrative headache of caring for them. It was a headache that grew during the early months of 1862, as spring campaigns in both the eastern and western theaters of the war produced fresh waves of prisoners. Even before that the numbers had grown well beyond the capacity of Richmond's makeshift prisons. As a result, Confederate officials had reached out to the leaders of states farther south and west. In some cases they had virtually begged governors to find them some space to house the captured Yankees. Their success was mixed, but by the time exchange became a reality the South had a nascent network of prisons in place. Many of those depots were destined to be again pressed into service. The cartel, plagued with controversy from the very outset, would not survive. This would lead to problems for prison keepers north and south. The Union, however, had in place a commissary general of prisoners to address those problems. Col. William Hoffman, a career officer, held the post virtually the entire war. The Confederate government would not create such a position until November 1864. As a result, Confederate prison policy would continue to evolve on a makeshift basis, and the Confederacy would still be unready when it was forced to deal with a second, and much larger, wave of captives in blue.

2
"A very inconvenient and expensive problem"
The Search for New Prisons

"Everybody is asking, 'What is to be done with the prisoners?'" According to the *Richmond Whig* of August 5, 1861, that was the burning question on the minds of residents of the Confederate capital. Answers ranged from sending them farther south to releasing the "better behaved" to go home, relate their experiences, and "frighten away others." Some suggested that Yankee shoemakers be required to "earn their grub" by turning out footwear for Southern soldiers. Although the specific recommendations varied, everyone seemed to agree that something had to be done. As the *Examiner* noted on September 7, "Few are fully aware of the trouble, care and annoyance which their safekeeping devolves upon those entrusted with that duty." Evidently those officials agreed. On October 5 Huger asked what he was to do with fifty prisoners, taken from a Federal steamer, he was holding in Norfolk. Adjutant and Inspector General Samuel Cooper pleaded with him to retain them. "We are too much crowded here already," Cooper explained.[1]

By then Winder and Benjamin had begun to take steps to relieve the crowding, seeking states that would accept a few of their surplus prisoners. Their luck was decidedly mixed, but officials in a handful of states each agreed to take a handful of prisoners. On September 10 Capt. Gibbs left Richmond with the first detachment, a group of 150 prisoners bound for Charleston. Among them was Dr. Gray, who termed the first leg of the trip, to nearby Petersburg, "a pleasant ride." There the group changed trains. The prisoners spent the night at Weldon, North Carolina, crowded into a single room that was "almost stifling." Gibbs paroled the officers to the limits of the community. They rushed to secure hotel rooms and enjoyed "good beds which few had known for months." The train reached Wilmington the next night, but everyone had to remain on the freight cars. "God forgive the cowards guilty of such an outrage," Gray wrote. They arrived at Florence, South Carolina, at about 8:00 on the night of September 12, changed trains, and continued on to Charleston.[2]

The train bearing its human cargo pulled into Charleston at about 5:45 on the morning of the 13th. The local press had informed the populace that the Yankees, "including the redoubtable Col. Corcoran," were on their way. The early hour, however, precluded a large crowd. After debarking from the train, the prisoners formed into two columns. Surrounding them were nearly a dozen guard outfits, including local militia and a company of Louisiana soldiers that had accompanied them from Richmond. "They all wear uniforms," the *Charleston Mercury* wrote of the prisoners, "although some of these are in a somewhat dilapidated condition." The *Mercury* added, "When they first arrived they were generally taciturn, but during the day became communicative, in some instances, even loquacious." The paper was pleased with their good behavior. "A Richmond paper had mentioned these prisoners as having been 'selected chiefly from among those who had evinced the most insolent and insubordinate disposition,' but their deportment . . . was generally as orderly as could be desired."[3]

The prisoners marched about a mile and a half to the local jail. This was to be their temporary home until Castle Pinckney could be prepared for their reception. Gray was among a group of thirty-four officers locked up in a corridor he described simply as "pretty hard." The prisoners received no rations until noon. They consisted of "an insufficient quantity of crackers, sugar, poor coffee & fried bacon." In the evening more crackers arrived, along with some rice. Gray slept "tolerably well" his first night despite being pestered by mosquitoes. The rations remained about the same during the captives' brief stay at the jail. The one bright spot was the opportunity to exercise in the jail yard.[4]

On September 18 the prisoners boarded the steamer *Cecile* for the short trip to Castle Pinckney. Located on the southern tip of a small island in Charleston Harbor, Castle Pinckney had been built in 1809. It was named for Charleston native and Federalist politician Charles C. Pinckney, George Washington's minister to France and a two-time presidential candidate. According to the *Mercury,* the prisoners "seemed highly delighted" with the facility. This may have been stretching things, but Chaplain Eddy found the castle superior to the prisons of Richmond. "Our condition is much improved here," he informed his wife. "We have plenty of air, & go out upon the island when we please." Dr. Gray was much less impressed. "It did not look inviting," he wrote. "The area [is] filled with all manner of rubbish & the casemates small & dark with the embrasures walled up save a little slit for an air hole." As time went on Gray, who arrived ill at Castle Pinckney, came to appreciate certain aspects of life on the island. For one, the freedom to roam allowed the prisoners to supplement their rations with crabs and oysters. There was also a number of books available and, thanks to a black resident of Charleston who visited the castle to trade, the captives received smuggled newspapers.[5]

Gray's opinion of Castle Pinckney may have been ambivalent. He and his fellow prisoners were nevertheless "disturbed" when they learned on October 30 that they were heading back to the jail. The castle had proved too small to accommodate the Yankees, and that afternoon they boarded another steamer for the return trip to Charleston. Soon the prisoners were complaining of cold weather there. "Everyone shivering & swearing no wood & no prospect of any," Gray wrote on November 25. "Burning everything superfluous." They went three days without fuel before receiving a supply on the 27th. Chaplain Eddy also found cause for complaint. In a letter smuggled out of the jail on December 4, he informed his wife, "We are now, and have been for some time living on less than half rations." Meat, hard crackers, rice, and small issues of soap and vinegar composed the rations. The prisoners also received one candle and one pound of coffee a week. Two officers in his mess had cots. The others slept on sacks filled with straw. As was the case with Gray's mess, rations of wood were sporadic. Eddy conceded that the officers' situation was far superior to that of the enlisted prisoners. "Many of the men are in a famishing condition, living on three crackers a day. Many of them sleep without any covering on the bare floor."[6]

As December arrived Gray believed that the Confederates were "'letting up' in the severity of our captivity." He attributed the change to word from the North that the privateers were not to be hanged. Whatever the cause, the prisoners were allowed visitors and given the opportunity to procure items from outside the prison. The added courtesy even extended to the privilege of "getting drunk with our friends." Gray noted a few specific instances of this happening, particularly as part of the prisoners' observance of Christmas. The officers held a number of parties to celebrate the holiday, whiskey flowing freely at all of them, according to the doctor. Gray's mess enjoyed "turkey & 'fixins' [and] egg nog of my manufacture." Capt. Theodore Boag, who commanded at the jail, was the guest of honor for another mess.[7]

New Year's Day 1862 found Chaplain Eddy, Dr. Gray, and some 150 other prisoners en route for the jail in Columbia, South Carolina. The Charleston jail continued to serve as a military prison, however. On March 18 Lt. Col. Frank T. Bennett of the Fifty-fifth Pennsylvania arrived. Bennett's outfit had been serving along the coast of South Carolina. It was part of Gen. Thomas W. Sherman's

Expeditionary Corps, which had been sent south to secure bases for the Union's blockading squadron. "The men who captured us seemed to vie with each other in rendering us as comfortable as possible," Bennett wrote. They shared their rations with the prisoners and provided Bennett with a horse for the long trip to their camp. Once they reached camp a Confederate captain saw to it that they received "an excellent meal" and a glass of whiskey. Two days later they went to the depot for the ride to Charleston. The Rebel officers escorted the prisoners into the telegraph room so they could escape the gaze of curious citizens. Once inside the Confederates shared some more whiskey with the captives.[8]

Their treatment worsened when they reached Charleston. "The four bare walls and grated windows . . . struck a chill into us," Bennett noted in his diary. He and his fellow prisoners improved their condition by paying $2 for a mattress and two blankets. Their sleep was interrupted by the nighttime visits of "mice, bugs, roaches, horrid crawling things, Ugh!" The next morning they received a different group of visitors, "criminals here confined, who walked unceremoniously into our cell, to see the Yankee prisoners." One of them informed the Unionists that their cells were unlocked during the day, during which time they had the freedom of the halls and the small jail yard. He also "posted us as to the character of our fellow prisoners, thieves and cutthroats fine associates!" Despite this initial assessment, Bennett and his comrades grew fond of their fellow prisoners. They proved to be "very kindly disposed towards us," smuggling in the daily newspapers for the Yankees' benefit. They hired one of them, "a large Irish woman confined here for stealing," as a cook. "She is not the most cleanly person in the world," Bennett observed, "but we manage to gulp down the dirt with very good grace." The prisoners also liked the local sheriff, "a pleasant man," who did all he could to make them comfortable. They especially looked forward to his Sunday visits, which allowed time to pass more rapidly than "the minutes of the dull monotonous week."[9]

On November 23, 1861, Secretary Benjamin asked Governor Francis W. Pickens of South Carolina if he could find a location in the interior of the state to house a few hundred prisoners. Three days later Pickens replied that the jail in Columbia could hold 200. Within a few days there would be room for another 200 "of the better class" at the fairgrounds. Benjamin immediately sent word that he would ship out 200 in two or three days. At that point the governor decided he had acted a bit hastily. Responding the same day to Benjamin's message, Pickens wrote that the jail could only hold 150. He further requested that they be delayed a few days "as [the] jail will have to be put in proper order by the mayor." The secretary agreed to the reduced number and the delay, informing the governor that he could expect 150 Union prisoners on November 2. When they finally showed up, the captives made a poor impression on the Columbia correspondent of the *Charleston Courier.* "This set contains some of the poorest looking specimens of humanity we have yet seen," he wrote. "The majority are foreigners."[10]

Upon reaching Columbia on January 1, Dr. Gray and his comrades found "the girls pretty, the officers who received us gentlemen, & our quarters small but clean & otherwise very good." They were equally pleased to learn that they could send out for anything they could pay for. "So we spent a rollicking singing drinking New Year's evening after all; our guard officers enjoying it as much as we." Chaplain Eddy was less impressed, writing, "A drunk in the eve—stool—no bed."[11]

Dr. Gray continued to enjoy special treatment at Columbia. "The yard is very small . . . and the privy abominable," he wrote. Still, Gray observed, "On the whole [we] have gained mightily by our last move." Thanks to a recommendation from officials in Charleston, the post surgeon, who was also mayor of Columbia, made the doctor his deputy. This resulted in comfortable private quarters and occasionally in "a bottle of fine 'blockade-run' brandy." Both Gray and the surgeon were members of the Masonic Lodge. On at least two occasions, Gray attended meetings of the local lodge, where he received "a warm cordial welcome." Following his second visit, his hosts treated Gray to an evening on the town, returning to the prison at 3:00 A.M.[12]

From the time the first prisoners arrived at Columbia, the *Charleston Mercury* had complained of the "singularly lenient treatment" they received. On February 24, 1862, the paper wrote, "The culpable lenity with which Yankee prisoners in Columbia have been treated, has produced its legitimate fruits." Three days earlier thirteen prisoners had made their escape from the jail. Col. John S. Preston, who had been in command at Columbia since January 28, may have tacitly agreed. In any event, according to Hiram Eddy, life at the jail became much more strict. "Officers locked up for the first time—double guard—no going out." On March 3 the *Mercury* reported that nine of the escapees had been recaptured, and a group of citizens was in pursuit of three others.[13]

Both Gray and Eddy were gone by the time Lt. Col. Bennett arrived at Columbia from Charleston on May 6. His views of the facility were decidedly less positive. "We were incarcerated in a black looking place [compared] to which Charleston jail is a palace," he noted. The prisoners were not allowed outside unless a guard accompanied them. Communication with the outside was prohibited, as were newspapers. To make matters worse, Bennett and his comrades were guarded by a sergeant who was "ignorant boorish and dumb." On one occasion he took some money from a prisoner, promising to buy some items the mess needed.

Then he disappeared. "We do not dread the loss of our money so much as that he may return," Bennett wrote. "In fact I would give him two dollars more to stay away." Much to the prisoners' chagrin, the sergeant returned five days later. His disposition had not improved. Col. Preston had relented and allowed the prisoners the freedom of the jail and the yard if they signed a parole agreeing not to escape. The sergeant flaunted his authority by delaying the captives' release into the yard in the mornings. This prompted Bennett to write a note to Preston. The commander overruled his sergeant. The prisoners secured entrance into the yard at 5:00 A.M., "but our sergeant has become more unpleasant in his manner to us."[14]

Bennett termed Preston "very gentlemanly in his bearing." He particularly appreciated the "slight taste of liberty" the paroles represented. The lieutenant colonel also enjoyed looking out his windows in the evenings and observing the passing parade of humanity. "There are a great many pretty girls in this little town and they dress with good taste and wear jaunty little hats with feathers," he noted. Occasionally he could hear music from an unnamed instrument emanating from a nearby home. Still, there was little to break the monotony of prison life. After two weeks at Columbia, Bennett described a typical day:

> In the morning I arise at five o'clock, bathe take breakfast at seven. After breakfast a short walk in the yard. Then to my room where I read, and write, or sketch, or attempt it until twelve or one. Then lunch of bread and molasses. After lunch I wander about uneasily sometimes to the window; then in and out of the room and down the hall until four. This is the largest part of the day. At four dine, look out of the window at the street until six, when I go into the corporal's room, and sitting by the bars, listen to music from a neighboring house, and dream of home until nine.[15]

In attempting to relieve the crowding in Richmond, Confederate officials also looked far to the west. On the afternoon of September 21 a detachment of Union prisoners left the Confederate capital bound for New Orleans. Among their number was Willard Wheeler, who recorded that their train reached Petersburg at about dusk. The prisoners changed to a different railroad and continued south. Traveling through North Carolina the next day, the Yankees got their first look at cotton plants. "The people here seem very bitter against us but some of them seem to have considerable sympathy for us," Wheeler wrote as the train rolled through South Carolina. "Many of the women were effected to tears at our condition." On the 24th the prisoners reached Atlanta. The next day they passed through Montgomery. Their progress then slowed. The prisoners did not reach Jackson, Mississippi, until September 29. There, according to Wheeler, the citizens were largely sympathetic. "Jackson seems to be very much imbued with a Union sentiment," he observed. "Many gathered around us and secretly hinted their deep sympathy for us."[16]

The prisoners finally arrived at their destination the following morning. It is not clear how many there were in this contingent, but by January 16, 1862, there were five hundred in the Crescent City. Maj. Gen. Mansfield Lovell, the Confederate commander at New Orleans, termed them "a serious nuisance" and asked Benjamin if they could be exchanged. This was impossible, but on February 6 the prisoners moved on to Salisbury, North Carolina. New Orleans would not long remain in Confederate hands, and this ended its career as a military prison—at least for Union prisoners.[17]

Wheeler and his fellow captives were housed in the parish prison, a large three-story building. Female criminals, "the lowest and most degraded I ever saw," occupied the third floor. The military prisoners stayed on the lower two. They were in cells nine and a half feet by thirteen and a half, seventeen to a room. Two small openings provided ventilation, but the captives could go outside into the prison yard during the day. Beef, bread, soup, and tea composed the rations, which were issued twice a day. Wheeler wrote that the fare was better than it had been at Atkinson's, adding, "We feel better pleased with our situation here than we did at Richmond." The prisoners were able to wash at a water tank daily. Otherwise they occupied their time sleeping, reading, singing, and exercising. "The principal employment," Wheeler wrote, "is to cut rings and various fancy articals out of the white bones we get with our beef and many beautiful specimens of Yankee ingenuity are formed of these rough bones [with] an old dull jack knife." This was more than just an activity to occupy the prisoners' time. Confederate guards purchased many of the rings and carvings they turned out, gaining the craftsmen a few dimes "for luxuries and extra bread."[18]

These diversions notwithstanding, the prisoners were never able to escape the boredom and extreme loneliness of prison life. Thoughts of home were especially acute on Sundays. On one Wheeler wrote, "It is the Holy Sabbath and my thoughts turn involuntarily homeward, and I think of loved ones there who are no doubt sighing for one far away." Similar emotions surfaced on December 25, when "the familiar old 'Wish you Merry Christmas' went around among the boys. . . . How we thought of our Mothers and Fathers and all the family circle gathered around the Christmas dinner," Wheeler lamented. Only one thing was able to shatter this loneliness. On at least two occasions during the captives' stay in New Orleans, mail from home arrived. The first delivery came on November 2 and included letters for other members of Wheeler's company. Of the occasion he wrote, "Our company were almost wild with excitement and we soon collected in our room and each in turn read his letters." Wheeler's turn came on January 2, when he received a letter from his parents. "Oh how eagerly did I read it over and how glad was I to hear from them to know that they were all well," he wrote. Mail was scarce, however, and many prisoners turned to their faith for comfort. Occasionally the more pious among them gathered for services or Bible studies. On one occasion a local Anglican clergyman came to preach to the prisoners, but the visit did not go well. When he offered up a prayer for Jefferson Davis the majority of the congregation walked out, and a few hissed.[19]

If the New Orleans prison fell a bit short of meeting the captives' spiritual needs, it did not come close to relieving Richmond of its crowded prisons. On October 23, the same day he appealed to Governor Pickens of South Carolina, Secretary Benjamin sent similar messages to the governors of Alabama and Georgia. "Will pay a fair rent for the property," he assured them both. Governor Joseph Brown of Georgia offered a slave market in Macon, which would hold two hundred, but there is no evidence of the facility being used. Governor Andrew B. Moore of Alabama replied that he could not find any buildings suitable for prisoners, although he promised to keep looking. This did not sit well with the harried secretary, who believed he knew otherwise. Benjamin wrote back, "I am told you have at Tuscaloosa, the former capital, not only legislative buildings but an insane asylum and a military institute—all unoccupied. We are greatly embarrassed by our prisoners, as all accommodations here are required for our sick and wounded." The desperate secretary concluded, "It would be a great public service if you can find a place for some if not all of our prisoners."[20]

Moore apparently looked a little harder, because on October 28 Benjamin instructed Maj. James L. Calhoun to make arrangements to receive prisoners at Tuscaloosa. Three weeks later he dispatched Capt. Elias Griswold to take charge of the prison. When Griswold arrived he found the facility, an abandoned paper mill, "utterly untenable." There was no flooring on the first story. The grounds were low and damp, the walls were moldy, and the building lacked windows. On top of all that, there were no means for building fires for heating or cooking. Despite their desperation, Confederate officials would not house prisoners in such a place. Griswold was ordered to rent the asylum if it was available and see about renting hotels in the city. This attracted the attention of John Gill Shorter, who had succeeded Moore as governor. "Better send no prisoners to Tuscaloosa," he wrote

Benjamin on December 20. "Accommodations exhausted. Lunatic Asylum will not be leased."[21]

As Shorter's message indicated, Union prisoners had already arrived in Tuscaloosa. Elisha Rice Reed was among a group of 150 that left Richmond on November 22. They reached Montgomery three days later, where 350 more captives joined them. The entire group arrived in Tuscaloosa on December 5. They were under the command of Sgt. Wirz, and according to Reed, the "Dutch Sergeant" helped them secure comfortable quarters. The U.S. Hotel was unoccupied, but its owner was reluctant to turn it over to Yankee prisoners. As Reed recalled it about a month later, Wirz informed him, "I'll call out my one hundred and fifty guards and take it by force. If they can't do it, I have five hundred Yankees and they'll *fight like hell.*" Reed described the hotel as a four-story brick building. He was one of 155 prisoners in a fifty-by-sixty-foot room that had been used as a dining hall, ballroom, and theater. "As soon as it is dark we begin to spread our blankets on the floor and roll ourselves therein," Reed wrote. The floor did not make a comfortable bed, and the men suffered from callused hips. The best thing about the location was the climate. By the time they reached Alabama, many prisoners were lacking coats and shirts. "Fortunately for the poor Yankees it is not very cold here in the 'Sunny South,'" Reed observed on January 8. Often the prisoners had the windows raised.[22]

Although the exact numbers are not known, Tuscaloosa soon became a concentration point, albeit a temporary one, for western prisoners. On December 14, 1861, Maj. Gen. Braxton Bragg, commanding the Department of Alabama and West Florida, ordered all Federal prisoners at Montgomery to Tuscaloosa. Those confined at Memphis followed on March 9, also under Bragg's orders. The latter group consisted of 214 captives. Of that total, 118 had been taken during the Federal campaign against Fort Donelson. A few chose to depart early. During the night of March 3–4, fourteen made their escape. They got away by crawling out onto an adjacent shed and climbing down to an alley. Prison officials did not discover the escape until the 6th. They still managed to recapture at least half of them.[23]

Among those making the trip from Memphis to Tuscaloosa was Nathaniel C. Kenyon, an officer with the Eleventh Illinois. Along the way he complained of crowded freight cars and rations that were scanty and often spoiled. The captives traveled by rail to Corinth and then on to Mobile, where they boarded a small steamer for the trip up the Alabama River. The privates stayed below, while the officers remained on the upper deck. This produced difficult sleeping when a heavy thunderstorm blew up, followed by a cold wind. The boat reached Tuscaloosa on the afternoon of March 16. Kenyon pronounced the quarters there "comfortable." The new arrivals received plates but no utensils. Rations were skimpy, but the men were able to supplement them somewhat by purchasing coffee. Their living conditions improved considerably on March 26, when the Confederates provided them with cots and mattresses. The next morning Kenyon wrote that he had enjoyed "a first rate night's rest."[24]

Sgt. Wirz remained, and the prisoners' opinions of him were decidedly ambivalent. A creature of duty, he did all he could to see to the prisoners' well-being while at the same time enforcing prison rules rigidly. Soon after securing the U.S. Hotel for the Richmond prisoners, he took away their meat rations because one of them had broken down a door. Later, after Capt. Griswold was the recipient of disrespectful language, Wirz placed two guards at the door and announced that only one prisoner would be allowed out at a time. He further ordered the sentries to "kill all they can and the easiest way they can" if the captives attempted to make a charge. Elisha Reed was particularly upset when the sergeant ordered the prisoners to turn over their files, which they used for carving bones. "He *never* will get *mine,*" Reed asserted. "I'll *smash* it." Despite all these complaints, Reed was upset when Wirz left for a few days for a visit to New Orleans. "How we hated that man in Richmond but now he is the best friend we have," the Wisconsin soldier wrote. Kenyon's feelings were similarly mixed. "We have a Sgt. Wertz over us as big a tyrant as ever ran," he wrote his second day at Tuscaloosa. Two days later he termed him "quite gentlemanly to what he had been." Kenyon further credited Wirz with securing bedding for the prisoners. Two weeks later his opinion of the sergeant again shifted as Wirz got "very red in the face" over "an alleged infringement of the rules."[25]

Although Wirz may not have been responsible, the prisoners who arrived from Memphis and Montgomery were treated more strictly than their eastern predecessors. "What the rules are no one of us knows," Kenyon wrote. "We hardly dare make a move for fear we may transgress some unknown rule." Kenyon recorded two instances of prisoners being placed in irons. A captain received the punishment for talking to prisoners in an adjacent room. On another occasion a man complained of getting too little to eat. He not only found himself in irons but was also restricted to a diet of bread and water. Lt. Frank Hughes of the Thirty-seventh Indiana wrote on May 17 that five or six prisoners were in irons "for attempting to run away."[26]

Kenyon recorded one shooting during his time at Tuscaloosa. On April 15 a prisoner was shot for putting his head out a window. His body fell out and struck the pavement below. In a letter to his wife, a Shiloh prisoner confirmed Kenyon's account. "One of the boys went to the window and looked out and one of the guards shot his brains out," Elias Perry wrote. "The officer that was in command," presumably Wirz, "came up to where we was and cursed and swore that if we dident quit looking out of the windows that we would all be served the same way." Former Tuscaloosa prisoner J. B. Dorr of the Twelfth Iowa Infantry reported to his superiors that two prisoners had been shot for looking out their windows. A third was shot when he and a fellow captive were sent out under guard to secure water. The prisoner had been in the habit of visiting a nearby house to buy milk while on such details. On this occasion the guard ordered him to come back. Dorr conceded that the sentinel did not fire until after a second warning. Writing home on May 22, Isaac Morgan of the Thirty-seventh Indiana informed his family that three escaped prisoners from Tuscaloosa had recently reached his camp. They reported that there were eight hundred prisoners there. "They say that they was badly treated and if any of them stuck his head out of the window he was likely to be shot." The escapees also reported that there had been three shootings while they were there.[27]

As the spring campaigns of 1862 got under way, the South found its prison system strained even more. On April 6, 1862, Union and Confederate forces met near a small meetinghouse along the Tennessee River. The result was the first major battle in the western theater. When the battle of Shiloh ended on the 7th, the South had suffered a defeat. In the process it also gained nearly three thousand prisoners. Among them were Privates Willard Felton and Levi Minkler of the Eighteenth Wisconsin, an outfit that suffered 280 casualties, including 174 captured. The Badger State captives followed a circuitous course over the next week, journeying through Corinth, Jackson, and Mobile before ending up in Montgomery in mid-April.[28]

At first rations were skimpy at the prison, which Felton described simply as "a brick house." On April 22 he reported that rations were improving and by the 23rd he wrote, "We get enough to eat now at present such as it is." By mid-May the rations were again limited to the point that "some of us have to go hungry." Felton did not blame his captors, however, writing, "The south is not able to keep us." On May 1 he noted briefly that a Union lieutenant had been shot and killed by one of the guards. Minkler did not offer any details of the incident either, but he termed it "a cold blooded murder." Soon after that Minkler became ill. On May 22 he entered the hospital. The next day he recorded four deaths there. Two more died on the 26th. On the 27th he wrote, "I still have my hopes." It was Minkler's last entry. He died on June 16, far from the fields of Wisconsin.[29]

Beginning on May 14, prisoners from Tuscaloosa began leaving to join the Shiloh captives in Montgomery. Nathaniel Kenyon was among a contingent that departed on the 15th. They arrived on the 21st amid swirling rumors. One had all the prisoners being paroled "as fast as possible." Another claimed that only the privates were to be paroled. "This state of suspense is awful," Kenyon observed. Beyond doubt, in Kenyon's opinion, was the poor treatment the prisoners received in the former Confederate capital. The Shiloh prisoners, numbering nearly six hundred, were confined in a "cotton shed," which was "dirty, lousy, and almost everything else disagreeable." Frank Hughes agreed, terming the facility, "the filthy stinking old cotton ware House." Moses T. Anderson of the Fifty-ninth Illinois, who spent only one day in Montgomery, wrote that the city was "beautifully situated" and that the prison was "a filthy hole." Sick prisoners, Kenyon observed, were "in an awful position, lying on the hard floor, no care and nothing to eat that is fit." Rations for the rest of the prisoners arrived raw and generally consisted of "black eyed beans and stinking beef." When the captives received cornbread it was "made from corn and cob ground all together."[30]

Montgomery was not the only destination for the Shiloh prisoners. Col. Madison Miller of the Eighteenth Missouri was among a group of officers that went to Talladega, Alabama. Their prison was a Baptist college, where the prisoners were "guarded by the hardest lot of Butternut recruits and fed on the hardest fare." Cpl. Charles Whipple Hadley of the Fourteenth Iowa was among a group of approximately 650 that marched to Corinth on April 7. The captives reached Memphis the next day. There they remained until the 12th, when they boarded freight cars for Mobile. Although curious spectators turned out at virtually every community "to get sight of a lot of live Yankees," Hadley noted, "All along the road we were as a general thing treated well." April 16 found the prisoners in Mobile, where they stayed in "a large cotton ware house." According to the *Mobile Tribune,* Hadley and his comrades were "a rough looking set of fellows, and just as filthy as it is possible for men to be." Their rations at Mobile consisted of sacks of flour and cornmeal. The Confederates did, however, supply them with cooking and eating utensils.[31]

On April 18 the prisoners were given an hour to cook their rations and told they would again be on the move. This time it was by steamer up the Alabama River. Their destination was Cahaba, where they arrived on the 21st. "We are . . . quartered in a large unfinished ware house situated on the [river] bank," Hadley wrote.

This almost certainly was the brick warehouse begun by Samuel Hill on the eve of the war. Because of circumstances both economic and military he never completed the facility. In 1863 it would become an important military prison. In the spring of 1862 it was a temporary holding facility. Hadley and his comrades remained for two weeks. Their first impressions of their imprisonment in Cahaba were positive. "The ladies of the town sent in a beautiful supply of cornbread & meat," he wrote the day of his arrival. "We shall long remember our breakfast, for we were hungry as dogs." The next day five hundred more prisoners arrived from Mobile, crowding the facility and apparently making it impossible for the women of Cahaba to supplement the prisoners' rations. They now had to make do with cornmeal, "very poor" pickled beef, and a cup full of mush, all issued without salt. Even these rations ran short on the 24th, but that was the only day at Cahaba that Hadley mentioned the inability of the Confederates to keep all the men fed. Water arrived via a pipe from the town's reservoir. Meanwhile, the prisoners found means of providing both mental and physical stimulation. A debating society discussed whether the pen or the sword exerted a greater influence. The sword won. Other prisoners erected a "gymnasium horizontal pole" for recreation.[32]

On May 2 Hadley and many of his fellow prisoners made yet another move, for many their last as captives of the Confederacy. This time they were bound for Macon, Georgia. They were not interned in the dank holding pens of the slave market that had been offered. Rather they went to the former fairgrounds, a site christened Camp Oglethorpe in honor of the founder of the state. Hadley termed it "a splendid place." The ground was well sodded, pine trees provided shade, and he concluded, "We shall enjoy our selves." The *Macon Telegraph* was less excited about their arrival. "At a time when it is difficult to feed our own population, we are to be blessed with the presence and custody of 900 prisoners of war!" the paper shrieked. Ten days later the *Telegraph* reported that it cost about $1,000 a day to keep the prisoners, terming them "a very inconvenient and expensive problem." Many were "nearly naked," and the paper placed the cost of properly clothing them at $20,000. Still, if the prisoners were to remain, they would have to be clothed "out of a due respect for the customs of every civilized country." The paper suggested paroling them, saving the Confederacy "a useless expenditure."[33]

In the meantime Macon had some nine hundred prisoners to care for. On May 7 Dr. J. B. Hinkle, Camp Oglethorpe's surgeon, reported that between two hundred and three hundred were on the sick list. Dysentery and diarrhea were the prevailing diseases, with others suffering from bronchitis and pneumonia. Through the pages of the *Telegraph,* he appealed to the citizens for donations of mattresses, quilts, and other supplies for the hospital. The people apparently responded, because three days later Dr. Hinkle offered his thanks for the "very liberal and generous donations." Later in May, Macon citizen J. W. Fears raised $295.35 to help clothe the one hundred destitute prisoners at Camp Oglethorpe. He was able to provide shirts for all of them and had a large fund left over to donate to needy families of Confederate soldiers.[34]

By the time the funds were raised, the need to provide for the sick had become great. On May 15 Hadley noted in his diary that the health of the camp had been declining and that "deaths are quite frequent now." That day he attended a funeral service for five prisoners who had recently died. By the next evening four more prisoners were dead. "It is hoped we will get out of this soon for a great many are sick," Hadley wrote.[35]

The Iowa prisoner was lucky. On May 22 he was part of a large group that left Macon on parole destined for the Union lines. According to the *Telegraph,* "The prisoners were highly edified with the tidings." The Macon paper expressed its pleasure with their departure as well. That happiness proved to be short lived. Eight days later a contingent of captives from Montgomery arrived to take their place. "Loose them on their oath and let them go," the *Telegraph* again advised. If this was not practical they should be put to work fortifying Confederate army camps.[36]

Among the Montgomery prisoners sent to Macon were Nathaniel Kenyon, Frank Hughes, and Charles Van Riper. Like those who had come before them, all three recorded positive first impressions of Camp Oglethorpe. Most impressed was Van Riper. A member of the Twelfth Michigan captured at Shiloh, he wrote, "It is a paradise compared to the cotton sheds of Montgomery. We have nice shade trees and [a] pleasant green to walk on and the officers in command try to make it comfortable." There were two or three "fine springs" of water there, Kenyon noted, and he concluded that it was "the best place we have been yet." He found the buildings crowded, but he and some other prisoners willingly "put up our establishment outdoors." Hughes considered Macon to be a pretty town and his new prison "a very beautiful camp," adding, "We find comfort here to what we have had." Wood was in short supply, but the prisoners were able to secure a small supply by scavenging and by climbing trees and breaking off dead limbs. Elias Perry, who arrived in late May from Tuscaloosa, later informed his wife that the food at Camp Oglethorpe was sufficient in quantity if not in quality. "The corn meal was corse enough for cow feed & the Bacon semed to [be] 3 or 4 years old."[37]

Before long, Kenyon and Hughes were reporting that crowding in the camp was getting worse. On June 19 Hughes recorded the arrival of five hundred more prisoners. Four days later Kenyon wrote that the prison population was thirteen hundred. Although he had chosen to remain outside the camp buildings, he added that "many of the men [are] lying out in the open air without covering or shelter." By then he was frequently recording the deaths of prisoners. On June 15 he placed the number at one per day, a statistic confirmed by Van Riper. When a man from his regiment succumbed, Kenyon wrote, "I was in hopes that after passing through that hard fought battle [Shiloh] none of us would die in prison." His entry for June 25 was far more graphic. "I helped put two men in their coffins last evening. They had lain so long they were fly blown and the stench was almost unbearable." Kenyon's assessment of the situation was confirmed by Moses Anderson, who arrived at Camp Oglethorpe in early July. He, too, placed the number of prisoners at thirteen hundred. On the 13th he wrote, "There is considerable sickness here. They have poor facilities for taking care of the sick. There are one or two of the poor fellows buried every day."[38]

A number of prisoners chose not to wait around to die, and escape attempts were common. According to Charles Hadley, the original guards at the camp, a detachment of South Carolinians, were "brutal." A new group replaced them on May 11. "They are rather an ignorant set of fellows," Hadley wrote. "One of them did not know there was such a state of Iowa, although he was about 40 years old." Beginning in mid-June, Lt. Hughes noted that the prisoners were taking advantage of their guards' ignorance to make almost nightly escapes. Six or eight got away during daylight hours on the 17th, he wrote, and more were planning to escape that night. Somehow the prisoners had figured out a way to cover for the escapees during roll call. "Noon [None] reported absent yet our Yankee tricks Work well," Hughes wrote on June 18. At least fifteen took advantage of a rainy day on the 28th to get through the guard line. Another storm two nights later enabled more to escape. "Sentinels all doubled and thrippled all instructed to shoot without halting any one coming within Six paces of their line," Hughes wrote. The result of their increased vigilance, the lieutenant continued, was the discovery the next morning that "the Corporal of the Guard was shot by a Sentinel supposing him to be a Yankie."[39]

At the same time, the "Yankee tricks" apparently played out. On July 1 Kenyon wrote that prison authorities had checked the rolls and discovered "quite a number of escaped prisoners." As a result, those remaining faced "more restrictions." The next day Hughes wrote, "The guard is more strick in vigilance." That evening one of them shot and killed a prisoner. According to Hughes, the victim had been sixty feet inside the guard line. Kenyon claimed the shot had been fired "without cause or provocation." The Confederates meanwhile were doing all they could to retrieve the missing prisoners. The *Macon Telegraph* published names and descriptions of escapees, and prison officials pressed bloodhounds into service to track them down. On two occasions Lt. Hughes wrote of prisoners being brought back in chains. They were confined in tents at the guard post.[40]

In July Confederate officials decided to send the officers at Camp Oglethorpe and other western pens to Madison, Georgia. Although no official reason was given for the move, it may well have been an attempt to discourage escapes by separating officers and men. On the morning of the 9th, 113 officers left Macon, arriving at Madison that night. They were confined on the second floor of a cotton factory, where 60 of their fellow officers and 50 citizen prisoners from Tennessee greeted them.[41]

Nathaniel Kenyon found the rations at Madison to be worse than at Macon. They consisted of "heavy bread half baked and a small allowance of meat, about 4 mouthfuls apiece with something they call coffee made from rice or corn." Eventually the prisoners were allowed to supplement their fare by purchasing sweet potatoes for $13 a bushel.[42]

The men were allowed outside for exercise, but an incident in early October jeopardized that privilege. One of the officers wrote on a wall, "Dixie, the land of snakes, scorpions and traitors." Prison officials threatened to place all the officers in close confinement if the inscription was not removed. Nine officers, including Gen. Benjamin Prentiss, and a political prisoner were taken to the Madison jail after an unsuccessful escape attempt during the night of September 13–14. The group had hidden in the cellar until darkness fell. The men's attempt to loosen a board in the fence attracted the attention of the guards, foiling the plot. They remained in close confinement at the jail for a week. Charles Van Riper, one of the men confined, wrote that the cell was about sixteen feet square. Two small windows, each ten by eleven inches, provided ventilation. "Allmost suffocated for the want of pure air," Van Riper wrote during their last day at the jail. Five members of the group, he added, had become ill as a result. The ten would-be escapees were segregated after they were returned to the cotton factory.[43]

In July 1861 the Confederacy's search for prison space led Secretary Walker to ask Governor John W. Ellis of North Carolina if he could find a suitable site. Unfortunately the governor died before he had the opportunity to receive the message. The acting governor, Henry T. Clark, quickly recommended Salisbury as a likely location. It offered railroad access, cheap prices for supplies, and a "very large and commodious building" that could be had for little cost. He added, "Should this be decided upon it had better be withheld from the public until the purchase be made."[44]

Home to some twenty-four hundred souls, Salisbury was the fifth-largest community in North Carolina. The facility that Governor Clark suggested was a large cotton mill that had been established in 1839 and abandoned in 1847. An inspector dispatched by the governor reported that the lot comprised sixteen acres. Large oak trees provided shade, and there was an ample supply of good water. In addition to the main factory building, there were six brick tenements of four rooms each, a superintendent's house, and three or four outbuildings. The buildings had fallen into disrepair but could be put in proper order for $2,000. The entire property could be purchased for $15,000.[45]

Despite the optimistic report, complications soon arose. Guards could not be found, and details of the purchase proved difficult to settle. After Walker resigned on September 16, the Confederate War Department appears to have forgotten about Salisbury. On October 25 Clark sent a reminder to Secretary Benjamin, offering to assist in reopening negotiations to purchase the site. By then Walker's successor was scrambling to find prison space, and he informed Clark that the offer "greatly relieves this Department from serious embarrassment." The deal was struck on November 2. Five days later the Confederacy authorized $15,000 for the purchase of the property.[46]

Clark warned Benjamin not to send prisoners too quickly. The buildings had to be made secure, and guards were still not available. Confederate congressman Burton Craige also urged delay. Learning that a group of Richmond prisoners was being sent to Salisbury on November 27, he advised Benjamin, "If such an order was issued it ought to be countermanded for the place is wholly unfit for their safe-keeping." Meanwhile officials were working to prepare the Salisbury prison for Union prisoners. On November 11 the *Carolina Watchman,* a Salisbury newspaper, reported that the buildings were being fitted up to receive a thousand or more captives. "Our citizens don't much like the idea of such an accession to their population," the paper reported, "nevertheless they have fully assented to their part of the hardships and disagreeables of war, so bring them along." *Watchman* editor J. J. Bruner was less sanguine a month later when he observed workmen preparing the prison buildings. He predicted that the cost of readying the facility and caring for the prisoners bound there "must be a frightful sum."[47]

The problem of finding guards disappeared late in November when Rev. Braxton Craven, president of Trinity College, arrived. He brought with him the Trinity Guards, a company composed of students Craven had recruited. They received their first prisoners, a contingent of 120, on December 9. Some arrived on parole and were allowed the freedom of the town, a policy the *Watchman* strongly opposed. The paper observed that the paroled men could "set on foot serious mischief."[48]

According to Rev. A. W. Mangum, a former Confederate chaplain residing in Salisbury, the early prisoners seemed "generally well clothed & quite cheerful." They told him they liked both Salisbury and Rev. Craven, although all would prefer to go home. "They are in a perfect bustle all the time," he informed his sister. The captives made rings out of cow horns or whatever materials they could find. One, Mangum had heard, made a miniature ship and sold it to a local resident for $10. Some of their diversions were less positive. "Sometimes they fight one another & are chained & closeted for it," Mangum noted. He also expressed concerns about the Trinity Guards. "I should not wonder if [the prisoners] get out one of these days for it is an awkward charge that guard them," he wrote.[49]

Officials in Richmond apparently harbored similar concerns. On January 11 the War Department ordered Maj. George Gibbs, who was becoming the Confederates' leading prison troubleshooter, to Salisbury. He was to take command of the prison and raise three or four companies to guard it. The force was necessary because Salisbury's prison population was about to increase dramatically. On January 4 Craven reported that the camp housed only 295 captives. By March 14, according to Rev. Mangum, a recent accession had brought the total to 1,390. On April 22 Governor Clark wrote to George W. Randolph, who had succeeded Benjamin as secretary of war, that there were between 1,500 and 2,000 prisoners at Salisbury. Feeding them was becoming increasingly difficult, Clark complained. He added, "It is further represented to me that the government of the prisoners and discipline of the guard are both somewhat demoralized." Much of the problem he attributed to Gibbs, who had received a promotion to colonel and secured permission to raise a regiment for field service. In making his preparations, Clark suggested, Gibbs had "perhaps relaxed his attention and discipline." He was also recruiting members of the Salisbury guard force for his new unit. This the War Department was able to stop, ordering three companies to remain behind at the prison.[50]

What Richmond officials were not able to do was stop the prisoners at Salisbury from escaping. Although surviving Confederate records do not mention escapes from the prison during this period, the local press suggested that they were common. "Again we warn the public to keep a sharp look out for runaway yankee prisoners," the *Watchman* advised on March 24, "for it seems to be impossible for the guard at the prison to prevent their escape." The paper reported that "eight more" had recently been recaptured. Editor Bruner criticized prison officials for allowing the escapes to take place and for failing to report them to the public.[51]

Whatever problems Salisbury prison posed for local residents, Union captives arriving from other facilities generally found it to be an improvement. Willard Wheeler, transferred from New Orleans in February, wrote that the quantity of rations was better, though not the quality. Bunks, he discovered, were four tiers high, each with a straw tick. "We are not held quite as closely here as at Richmond or Tuscaloosa," Elisha Reed observed. "I like the quarters here better than any thing previous." Reed traded his watch for a violin and $5. As a result, "I now have plenty to eat and plenty of recreation."[52]

The Salisbury prisoners gained extra opportunities for recreation in April when the Confederates gave them greater freedom of the prison yard. According to prisoner Budd Walcer, the privilege was granted only after the captives gave their word of honor not to attempt to escape. John Crocker, who had been confined in Libby, observed, "This gives us the pure free air which we now know how to prize and enjoy." Hiram Eddy, the Connecticut chaplain, took advantage with relish. "Played a game of base ball in the morning & two of hand ball in the P. M.," Eddy wrote on June 9. On one occasion he interrupted his ball playing to watch a cockfight staged in the prison yard. Even editor Bruner approved of the greater liberties. "The experiment thus far has proved every way favorable," he wrote on May 12, "especially on the health of the men, which exhibits a decided improvement."[53]

The prisoners were even allowed to stage an elaborate Fourth of July celebration, complete with a professionally printed program. Chaplain Eddy opened the ceremonies with a prayer. Numerous poems, readings, and musical numbers followed, including such patriotic songs as "The Star-Spangled Banner" and "Columbia, the Gem of the Ocean." Sports and games occupied the afternoon hours. There was a sack race, a foot race, a baseball game, and a fencing match. The day's events closed with a "[c]hase for a greased pig, which afforded a great amount of fun."[54]

Removed from whatever rare moments of fun crept into prison life were Salisbury's political prisoners. These individuals were suspected of various degrees of disloyalty to the Confederacy. Many had arrived from Richmond and were accused of being "bridge-burners, spies, and domestic traitors." According to Charles Gray, they were confined in "a tumble down shanty or two." The Confederates segregated them from the military prisoners and denied them the fresh air of the prison yard. In a letter smuggled out of the camp, John Crocker wrote that the political prisoners were "closely confined and densely packed" and received only half the rations that military prisoners did. "The officers we find here tell us that dead ones are brought out daily," Gray wrote the day of his arrival.[55]

Although prison rumors could be exaggerated, conditions under which the political prisoners were held were bad enough that many risked escape attempts. In late June they began work on a tunnel, but prison officials discovered it, thanks to a "spy," Gray wrote. Undeterred, a group of captives scaled the wall with ladders on the night of the 29th. In reporting the escape, the *Watchman* inadvertently revealed much about their treatment as it advised readers to be on the lookout. "They are very dirty and ragged and may be known by this." On July 17 seven more absconded, taking advantage of "a dark and stormy hour" to run the guard. The sentries nevertheless managed to fire a few shots, reportedly wounding two of the escapees.[56]

The political prisoners would remain, but for the military captives, freedom was on the horizon. Political pressure on the Lincoln administration would soon result in an exchange cartel that would finally return most of them to the North. The agreement would prove short lived, but for most Yankees—and Confederates—taken in 1861 and early 1862, it would last long enough to see them safely home.

3
"Fresh air tastes delicious"
Virginia Prisons and the Road to Exchange, 1862

Despite their energetic efforts, Gen. Winder and other Confederate officials were never able to find sufficient prison space outside Virginia to relieve Richmond of all its Yankee captives. This meant Winder would have to locate more facilities in the capital city. In early March 1862, with the spring campaigns soon to get under way, he went looking. The general quickly settled upon the three connected warehouses of Luther and George Libby. Each building was three stories tall, and each floor contained three rooms approximately 103 by 42 feet. On the 7th the *Richmond Dispatch* announced that the government planned to utilize the facility. The first transfer of prisoners, some five hundred in number, took place on the 26th.[1]

From the standpoint of Confederate officials, the move made a great deal of sense. The Libby warehouse was located on Cary Street, "a locality secluded from observation," the *Dispatch* noted. This translated into fewer problems for the guards. The Main Street facilities had been spread out over a wide area. Now the Union captives would be confined in three connected buildings. This, too, would make the guards' lives easier. The site also offered logistical advantages. Sudden large contingents of prisoners would no longer have to be herded down busy Main Street. Both prisoners and supplies could be shipped via the James River, which was located behind the Libby buildings. The *Dispatch* also believed the facility would be an improvement for the captives. "We are inclined to think that the arrangements not only for their safe custody, but comfort, are well nigh as perfect as they can be," the paper suggested.[2]

It is extremely unlikely that the editor of the *Dispatch* ever spent much time in Libby prison. Those who did offered a far different opinion. Among the initial contingent of captives to arrive there were Charles Carroll Gray and Hiram Eddy. Their Southern sojourn had already taken them from Richmond to Charleston to Columbia. In February they had returned to Richmond, once again occupying prisons on Main Street. Gray did not consider the move to Libby an improvement, nor did he believe the arrangements for his comfort were "well nigh perfect." Instead, he wrote that he and his comrades had been marched to "a more dismal ware-house." He added, "Room large, low, damp, dirty, cold & dark." Eddy's initial remarks were more subdued, although he did concur in Gray's assessment that the facility was damp. The chaplain's first real complaint came four days later. The Confederates had told him that he would be allowed to conduct Sabbath services, but when the time came they refused. The lack of ventilation combined with the habits of his fellow prisoners also caused Eddy consternation. "Suffocated with smoke today," he wrote on April 9.[3]

At first the cavernous warehouse offered the captives a little more elbow room. This advantage disappeared within a few days as hundreds more arrived to join them. Crowding, however, proved to be just one of a number of grievances the prisoners had with their new home. Among them was the lack of windows. "There are only three windows to the room," Eddy wrote, "& those on the end." New Yorker John Crocker, who termed Libby "the most execrable place I ever was in," wrote that his first-floor room had but two windows, also at one end. William Wilkins, who arrived in August after being captured at the battle of Second Manassas, noted that there had been windows at the other end of the room in which he was confined. They had been closed up "to prevent a draft." Of course, for the prisoners arriving in the late summer at a crowded warehouse, a draft would have alleviated a great deal of discomfort. This was especially true of the prisoners confined on the top floor. One of them was James A. Bell, a civilian government clerk captured at the Manassas battlefield. "The days were suffocatingly hot, owing to the sun's rays on the metalic roof," he wrote soon after his release in late September.[4]

An even more common complaint was the sticky accumulation of a variety of substances on the floors of the warehouse. With no organized prison administration in place, the Confederates had not even made the simplest preparations to house prisoners at Libby. Wilkins termed the substance a "thick black greasy slime" that was an inch deep. Bell described it as "an oozy compound of filth, from which arose a stench more intolerable than I ever before inhaled." In a letter smuggled to his wife, Crocker explained, "The room for a long time had been used as a packing house for packing, ham, bacon and pork. The grease, salt and dirt, that had accumulated from year to year on the floor was so thick and hard it was impossible for us to sweep it, or hoe it, or even to shovel it up." Eddy wrote, "The floor is perfectly saturated with fat & grease. This makes it impossible to get the floor clean." He added, "In walking, this vile stuff adheres to the shoes." Although a few prisoners had camp beds for sleeping, most had to sleep on the floor. Among them was George Parker of the Twenty-first Massachusetts. "They wouldn't give me so much as an old rag to lay down on to keep me out of the filth," he explained in a letter to his mother. "When I got up in the morning it was like pulling two sticking plasters apart."[5]

Lice added to Parker's nighttime woes. "I couldn't sleep there at all," he wrote. "I felt crawly all over." Each morning, as it grew daylight, "One [prisoner] after another would drop down on the window seat, pull off their shirt, turn it inside out and commence picking off the lice or as it was called there '*skirmishing.*'" According to Bell, the vermin were inescapable. "The floor, walls and every place was lined with them, even the food that we ate was not free from their odious presence." Daniel Cooledge of the Second Vermont blamed the creatures for much of the mortality at the prison. "Vermin and maggots are taking the life of many a poor fellow," he wrote in a July diary entry.[6]

The Federal officers occupied the first floor of the facility. Although the Confederates may have considered this a privilege, believing this to be the most comfortable level, events proved otherwise. There was no plastering to the ceiling, simply a board floor overhead, "and the noise and confusion caused by so many men over our heads was terrible," Crocker wrote. "The poor fellows above were crammed in so thick they could hardly stand. They were very uneasy and constantly jumping, dancing stamping, pounding, and engaged in various employments for exercise, all of which, annoyed us beyond measure."[7]

The officers soon found out that the noise was not the worst thing emanating from above. Privies had been installed at all levels, connected by pipes that ran to the ground. Occasionally the privies would overflow. At other times the pipes burst. As a result, Eddy noted, "We are the sewer for near 400 men above us." Added Crocker, "The entire filth from the sinks and closets . . . came constantly pouring down into our room, impregnating the air and creating the most nauseating and filthy atmosphere that I ever breathed." On one occasion the pipes burst as Eddy was composing a letter to his wife, spilling their contents close to where he was writing. "Every man lit his pipe & smoked for his life," he noted. Despite their efforts, "[t]he awful stench is still in the room." Arriving in August, Wilkins observed, "The walls are smeared from the floors above with the slops & excretions of the hundreds of men confined over head."[8]

As bad as conditions were for captured Union soldiers, they were even worse for the civilian prisoners housed in Libby. As at Salisbury, the evidence against them varied greatly, but Winder believed it was flimsy in many cases. In August 1861 he urged Secretary Walker to appoint a commission to investigate their cases. Many, he felt, would be released as a consequence. "By this course justice would be done and [there would be] a great saving of expense to the Confederate States." Walker acted upon the recommendation, naming J. Randolph Turner and James Lyon commissioners. When Benjamin succeeded Walker, he went further, releasing virtually all of the suspects.[9]

More quickly arrived to take their place. In early May Eddy wrote that there were hundreds in Libby. Some served as cooks, and others worked in the prison hospital. Many were over sixty years of age. A member of one contingent, arrested in January in Fairfax County, told Eddy that when the men were taken, they had not been permitted to return to their homes for clothing or money. They then had to endure an eight-day march, during which two of them fell dead along the road. By the time James Bell reached Libby, many of them had been there for nine months, some for over a year. "Among them are men of wealth and intellectual refinement whose classical features and dilapidated apparel form a sad contrast," he wrote. "The privation, sufferings and anguish of mind endured for so long a time by these men, deprived of their personal rights, had reduced them to the verge of idiocy." After evincing "signs of aberation of mind" for weeks, one had jumped from a second-story window. He survived the impact, but not the shots of the sentries.[10]

On March 3 a building formerly known as "McDaniel's negro jail" was converted into "a secure retreat for the Unionists of Richmond, and for politically dispeptic characters from other portions of the state." It was rechristened Castle Godwin, in honor of Capt. Archibald C. Godwin. The future Salisbury commander was then serving as a provost marshal under Winder. On March 2 he initiated a crackdown, arresting nine prominent citizens of Richmond. "It is inferred that they are charged with conspiring against the government, upon what evidence has not yet transpired," the *Dispatch* explained. By June 11 there were 128 prisoners confined there, and by August 14 the number had reached 250.[11]

The dramatic increase in the number of inmates strained the capacity of the small facility, and once again Winder was scrambling to find roomier quarters. He settled on three buildings located just two blocks from Libby. Greanor's tobacco warehouse, Whitlock's warehouse, and Palmer's factory were appropriated and collectively given the name Castle Thunder. The move took place on August 18, and according to the *Richmond Enquirer*, it was "conducted with admirable expedition." Greanor's had been used previously as a prison and was, as a result, "massed with filth." It was thoroughly cleaned and whitewashed and was, the *Enquirer* insisted, "in 'apple-pie order' " to receive the prisoners.[12]

The prisoners confined in Castle Godwin and Castle Thunder arrived there under a variety of charges. Lists of those held published in the *Richmond Dispatch* during the month of April included individuals accused of "treason," "disloyalty," and "suspicion." A Fredericksburg resident had been charged with using "treasonable language." A Texan and a Georgian were listed as spies. In April a group of employees at a "lithographic establishment" found themselves in Castle Godwin after striking for higher wages while working on a government contract. Many occupants of the two prisons arrived there under much less serious charges. On a day in which about a half dozen offenders arrived at Castle Godwin, the *Dispatch* conceded that "most of them were for trivial offenses." Whiskey sellers made up a sizable percentage of the offenders. Even those guilty of loitering were not immune. In September the paper reported that "a number of loafers and men of leisure" were taken to Castle Thunder. They remained for about two weeks.[13]

If the Richmond press is to be believed, Confederate soldiers were the dominant group at Castles Godwin and Thunder. On September 18 the *Dispatch* reported that they made up five hundred of the six hundred prisoners lodged at Castle Thunder. Most were charged with desertion. Their presence led to a blame game between Confederate generals. Field commanders such as Joseph Johnston and Daniel Harvey Hill complained that Winder was augmenting his own command with deserters he had rounded up. Winder responded that he did not have sufficient forces to return these stragglers to their units. The *Dispatch* implicitly sided with Winder. The paper charged that Confederate officers had concluded that the prisons were "nothing more nor less than a hospital for incurables." Whoever was to blame, the military and civilian prisoners soon taxed the capacity of Castle Thunder.[14]

With the start of the spring campaigns of 1862, a wave of new military prisoners taxed the capacity of Libby prison as well. In March 1862 Gen. George B. McClellan landed some one hundred thousand soldiers on the peninsula between the York and James rivers. His plan was to move west up the peninsula, capture Richmond, and win the war. He did not, and the failed campaign that followed placed several thousand prisoners in the hands of the Confederates. As a precaution, the Confederates sent all the Union officer prisoners, a total of sixty, along with "fifty of the hardest subjects" at Castle Godwin, to Salisbury as McClellan approached. This did not begin to compensate for the tide of captives that was soon headed for Richmond. The first significant batch, some five hundred in number, reached the

Confederate capital on June 2. They had been taken the two previous days at the battle of Seven Pines. There followed a brief respite until the Seven Days' campaign of June 25–July 1. When it ended, Richmond was safe, Robert E. Lee had emerged as a Confederate hero, and a deluge of prisoners was on its way to Richmond. By July 2, the *Richmond Examiner* reported, four thousand had arrived at the capital. Fourteen days later Gen. Winder reported that 7,847 Union prisoners were being housed in Richmond.[15]

Once again circumstances forced the harried "warden of Richmond" to find more places to house the unwanted Yankees. Two warehouses became Scott's and Pemberton's prisons. The Warwick and Barksdale mill, acquired on July 1, could reportedly house 4,000 men. On the evening of July 4, all Union officers held in Richmond, about 120, were taken to Smith & McCurdy's factory. Among those observing a gloomy Independence Day were Generals John Reynolds and George McCall. Both had previously enjoyed the hospitality of the Spottswood Hotel.[16]

Despite the acquisition of the new facilities, Libby remained extremely crowded. "The floor is so thronged with prisoners that it is difficult to turn around," one wrote on August 16. Still more arrived two days later, "until every inch, almost, of standing ground is occupied." The men received some relief on the 19th when teamsters and other civilian prisoners were removed, but the facility was still strained nearly to capacity.[17]

It had become apparent that the factories and warehouses of Richmond were no longer sufficient, forcing Winder to expand the scope of his search. Among the locations he settled on was Lynchburg, Virginia. It is unclear when the Confederates first utilized the site, but it was likely early June 1862. Ziba Roberts of the Twenty-eighth New York was part of a detachment of prisoners that arrived on the 11th. They had been captured May 25 in the Shenandoah Valley. The Lynchburg prisoners remained in a field until the 17th, when they were taken to the fairgrounds. The captives had apparently not been searched very thoroughly because on his second day there Roberts sold his revolver to an Illinois soldier for $7.50.[18]

Roberts offered no description of the camp, but Charles H. Blinn, who also arrived at Lynchburg on the 11th, preferred the field where they were first held. "The place is not as healthy as the one we vacated," he explained. There was but one well to provide water for the 2,260 prisoners there. After only four days at the fairgrounds, Blinn wrote that four to seven were dying each day. He was not alone in his views, nor were those views limited to Yankees. Winder had sent Col. George Gibbs, the former Salisbury commander, to take command at Lynchburg. On the 18th Gibbs informed the general that the fairgrounds were "entirely unsuited to the purpose." The prisoners were all housed either in open stalls or tents they had constructed from their blankets. There was no lumber to erect barracks or a hospital, nor was there wood to be used as fuel. Because of confusion between local officials, the prisoners had gone twenty-four hours without receiving any rations.[19]

Winder acted decisively, ordering Gibbs to appoint a quartermaster. He instructed Capt. John Galt, the commissary of subsistence at Lynchburg, to furnish rations on Gibbs's order. He further ordered Galt to stop shipments of flour, corn, bacon, and cattle from Lynchburg and impress however much was required for the prison.[20]

The same day that he sent his message to Winder, Gibbs promised the men that they would soon have better rations. The commandant, whom Blinn termed "a gentleman," was true to his word. On the 20th Blinn wrote, "Our rations are now more ample than they have been since our capture." The next day the sick prisoners received wall tents. On the 24th the Confederates issued "a quantity of old tents of every description," causing the camp to "present a 'Yankee appearance.'" The camp also received a doctor. Roberts visited him on several occasions, receiving ointment for an injured foot, pills for diarrhea, and to have a tooth pulled.[21]

When not attending to his medical needs, Roberts put his Yankee entrepreneurial skills to work to better his rations. In addition to his revolver, he also sold his watch and his pocketbook. He used the funds to purchase bread, onions, blueberries, and huckleberries. The berries enabled the New Yorker to make pies for his mess. On July 9 Roberts earned a special reward for his physical labor. After he worked all morning chopping wood for the camp, the quartermaster provided him with a drink of whiskey.[22]

The most fateful decision Winder made in his 1862 search for prison space occurred in July. On the 9th the *Richmond Dispatch* reported that Confederate authorities were considering utilizing Belle Isle, an eighty-acre island in the James River, as a military prison. Two days later the *Richmond Enquirer* reported that "a large number" had been moved to the site. The capital city press gushed as it extolled the virtues of the island. The *Enquirer* termed it "a very pleasant spot." Noting that a number of wounded prisoners had been sent there, the *Dispatch* concluded, "Here, with the advantage of fresh air and plenty of water, their chances of recovery are much increased." Speaking of the prisoners in general, the *Enquirer* observed, "Their friends in the North may be perfectly satisfied that they will pass a pleasant summer at Richmond." Both the *Dispatch* and the *Examiner* claimed that the prisoners had "excellent tents" to protect them from the elements.[23]

As was the case with Libby, the newspapers' views differed distinctly from those of the prisoners at the site. On July 14 the *Dispatch* reported the "salubrious and pleasant spot" was already home to three thousand Yankees. Among those arriving that day was William Collin, a corporal with the Fifth Wisconsin. "We are very thick on the Island," he wrote, adding, "We are very short of food." By the 29th Collin had concluded, "This is becoming an awful place. Many are dying every day." Arriving in mid-August from Salisbury, Simon Hulbert wrote, "About six men dies every day with starvation & exposure to the cold & wet having to lie out upon the ground." Writing to his brother from a parole camp shortly after being exchanged, Albert Irwin recalled, "Our suffering from exposure and *hunger* while we remained on the island were awful." His estimate of the mortality rate was close to Hulbert's. "The deaths averaged *five* pr. day, and on one morning I saw nine coffins leaving camp."[24]

The causes of the suffering on Belle Isle were many, beginning with the fact that Confederate officials had simply shipped the prisoners with no plan in place of how to care for them. Among the problems was terrain. The prison was on the lower portion of the island, an area that was sandy and bug infested. One former prisoner even wrote that he amused himself by watching ants emerge from their sandy hills and return with lice the prisoners had picked off. The upper portion, home to Confederate quarters and artillery, was much more comfortable. It sat considerably higher and was lush with vegetation. Despite the claims of the local newspapers, the vast majority of the prisoners had no shelter. Even the *Dispatch* seemed to concede this point on September 1, noting, "In dry weather the prisoners can get along excellently; but in rainy, wet weather . . . many more desirable stopping places can be thought of." On August 22 Hulbert wrote, "I got a good wetting last night. Slept on the ground in the open air with nothing over me but . . . my coat." Although a few tents arrived a week later, they were not nearly enough to supply all those in need. Fortunately for Hulbert, some of his friends were among the lucky ones, and they invited him to share their shelter. Still, when Irwin arrived in September, he wrote that he was one of hundreds of prisoners sleeping on the bare ground.[25]

Another problem for the Belle Isle prisoners was a lack of rations. As early as July 19, the *Dispatch* complained of the cost of feeding the prisoners. On September 1 the paper asserted, "It takes an enormous quantity of victuals to feed so many hungry mouths as are to be found on Belle Isle, and the onerousness of the burden to the Government is not lessened when we reflect that all of the consumers are non-producers." This may have been so, but the prisoners were unanimous in the view that their individual rations did not constitute "enormous quantities." On August 16 Collin wrote, "Since we have been on this Island we have had just enough to eat to keep the breath in us & that is all." Two days later his diary entry read, "We are most dead this morning *nothing* to eat for twenty-four hours." A ration of bread, one-quarter pound per man, arrived at noon. According to Irwin the rations included a half pound of bread daily, a small piece of beef two or three times a week, and occasionally a half pint of soup that he described as "dish water." Hulbert's diary entries confirmed that description, except that he termed the bean soup "greasy water." The New York soldier added that the rations, prepared across the James in Richmond, did not always arrive. "We all sit on the shore after we get our breakfast & watch the boat to see if we are going to have any supper," he noted. "Sometimes the cooks in the Bake house over in the city get drunk & then we have to go without Bread."[26]

Prisoners who had money could supplement their rations through purchases, but the prices were high. Collin was among a group of captives who pooled their funds and bought a barrel of flour for $22. "We have been living *high all day,*" he wrote the day of the purchase. Unfortunately, later that day a mob rushed through the camp, stealing as much flour as possible and upsetting the rest. Collin and his friends lost most of their supply. They were able to purchase a little more within a few days, consuming some themselves and raising funds for future purchases by selling "flapjacks" to their fellow prisoners.[27]

When not searching out locations to house the ever-growing number of Union prisoners, Winder spent the summer of 1862 trying to staff his burgeoning prison system. Henry Wirz had by then returned from Alabama. On August 27 Winder placed him in charge of all Richmond prisons, a command replete with challenges. One day after assuming the position, Wirz informed his boss that there were only fifteen muskets available for the guards at Libby, "whilst it requires forty to arm every man on guard." On the 31st he told Capt. Norris Montgomery, commanding Belle Isle, that another two thousand prisoners would arrive there the next day. "This will make it necessary to extend your lines," Wirz counseled. He asked Montgomery to inform him if he needed more men. The captain had apparently located weapons, because he promised to send Montgomery one hundred guns. Most interesting, considering Wirz's future reputation, was his reaction to a September 5 shooting incident at Libby. A prisoner had "amused himself" by sticking his head out a window and verbally abusing guards, who ordered him to desist. The sentinel fired, hoping to frighten the man. The ball, however, passed through the ceiling and killed a citizen prisoner on the level above. Although the shooting was accidental, Wirz immediately had the guard placed under arrest and sent to Castle Thunder.[28]

In September Wirz returned to Alabama "to hunt up the missing records" of Federal prisoners as part of the exchange process. Capt. George Washington Alexander assumed Wirz's post until October 27, when Capt. Thomas P. Turner took command of Richmond's Confederate prisons. By then prisoner exchanges had cleared Belle Isle and most other Richmond prisons, and Turner basically became the commandant of Libby. He would retain the post for the remainder of the war. His second in command was Richard R. Turner. As time went on, "Dick" Turner would gain a reputation among the prisoners as a hot-tempered and cruel keeper. The two Turners, both in their early twenties, were not related.[29]

Despite the future reputations of Wirz and Richard Turner, it was Alexander, placed in command of Castle Thunder, who first became a controversial figure following allegations of abuse. The castle housed a variety of prisoners, many of the worst stripe. In addition to Confederate deserters, there were suspected spies and other disloyal persons, criminals, and all offenders under sentence of death. The last group had nothing to lose, and escape attempts were common. Newly sentenced inmates and the weaker of those incarcerated were routinely beaten and robbed. On November 1, 1862, several prisoners somehow secured "several pounds" of gunpowder, which they ignited with a fuse they had also obtained. According to the *Dispatch,* the explosion "raised considerable alarm, shook the building, and broke a number of panes of glass." Miraculously, nobody was injured by the blast.[30]

If reports in Richmond newspapers can be believed, escape attempts at Castle Thunder took a variety of forms. In October 1862 there were two attempts to get out through a window. In the first case a group of prisoners made a rope of cotton sheets to allow a fellow inmate, who had been sentenced to be shot, lower himself to freedom. Guards caught them before they had completed their project. A few nights later a deserter from the First Virginia escaped through a second-story window, making it down to the street and past the patrols. Several sentinels found themselves under arrest as a result. In December a group of prisoners confined on the first floor smuggled in some hoop iron. The men loosened a few bricks before the guards discovered them. On the 29th the *Enquirer* reported that a group of about 150 prisoners had conspired to "assassinate the sentinels and secure their escape." The leader of the plot was David Welsh, "a Yankee murderer and thief." Prison officials discovered the plan. Welsh was "punished with stripes, placed in irons, and is now kept on bread and water."[31]

Occasionally the prisoners resorted to deviousness to secure their escape. On December 27, 1862, the *Dispatch* reported that one John Gormley "was disposed to have a Christmas spree with an old friend who was a prisoner in Castle Thunder." Gormley arrived at the castle and wove a woeful tale that two of his friend's children had died of some form of fever. "His long face and sorrowful words had the desired effect, and the prisoner was released to attend the melancholy ceremony," the paper explained. Officials somehow discovered the trick, and soon both men were lodged in the prison. Another escape was conceived by some "desperate cases" who determined to bribe a guard, notwithstanding the fact that they had no money. One of them whispered to a likely sentinel that the would-be escapees would pay him $50 apiece if he would look the other way as they scampered out through an open window. The guard agreed after enlisting a colleague to assist him. As the first prisoner made his exit, he informed the trusting guard that the last man out had his money. About seven got through before the sentinel began to realize that he had been duped. The gullible guards were soon in irons.[32]

In dealing with the miscreants placed under his charge, Alexander resorted to harsh punishments. Whippings were reportedly common. Prisoners were occasionally bucked and gagged. Under this procedure, a piece of wood was placed crosswise in the prisoner's mouth and tied in place. His arms were then tied behind his back and attached to another piece of wood behind his legs. There were also reports of guards forcing prisoners to wear "barrel shirts" or suspending them by their thumbs.[33]

The *Enquirer* approved of the whippings, writing, "The mode of punishment is most appropriate, and if generally adopted towards rogues, would save the courts, civil and martial, much trouble." The *Dispatch* agreed, observing, "The introduction of corporal punishment has had a most salutary effect on the manners of the inmates, some of whom are very hard cases."[34]

Not everyone viewed Castle Thunder so blithely. Among the skeptics was the Confederate House of Representatives, which in April 1863 appointed a committee to investigate the treatment of prisoners. For nearly three weeks the committee heard from a variety of witnesses. Inmates, prison officials, and detectives from Winder's police force all offered testimony. Some told grisly tales of men being hung by their thumbs for up to eight hours, bucking and gagging that lasted for as long as two hours, and whippings involving fifty lashes as Alexander urged guards, "Lay it on!" Others told of escaping prisoners who could have been easily retaken being shot down instead. Following the gunpowder incident, Alexander had allegedly placed a number of men outside in the cold and rain for two days because they would not reveal the names of the perpetrators. Alexander produced a number of defense witnesses who testified to the commandant's humanity and the incorrigibility of the inmates. One of them claimed that a prosecution witness, a hospital steward, was motivated by hatred of Alexander, who had put him in a cell for insubordination. Alexander's star witness was Gen. Winder, who noted that he had given the orders "to punish these ruffians severely and if necessary to resort to corporal punishment."[35]

In the end the committee exonerated Capt. Alexander by a vote of three to two. Each of the dissenters offered a minority report. W. D. Simpson termed Alexander's methods "illegal and improper" but agreed with the majority that no further action should be taken against the captain. The other, Thomas S. Bocock, who was Speaker of the House, concluded that Alexander's punishments had been "not only degrading and cruel but barbarous and inhuman." He added, "Firmness and promptness are very different from torture and inhumanity." Bocock concluded that Alexander "deserves in my opinion the severest censure at the hands of Congress."[36]

As the summer of 1862 wore on it began to look as though Castle Thunder's incorrigibles might be the only prisoners remaining under military authority in Richmond. For the prisoners of war held at Libby, Belle Isle, and other locations in the South, the prospect of exchange and a return to the North grew much more promising. It was a prospect that the Lincoln administration had been resisting for nearly a year. Public and political pressure in favor of exchange had finally caught up with them. In July Union officials finally agreed to begin serious negotiations. By the end of the month a cartel was in place that would bring an end to the captivity of thousands of prisoners in both Northern and Southern camps.

Informal exchanges between individual commanders had actually been going on since the war began. Indeed, as the conflict began, the Union garrison at Fort Sumter had not only been paroled but provided transportation home. By the fall of 1861 Maj. Gen. John E. Wool, the Union commander of Fortress Monroe, and Maj. Gen. Benjamin Huger of the Confederate Department of Norfolk were exchanging captives regularly. The numbers seldom reached one hundred, and Wool was careful to make clear that these were individual exchanges. He did not allow the discussions to evolve into the topic of a general exchange between the belligerents. Perhaps the most unusual arrangement involved some 250 Confederate prisoners from Fort Warren in Boston Harbor. They were sent south to obtain the release of Union prisoners of equivalent rank, thus securing their own exchange.[37]

Western theater generals also agreed to limited exchanges during the first year of the war. Among them was Gen. Ulysses S. Grant, who would later become a determined foe of the practice. During the fall of 1861 Grant made a number of exchanges with Gen. Leonidas Polk. He was quick to point out, "I recognize no Southern Confederacy myself." To make sure the point was not lost, Grant instructed a subordinate who conducted one group of prisoners to a flag-of-truce steamer to "avoid all discussions upon the rights of belligerents." The following February, when the capture of Fort Donelson in Tennessee placed fifteen thousand prisoners in his hands, Grant recommended a policy of immediate parole. "I am now forwarding prisoners of war to your care and I shall be truly glad to get clear of them," he explained to a staff officer at department headquarters. "It is a much less job to take than to keep them."[38]

Although Grant's campaign against Forts Henry and Donelson made him a hero in the North, his stature was not yet to the point where his policy recommendations were seriously considered. The Lincoln administration held fast to its desire to avoid any action that might imply a recognition of the Confederacy. With the January 1862 appointment of Edwin M. Stanton as secretary of war, Lincoln added an equally determined foe of exchange to his official family. This posed a serious problem for Union soldiers held in the South and for a Confederate government that was having a difficult time trying to care for them.

In January 1862 Secretary Benjamin attempted to expand the scope of prisoner exchange. In a message to Gen. Joseph Johnston, commanding the Department of Northern Virginia, the secretary of war wrote that he was "hourly assailed by propositions from different quarters for partial and individual exchanges." He added, "We cannot consent to continue a system so partial in its operation, so cumbersome in detail and so difficult of execution." Benjamin wanted Johnston to send a message to Union general-in-chief George B. McClellan proposing "some general system of exchange." Johnston complied but he received no response from McClellan.[39]

As January ended Benjamin learned that New York congressman Hamilton Fish and Methodist bishop Edward Ames were heading south. Although he did not know the details, through newspaper reports he learned that they were being sent on a mission "in relation to the prisoners of war held by us." He instructed Huger to find out what they were up to and to communicate those findings to the War Department.[40]

On February 4 Huger made his report. Fish and Ames had been dispatched by Secretary Stanton. They were to visit Union prisoners held in Richmond and elsewhere, determine their needs, and "supply their wants and provide for their comfort according to your discretion." A government fund had been placed at their disposal for the purchase of clothing, medicine, and other needed items. Stanton further instructed the two men to make a list of all Union prisoners and describe "their present state and condition." The list was also to include "all other particulars that may be interesting and proper for their families to know or useful to be known by this Government for the purpose of effecting their exchange or release."[41]

Benjamin latched onto those final few words, seeing them as an opportunity to expand the mission beyond anything Stanton intended. Davis and the Confederate cabinet agreed, and on February 6 the secretary of war sent a letter through Huger to Wool. It announced that Benjamin was sending two commissioners to Fortress Monroe to meet with Ames and Fish. "These honorable gentlemen . . . propose to spare Messrs. Ames and Fish the necessity of travel to Richmond and other places in the South by agreeing at once to the restoration of all the prisoners to their homes on fair terms of equal exchange," he wrote. Ames and Fish immediately realized that Benjamin's letter "embraces matters not intrusted to us," and they asked Stanton for instructions. His reply was blunt: "Leave to pass through the opposing lines having been denied you[,] you will consider your mission terminated and you will return at your convenience to this city."[42]

Stanton realized that the termination of the Ames-Fish mission would not end the Northern demand for an exchange agreement. Indeed, with the failure of the effort to feed and clothe Union captives, that demand was likely to grow. State legislatures, concerned over favorite sons held in Confederate prisons, were passing resolutions demanding a cartel. So, too, were both houses of the U.S. Congress. Newspapers generally friendly to the administration, such as the *New York Times,* would soon add their voices to the clamor. With his options limited, Stanton on February 11 instructed Wool to inform Huger "that you alone are clothed with full powers for the purpose of arranging for the exchange of prisoners." The secretary gave his negotiator a great deal of latitude in devising the terms for exchanging soldiers of different grades. Significantly, in light of the subsequent negotiations, Stanton authorized Wool to agree that "all the surplus prisoners on either side be discharged on parole." He even added a sweetener, ordering Wool to inform the Confederates that their privateers were being held as military prisoners.[43]

Benjamin was anxious to make another effort to obtain an exchange cartel. On February 18 he ordered Brig. Gen. Howell Cobb to meet with Wool to work out an agreement. In response to the Union's shift on policy concerning privateers, Benjamin instructed Cobb to tell Wool that the prisoners held as hostages had been released from close confinement. The two negotiators met on February 23. By the end of the day they had agreed to every point except one. Benjamin's instructions to Cobb included the clause, "That all prisoners delivered up on parole by either party shall be so delivered on the frontier at the expense of the captors." The word "frontier," which could have implied recognition, troubled Wool, and he wired Stanton for advice. Terming the proposal "obnoxious in its terms and import," Stanton ordered Wool to "make no arrangement except for actual [individual] exchanges." Cobb offered to remove the clause in question, but Wool stuck to the letter of his orders. The Southern negotiator believed he knew the reason. On February 16 Gen. Grant had taken Fort Donelson, along with its fifteen thousand prisoners. "Before the agreement could be reduced to writing . . . the casualties of war reversed this state of things and gave the United States the largest number of prisoners," Cobb informed Benjamin. "With this change of things the United States changed their policy and deliberately abandoned their own proposition."[44]

Whether calculated or not, the Union's change of heart was not destined to last. The clamor from the public, the press, and elected officials continued to grow. As summer arrived the "casualties of war" again "reversed," this time in favor of the Confederates. The failure of McClellan's Peninsular campaign and the resulting flood of Union prisoners suddenly made exchange more palatable for the Union and more urgent for the Confederacy. On July 3 Lee urged Randolph to allow Cobb to make another attempt with Wool. Randolph gave his approval the next day, noting, "The sooner it is done the better, as the number of prisoners is increasing to an extent that threatens serious embarrassment." On the 9th Lee offered to send wounded Union prisoners through the lines on parole. Although the Confederates had given them the best care they could, Lee informed McClellan, "I learn with regret that they are dying rapidly." McClellan forwarded the message to Stanton. "I commend to your attention the humane spirit evinced by General Lee," he wrote, "and I also beg leave to commend to your consideration a mutual release of all prisoners upon parole, exchanging as far as may be practicable."[45]

The next day Stanton ordered Maj. Gen. John A. Dix, then commanding at Fortress Monroe, to "negotiate a general exchange of prisoners with the enemy." Despite the timing, McClellan's endorsement of the policy likely did not prompt the decision, although it may have helped confirm it. On July 8 Stanton had informed Dix that the assignment was soon to come. Dix advised McClellan that he also had a brief conference with Lincoln concerning the appointment. On the Confederate side, illness prevented Cobb from resuming the negotiations. In his place Lee appointed Maj. Gen. Daniel Harvey Hill. Over the next week, the two generals held a series of meetings at Haxall's Landing on the James. Despite the difficulties of the earlier negotiations—and Hill's reputation for stubbornness—the pair quickly reached an agreement. Signed on July 22, it was based upon an exchange cartel used by American and British forces during the War of 1812. A sliding scale of various values was to be used when exchanging prisoners of different ranks. Excess prisoners would be paroled and not be permitted to take up arms until properly exchanged. Finally, the terms stipulated that disputes were to be "made the subject of friendly expressions in order that the object of this agreement may neither be defeated or postponed." It was a clause that would prove to have a painfully short shelf life.[46]

It did not take long for word of the cartel to reach Yankee prisoners in the East. "Hear that arrangements are being made for a general exchange of prisoners," Frank Bennett wrote from Columbia on July 24. "I pray God that it may be true." Confirmation arrived on August 4. "We are becoming very impatient and anxious to be off," he noted. A number of officers confined in Richmond learned of the cartel on July 25, when one of their number received a letter from a friend in the Virginia state government. "Puts the prisoners in good heart," one of them wrote. Five days later they read the terms in a Richmond paper. At Salisbury Simon Hulbert first wrote of exchange rumors on July 14, observing that they were daily occurrences. By August 10 he was confident enough to write, "I feel that my prayers are being answered." The prisoners were not the only ones celebrating at Salisbury. On July 21 guard James Lowry informed his mother, "There is to be a general exchange of prisoners. It has caused a great deal of excitement among the boys here."[47]

The cartel was a mixed blessing for Gen. Winder. On the positive side of the ledger, it allowed him to remove all prisoners from Lynchburg, Salisbury, Columbia, and points farther west. At the same time he was faced with a logistical nightmare as Richmond became the focal point for exchange in the East. Winder was charged with forwarding to Col. Robert Ould, the Confederate agent of exchange, prisoners to be paroled. At the same time he was responsible for receiving and forwarding Confederate prisoners. Meanwhile prisoners he had sent away because of overcrowding were headed back to Richmond. On August 6 the *Dispatch* announced that over three thousand prisoners from Lynchburg and Salisbury were on their way to the Confederate capital. Over the next five days nearly twenty-five hundred arrived from Lynchburg. The last of the Salisbury prisoners reached the Confederate capital on the 16th. The same prisons that had been established to relieve overcrowding in Richmond were now returning their captives to a city no better prepared to handle them than it had been before. Fortunately, for both them and the Confederates, their second sojourn in Richmond was destined to be brief.[48]

Although some of the prisoners bound for Richmond went to Libby, most were sent to Belle Isle. By September 1 even the *Dispatch* conceded that "the place is crowded." One of the prisoners arriving at this time was Charles Gardner of the

First Maine Cavalry, who arrived as part of a contingent from Lynchburg. "As we crossed the bridge and approached the prison yard, such a sight met my eyes as I never saw before and never want to again," he later wrote. "I thought we were hard looking but we did not compare with those poor fellows. . . . Some of them were living skeletons with just life enough to crawl, and some were nearly idiots." The situation was especially dire because more prisoners were on their way, the result of Gen. Lee's victory over John Pope at the battle of Second Manassas.[49]

Exchange moderated the prison crisis in Richmond temporarily, but it never entirely solved it. The first shipments out of the city included Union sick and wounded, which relieved Confederate officials of the expense of caring for them. Some eight hundred wounded captives departed on July 26. Smaller numbers left during the next two days. At the same time more wounded Yankees were reaching Richmond from McClellan's army on the peninsula.[50]

The next large shipment of Union prisoners left Richmond on August 5. Three days earlier Confederate officers had visited Belle Isle in order to ascertain which prisoners were "most prostrated by sickness." The task was difficult, the *Dispatch* reported, "as simultaneously with the announcement, over 4,000 men were taken violently ill." Despite the complications, three thousand left the island for Varina, the nearby plantation being used as the point of exchange. The prisoners, all enlisted men, marched past the prison where many of their officers were still held. As they did, the men "cheered their imprisoned compatriots . . . and otherwise testified their respect for them." One officer who was glad that they did was Samuel Jackson. The Pennsylvanian saw several men from his regiment, including his brother. "They are looking pretty hard, but in fine spirits, rejoicing over the event of their release from prison," Jackson observed.[51]

One group of prisoners did not rejoice—the officers who had served under Gen. John Pope. In June Pope had been named commander of the newly christened Army of Virginia, an amalgam of forces in western Virginia. He earned the assignment based on a successful record in the western theater. Upon taking command he promptly reminded his new army of both his successes and its failures. "I have come to you from the West, where we have always seen the backs of our enemies," he puffed in his introductory orders. On July 23 Pope issued General Orders 11. They called for the arrest of all disloyal male citizens within Union lines. If those citizens agreed to take an oath of allegiance to the United States they would be allowed to remain. Those unwilling to do so would be conducted to the Confederate lines. If they returned they would be "considered spies and subjected to the extreme rigor of military law." Anyone deemed guilty of violating the terms of the oath of allegiance "shall be shot and his property seized and applied to the public use."[52]

Pope's orders came one day after Dix and Hill signed the exchange cartel, and they immediately jeopardized the agreement. On August 1 the Davis government issued its own set of orders. General Orders 54 proclaimed that Pope and his commissioned officers were "specially declared to be not entitled to be considered as soldiers, and therefore not entitled to the benefit of the cartel for the parole of future prisoners of war." If captured they were to be kept in close confinement and held as hostages subject to hanging "in the event of the murder of any unarmed citizen or inhabitant of this Confederacy." In a message to Gen. Lee, Davis made it clear that only the officers under Pope's command were included in the order. The president further asserted that the offensive orders "would justify our refusal to execute the generous cartel by which we have consented to liberate an excess of thousands of prisoners held by us beyond the number held by the enemy." This Davis declined to do, although his motives were likely more practical than altruistic.[53]

The battle of Cedar Mountain, fought on August 9, gave the Confederates their first large contingent of prisoners from Pope's army. Among them was one brigadier general, Mexican War veteran Henry Prince. Twenty-seven captured officers reached Richmond on the 11th, and some twelve more arrived during the following week. Their presence in the capital allowed the Richmond press to give vent to their hatred of Pope. "They have all, Gen Prince included, been placed in Libby prison," the *Enquirer* reported, "and will in a few days be separately confined, to be treated, and finally punished as felons, should the brute Government of the North persist in claiming the right to murder and pillage." According to the *Whig,* Prince appeared before Winder, asking to be treated as a prisoner of war. The general denied the request. "The illustrious Prince was then conveyed to the prison, where, with his brother officers, he will enjoy 'close confinement,' until the villainous orders of the land pirate Pope are revoked by competent authority." The *Dispatch* gloated, "They have not been permitted to associate with the [other] Federal officers, and appear very downcast at the prospect before them."[54]

According to George Parker of the Twenty-first Massachusetts, the Confederates' contempt for Pope ran deep. Captured at the battle of Second Manassas, Parker was paroled in early October. In a letter written from a Union parole camp, he told his mother, "As to 'Pope' if they had got hold of him he would have been shot a dozen times on his way to Richmond. They tell most horrid stories of his cruelties to the inhabitants of the places his army occupied." Parker was not under Pope's command, and soon after their arrival at Libby, he and twelve other officers of the same status were separated and put in a different room. Not only were their new quarters superior, but prison officials made it clear that this room was set aside for officers eligible for exchange. "I left a sad looking lot of faces in that room when I came out," Parker recalled.[55]

Among the Pope officers at Libby was William D. Wilkins, a captain of U.S. volunteers who had served on the staff of Gen. Alpheus S. Williams. He was captured at Cedar Mountain and arrived at Richmond on August 11. Like those who had preceded him to Libby, he complained of the "thick black greasy slime" on the floor and the "horrible odor" from the faulty privies in the rooms above. "The floors, walls, clothes and bodies of the men swarm with vermin," he added. About two hundred prisoners were crammed into the seventy-by-thirty-foot room. Wilkins further complained that he and his fellow officers were incarcerated along with "deserters, captured teamsters, idiots, lunatics, thieves, counterfeiters, and a few of our sutlers." He was unable to sleep the first night because "[m]y bed is 10 feet from the open privy & is surrounded by those of naked filthy teamsters, who steal all they can lay hands on."[56]

It did not take long for Wilkins to learn exactly how Confederate officials felt about officers who had served under Pope. They were soon plagued by "crowds of gazers anxious to see 'Pope's Sepoys.'" When prison officials received a delivery of thirty-six coffins on August 16, they gleefully informed Wilkins and his comrades that this was "just the number of Pope's officers." On the 24th another shipment of Pope prisoners, most of whom were wounded, reached Libby. One of them, a New York officer, reported that they had spent thirty-six hours in the Staunton jail in a six-by-ten-foot room that was virtually unventilated. After nearly suffocating, they were released and placed in handcuffs for the trip to Richmond, "not for any resistance or attempt to escape but because they were of Pope's army."[57]

According to Wilkins, their treatment grew worse when Capt. Wirz assumed command. "We have a new Military Commandant appointed over us a Dutchman named Wirtz, who strives, with devilish ingenuity, to aggravate the hardships imposed by his predecessor," he wrote on August 28. The previous day Wirz had issued orders to the officer of the guard to see that "nothing is carried into the room" occupied by the Pope officers. They also could not "stand about the door or converse with any other person." Wilkins especially resented the fact that he and his fellow prisoners would no longer receive newspapers, which had been smuggled to them by a friendly guard.[58]

Despite this initial observation, conditions in Wilkins's room improved under Wirz's command. "Our treatment by our jailors has bettered in the last few days," he noted on September 6. All the prisoners had received cots or bunks, and the Confederates had installed a cook stove in their room. An acquaintance living in Richmond was allowed to provide Wilkins with towels, handkerchiefs, soap, and a toothbrush on one occasion and a Bible and some magazines on another. Most important, mail soon arrived for the prisoners from Pope's command. On September 18 Wilkins received four letters from his wife and one from his sister. They informed him that all family members were well. "Now a great burden is lifted from my mind," he wrote, "and the day will pass far more easily than I had hoped for."[59]

Still, all was not well with the officer prisoners of the Army of Virginia, and as time wore on they grew bitter over their confinement. Much of their invective was directed toward the Lincoln administration. "I cannot see that our Gov't has taken a single step to effect our release, or ameliorate our condition, either by protest or retaliation," Wilkins wrote on August 26. "We are forced to the sad & painful belief that our Gov't have forgotten or abandoned us." The prisoners harbored "a bitter desperate feeling" against a government that "has cruelly & shamefully neglected us." When a group of prisoners from the Army of the Potomac was released on September 11, Wilkins wrote, "We have tasted to day the bitterest cup yet." The fifty-four officers had only been in Libby for two days. "Let Gov't now exchange an equal number of rebels for these officers, & there are many of us here who will never draw a sword in its service again," Wilkins asserted.[60]

When not castigating the government, the prisoners often took their frustrations out on each other. "I observe . . . that my fellow prisoners are becoming more quarrelsome rows spring up on slight offense & are sometimes prosecuted to blows," Wilkins observed on September 6. Nine days later, two events further soured their dispositions. One was the announcement that another forty-five recent arrivals from the Army of the Potomac were about to be paroled. The other was the revelation that a large number of officers had sent a petition to Winder claiming that they were not members of Pope's army. This, Wilkins wrote, "is not only undignified, but untrue." He added, "Much bad feeling exists & the room to-day is as quarrelsome as a kennel of hungry dogs."[61]

Pope's defeat at Second Manassas eventually ended his officers' confinement. He was soon on his way to Minnesota to battle rebellious Sioux Indians, and the orders that had so offended the Confederates were rescinded. Southern officials formally responded in November by withdrawing those portions of General Orders 54 that applied to Pope's officers. Wilkins and his fellow officers did not have to wait that long, however. On August 23 the Michigan soldier wrote, "With inexpressible joy & happiness to God, I now note one of the happiest moments of my life." Wilkins had just signed his parole. He departed Libby the next morning, noting, "Fresh air tastes delicious."[62]

The people of Richmond were nearly as relieved as the prisoners themselves as exchange got under way. When a detachment of 3,300 left in September, the *Dispatch* estimated that the savings to the Confederate government would be $4,000 per day. Meanwhile Belle Isle had undergone "a fumigation for purification purposes." The tents that had housed the Yankees were taken down, although the guard camp remained in place in case it was needed again. By early November the *Dispatch* reported that only 224 prisoners of war remained at Libby. Castle Thunder housed 290 prisoners "of all kinds."[63]

Beyond Richmond, parole and exchange followed a widely varied timetable. To the west, the Confederates paroled some nine hundred privates at Camp Oglethorpe on May 22, two months before the Dix-Hill Cartel was signed. Among those departing was Cpl. Hadley, one of a handful of noncommissioned officers sent with the privates. "The boys are all in good spirits," Hadley wrote as the group departed for a Nashville parole camp. The officers at Madison remained until October 7, when they boarded trains for Augusta. They reached Richmond three days later but remained only two days before continuing on to the Union lines. As their steamer chugged toward Fortress Monroe, Nathaniel Kenyon noted, "It really seemed as though we could hardly realize our change from the confines of hell almost into the hands of our own government."[64]

October 7 was also the day of departure for a number of prisoners at Columbia. It had been over two months since Frank Bennett and his fellow captives had learned of the exchange cartel. On October 4 he confided to his diary, "Almost lost hope." It was just a few hours later that Bennett learned that "marching orders" had been issued for the prisoners to head north. "A crazy party the news has made us," he wrote. "Thank God! Thank God! I shall soon be with my family." The trip to Richmond Bennett described as a "merry ride. Get out at stations and run around as we please. Whiskey plentiful and drank in quantities."[65]

For the Salisbury prisoners, exchange generally involved a melancholy layover at Belle Isle. Simon Hulbert had no way of knowing what lay ahead when he received orders on August 14 to be ready to leave the next morning. "Providence has finally smiled upon us at last," he wrote. "Our boys are all wide awake to night & there is not much sleep in the old cotton factory." The trip to Richmond took only two days, but Hulbert remained on Belle Isle for nearly a month. Even exchange did not fully satisfy Hulbert, who observed as he headed north, "We are under a more strict guard than when I was a prisoner."[66]

Hulbert's complaint was destined to be repeated by a large number of paroled Union soldiers. Hoping for a furlough home, almost all found themselves instead bound for a Northern parole camp. This made for a bitter homecoming, one that would result in hard feelings between the U.S. government and the soldiers who had served it loyally. To their great relief, these soldiers were no longer prisoners in a hostile land. To their disgust, neither were they yet entirely free.

4
"This prison in our own country"
Union Parole Camps

On June 28, 1862, a month before the signing of the Dix-Hill Cartel, the U.S. War Department issued General Orders No. 72. The goal of the orders was to address what Secretary Stanton considered a serious abuse of the nascent parole system. The Confederates had begun paroling a number of western prisoners, including some two thousand taken at Shiloh. They had also initiated a policy of paroling prisoners in the field, immediately after a battle. It did not take long for Union soldiers to realize that capture no longer meant months of confinement in a dreary Confederate prison. Rather, its likely result would be a lengthy furlough and a pleasant trip home until exchanged.[1]

The orders announced that neither discharges nor furloughs would be granted to paroled prisoners. All furloughs previously issued were revoked, and all prisoners "now at large on their parole or who may hereafter be paroled" were ordered to report to one of three parole camps designated by the War Department. Those from the East would go to a facility near Annapolis soon to be christened Camp Parole. Parolees belonging to Virginia, Kentucky, Ohio, Tennessee, Indiana, and Michigan regiments were ordered to Camp Chase near Columbus, Ohio. Benton Barracks, located near St. Louis, was designated for paroled soldiers from Illinois, Wisconsin, Minnesota, Iowa, and Missouri. Officers were ordered to "use their utmost exertions" to help publicize and execute the instructions. In a passage that later events would render ironic, the orders further stated, "And their Excellencies the Governors of the several States are respectfully solicited to lend their efforts to the same end."[2]

Benton Barracks was the first parole camp to receive large contingents of men. On July 13 Col. Benjamin L. E. Bonneville, commander of the post, reported that 1,167 had just arrived. They reached the camp "without officers and with extraordinary opinions of duties proper for them." With what would prove to be an understatement, Bonneville noted that supervising them under the circumstances was "a somewhat unpleasant task."[3]

Writing from a different perspective was Charles Hadley. The Shiloh prisoner was part of a contingent of parolees that arrived at Benton Barracks on July 10. They entered the camp, Hadley wrote, guarded by "Uncle Sams Ignoramous 23d Missouri." Once inside, "We have been used as if we were a disgraced lot of men." As an example, Hadley cited an incident that occurred shortly after their arrival. An officer was lecturing the paroled men on duty. When one of the parolees asked if Union officials planned to pay the released prisoners before asking them to do any duty, the officer ordered a sergeant to arrest the heckler. This the sergeant refused to do. Under the terms of his parole, he protested, he could not perform any military duty until properly exchanged. Upon hearing this, the officer ordered a corporal to take both men to the guardhouse. Citing the same parole oath, the corporal also refused. The officer then proceeded to arrest all three himself.[4]

Over the next few days, Hadley recorded similar incidents. On the 14th camp officials ordered three men from each company to stand guard duty. Only one man, an Illinois soldier, reported. Some twenty of those chosen for duty were nowhere to be found. The remainder, approximately sixteen, ended up in the guardhouse adorned by a ball and chain. The same day nine acting captains of detachments submitted a petition protesting the order requiring garrison duty from the paroled men. They argued that such duty violated their paroles and asked that their protest be forwarded to the War Department.[5]

It is not known whether the petition reached Washington, but a number of complaints from other quarters soon did. Robert Winslow, whose two sons were among the Benton Barracks parolees, wrote to Stanton on July 19. He complained that the paroled men were owed eight months' back pay and that they were being forced to perform military duty in violation of their paroles. He further objected to the fact that those who refused were sent to the guardhouse. "This ought not to be," he concluded, "and if the fact becomes public will do much to embarrass our operations in recruiting under the new call for additional troops."[6]

Soon public officials added their voices to the protests. Two days after Winslow lodged his complaints, Nathaniel Baker, Iowa's adjutant general, requested that the men from Hawkeye units be returned home on furlough. "Do not allow punishment to brave and gallant men who have done their duty," he implored. The next day Iowa governor Samuel Kirkwood forwarded to Stanton complaints he had received from constituent parolees. The governor conceded that he did not know which side was in the wrong, and he asked for guidance. "If the boys are in the wrong I will use my best exertions to set them right," he promised. Less than a week later, Kirkwood was feeling less cooperative. This time he took the matter to the top, asking Lincoln either to have the men exchanged or sent to Davenport until they were exchanged.[7]

On July 19 Gen. Henry W. Halleck attempted to settle the matter. A few days earlier, Halleck had been named general-in-chief of all Union armies, but he was still in St. Louis, where he was about to relinquish command of the Department of the Mississippi. Known as "Old Brains," Halleck had established a reputation as the army's leading authority on military law. He maintained it during the war largely by issuing rulings that supported the policies of President Lincoln and Secretary Stanton. Halleck's circular stated, "Paroled prisoners of war must do guard, police and fatigue duty on their own camps. This is not military duty in the belligerent sense of the word. It is simply for their own order, cleanliness, and comfort and not in violation of any parole not to bear arms against the enemy till exchanged." He also informed Baker of the policy, adding, "Those who refuse are mutineers."[8]

On July 28, Gen. William Scott Ketchum, who had been dispatched by Lorenzo Thomas, adjutant general of the army, to check into the situation at Benton Barracks, reported that all was well. "General Halleck's decision appeared to settle the matter and now there is no trouble," Ketchum wrote.[9]

Others were far less sanguine. One day after Ketchum penned his optimistic report, Hadley wrote that patrol guards were working outside the camp to keep the parolees in. The men were apparently no more willing than before to perform routine camp duties. On August 10 Hadley observed, "We were ordered to parade for inspection but it proved a farce as usual." If the string of general and special orders that followed is any indication, camp officials also saw little improvement in the state of things at Benton Barracks. On July 31 they found it necessary to issue general orders requiring the men to clean their quarters and bathe themselves and change underwear at least twice weekly. A month later more orders addressed "the almost universal filthiness of the grounds, quarters, [and] mess rooms." Subsequent directives required officers to remain in camp and to put an end to "disorderly proceedings and noise in the quarters of the paroled men after 'Taps.'" Following a spate of unspecified "outrages" committed by the parolees, camp officials ordered that the men's weapons be confiscated.[10]

As 1862 drew to a close, Bonneville reported that there were 501 paroled men present at the camp and 410 absent without leave. By February 1 absent men were in the majority. There were 818 parolees at Benton Barracks and 971 absent. Among officers, 75 were present and 16 absent. On February 20 the War Department addressed the problem by issuing General Orders No. 46. Stragglers who refused to report at Benton Barracks and the other parole camps, the orders stated, would be considered deserters. The orders, which were well publicized, had the desired effect. On May 15 Bonneville informed officials in Washington that 3,067 paroled men had reported at the barracks and only 578 remained absent. Officers were in short supply, there being only 114 present. Five days later, Bonneville reported that the number of enlisted men had grown to 4,300.[11]

Among those swelling the ranks of paroled soldiers at Benton Barracks was Cpl. Jackson Thompson of the Seventh Wisconsin Light Artillery Battery. Paroled the day of his capture at Parker's Crossroads, Tennessee, on December 31, 1862, Thompson reached St. Louis on January 8. He found a number of men from his unit already there. "The boys is all well suited here," he wrote. Despite that initial observation, Thompson was soon recording the departure of a number of his comrades for home on "French leave." On January 13 Thompson joined them, heading for his home in Rubicon, Wisconsin.[12]

Thompson remained there two weeks before leaving for Camp Randall in Madison. A former training facility, Camp Randall had served briefly as a Union prison. Except for another visit home, lasting nearly three weeks, Thompson stayed there from January 30 until April 7. Also present were Union recruits and a number of paroled soldiers, including twelve members of Thompson's outfit. While there they received pay and passed the time with card games and visits to Madison. "The boys all seem to feel in good spirits," Thompson observed on March 1, soon after arriving from his second visit home. "We have plenty to eat and drink." By the 20th bad weather had dampened their spirits. Thompson noted, "The boys is getting tired of staying here it snows hard."[13]

The same ambivalence marked Thompson's return to Benton Barracks. Baseball and card games occupied the men's time during the spring of 1863. "The boys is all contented here," he wrote on April 14, adding, "We have lots of fun here" in a subsequent entry.[14]

By the 22nd, however, Thompson was writing that the men's attitude was again changing. "The boys all getting tired of staying here," he observed. On May 4 he reported a riot in camp, though he did not provide any details. On the 17th Thompson and several others visited a park, where they took out their frustrations on a group of "Copperheads" and "whiped them out." It was not the last fight the men engaged in, nor was it the most serious. Following a July 4 altercation, Thompson reported that two men had been killed. By then many of the parolees were again heading for home. Thompson remained, contenting himself with sneaking out past the guard at night to gather cherries.[15]

Among Thompson's complaints about life at Benton Barracks were the fleas, which he claimed made sleep almost impossible. If the results of a sanitary inspection of the camp conducted in March are any indication, one would not have been surprised to find the camp infested with any number of unwanted creatures. Assistant surgeon E. L. Phillips conducted the inspection, submitting the results to Ira Russell, who was in charge of the Benton Barracks hospital. "The yards in the rear of the officers' quarters, contain large accumulations of litter," he reported, "and the contents of the privy vaults thereunto attached are becoming quite offensive." The quarters were dirty, while most kitchens were "filthy." The sinks were in a bad condition, which rendered them "exceedingly offensive." Pools of water dotted the camp, Phillips observed, "which [have] a green and unhealthy appearance." With much understatement, the inspector concluded that the conditions he had observed would "have a tendency to increase the amount of sickness here."[16]

To the east, paroled soldiers began arriving at Camp Chase in August. Located four miles west of Columbus, the camp had first been established as a training facility for eager Union recruits at the start of the war. When Gen. Grant captured Fort Donelson in February 1862, it became one of a number of western camps pressed into service as a Union prison. Its prison population was about 2,000 when the parolees began to arrive, but exchange would bring that number down to 756 by the end of the year.[17]

To Ohio governor David Tod the paroled Union soldiers were a greater headache than the Confederate prisoners had been. "It is with great difficulty we can preserve order among them at Camp Chase," he informed Stanton on September 5. Tod suggested arming them and sending them to Minnesota to help quell the Sioux uprising. Stanton liked the idea and promised to act upon it immediately. On the 17th he sent Maj. Gen. Lew Wallace to Camp Chase to take charge of the parolees. Brig. Gen. James Cooper, already in Columbus, received orders to assist him. Wallace was promised that other officers would be sent "as soon as possible."[18]

The situation he encountered at Camp Chase was so bad that Wallace would later assert that the order sending him there "was intended with malice aforethought to put me to shame." Of the men he wrote, "Such a sight I had never seen or imagined—men long-haired and bushy-whiskered, their faces the color of green cheese; most of them without head-covering of any kind, or coats or shoes; some in dirty cotton drawers and wrapped in old blankets in lieu of shirts." In a letter to the War Department, Wallace reported that the quarters were "uninhabitable, being filthy beyond description. Why a plague has not visited the camp this summer will always be a mystery to me," he added. Wallace concluded, "Two thousand of the men have disappeared, and if they have deserted they should not be blamed."[19]

Tod and Wallace joined forces to ask that the men be paid. Many had not received pay for over a year, Tod claimed, adding, "It will be impossible for General Wallace to bring them to any kind of order or discipline until they are paid." Wallace proposed to organize the Camp Chase parolees one regiment at a time. As they were formed, the units would be marched to Columbus to receive pay. They would then continue on to a new post, christened Camp Lew Wallace. Wallace established the camp, hoping that "by separating the willing from the unwilling a better state of feeling might be brought about." However, instead of providing incentive to remain, pay gave men the means to desert. Most waited until they had reached Camp Lew Wallace and left during the night. Some men were even bolder, dashing down a side street as they marched through Columbus. On September 26 Wallace begged Stanton not to send any more parolees to Columbus. "It is impossible to do anything with those now in Camp Chase," he complained. "Every detachment that arrives only swells a mob already dangerous."[20]

Members of the "mob" viewed the situation from a decidedly different perspective. Like the Benton Barracks parolees, their complaints began with orders to perform various camp duties. "There is great dissatisfaction among the paroled men," one parolee informed his parents. "Gen. Wallace requires them to perform camp duty, when their parole *positively says they must not perform such duty until exchanged.*" The men at Camp Lew Wallace were so upset, he added, that "there was a prospect of it terminating in a battle." The uncle of one Camp Chase parolee complained to Stanton that his nephew was among a group of paroled soldiers put on guard duty upon their arrival. "They refused to comply until exchanged and were reported to you as 'rebellious,'" the man wrote.[21]

As at Confederate prisons, boredom was a regular feature of life at Camp Chase. "How I wish we could get out of this miserable old camp," Lt. William Curry noted in his diary. "Nothing to drive away the weary tedium of camp life." Like many of his fellow parolees, Alfred G. Ryder of the First Michigan Cavalry resented being sent to Camp Chase. "I don't like this prison in our own country for those who have been as faithful as they know how," he wrote to his mother.[22]

The move to Camp Lew Wallace did not improve Ryder's spirits. The ground was low, he complained, making his tent susceptible to flooding. He also arrived to find most of his fellow Michigan soldiers gone. After about a week he decided to join them, "there being no hopes of any exchange and being disgusted here doing nothing." Curry was at first pleased at the change of base, terming Camp Wallace a "fine camp." Soon, however, he was noting signs of dissatisfaction among his fellow parolees and himself. "We are becoming very much demoralized here with no duty to do," he wrote as October closed. "Prize fights and black eyes are all 'the go' now." On November 6 he reported, "Boys have been playing the *Devil* generaly. Burn the guard house. Whip all the officers who show their heads." As for himself, "I am getting tired of this playing soldier."[23]

General Wallace was getting tired of playing soldier, too, at least with parolees. On October 18 he reported that all paroled prisoners at Camp Chase had been organized into regiments. "The order that brought me here is now fully complied with," he announced. If that was not enough to drive the point home, he added, "Having thus discharged all the duties required of me at this post I have no doubt of being permitted to take the field, with a command suitable to my rank."[24]

Wallace's departure left Cooper in command of the paroled soldiers. Orders he issued over the next several weeks suggest that Wallace had not fully complied with all the orders that had brought him to Columbus. In any event, he left his successor with a number of problems to address. On October 19 Cooper issued orders warning the parolees against burning rails and killing hogs belonging to neighboring farmers. A subsequent order dealt with "insults and outrages perpetrated in this neighborhood . . . on peacible citizens." Outrages were also perpetrated against the U.S. government. A number of parolees enrolled in different companies, using false names and drawing pay from all of them. Meanwhile, as new sets of paroled soldiers arrived, old problems resurfaced. As late as December 30, camp officials were penning orders informing parolees, "Any impression prevailing among any of the Paroled Forces that the terms of their parole prohibit them from performing the usual Camp Duties for their own instruction, discipline, or comfort must be corrected."[25]

By then the men were back at Camp Chase. As winter approached, both Wallace and Cooper had sought permission from the War Department to erect winter quarters at Camp Lew Wallace. Their requests were ignored until mid-December, when officials instead ordered the post abandoned. A small number of sick men remained behind under charge of a lieutenant and a detail of twenty-five men.[26]

As 1863 wore on, paroled prisoners continued to trickle in and out of Camp Chase. Between January 13 and May 14 forty-two groups were ordered away after being declared exchanged. The numbers ranged from seven to three hundred. Others departed without being exchanged. Between April and October seven hundred were arrested after failing to return from furloughs.[27]

Those who remained for any length of time were soon uttering complaints similar to those recorded by men who had already passed through. "The day seemed long and dull to me," Hiram Penland of the Nineteenth Michigan noted in his diary. He finally broke the boredom by starting out on foot for home. "Well it is not a very pleasant place," wrote Fernando Pomeroy of the Eighteenth Michigan upon his arrival April 1. He concluded that Camp Chase was "a verry poor place for amusement not anything to do." In the ensuing weeks, Pomeroy witnessed a number of fights and participated in at least one. On one occasion he wrote that a deserter had run past the guard and then shot a man in the arm. Watching numerous comrades depart on "French leave" led him to another conclusion, "to go home if I can or go to the bull pen." Fortunately a furlough prevented him from having to face that choice.[28]

Whatever challenges Wallace and Cooper faced with parolees at Camp Chase, they were mild compared to those encountered by officials at Camp Douglas. Like Camp Chase, the Chicago post had started as a training camp before being pressed into service as a prison following the capture of Fort Donelson. Its incarnation as a parole camp resulted from the surrender of the Union garrison at Harpers Ferry, Virginia, on September 15. Robert E. Lee was taking his Army of Northern Virginia into Maryland, dispatching Stonewall Jackson to seize a position that could have posed a threat to his rear. Jackson's men occupied the heights surrounding the valley town, placing the post in an untenable position.

Nevertheless, the Union soldiers believed their commander, Col. Dixon Miles, surrendered Harpers Ferry, and its approximately twelve thousand defenders, far too easily. Some suspected him of being drunk, others of being a traitor. "It is thought that we were sold at H. Ferry and I am inclined to the same opinion," wrote Capt. Valentine Barney of the Ninth Vermont. Charles Kline of the 115th New York was more blunt. "I think if [Miles] had been a loyal man we would not be here prisoners today," Kline wrote from Camp Parole. Mortally wounded, Miles never got to tell his side of the story. His death did not mollify the men who had served under him. "As we passed through Harpers Ferry we heard that our traitorous commander was dead," one wrote, "which to us was good news as he richly deserved his fate." Another simply noted, "I am glad he is dead." A quick parole did not assuage such feelings, and events in the days that followed only made the men's humor worse.[29]

It began with a four-day march to Annapolis, where the paroled soldiers arrived on September 21. Kline described it as a "hard march," while Barney simply termed it "fatiguing." Both reported that a number of men fell out of the ranks. Barney's company started out with ninety-six men but reached Annapolis with only twenty-five. Those unable to continue on were put on trains for the remaining miles of the journey. "We are encamped out in the woods here without tents," Kline wrote of the parole camp. On the 22nd the parolees learned that their stay in Annapolis was to be brief. "General Order Number One was read from the War

Department," Cpl. Charles E. Smith of the Thirty-second Ohio wrote. "That the prisoners taken at Harpers Ferry were paroled here to go into Camp Douglas at Chicago." The Buckeye soldier concluded, "This made some of the boys feel sad to think of going there without stopping a few days to see their relatives in Ohio, after having served their country about thirteen months faithfully."[30]

Smith was not the only soldier in his unit expressing that view. Adj. Gen. Thomas reported to Stanton that the men of the Thirty-second had made clear their intention to head for home as they passed through Ohio. The Confederates, Thomas explained, had left the Harpers Ferry men with the notion that their paroles included a provision stating that they were to be sent home. As a result, "This movement is very distasteful to them and many complaints are made that it is a violation of their parole."[31]

The men headed west under the command of Gen. Daniel Tyler, a strict old smoothbore not likely to brook any nonsense. A graduate of West Point, Tyler had resigned his original commission nearly thirty years before the outbreak of the Civil War. Now he was back, and upon his arrival in Chicago he took over command of Camp Douglas, relegating the previous commander to lesser duties.[32]

Only a small number of the parolees went into Camp Douglas. The post was largely filled with trainees, so the bulk of the paroled soldiers ended up in tents and stables outside the camp in an area known as the Fairgrounds. It was soon christened Camp Tyler. Kline was among its occupants. He found himself in a stable that had been home to trotting horses previous to his arrival. "They are comfortable quarters," he informed his family, adding, "leak pretty badly." His main complaint was the rainy weather and the thick mud it produced. Somehow, he wrote, the men were still able to run races and enjoy a "foot ball" their lieutenant had provided for them. The food was good, the men could go downtown for ten cents on city railway cars, and Kline concluded, "I can enjoy myself first rate." Nevertheless, "A number of the boys of our regiment have skedaddled and left for parts unknown."[33]

New York soldier Nicholas De Graff was less satisfied with the quarters at Camp Tyler. "They do not look very inviting," he wrote of the horse sheds he and the other soldiers were to occupy, "but all hands set to work forthwith to make them as comfortable as possible." The stalls, he added, were ten by fifteen feet, with eight men to a stall. Capt. Barney was also not impressed. He complained about poor rations and a lack of utensils with which to cook them. Eventually camp kettles and mess pans arrived. Barney and some of his men tore up a plank walk and installed a floor in their quarters, using the extra lumber to build bunks. He supplemented his rations by purchasing tomatoes and apples. This allowed the captain's disposition to improve. It remained good until winter approached. "The weather is getting to be pretty cold and the boys in camp are suffering considerably," he wrote on November 7. The quarters provided virtually no protection from the elements. "I don't know how long the government will keep us in this condition," Barney wrote his wife, "but it is an outrageous shame." Soon he was reporting one death per day, "but that is nothing as long as the government can get us kept here for 10¾ cents per day each."[34]

Even before the first frost of fall, rumors that the men would soon be sent to Minnesota to fight the Sioux soured their outlook. On September 28 Cpl. Smith wrote that such reports caused "much hard feeling against our government and our field officers." Three days later Barney observed, "I hardly think we will be sent there but if we are ordered I fear there will be a mutiny in the Reg. and I should not wonder if part of the officers would resign."[35]

On October 3 Tyler reported to Thomas, "The fact is these Harper's Ferry men are perfectly disorganized." Adding to the confusion was the fact that most of their officers were not present. Many outfits refused to perform any duty, and most of the willing ones were "far from being reliable." According to the general, Barney's regiment was the only one upon which he could rely. Unfortunately the Vermonters were unarmed. Through sheer force of personality, Tyler managed to bring a semblance of order to the situation. Much of that work went for naught, however, when, on October 5, the *Chicago Tribune* published the terms of the cartel. The parolees focused their attention on a clause in article 6 forbidding the men from performing "field, garrison, police, guard, or constabulary duties." As Tyler noted, "If we comply with this paragraph it appears to me it leaves little else for us to do with the men but feed and clothe them and let them do as they please." He predicted, "I shall have hard work to keep our men quiet."[36]

According to Cpl. Smith, Tyler was already having hard work keeping the parolees at Camp Douglas in line. The Ohio soldier recorded incidents of men attacking the fence each of the first four days of October. "The guards were not close enough to keep them in and they broke through and over wherever they pleased," he wrote on the 1st. By the next day, the guards sent from headquarters had apparently given up. "The guards stood and laughed at the proceedings," Smith observed as more sections of fence came down, "knowing they could do nothing more than tell them to stop." The men "went out [of camp] and in at pleasure," he added, noting that more than a few returned in the hands of the provost guard. According to Capt. Benjamin Thompson of the 111th New York, the city was a magnet to the bored parolees. "They took every opportunity to get down into Chicago, which seemed at that time to be one vast beer saloon," he wrote after the war.

As a result he and his fellow officers "had to hunt our men every night out of the saloons—and worse places—and try to get them back into camp."[37]

On October 20 Calvin Haynes of the 125th New York informed his wife, "They are trying to make the boys take guns and guard the camp but they swear that they will not do it if they shoot them." Meanwhile they were taking out their frustrations on Camp Douglas itself. According to Haynes, they had burned about one thousand feet of barracks, "and they will burn all the rest before the week is out I think." In any event, they had threatened to do so.[38]

The first fire broke out between midnight and 1:00 A.M. on October 17. "There was a strong breeze," Smith wrote, "and the roofs being covered with pasteboard and pitch burned finely." The blaze consumed eleven barracks. Pvt. Charles Belknap of the 125th New York wrote that the fire would have claimed more buildings had axmen not worked quickly to tear down structures in the path of the flames, staying their progress. Four nights later both Smith and Belknap were attending a prayer meeting when shouts of "Fire!" broke up the gathering. Smith reported that two small buildings were burned.[39]

When not firing their camp, the parolees found other ways to amuse themselves. October 22 was a particularly busy day. "Some of the boys got drunk and had a jovial time," Smith recorded. They found weapons belonging to some of the few men willing to perform guard duty, bent the bayonets, and filled the barrels with sand and acorns. Late in the afternoon a group of men from the Sixtieth Ohio attacked the major of the 126th New York "and gave him a pounding." That night an enlisted parolee put on a captain's uniform. He gathered some friends, and the entire group marched to the guard line. The phony captain informed the guards that they were being relieved by a new regiment and ordered them back to quarters. After they departed, the supposed relief hid their weapons and slipped away. When the sergeant of the guard came around with the legitimate relief guard, he found the line vacant of both weapons and guards.[40]

That night, Gen. Tyler reported, "the crisis came." He added, "I think we have won the victory and without any undue violence." Tyler assigned the blame to the Sixtieth Ohio, a unit so insubordinate that he placed the entire outfit under arrest. He wrote, "To my great gratification our paroled men with arms in their hands stood to duty and the Sixtieth Regiment caved in." Tyler brought in a company of the Sixteenth United States Infantry, and with it he hoped to restore order. "I claim this capitulation covers all the duties and I mean to enforce them," he concluded.[41]

Over the next three days Smith recorded a few incidents of parolees using bricks and rocks to fight off guards sent to arrest men for various offenses. Belknap and

De Graff reported cases of drunkenness. Otherwise Tyler's assessment that the camp had weathered the crisis held true. Meanwhile, Gen. Pope announced that the Sioux had been defeated, and the government began exchanging the men. As December dawned, Barney informed his wife that the Sixty-fifth Illinois and his Ninth Vermont were the only paroled units present. Both would spend their winter at Camp Douglas.[42]

Even the departure of the parolees was not without incident. As the 115th New York prepared to leave on November 20, men from other regiments greedily eyed the stoves in their quarters. One of the New Yorkers wrote, "As soon as we formed line a scrabble began for the stoves." So anxious were the men to secure them that they simply dumped out the fires inside. The men of the 115th had not reached their trains before their former quarters were in ashes.[43]

Although they refrained from burning their post to the ground, the men at Camp Parole were no more satisfied with their condition than were their fellow parolees to the west. One of the first to arrive was Henry Bemis of the Fifteenth Massachusetts, who reached Annapolis on July 19. Three days later he observed, "We do not have anything to do as the time is pretty long on our hands." Despite the boredom, Bemis and his fellow soldiers rejected one suggestion for passing the time. "The Officers tried to make us do guard duty around the camp but it was no go as we all hung together and would not do it." According to Jerome Robbins of the Second Michigan, it was not just the enlisted men who were opposed to such duty. He wrote that a Pennsylvania officer, "who has been in other wars," informed the men that they would be in violation of their paroles if they performed "any duties for our government."[44]

Of more immediate concern to the men was their government's failure to prepare for them. Although he and two comrades had a comfortable tent, Milton Woodford of the Seventh Connecticut informed his sister that others did not. "There are a good many who must suffer these cold days," he wrote in late October, "as there are not enough tents for all, and *some* of the men are in *very* destitute circumstances." Robbins also fared well, he noted in his diary, but he, too, was concerned for fellow parolees who arrived with nothing but the ragged clothes on their backs. Many could not secure tents or even blankets. "Our government has plenty," he wrote, concluding, "Surely some one must be to blame for this."[45]

The paroled prisoners also turned to marauding to secure sufficient rations. Simon Hulbert, arriving from Belle Isle, wrote that the men spent their days roaming the countryside in search of apples, pears, peaches, and "everything they can lay their hands on." Ziba Roberts went a step further, securing all the fruit he could then finding a comfortable barn to spend the night. Like others, he also went fishing for crabs in Chesapeake Bay. According to Bemis, a banner crop of blackberries supplemented many men's rations.[46]

On September 22 the marauding turned violent. The camp sutler, termed an "army vulture" by one parolee, had constructed a dining hall and storehouse and secured a stock of goods reportedly valued at $15,000. On this particular morning a private went there for breakfast only to be told that commissioned officers would be served first. He objected and was unceremoniously kicked out and placed under guard. Word of the incident quickly spread. Before long about a thousand angry soldiers were at the scene. They freed their comrade and proceeded to loot the establishment of food, cigars, tobacco, and anything else they could find. The sutler attempted to stop them until a champagne bottle, thrown by one of the rioters, hit him in the head. The men did not quit until they had dismantled his store and carted away the lumber for tent flooring.[47]

In a letter to a relative written on November 29, William Harrison of the Tenth New York Cavalry said of Camp Parole, "Law and order is not known, and crime goes unpunished." Both camp officials and diarists among the parolees supported his assessment. Chief among them was Lt. Col. George Sangster, Camp Parole's commanding officer. On at least eight occasions between September 10 and October 10, Sangster sent one or more parolees to the Annapolis jail for confinement. Among the myriad of problems he faced was desertion. On October 21, Sangster complained to the provost marshal of Annapolis that men were receiving civilian clothing from "some Jew store in town" before departing on the trains. Later he reported that he had apprehended a man who was selling forged furloughs for $5. According to Robbins, several men left by claiming to be members of units that were being exchanged or sent to other camps.[48]

Those who remained considered Camp Parole a dangerous place to live. "At night there is usually a fight, so it is best to stay in your tent," one prisoner wrote. The previous night, he explained, an ill parolee had emerged from his tent and was immediately knocked down by "one of these smart alecks," who stole the man's revolver. On October 24 Robbins observed, "Some fist fighting some yelling with sore noses & black eyes being the result but such scenes are [too] common to receive comment." Earlier Robbins had recorded a more organized form of violence "enacted by a gang of thieves & marauders." The men had robbed a few parolees of their pay, but their main targets had been small grocery stores erected by men who had managed to acquire some food items.[49]

Both Robbins and Sangster placed much of the blame for the disorder at Camp Parole on the effects of liquor. "Many of the [paroled] prisoners received pay which has instituted an enormous amount of gambling and drinking liquor," Robbins wrote on September 29. "Such has taken place today the gambling being pretty brisk and liquor taking effect a severe fist fight ensued." When another pay was issued six weeks later, the results were "gambling drinking & every thing attending to a reckless demoralized collection of thoughtless beings calling themselves human." Robbins was not alone in his disapproval. After yet another round of pay, Milton Woodford wrote, "Last night 'King Whiskey' was out in force. One man had his head split open with a club and another was badly pounded near my quarters. I shall be glad when the money is gone," he continued, "so that part of the roughs will have to be sober."[50]

Sangster fought a diligent battle to keep liquor out of his camp. When he arrested a number of parolees who had been selling it, he forwarded them to the headquarters of the Eighth Army Corps with the request that they be severely punished. Sangster also attempted to close down saloons that sold to soldiers, in violation of his orders.[51]

The commanding officer was sincere, but he was fighting a losing battle. When Col. Adrian Root succeeded Sangster in July 1863, he observed, "Numerous instances of gross intoxication are of daily and public occurrence among the paroled prisoners to the continued reproach of the camp." He informed Col. Carlos Waite, commanding Annapolis, that the men had no difficulty obtaining liquor in the city and recommended "all traffic in liquor" be prohibited there. Like Sangster before him, Root soon realized that paying the men quickly led "to the evil results." Following an issuance of two months' pay, "Drunkeness, disorder, gambling and desertion prevailed to an astonishing extent, and ordinary decency was ignored by many of the drunken men, who roamed through the streets of Annapolis apparently without restraint."[52]

It did not take long for reports of problems at Camp Parole to reach officials in Washington. On August 5 a group of officers representing parolees from ten states sent a petition to Secretary Stanton. Conditions at the camp, the officers protested, were hard on the health of men "not yet entirely recovered from the effects of hardships which were suffered while in Southern prisons." The officers asked that the paroled prisoners either be exchanged immediately or discharged from the service until they were exchanged.[53]

In November far more volatile messages reached the War Department. The first was sent to Stanton on the 18th from a soldier of the Forty-fourth New York. "Cannot something be done to lessen the perpetration of crime by the paroled soldiers kept at Annapolis?" he implored. "Drunkness, fighting, burglary, robbery, gambling, &c., are witnessed by us daily, and even murder is not of unfrequent occurence." There were fifty gambling stands in daily operation, he reported, and large quantities of liquor were being smuggled into camp. At night, the men were not safe to step outside their tents. The man virtually begged Stanton to do something about "the reign of rowdyism here."[54]

Six days later a petition with more weight behind it reached Col. William Hoffman, the Union's commissary general of prisoners. It was signed by forty-eight Wisconsin soldiers and forwarded to Hoffman by Governor Edward Salomon. The Badger State men asserted that Camp Parole was "not a fit place to stay in on account of its filthy condition and the want of proper discipline. Men are being assaulted, robbed and killed," they continued. "Drunkeness and gambling are raging to a fearful extent." Salomon wrote that the men's dire reports were corroborated by "agents of the State" who had visited the camp. The governor requested that the Wisconsin men be sent home until they were exchanged.[55]

Hoffman's response was twofold, and somewhat contradictory. He replied to Salomon that he had recently inspected Camp Parole and found the men well cared for. There were very few "deficiencies," and measures had been taken to address them. Hoffman did concede that portions of the camp were filthy, but he blamed the parolees for this condition. "Men in camps away from their homes make many groundless complaints," he lectured the governor, "in the hope to obtain through the interference of their friends a transfer to their own States." At the same time, Hoffman demanded that Sangster immediately inform him of his guard strength, the commands he had given to maintain order, and what system was in place for policing the camp. Finally, he wanted to know what was "the cause of [the] want of good discipline if such is the fact."[56]

In his reply, Sangster denied that any murders had been committed at Camp Parole. Whatever problems did exist, he insisted, were brought on by the lack of guards. Only 175 were on hand, and his requisitions for more had gone unanswered. The commander also forwarded transcripts of interviews with men who had complained to Stanton of murders in the camp. As reported by Sangster, they revealed that the men had no personal knowledge of such acts, but were basing their assertions on rumors they had heard.[57]

In March 1863 Hoffman made his final report to Stanton on the situation at Camp Parole. Once again, he concluded that the blame for any problems rested squarely with the parolees themselves. "The great obstacle in the way of a favorable state of things [at Camp Parole] is the anxiety of the men to go to their homes and their unwillingness to do anything to better their condition," he observed.[58]

Hoffman realized that the problems went deeper. A few days before penning his report to Stanton, he wrote to Col. John C. Kelton, the army's assistant adjutant general. To Kelton he conceded that there were "many things in the management of the camp that might be changed for the better." Specifically, he blamed paroled officers in the camp, who "exagerat[ed] in every way the unavoidable inconveniences" of the camp. This attitude, Hoffman believed, was quickly adopted by the enlisted parolees. However, in a subsequent message to Kelton, he requested that a new camp be erected. Hoffman wanted permanent barracks to replace the tents the parolees had been occupying. They had been in them during the harshest winter months, but Hoffman did not couch his suggestion in humanitarian terms. Rather he argued that the tents were easily destroyed, making barracks more economical in the long run. The fact that the barracks would also be more comfortable meant the parolees would have less cause for complaint. They would also allow the camp to be more compact, leading to better policing and discipline.[59]

On April 23 Hoffman ordered Capt. Gardner S. Blodgett, the assistant quartermaster at Annapolis, to begin construction on the new camp. A stickler for economy, the commissary general also urged Blodgett to use as much timber as he could find lying around Camp Parole. Hoffman kept a close eye on the project as the work continued over the summer. It was completed in August, and men occupied the new barracks on September 1. At the same time the guardhouse was filling with men who had threatened to burn their new quarters.[60]

In addition to constructing improved facilities at Annapolis, Union officials established a new parole camp at Alexandria, Virginia. Christened Camp Banks, it held as many as six thousand parolees. According to Simon Hulbert, who was transferred there from Camp Parole in September 1862, Camp Banks housed sick soldiers from the Army of the Potomac as well as parolees. This was confirmed by Pvt. William L. Aughinbaugh of the Fifth Ohio, who arrived at Alexandria in May 1863 after being captured at the battle of Chancellorsville. Former Libby prisoner Charles Grannis later recalled that Camp Banks was better organized than Camp Parole. Different army corps were separated, and conscientious officers were placed in charge of each.[61]

Surviving records suggest that, despite these positive memories, Camp Banks was plagued with problems similar to those at other parole camps. Local farmers complained of parolees milking their cows, cutting their trees, and stealing their vegetables. The sutler store was burned on at least one occasion. When a group of parolees was mustered for pay, Col. Gabriel De Korponay, the camp commander, requested a guard of one hundred men "for the purpose of keeping order and preventing the sale of spiritous liquor."[62]

It did not take long for the problems at the various parole camps to reach home. Soon governors of Union states were pressuring the War Department to let their home state boys return home until they were exchanged. Governor Salomon was one of seven chief executives who contacted either Stanton or Hoffman on the subject. Austin Blair of Michigan wanted Wolverine soldiers at Camp Chase sent to Detroit. J. F. Robinson asked that Kentuckians be sent from Columbus to Louisville. Like Salomon, Andrew Curtin of Pennsylvania cited poor conditions at Camp Parole. "All they say of their treatment is true and many of them would prefer to be returned to Richmond," Curtin asserted. Even President Lincoln became involved. Learning that two paroled regiments from Ohio and one from Illinois had been sent to Camp Chase, he suggested that Stanton return his fellow Illinoisans to their home state.[63]

No governor was more persistent on behalf of his constituent soldiers than Oliver P. Morton of Indiana. "Our accommodations are at least as good as those at Camp Chase," he informed Stanton in September 1862. This brought him only the war secretary's standard reply that sending men to their home states would simply offer them incentive for "shameful surrender." Morton did not give up, citing problems at the Ohio camp. His obstinacy paid off when a few Indiana regiments found themselves en route to the Hoosier State.[64]

As Stanton and Hoffman wrestled with the problems of the various parole camps, the agreement that created them was dissolving. From the outset agents of exchange on both sides accused each other of violating the terms of the cartel. Men were declared exchanged prematurely, they charged. Citizen prisoners and irregular troops put strains on an agreement that did not fully address their status. Eventually the South's adamant refusal to exchange black Union soldiers doomed the cartel, at least officially. The North's true motives are difficult to discern. Certainly, with the Union's tremendous advantage in population, exchange benefited the Confederacy considerably more. The headaches produced at the parole camps likely entered into the equation as well. Still, there is no substantial evidence that the Union's desire to protect its black soldiers was not sincere.[65]

The debates of the historians were decades away when the exchange cartel collapsed during the summer of 1863. For thousands of prisoners, Northerners and Southerners, it was anything but an academic exercise. Big battles were being fought, and many more lay ahead. Those unfortunate enough to fall into the enemy's hands would face months or even years of confinement. It was not a pleasant prospect for soldiers on either side, but for captives in blue, heading into a Confederacy ill equipped to provide for them, the future was far more bleak.

5
"The most villainous thing of the war"
Libby Prison, 1863–64

As 1862 came to a close, two major battles again sent thousands of Union prisoners to Richmond. One, the battle of Fredericksburg, fought on December 13, took place only about fifty miles away. The other, the battle of Stone's River, which lasted from December 31 through January 2, was fought near Murfreesboro, Tennessee.

By December 18, according to the *Richmond Dispatch,* 229 "abolitionists" had been brought to the Confederate capital. Many more followed, and by New Year's Eve 1,450 were crowded into Libby prison. Others, "badly wounded in every conceivable part of the body," strained the capacity of the city's hospitals. The second wave, arriving from Tennessee on January 16, brought 1,600 more prisoners to Richmond. Gen. Winder scrambled to find facilities to hold them. The day the Stone's River prisoners arrived, he reoccupied the Mayo factory and, despite bitter winter weather, reopened Belle Isle, where the prisoners were again housed in tents.[1]

In early March the *Richmond Whig* announced that another six thousand were on their way "from all parts of the South." By then finding places to house all the prisoners was not Winder's sole problem. The local press had long complained, "The expense to the Government in supporting this large number of non-producing vagabonds is . . . considerable." The March accessions forced Winder for the first time to take food from Confederate citizens' mouths to feed the unwelcome guests. Out of options, the general impressed supplies of flour bound for Richmond markets, an action that led the city's press to castigate him. The anger was not limited to editorialists. On April 2 Richmond erupted as rioting citizens charged downtown and smashed store windows in an attempt to secure bread. It took a company of soldiers, Mayor Mayo, Governor John Letcher, and finally President Davis to disperse the mob.[2]

Although threats and counterthreats were increasingly issued, the exchange cartel was still in place in early 1863. As a result, many of the prisoners who reached Richmond that winter soon found themselves headed to Camp Parole. George Gill of the First Kentucky, a Stone's River captive, arrived with the large contingent on January 16. He pronounced Libby "very neat and Clean," although he was soon complaining about the facility's lice. "They bite like Hell at night and therefore Disturb our repose," he wrote. "Curses on them." With neither a blanket nor an overcoat, the cold also troubled him. During his two-week stay, Gill traded his blouse for extra bread, and in a transaction unusual even by military prison standards, wrote a song for a fellow prisoner in exchange for tobacco.[3]

The lice also made themselves known to Charles Stone, who arrived at Libby on February 20. They were almost impossible to do battle with because they were equipped with armor which made them "iron clads, monitors invulnerable to any instrument yet known except the hammer or ax—[articles] not to be found in [the] Libby market." His room was lacking glass in many windows, boards covering some, others totally open to the elements. A fireplace at one end and a stove at the other supplied all the heat the men got in their one-hundred-foot room.[4]

On February 25, Stone recorded, another group of prisoners captured at the battle of Stone's River arrived at Libby. "They are a hard looking set of men," Stone observed. The captives were without blankets or overcoats, which they said the Confederates who captured them had confiscated. "They represent as having recd the most inhuman treatment on their way to Richmond," Stone added. On more than one occasion the prisoners had gone forty-eight hours without rations, and those they did receive often consisted of nothing more than meal and water. Stone concluded, "Their condition is good proof of their words."[5]

Stone's account of his own capture was quite different. Taken in Virginia, he recorded kind treatment at the hands of his Confederate guards. Stone and his fellow captives spent their nights at farmhouses, where they enjoyed good meals and hospitality. Their coats and blankets were not confiscated, but some sold them to Confederate soldiers they met along the way for as much as $20.[6]

Prisoners captured in Tennessee during the winter months recorded a variety of experiences. Gill followed a circuitous route to Richmond that took him first to Atlanta, then south to a point about fifty miles from Mobile. His contingent next headed north to Montgomery, back to Atlanta, and on to Dalton, Georgia; New Bern, North Carolina; and Lynchburg. The rations en route were good, including beef and chicken at Montgomery, although Gill supplemented them with purchases. The men were "well treated" by the Confederates. In fact, when one of Gill's fellow prisoners lost his cap as they rolled through the Carolinas, the Confederates stopped the train so he could retrieve it.[7]

Hiram Penland was captured on March 5 near Franklin at the battle of Thompson's Station. During his seventeen-day trip to Richmond he complained of rations that were skimpy and of poor quality. A bigger complaint was that he and his fellow captives had to sleep outdoors in cold, rainy weather. The prisoners had little protection from the elements, their coats and blankets having been taken. Capt. John Holmes of the Twenty-second Wisconsin, taken at Brentwood, Tennessee, on March 25, recorded more positive experiences, but only because he was an officer. At numerous stops on his march across Tennessee, Holmes and his fellow officers were confined in homes and hotels. The men slept outside during nights he termed "bitter cold." At Tullahoma the men had to surrender their coats and blankets. The enlisted soldiers also went without rations during at least one day of the trip.[8]

Although Holmes's fate is not known, Stone, Penland, and Gill were soon on their way to Camp Parole. They were among the last officers to depart from Libby. On May 25 Gen. Halleck informed all department commanders that no Confederate officers would be paroled or exchanged. The Confederates responded in kind. By then the spring campaigns were under way, and hundreds of prisoners taken during the Confederate victory at the battle of Chancellorsville were arriving in Richmond. Gettysburg would soon result in thousands more. Meanwhile, commanders in the western theater were also forwarding to Richmond any captives that fell into their hands. Following the battle of Chickamauga in September, Winder impressed two other facilities, Grant's factory and Smith's factory, to handle the overflow. The majority of the officers would spend their summer, fall, and winter in Libby or one of the other warehouses. When they departed, it would not be on exchange but for Danville, Macon, or another prison to the south.[9]

Like those who had arrived before them, the newest Libby residents found lice in abundance. On June 23 Col. William T. Wilson of the 123rd Ohio entered Libby, having been captured nine days earlier at the second battle of Winchester. "Very much *encouraged* to see a venerable Lt. Col. pick a creeper from his pants and proceed to slaughter it," Wilson wrote of his arrival. The next day Wilson was engaged in the same pursuit. According to Lt. Louis R. Fortescue, a Gettysburg prisoner, lice hunting was "one of the greatest institutions of this place." As soon as the prisoners arose each morning, he explained, they stripped off their clothes and began "skirmishing . . . making very minute examinations of the seams and snug corners where those detestable critters are supposed to be hiding." The nuisance was not limited to Libby. After being transferred to another prison in Richmond, Wisconsin soldier Harlan Howard estimated that there were 27,800 vermin in his room, or 100 per prisoner. "Mortality among them very great," he noted, "but fear they multiply rapidly."[10]

An even greater source of complaint was the Libby rations. "We have roll call for breakfast, corn bread for dinner and go to bed for supper," one Libby prisoner wryly observed. Fortescue wrote in July that the twice-daily rations added up to half a loaf of bread, three ounces of meat, and a cupful of soup. The soup, he added, came with bugs. The same week George W. Grant of the Eighty-eighth Pennsylvania put the daily ration at one-fourth to one-half a loaf of bread and four to eight ounces of meat. The officers also received rice soup, which Grant agreed was "more bugs than rice."[11]

The rations grew skimpier in late October. On the 27th Capt. Nathaniel Rollins of the Second Wisconsin wrote that they had been reduced to bread alone. That was supplemented the next day with bacon "so maggoty that no one would buy it unless they were starving." A Michigan prisoner added that the bacon was only about two inches square. The prisoners did not blame their captors. Diarists noted that Richmond newspapers were reporting severe food shortages in the city. In a letter likely smuggled out of the prison, Lt. James Higginson of the First Massachusetts informed his family that prison officials had told the prisoners that they could find neither beef nor bacon. They were issuing sweet potatoes as a substitute. One Libby prisoner summed up the situation succinctly when he wrote, "This Confederacy is in a bad way for Provision for her prisoners."[12]

Officials in Richmond would certainly have concurred with this assessment. On October 28 Winder's prison commanders informed him that they had not received any beef that day to issue to the prisoners. At Castle Thunder, Capt. Alexander felt that a ration must be issued quickly to "insure discipline and, I think, prevent violence." Winder agreed, and he warned James A. Seddon, the latest Confederate secretary of war, "No force under my command can prove adequate to the control of 13,000 hungry prisoners." Winder repeated the warning on November 10, when only twenty-five hundred pounds of beef arrived for Richmond's 14,000 prisoners.[13]

Prisoners with money could enhance their rations with outside purchases. Capt. William Noel of the Fifth Maryland helped maintain his good health for a time by sending out for vegetables. His money ran out quickly, however, forcing him to subsist on prison rations. "I begin to feel ravenous," he wrote after a few days. Col. Wilson's mess purchased bread, pepper, and even blackberries on various occasions. Other groups of prisoners bought sugar, tobacco, coffee, soap, chickens, sweet potatoes, and butter. The purchases were not limited to edibles. Alonzo Keeler of the Twenty-second Michigan battled the boredom of prison life by sending out for a set of books.[14]

The items did not come cheap. It took $16 to buy one mess half a bushel of potatoes. Another paid $3 for a pound of butter and 12¢ apiece for eggs. Fortescue wrote that during a four-week period his room of three hundred men spent $11,000 for provisions. The prisoners could convert their greenbacks for Confederate money at a rate of $8 Confederate for $1 Union during the summer of 1863. These transactions were supposed to go through prison officials, but occasionally guards would smuggle bread for prisoners who had managed to sneak in greenbacks. They adamantly refused to accept Confederate money. Harlan Howard claimed that these dealings led to a change in the guard outfit. "Old were become-ing too *corrupt,*" he observed. Howard himself was not free of corruption. He devoted many hours to making counterfeit $5 bills to give to the guards in return for bread.[15]

Boxes of supplies sent from the North also allowed the Libby captives to improve their condition. "Rec'd box from Home to day containing crackers, cans [of] fruit, Daily Papers, Periodicals, Candles &c.," Capt. Noel wrote on November 28. A subsequent shipment included ham, beef, molasses, and most important, photographs of his wife and his sister. Col. Wilson's regiment remembered him with a "fine box" containing coffee, sugar, butter, and canned fruits and meats. Louis Fortescue's family made sure he was well clothed with a shipment that included shoes and a full suit of clothing. In addition to food items, Alonzo Keeler's father sent him a box with an overcoat, medicines, and several books inside. Nothing was wasted. Keeler made a seat and a table from the box itself.[16]

Although seemingly innocuous, the boxes soon became a subject of controversy. Among the prisoners at Libby was Gen. Neal Dow. Before the war, Dow had gained a certain measure of fame by securing passage of a prohibition law in his home state of Maine. In early December a few boxes containing cans of liquor arrived. The result was a noisy, drunken party. This so offended Dow that he reported the incident to prison officials, who immediately instituted a policy of breaking open any cans that arrived.[17]

Dow had already been involved in a much more important controversy involving boxes. In November Robert Ould, the Confederate agent of exchange, agreed to a plan proposed by Gen. Sullivan Meredith, his Northern counterpart. Under the agreement, the Union government would send clothing to Richmond to be distributed to the prisoners. Dow was placed in charge of the distribution, a choice the Confederates soon came to question. After taking the first shipment to Belle

Isle, he complained to Ould about "the most wretched condition" prisoners were in there. He secretly sent a similar report to Washington, asking that the government hide $100,000 in counterfeit Confederate money in the next shipment. It is not clear whether Southern officials learned of Dow's request. It is clear that they had had enough of the general. Calling him "an utterly inefficient agent of distribution," Ould added that Dow had "shamefully broken his word of honor in not confining himself exclusively to that work." Confederate authorities concluded to put a board of U.S. officers in charge of subsequent distributions.[18]

More serious concerns soon scuttled the agreement. On November 13 Meredith forwarded to Ould a message from his superior, Gen. Ethan Allen Hitchcock. Ould was informed that the Union shipments to Richmond in no way relieved the Confederates "from the obligation to treat prisoners of war according to the laws of civilized warfare." Put simply, Hitchcock continued, the failure of Union supplies to arrive would not be an excuse if the South refused to feed its prisoners. Understandably offended, Ould replied, "We recognize in the fullest form our obligations to treat your prisoners with humanity and serve them with the same food in quantity and quality as is given to our own soldiers." If those rations were scanty, Ould went on, it was the fault of the Union's blockade of Southern ports. On the 25th, during a personal meeting with Ould, Meredith produced two recently paroled Union surgeons, who claimed to have been told that portions of the shipments had been diverted to Gen. Lee's army. Hitchcock and Meredith later backtracked, thanking Ould "for the efforts we believe you to have recently made in behalf, and for the relief, of Union prisoners." This acknowledgment proved to be too little and too late. On December 11 Ould informed Meredith that the Confederates would accept no more shipments. They had been, he asserted, the subject of too much "vilification and abuse."[19]

At Libby the news hit like a thunderclap. On December 14 the prisoners learned that no boxes of any kind would be allowed, nor could they make any more purchases. "So here goes for Corn bread and water," Col. Wilson worried. The prisoners were allowed that day to send out for items, and estimates of the purchases ranged from $10,000 to $30,000. The Libby captives soon learned that the order did not apply to boxes from home, only those sent by the government. Purchasing was again allowed about a week later. This enabled one mess to enjoy a Christmas dinner that included roast turkey, mashed potatoes, applesauce, and pumpkin pie. Another group feasted on oysters, potatoes, salmon, turkey, corn, and peach pie.[20]

Even when the prisoners secured enough food, cooking it was often a problem. The rooms generally had only two or three stoves to serve 250 or more men. One prisoner complained, "All our time is occupied in cooking during daylight." The problem was so acute that Capt. Noel's mess eventually decided it was worth a substantial investment to secure relief. In early December some thirty officers pooled their money and purchased a stove for $350. This did not guarantee that there would be sufficient fuel to feed the stoves. Wood shortages were frequent at Libby. Window glass was missing in some of the rooms, and by late September Louis Fortescue was writing of men staying up at night and stamping on the floors to keep warm. By November the prisoners were burning their boxes and furniture. The following month at least one Christmas dinner was cooked with wood that had previously been covering the windows.[21]

Most Libby prisoners appear to have had one or more blankets with which to battle the cold, but keeping them was sometimes problematic. Prison officials had a strangely prickly attitude toward prisoners who lay upon the floors with their blankets during daylight hours. Anyone caught had his blanket immediately confiscated. Even illness was not considered a sufficient excuse. On September 20 Dick Turner went through the prison, confiscating blankets as he went. There was a good deal of grumbling at first, but the prisoners eventually realized that equality was the goal. Anyone having more than two blankets saw the excess confiscated. They were redistributed to those having none. "This is all right," Capt. Noel concluded, "as some have more and I am sorry to say the officers who had plenty would not give them to those without." The Confederates were thorough in their policy. Capt. William H. Powell of the Second West Virginia Cavalry was in close confinement, charged with murdering a Confederate soldier and burning many homes. Despite the seriousness of the charges, Powell received two blankets. The charges were later dismissed.[22]

In addition to the physical discomforts of prison life, the officers also complained of the boredom that was a constant feature of captivity. "This place is becoming very dull and monotonous," Fortescue observed after six weeks at Libby. Robert Cornwall of the Sixty-seventh Pennsylvania wrote, "Time here is a burden, a tormentor, a bore." Col. Wilson feared that confinement might produce long-term effects. Noting that a number of prisoners did not rise before noon, he asked, "What will they be fit for when they get out if such habits adhere to them? Prison life is calculated to induce a careless restless indolent disposition."[23]

Nothing improved the prisoners' dispositions more than the arrival of letters from home. "You should see the rush when the mail is brought upstairs," one prisoner wrote. "It is carried to one of the rooms and some one calls out the letters hundreds collected around eager for news of home." Those whose names were called out felt very fortunate. "This evening my joy knew no bounds—a letter from home—all are well—thank God for it. Oh my soul," wrote John Kay of the Eighth Michigan Cavalry. Col. Wilson received four letters from his wife while suffering through a week's illness and needing "something to cheer and stimulate me. Nothing could so fully meet my case as a letter from my dear Lou." Robert Cornwall saw them as a necessary survival tool. "These letters do me so much good, and though they remind me forcibly of my dear little family at home and make me long to be in their midst once more, yet they in some way impart strength to me to bear against my thronged yet solitary condition." After receiving a letter from his cousin, Pennsylvania soldier Wilson Paxton wrote back, "Its a perfect god send to receive letters in this place. if I dont get one or more every mail I feel pretty blue. Yours saved me from going to bed last night feeling as though I had been forgotten by friends at home."[24]

Feelings of home were especially strong on Sunday. "I lay and think of home," a prisoner wrote on one lonely Sabbath, "and wonder what my friends are doing to day if they think of me." A number of pious captives attended Sunday services held in the prison, although at least one questioned their effectiveness. "We have preaching and prayer meeting of a Sunday, but there is need of revival," Capt. James Love of the Eighth Kentucky informed his future wife. "Libby is very profane in its practice!"[25]

On the evening of October 6 prison officials called out all the chaplains and announced that they were to be paroled and sent back to Union lines. The result was abbreviated services conducted by prison volunteers. Confederate officials attempted to fill the void by allowing local ministers to preach to the Libby prisoners. Although Alonzo Keeler felt one had delivered "an excellent sermon," other captives were less enthusiastic about their presence. Louis Fortescue summed up the views of many by writing, "They pray for our destruction on Sunday in their churches and on Monday wish to pray for our salvation." The result was a meeting that produced "great excitement." When it ended the majority had voted to continue allowing the "Rebel preachers" to visit.[26]

In addition to spiritual comfort, the prisoners also longed for news about the war. Despite occasional crackdowns, the prisoners generally managed to smuggle in both Confederate and Union newspapers. One officer wrote that his mess got Richmond papers almost daily. He complained, however, that they contained "but little news."[27]

Because of the frequent availability of newspapers, the prisoners often learned quickly about important events. On July 5, two days after the battle of Gettysburg ended, news of the Union victory "made the old prison ring with 'Three cheers' for [Gen. George G.] Meade," the victorious Union commander. By July 8 rumors of the Confederate surrender of Vicksburg, which had taken place four days earlier, reached the Libby captives. The news was not always good. On September 22, two days after the battle of Chickamauga concluded, Capt. James Penfield of the Fifth New York Cavalry wrote, "Rebs Jubilant" over the initial reports. By the 24th the papers were reporting an overwhelming Confederate victory, prompting Penfield to comment, "I do not believe all this."[28]

The reports from the Chickamauga battlefield proved accurate. Other prison rumors did not. One had Jefferson Davis captured by Union cavalry. Frequently reports reached Libby that the exchange cartel was about to be resumed. Such rumors produced "[g]reat rejoicing," but invariably led to disappointment. "Rumors of exchange & how silly we are to put confidence in them," Keeler observed on November 10. However, when another report arrived on December 21, he wrote, "At night news of Exchange came so reliable that all the prison seemed a place of complete happiness."[29]

Newspapers were not the only popular reading material in Libby. Anything that helped pass the long hours was viewed as a godsend. "I very fortunately today got hold of a couple of novels," Fortescue wrote on October 16. "I shall now hunt some quiet corner if such a thing can be found and settle myself down for a few days, at least." Keeler had been at Libby less than two weeks when he invested $10 in four works of philosophy. Occasionally back issues of such magazines as *Harper's* or *Atlantic Monthly* made their way through the lines. After securing a collection of old magazines, Col. Wilson happily noted that they contained "a large amount of excellent matter."[30]

Classes also allowed the prisoners to pass the time and gain mental stimulation. Foreign-language classes, particularly in French and German, were popular with the captives. A number also studied phonography, a form of shorthand. Robert Cornwall briefly attended a dance class offered by a cavalry officer. The effects of captivity and inactivity quickly showed themselves, and he attempted only a few steps before exhaustion forced him to quit.[31]

The prisoners also attended lectures delivered by their fellow officers. Gen. Dow gave a number of temperance talks. Other topics ranged from Cuba to mesmerism. In early 1864 a major from the Fifth Ohio Cavalry offered a lecture on spiritualism. According to an audience member, "[He] spoke first of the probability of spiritual manifestations, secondly of the many manifestations that he had witnessed, and lastly of the doctrine of spiritualism."[32]

On July 29 the prisoners organized the Libby Lyceum, an educational fraternity that hosted lectures and held debates. One prisoner termed it "a very good preventative for the blues." One of the topics debated was whether fear of punishment had a greater effect than hope of reward. On other occasions the debaters considered whether capital punishment should be abolished and "[w]hether wearing a beard is beneficial to the health." On all three occasions the judges ruled in the affirmative. By the following spring the debates had grown longer, often stretching over several nights. On the topic of whether "the Periodical Press has a greater influence over mankind than the Pulpit," the judges came down on the side of the negative. When the question of black suffrage was debated, a number of prisoners protested that it was "not a proper question for discussion." The debate continued despite their protests but was decided in favor of the negative.[33]

Musical entertainment offered an occasional escape from the boredom of prison life at Libby. Some prisoners pitched in so one of their comrades could purchase a violin for $18. On one of the floors a chaplain who sang tenor often joined with a "fine" bass singer to treat their fellow prisoners to an impromptu concert.[34]

More organized entertainment was offered by the Libby Minstrels, who presented their first performance on October 12. According to one member of the audience, "The participants acquited themselves very highly, and the affair passed off very pleasantly." The group put on another show five nights later, attracting an audience of some eight hundred prisoners. Capt. Noel attended the minstrels' Christmas Eve concert, describing it as a "big affair." Although one prisoner wrote that the entertainment "was very creditable," not all were pleased with such gaudy spectacles. "They indulge in too much vulgarity," Col. Wilson complained, "and I do not feel like having the sacred thoughts of home marred by even the *shadow* of evil."[35]

A few months earlier Confederate officials detected more than just the shadow of evil when the prisoners celebrated the Fourth of July. They erected a speaker's stand and on it proudly displayed an American flag made from red denim and a white shirt. One of the officers was in the middle of a patriotic address when a sergeant arrived, took down the flag, and called a halt to the proceedings. This was done, Col. Wilson asserted, "by order of the tyrant Turner." The prisoners got a little revenge that night by lustily singing patriotic songs. They got even more the next day when they celebrated news of the victory at Gettysburg.[36]

Numerous other activities occupied the long hours of confinement. "What a crowd!" one prisoner observed. "Nearly all busy at something—cooking, reading; games—bones work—writing—washing—hunting." The "bones work" involved carving various knick-knacks out of discarded bones. James Love termed it "the fashionable method of killing time here," noting that many prisoners demonstrated a “considerable display of ingenuity.” Those who could acquire gutta-percha resin also turned out small pieces of art. Perhaps the most impressive accomplishment was the homemade clock manufactured by one of the Chickamauga prisoners. (Confederate prisoners in Northern camps turned out handmade merchandise in much greater quantities. Their money was useless in Union territory, forcing them to put their skills to work to raise funds for visits to the sutler shop.) Card games were also popular with the prisoners, as was chess. In March 1864 the occupants of the middle upper-floor room took on their comrades in the east room in a chess match. The east room carried the day.[37]

Not all prisoners approved of the ways in which many of their fellow captives chose to pass the time. “Considerable Gambling in our room,” Capt. Noel observed. “I despise to see it.” According to Fortescue, gambling was “quite an institution” at Libby. “Some of the officers came here with a considerable pile of money but are now penniless.” Lt. George Lodge of the Fifty-third Illinois believed many of the prisoners were addicted to gambling. “They never appear at ease nor satisfied unless they are at it,” he noted.[38]

Noel was even more offended by what he termed “huckstering” on the part of his fellow prisoners. Officers with abundant funds purchased fruit, crackers, and other commodities by the barrel, then sold them by the piece at inflated prices. They even sold the empty barrels to be used as seats. Fortescue termed the Libby inmates “the most . . . selfish set of men that could possibly be got together.” On September 1 he wrote that a surgeon had his wallet, containing $180, stolen. “I shall be much pleased when rid of the society of such men,” Fortescue concluded.[39]

Col. Wilson complained of a “detestable” game in which the Libby prisoners indulged. As he described it, “One holds a hat while another of the crowd inserts his head in it, when some one of the crowd applies his open hand to the fellows posterior with such force as to raise the victim almost off his feet; if he fails to guess who struck him in goes his head again.” If the man guessed correctly, the person who struck him took his place. “Human cockfighting” was another popular diversion. The participants’ hands were tied behind them, and sticks were placed through their arms and legs. This apparently made them hop like a chicken. One prisoner termed the contest “plenty of fun,” while another observed, “The cheers are uproarious.”[40]

As 1863 came to a close, several officers decided that their colleagues had “behaved very disgraceful, singing obscene songs” at night. Col. Wilson was chairman of a meeting called to address the problem. He gave a brief speech, after which the group adopted resolutions threatening to report future bad conduct to the military authorities in Washington. The colonel declared the meeting a success. “We have had very good order during the last two nights and all except a few black guards are delighted with the result."[41]

Bad behavior was not limited to prisoners. John Kay, who was in the Pemberton prison, wrote that all the guards were drunk on Christmas night 1863. James Higginson observed, "As a rule the officers & soldiers who have fought us treat prisoners with great kindness, but civilian authorities & officers & soldiers who have never been in the field behave like brutes very frequently." It was a common observation from prisoners in both Union and Confederate camps. One of the most telling comments about the Libby guards was Robert Cornwall's January 7, 1864, diary entry, "The guards around the prison ask us for bread." Cornwall added, "I am afraid the Confederacy will rot down over our heads."[42]

The prisoners did record a few instances of punishments for various infractions. A Capt. King of the Twelfth Pennsylvania found himself in a cell for two days after he had spit on the floor. When a group of about sixty officers made too much noise one evening, Dick Turner made them stand silently for several hours. One diarist wrote that the tipping point may have come when the assembly sang "We'll Hang Jeff Davis on a Sour Apple Tree." Prison officials were also adamant about preventing communication between the floors of the prison. A captain found himself under arrest after he received a message from a room below. Guards soon sealed the holes between the floors to prevent any further communications.[43]

Roll call was frequently a source of controversy between the prisoners and their Confederate keepers at Libby. As Fortescue described it, "One of the greatest humbugs of the age is the prisoners roll call in Libby. We are obliged to form a line 'four deep' twice a day and be counted by an insignificant looking cuss approximately 20 years of age." The prisoners were less than eager to engage in the procedure, and their unwillingness to cooperate often led to threats of punishment. On one occasion, according to Lt. Lodge, "the little snotty *pup* who calls the roll" made the prisoners stand in line an hour for not falling in quickly enough. He added that "insults and indignities" were a daily feature of roll calls. Lodge conceded, however, that things would go much more quickly if the prisoners would cooperate. He nevertheless found it highly amusing when the prisoners gained some revenge by climbing over a skylight so they would be counted twice. "Two days have now been spent in vain endeavours to find out how many prisoners they have here," Lodge chuckled. "It is great sport for us thus to outwit them."[44]

Charges of actual physical abuse of the Libby prisoners were rare but not unheard of. Capt. Penfield wrote in his diary that Dick Turner struck an arriving prisoner in the head when the prisoner claimed that Turner had no right to confiscate a piece of shell from him. Kay wrote that he had seen Turner "beat and pound one of the prisoners—then drew his pistol threatening to shoot any one who said a word." According to Nelson Purdum of the Thirty-third Ohio, a prisoner "was bucked [and gagged] for cutting the window."[45]

Shooting incidents were rare at Libby, but when they did occur, they often involved prisoners looking out the window. Capt. Noel had been at Libby only four days when a guard fired at a surgeon who was gazing at the Richmond scenery. The ball lodged in the window frame.[46]

Noel also witnessed the next shooting incident at Libby, which occurred on October 1. He was among a group of prisoners who watched as a Confederate guard fired and hit three of his own comrades. One died, and another had to have his arm amputated. The *Richmond Examiner* reported that the guard had exchanged angry words with two of his fellow guards before the shooting occurred. The bullet first hit the second man with whom he had argued. This was the wound that required amputation. It then struck a second sentry, breaking his arm before lodging in the abdomen of yet another Confederate. The third victim was carried to a boardinghouse, where he died the next day. The shooter was taken to Castle Thunder to await trial. Noel was unsympathetic, writing, "We cared little how many of them were killed."[47]

On March 1, 1864, prison officials tightened the restrictions on looking out the windows. They reiterated their order that anyone seen near them would be shot. They also forbade the prisoners to hang clothes from the windows, threatening to confiscate them. The orders came against the backdrop of the Judson Kilpatrick–Ulric Dahlgren Raid on Richmond. The cavalry raid was intended to free the prisoners held in Richmond. It failed, and papers allegedly found on Dahlgren's body afterward indicated that the plans also called for the destruction of the city and the murder of Jefferson Davis and his cabinet. Many of the raiding officers ended up in Libby. They were placed in a particularly dank cell and fed on bread and water. Buckets, removed once a day, served as sinks.

The Libby orders were intended to prevent the prisoners from signaling to Union sympathizers while the raid was in progress, and prison officials enforced them strictly. Before March was over there were at least four shooting incidents at the prison. The first came only a few hours after the restrictions went into effect. The victim proved to be a detective planted in the prison by the Confederates. Thus, as one prisoner gleefully wrote, "The nefarious order of the prison authorities . . . recoiled on themselves beautifully." He added, "I am sorry for the wife and three children he leaves."[48]

On March 5 a sentry fired at a prisoner while he was at the sinks. The ball passed through his ear and struck the brim of his hat. "One inch farther would have sent him to eternity," one prisoner noted. Robert Cornwall came close to being the victim on March 20. He and two comrades were cooking their supper when a charge of ball and buckshot blasted through the window. A Lt. Kupp suffered minor buckshot wounds to the face and neck. The month's final shooting occurred on the 28th at Crew's Prison. The guard claimed that he had warned the prisoner away from the window before the shooting. A second guard backed up his account. The prisoner was killed.[49]

As the raid got under way, the Confederates threatened to kill all the Libby prisoners in one tremendous blast. With the approval of Gen. Winder, Maj. Turner had a trench dug beneath Libby and had two hundred pounds of gunpowder placed in it. Turner let the prisoners know that if they made any attempt at an uprising they would "all be blown to Hell." Winder and other officials later claimed that they never planned to detonate the mine. Their intention was simply to intimidate the prisoners and prevent them from cooperating with the raiders. Indeed, a Confederate congressional committee later concluded, "The real object was to save their [the prisoners'] lives as well as those of our citizens."[50]

At Libby the prisoners' reactions took many forms. Neal Dow refused to believe the report at first, "not that I think the act too atrocious for these men to commit." Rather he did not feel they would risk the Union retaliation that would be sure to follow. Lodge termed the action "the most villainous thing of the war." Col. Wilson wrote, "This villainy is worthy of the black hearted scoundrels." Lt. Cyrus Heffley of the 142nd Pennsylvania reacted similarly to Dow. "I have seen very few symptoms of fear," Heffley wrote, "not that Maj. Turner would be too much of a gentleman to do a thing of that kind, but he would not dare to put the match to it. Our gov't holds too many of their men." Lt. Cornwall summed up the situation: "'Gunpowder on the brain' is a very prevalent but not very alarming disease in Libby just at present." Whether the prisoners were alarmed or not, the failure of the Union raiders rendered moot the question of whether Turner would have lit the fuse.[51]

Sentries and threats notwithstanding, escapes were not unheard of at Libby and the nearby prisoners' hospital. On October 23, 1864, two officers escaped from the hospital wearing the uniforms of Confederate surgeons. The uniforms had been in bad shape, and one of the prisoners, a tailor, volunteered to work on them. He did, then gave one of them to a friend, and the pair walked out of the hospital. When Union surgeons left on parole on November 24, a major left in place of one of them. The Confederates quickly detected the ploy, and the officer was back at Libby two days later. On December 11 two prisoners escaped from the hospital. Unfortunately the prison diarists who noted the incident added no details beyond the fact that they had done so "with great success."[52]

As January ended a few prisoners made their escapes by simply walking out of the prison. A number of diarists wrote of the escapes. Although their accounts vary a great deal in details, most wrote that two left on the 29th and another three departed the next day. Workers were installing iron bars to the windows, and according to a majority of the diary writers, the first pair put on the workmen's jackets, blackened their faces, and strode boldly through the sentry post. This inspired the three who walked out the next day. "If I can get clothes I will try my luck soon," Col. Wilson wrote. He did not get the chance. Somehow the Confederates learned of the escape, Cornwall suspecting "some death-deserving *traitor.*" A spate of roll calls followed, but the prisoners had by then perfected their tactics. "Every time they count they have a different number," Wilson gleefully observed on the 31st, "and this evening they have 40 more than they can account for." It is not clear how many were recaptured, but those who were found themselves in the Libby "dungeon."[53]

One of the most dramatic and successful escapes of the entire war, North or South, took place on the night of February 9–10, 1864, from Libby. Col. Thomas Rose of the Seventy-seventh Pennsylvania was the mastermind of the plan and the supervisor of the project. Rose had been captured at Chickamauga on September 20. He escaped en route to Libby but was retaken after enjoying only a day of freedom. According to Frank Moran of the Seventy-third New York, who joined Rose in the effort, "From the hour of his coming, a means of escape became his constant and eager study."[54]

Rose quickly began surveying the scene in the Libby neighborhood. Workmen descending into a sewer across the street attracted his interest. The only way to get to it, he concluded, was by digging a tunnel commencing at the prison's cellar. Because of the crowding caused by Rose and his fellow Chickamauga prisoners, Libby officials had allowed prisoners into the basement to cook their meals. Looking around, Rose further determined that the starting point should be a room in the north end covered with about two feet of straw. Because rats sought shelter in the straw, prisoners had christened the room "Rat Hell." As he was examining the room one day, Rose made the acquaintance of Maj. A. G. Hamilton of the Union Twelfth Kentucky Cavalry. Hamilton would prove to be a loyal lieutenant to Rose for the remainder of the project. With a broken shovel they found and two case knives, the pair began their tunnel.[55]

They soon encountered a serious setback. Shoring up the security of the prison, officials closed the downstairs kitchen and nailed up the stairway leading to it. Rose and Hamilton remained undaunted. Using a wedge whittled from a piece of pinewood, they pried up a floorboard, gaining access to a different basement room in the central part of the building. They reconnoitered this room for several nights. The pair first decided to use the room as a launch point for a mass escape directly onto the streets of Richmond. Only two guards patrolled the south side of the building. They could be easily overpowered, but there was a great danger that the scuffle would alert others. Despite the risk, they determined to make the attempt with a large group of prisoners they had recently enlisted into the project. As the group was ready to depart, a man left behind as a lookout signaled that a body of Confederate soldiers was heading to the building. The would-be escapees scrambled back to their rooms. Rose abandoned the plan, and the rest of the group began to give up their hopes of escape.[56]

Rose used this respite to seek out Hamilton once again. Somehow, the colonel insisted, they must find some other means of reaching Rat Hell. Hamilton found it, by means of a kitchen fireplace. Soon a tunnel was wending its way toward the sewer Rose had noticed weeks before. Geology worked in their favor, a Confederate officer at Libby later recalled. The dirt had enough sand to make tunneling relatively easy. At the same time it contained enough clay that mine props were unnecessary. At first Rose dug and Hamilton dragged out the dirt, which was placed in a wooden spittoon attached to pieces of clothesline. The dirt floor of Rat Hell solved the problem of disposing of dirt from the tunnel. The officers worked between 10:00 P.M. and 4:00 A.M., thus keeping the project secret not only from the guards but from their fellow prisoners. They soon realized that they needed more help and recruited thirteen more men. More disappointments soon followed. The tunnel's path to the sewer took it underneath the James River canal. Water trickled in at first, then broke loose in a torrent that nearly drowned Rose. The group then dug toward a smaller sewer that connected with the main one. Freedom appeared imminent until they discovered that the main sewer was made from seasoned oak, "hard as bone," that their tools could not penetrate.[57]

The discouraged party, sick after thirty-nine nights of working in the stench of the nearby sewer, was largely ready to give up. Rose and Hamilton were not. They next set their sights on a yard between two buildings across the street. This meant the escapees would emerge in view of the guards, but perhaps far enough away that they could quickly disappear into the shadows. Rose decided it was worth the risk, and he reassembled much of the old company. The work resumed, and as it neared completion Rose did yeoman work, digging an entire day, as other prisoners covered for him at roll call, to complete the project. He broke through at about 3:00 A.M., gasping for air as he dug upward. Rose and Hamilton wanted to escape at once, but their comrades persuaded them to wait for the next evening.[58]

At 7:00 P.M. on February 9 the egress began. The plan was for a few men at a time to depart, but within two hours word had spread, and there was a rush for the tunnel. Despite the confusion, the Confederates did not become alerted to the activity. Prison officials did not learn of the escape until roll call. At first they suspected bribery. They rounded up the entire guard detail and placed everyone under arrest. When a thorough search revealed no greenbacks, they went hunting for a tunnel, which they soon found. This disappointed Col. Wilson, who had planned to go out that night. He complained, "The rush was so great and so little system used that we failed to get the number that passed out and hence could not fool the rebs at roll call."[59]

In all, 109 prisoners passed through Col. Rose's tunnel that night. By the end of the day on the 12th, some 20 had been returned to Libby. More came in over the next several days, ending up in the prison "dungeon." Their stays there were generally brief, as the cells were frequently emptied to make room for those recaptured later.[60]

Fifty-nine Union soldiers eventually made it to Union lines. Forty-eight were recaptured, and two drowned during their dash to freedom. Among those making good their escape was Maj. Hamilton. Among those captured was Col. Rose, taken within sight of Union pickets. He was, however, soon exchanged. Col. Abel Streight, a Union cavalry commander, also made his way to safety. As the Confederates went chasing after the escapees, Streight was safely sequestered in the home of a Union sympathizer. Elizabeth Van Lew, who had aided a number of previous escapees, was involved in the effort to hide Streight and at least three of his comrades. The Union army also did what it could to assist the officers headed their way. As soon as the first of the escapees arrived, cavalry patrols went out to pick up all they could. One detachment returned with eleven of them. They also soon learned, likely from Mrs. Van Lew, that Streight was "concealed in Richmond."[61]

Most of the Libby prisoners left behind following the big escape of February 10 were not destined to remain there long. In 1864 the spring and summer campaigns of Ulysses S. Grant would make Richmond an untenable place to keep prisoners. Many would soon be on their way further south. So, too, would the enlisted men on Belle Isle. The winter of 1863–64 was an unusually harsh one. For the men on Belle Isle, the trip south would mark the end of a winter of unimaginable suffering.

6
"It looks like starvation here"
Belle Isle, 1863–64

As long as the exchange cartel remained in effect, Belle Isle remained an unpleasant, but generally temporary, place to be confined. After being closed following the big exchange of September 1862, the facility reopened in January to accommodate prisoners from Fredericksburg and Stone's River. Most of them were gone by early May, when the battle of Chancellorsville resulted in another large group of prisoners bound for Richmond. The majority of them stayed only until the 13th, when they began the thirty-four-mile march to the point of exchange. Belle Isle was again vacant, but the tents remained in place in case they were needed.[1]

They soon were. A trickle of prisoners reached the island in June, and in the wake of Gettysburg, the trickle became a flood. More exchanges followed, but with the difficulties that were quickly developing, arrivals began outnumbering departures. On September 1 the *Richmond Examiner* reported that there were between four thousand and five thousand Yankees on Belle Isle. The prison, the paper added, was "beautifully laid out." When Maj. Isaac H. Carrington conducted an inspection of Richmond prisons in mid-November, he reported that there were sixty-three hundred Union prisoners there.[2]

The captives entered the pen with very little. Strapped for resources, the Confederates searched every man they captured. Items of military issue, such as canteens, haversacks, belts, and rubber blankets, were virtually always taken. Personal items sometimes were and sometimes were not, depending, it seemed, upon the whims of the individuals conducting the search. Among the unlucky ones were the men who entered Belle Isle with Henry G. Tracy of the Eighteenth Connecticut. Tracy wrote that they lost silver pencils and gold pens during the search process. Nathan Webb of the First Maine Cavalry was searched at Libby before being sent to Belle Isle. He noted that Dick Turner treated a prisoner "favorably" if he saluted and addressed him as "sir." "If otherwise it would go hard with him," Webb added. In one case an impertinent prisoner ended up in the Libby dungeon after Turner had confiscated everything he could find.[3]

For the arriving prisoners, first impressions of Belle Isle were universally negative. "We were put in a field of about 3 acres," wrote Wisconsin soldier Horace Smith. "Not a spear of grass growing. It is nothing but sand full of lice and vermin." Smith had been at Belle Isle about three weeks when he concluded, "I would give anything I could get for the privilege of eating and sleeping with the hogs at home." Webb put the prison portion of the island at about two and one-half acres. An eight-foot-deep ditch, he noted, surrounded it, with an embankment built up around the ditch. For John Boudwin of the Thirteenth Massachusetts, the limited space was a major factor in the discomfort of the prison. He lamented, "If we only could enjoy the privilege of the Island it would be of some comfort but here we are pushed In like so many sheep in a pasture." William Tippett of the Union First Virginia and William Dolphin of the Second New York Cavalry both reached Belle Isle in September, and the two new prisoners recorded similar first impressions. "This place is the worst that I ever imagined. Hell is hardly a name for it for here a man suffers cold hunger & thirst all the time," Tippett wrote. Dolphin was even more succinct. "Bell Island [is a] Lousy dirty hole. Hell is a palace to it."[4]

At between four and five acres, the prison portion of the island was slightly larger then the diarists' estimates. Webb was correct about the depth of the ditch that surrounded the prisoners. Guard posts could be found every forty feet along the embankment that followed it. The cookhouse, a hospital, and quarters for Confederates sat outside the prison. Near the hospital was a cemetery.[5]

As Smith mentioned, lice were a major problem for the Belle Isle prisoners, especially during warmer weather. After only two days there, he added, "We have regular louse hunt[s] twice a day. Strip our clothes off and look them over." George Hegeman of the Fifty-second New York put the number of daily hunts at two or three. The ground, he wrote, was "alive with vermin," creating a situation "worse than [the] Egyptian Plague." Webb agreed, writing, "The ground litterally crawls with great body lice" as well as numerous fleas. A soldier from the Eighteenth Connecticut summed up the disgust the prisoners felt. "Now in any other place than that we were in, we would be ashamed to be seen looking for lice on our clothes, but it is a matter of course to have lice in Richmond." It annoyed him that "some [prisoners] are so lazy that they allow the lice to get so thick on them as to be seen crawling on the outside of their clothes."[6]

Lice were a minor nuisance compared to the almost constant hunger endured by the men. After arriving on June 24, Henry Tracy recorded his daily rations for his first week of captivity. Twice a day he received one-fourth of a loaf of bread with a small piece of meat in the morning and bean soup in the afternoon. According to Boudwin, the rations were no better by August. On the 8th he wrote, "Received ration of bread and meat and very small ones at that only enough to keep a man wishing for more." In the days that followed, he frequently noted, "Bill of Fare Bread & Meat & Bread & Soup." On the 25th Boudwin wrote that both the bread and meat rations had been reduced. By November, as the Confederates struggled to feed the prisoners, sweet potatoes were being issued occasionally. Nevertheless, after receiving breakfast at 1:00 P.M. one day, a prisoner concluded, "It looks like starvation here."[7]

The poor quality of rations on Belle Isle was nearly as big a source of complaint as the low quantity. When John Whitten of the Fifth Iowa arrived on December 9, he wrote, "Drew soup but we could not eat it." After three hungry days his diary entry instead read, "Drew soup in the evening but could hardly eat it." According to William Tippett, the rice soup contained about ten grains to a quart of water. The bean soup was "more bugs than Beans." On November 6 he wrote, "Sour Bread & stinking Salt Beef for Breakfast." Horace Smith wrote in a similar vein. "Our meat is boiled without any salt. . . . Our soup is made of dirty river water with scarcely rice or beans enough to know what it is intended for. A great deal of the rice is full of bugs and worms and they all are boiled together." Nathan Webb elaborated on July 7, "This morning I saw the negro cooks fill up the boilers with the water, then skim off what dirt they could handily. We find in our soup sticks, rocks, rags, and all kinds of filth. Our bread this morning was corn bread, ground cob and all, mixed with water, without salt or anything else."[8]

Although they had far less access to information than did the officers at Libby, many Belle Isle prisoners realized the Confederacy was not entirely to blame for the short rations. "I think [they have] pretty near run short of food in the confederacy," Tippett observed. "Seems to take all they can get to feed what prisoners they have got here." Another prisoner was somewhat less certain, writing, "This so called Confederate government must be in very straited circumstances or devoid of all civilized intentions to treat prisoners of war in the manner we are treated. I am inclined to think the former the principal cause while the latter doubtless has its influence." William Dolphin was again succinct, writing, "The Rebs can hardly get enough to keep us alive."[9]

John Winder would have agreed with Dolphin. Unfortunately he had been left in the dark concerning who was responsible for getting food to the prisoners for whom he was responsible. In late October, when Winder reported the shortages to

Seddon and warned of a prisoner uprising, he noted, "I look to the Quartermaster-General for any failure that may take place." He did not know that several weeks earlier Seddon had met with Quartermaster General Alexander Lawton and Commissary General Lucius Northrup. At that meeting the job of feeding the prisoners had been transferred from Lawton to Northrup. Only after Winder's dire warnings did Seddon bother to inform him of the arrangement. Complicating the situation was an abiding hatred between Winder and Northrup. As prisoners went hungry at Belle Isle, the responsibility of caring for them rested with two officers who were very unlikely to cooperate in reaching a solution.[10]

This left the prisoners to find any means possible to supplement their meager rations. At least one group dug wild onions to "put in our swill for supper. Tasted bully," was the verdict. An Ohio soldier managed to catch "3 fine pickeral" from the James River. A much greater windfall came to some of the men when a hog wandered into their tent late one night. "The pork is very good," one of them concluded. Other measures were less palatable. As the rations grew skimpier, men dug up discarded bones and sucked the marrow from them.[11]

According to the postwar memoirs of Aaron Bachman of the First Pennsylvania Cavalry, the prisoners consumed seven dogs during his time at Belle Isle. Most of them were poodles belonging to officers of the camp. Prison diarists confirmed three of the incidents, and one wrote that small pieces of dog meat were available for $1, "dogs being killed when ever catched." The most famous such incident occurred on December 26, 1863. The animal in question belonged to Lt. Virginius Bossieux, the camp commandant. One prisoner sharing in the bounty wrote, "I consider it wholesome and nourishing without the taint one would naturally suppose dog meat had." Bossieux was less open minded. According to Bachman, several men were to have been exchanged that day, but the commander refused to let anyone depart until the guilty party was revealed. The man was turned in quickly and made to eat a pound of raw dog meat.[12]

Stealing from their fellow prisoners or the Confederates was another option. The normally laconic William Dolphin devoted one of his lengthiest diary entries to a "Gallant Charge upon a Pork Barrel" he and some fellow prisoners made on November 29. They actually stole two barrels, garnering about sixteen pounds of pork. Although they got caught and were "whaled like Hell" by a Rebel sergeant, it was worth it. "Had enough for Once," Dolphin concluded.[13]

Most of the stealing was done by gangs of prisoners termed "Raiders" by their fellow captives. Although they stole tents and other items, bread was their most frequent target. John Boudwin wrote of almost nightly raids during late August and early September 1863. One night the victims raised such a noise that the guards came in and "very roughly handled" all the Raiders they could find. On another occasion Boudwin and two comrades found a thief who had stolen some items from them and "gave him a good Thrashing which he wont forget for some Time." Numbers, however, did not always guarantee safety. After Jacob Coburn was made sergeant for his squad of one hundred prisoners, he became responsible for delivering their rations. As he and some selected men attempted to do so one day a gang of Raiders descended upon them. They made off with four loaves of bread, meaning sixteen prisoners had to go without.[14]

Theft was not limited to the prisoners. Guards explained short rations by insisting that citizens had stolen bread being brought from the city over to the prison. Hearing a commotion across the James River one afternoon, Webb looked over to see just such an incident transpire. A mob of women surrounded the cart that delivered the prisoners' bread to the flatboat that was to bring it across the river. The women soon cleaned it out. "We shall probably go without our supper," Webb concluded.[15]

For some Confederates, a camp of hungry prisoners represented a tempting entrepreneurial opportunity. Several prison cooks were placed under arrest after they were caught stealing bread and salt from the quartermaster, which they then sold to the prisoners at inflated prices. One diarist wrote that their price for salt was 25¢ a tablespoon. Guards brought in bread, pies, tobacco, and liquor, which they sold to those few enlisted prisoners with money. These transactions entailed a great deal of risk. Regulations, of course, prohibited such ventures, and camp officials kept their eyes open for violations. According to Horace Smith, guards caught selling to the prisoners were bucked and gagged for half a day. On October 5, 1863, the *Richmond Examiner* reported that a guard had been sent to Castle Thunder for leaving his post and trading with the Yankees.[16]

Prison entrepreneurs gathered on Broadway, the main street running through the camp. George Hegeman often went there to trade. On one particularly good day he returned with a ration of meal and a piece of soap. Prices, he noted, were 40¢ for a quart of meal, 30¢ for a spoonful of salt, and $1 for a pint of beans. Tobacco came in 50¢ and 75¢ "plugs." Prisoners lacking money adopted whatever means they could to raise funds. Jacob Coburn was successful for a time boiling discarded bones and selling them to his hungry comrades. When that business slowed, he sold his Masonic pin for $10 Confederate. He invested the proceeds in rice and molasses, selling a portion for a profit and supplementing his rations with the rest. The winter of 1863–64 forced the prisoners to choose between food and comfort. William Dolphin chose the former, selling his "old Boots" for a ration of sweet potatoes. A friend of William Tippett's sold his coat for $18 Confederate during a very cold January. Horace Smith and two friends chose the opposite approach, saving their rations until they had the $5 they needed to purchase a blanket.[17]

The question of comfort was an important one because a large number of Belle Isle prisoners lacked shelter. Newell Burch had been there one week when his diary entry read, "Cloudy & showery, lie in the sun dirt & rain & take it." Confederate officials attempted to provide shelter for the prisoners, but they never kept up with the increase in the prison population. Jonathan Boynton of the 157th New York, captured at Gettysburg, later recalled that he and a friend occupied a small space between two tents for his first month at Belle Isle. He then shared a Sibley tent with twenty other captives. Horace Smith was without shelter for just over a week before prison officials issued a number of tents on August 4. He termed them "poor things but good enough for prisoners I suppose." Three days after they were issued, a large number of prisoners arrived from the West. As a result, Smith estimated that nearly one-third of the Belle Isle captives were still without tents.[18]

For the early Belle Isle prisoners the lack of shelter meant they had no protection from the pounding sun. As autumn approached cold nights became a greater source of suffering. "The men that are without Tents suffered considerable last night and this morning from the cold wind & rain," Boudwin wrote on September 19. Two men, he added, had been found dead that morning, victims of exposure. Arriving on November 1, William Robinson, a Chickamauga captive, estimated that there were forty-five hundred prisoners on the island. Half of them, he estimated, had tents. Confederate officials continued their efforts to find enough tents for the captives, but demand stayed ahead of supply. Robinson's squad received tents on the 9th. John Whitten, who arrived December 8, was in a tent three days later. On January 17, 1864, John Kay was transferred from a warehouse in the city to Belle Isle. It took him four days to receive a tent. The day he did another large contingent of prisoners arrived. "No tents for them, but the blue sky and cold ground," he wrote.[19]

Firewood was also scarce at Belle Isle. During one rainy November evening, the shortage was such that it was issued only to men without tents. "We are shivering in the tent today," Hegeman wrote on December 19. "I am thankful my dear ones at home are ignorant of what I have to endure here." As the bitter January of 1864 arrived, Coburn wrote, "The weather is growing colder and wood seems to be failing us. . . . I have frozen my feet already lying in bed and if the weather gets much colder I fear we shall nearly freeze to death or suffer worse than death." On January 21 Michael Dougherty arrived at Belle Isle from the Pemberton prison. "It is a shocking place," he wrote. "Froze hard last night. Morning verry cold. Had no shelter. About 600 of us had to sleep in the open air. . . . Several had their feet frozen and some died in Camp from cold." As late as February 15, John Kay wrote that there were between two hundred and three hundred men without tents that rainy night.[20]

In early November Gen. Dow arrived to distribute the clothing sent by the Union government. William Tippett got a blanket, a cap, a pair of shoes, and stockings. "Slept very warm and comfortable," he noted. He also asserted that the Confederates consumed about 90 percent of the food sent later that month from the North. William Dolphin concurred, writing, "The Rebs fed their guards out of our Government rations of Pork." Jacob Coburn wrote, "Government has actually sent us some rations. But the rascally rebel officers permitted their own soldiers on guard around us to be well filled with it before the hungry prisoners got a taste." His disgust was not limited to Rebels. Although grateful for the clothing, he added, "But much irregularity prevailed and all kinds of rascallity among our own men in getting more than was their due."[21]

As Dow returned to Libby, John Hussey of the U.S. Christian Commission, who had assisted him in Richmond, headed north. He brought with him Dow's declaration that the Belle Isle prisoners were "suffering beyond endurance." At Dow's insistence, Hussey reported there were fifty-four hundred prisoners on the "low and unhealthy" island. Over half the prisoners, he continued, lacked shelter, and many were without clothes or blankets. "They are on half rations, have no fuel of any kind, no soap is issued to them; they are consequently very filthy of necessity," Hussey concluded. Dow had predicted that daily deaths would reach one hundred by New Year's.[22]

Dow's assessment was corroborated by exchanged surgeons, whose reports of the "Horrors" of Richmond prisons hit the Northern press the same month that Dow's observations reached Washington. Exchanged prisoners provided further evidence. The cartel was dead, but a trickle of individual exchanges was still taking place. Confederate policy mandated sending north the worst cases of ill prisoners capable of traveling. The condition of these returning prisoners shocked Union officials. Republican politicians photographed many of them, and their pictures of emaciated parolees helped lead Northern officials toward a position of retaliation against Confederate prisoners. At least one Union soldier had doubts. Frank Wilkeson of the Eleventh New York Artillery Battery later recalled, "By far the largest portion of [the returned parolees] were in good condition and fit for service. It is true that many of them were diseased and almost dead when they were delivered to us, and these soldiers were grouped and photographed, very unfairly I think." Still, when the generally unemotional William Hoffman visited

Camp Parole, the condition of the returned prisoners shocked him. "Some of these poor fellows were wasted to mere skeletons and had scarcely life enough remaining to appreciate that they were now in the hands of their friends," the commissary general reported.[23]

Confederate officials were not unaware of the conditions on Belle Isle, nor were they totally unconcerned. In mid-November Winder received a report from Maj. Isaac Carrington stating that Belle Isle was thoroughly drained and policed. The only problem he cited was that some tents were "dilapidated" because of either weather or the prisoners' carelessness in building fires. This did not explain why, beginning in October, deaths at the prison exceeded one hundred per month. Winder called upon William A. Carrington, Richmond's medical director, who was not related to the major, to conduct his own inspection.[24]

Carrington first asserted that Belle Isle was "as well managed as possible under the circumstances," then went on to cite several examples of mismanagement. The camp was overcrowded, and the prisoners had neither enough blankets nor fuel. Carrington added, "They sleep on the ground and are exposed to all the vicissitudes of temperature incident to our climate." Much of the mortality Carrington attributed to "the depressing moral influence the prisoners labor under." Having been told that there was no hope for exchange, "They die from slight diseases, having lost all hope."[25]

A March 6, 1864, report from G. William Semple, Belle Isle's prison surgeon, was even more damning. The camp, he pointed out, was designed to accommodate about three thousand prisoners, but for several months six thousand to ten thousand occupied it. As a security measure, the men had not been allowed to visit the sinks at night. This had resulted in "deposits of excrement . . . in the streets and small vacant spaces between the tents." Overcrowding made it nearly impossible for the camp to be adequately policed. Rations, Semple reported, consisted almost entirely of bread, rice, and peas or beans. The bread, made from cornmeal, was not sifted or bolted, leading to diarrhea and dysentery. John Wilkins, the surgeon in charge at Richmond's General Hospital No. 21, added graphic confirmation. "The daily list of deaths is regulated by the number admitted each day from Belle Isle," he bluntly reported. In February, he went on, twenty-five Belle Isle prisoners had died fewer than twenty-four hours after they arrived. Many arrived in a shocking state. Wilkins explained, "It is so common an occurence for the patients sent from Belle Isle to be speechless or delirious and be unable to give their names &c. that I have requested the surgeon in charge . . . to pin their names, companies, and regiments of desperate cases on the lapel of their coats."[26]

The prisoners, of course, were sadly aware of their state. Some became hardened to it. "There is a good many men sick and the men are dying off very fast," John Whitten wrote on December 10. In a January diary entry, George Hegeman simply recorded, "17 deaths reported yesterday." John Kay was less sanguine. "Went past the hospital tent, saw the poor sick emaciated men lying in blankets and on the ground," he wrote on January 25. "Oh! how much of wretchedness, I have seen here this morning, how many poor sick and dying men, how many skeleton forms, they are starving us on this Isle."[27]

John Boudwin did not place all the blame on the Confederates. On August 13 he wrote, "During last night two men died in Camp and all owing to want of care and medicine and the fault of our Government in not using some means to get us out of this cussed place." Two weeks later he noted that several of his comrades harbored similar feelings against the Union government. "A great many of them say they will not do another days duty while they are in the service and I don't blame them much." Jacob Coburn tried to battle his feelings. "I do not intend to think hard of my country or her rulers," he wrote, "but this suffering is very trying to the soul." By the following summer, when Andersonville had replaced Belle Isle as the Confederacy's worst prison, few prisoners would suppress such emotions.[28]

Loneliness and boredom only compounded the prisoners' frustration. "This is a verry quiet place & one finds little to write about in a diary," Boudwin lamented. As at every other prison, these feelings were most acute on Sunday. "I would like much to be at home to day with my family—but I can't so I will try to be content," William Tippett wrote one lonely Sabbath. As 1863 ended, and he faced the prospect of another year in prison, Tippett again tried to be philosophical. "I am suffering for God and my Country and I will try and bear it with as good a Heart as I can under the Circumstances," he wrote. Nathan Webb viewed loneliness as a potential sign of personal weakness. "I fear that my mind is getting weak," he worried. "Lately I have thought of home and getting released all the time. My brain has been constantly exercised upon that one thing, till without effort I can not turn my mind upon anything else."[29]

With fewer resources than the officers in Libby and other Richmond warehouses, the Belle Isle prisoners were limited in their options for battling the boredom of prison life. Horace Smith provided a succinct account of daily life on the island. "Louse hunt twice a day, swallowing our little rations, whittling bones and occasionally a fight occurs in clash among the gambling class over a *dice board* but the boys are not stout enough to pound each other very bad."[30]

In warm weather, the opportunity to bathe in the James offered the men one diversion that even their officers did not enjoy. Webb was part of a group of fifteen that received the chance on July 3. He remained two hours, terming it "the most luxurious bath I ever enjoyed." Nearly as important was the opportunity to wash his clothes. Twelve days later, with the prison nearly empty thanks to exchange, Webb wrote that the entire camp enjoyed a dip in the river. Between July 5 and 12, Henry Tracy's diary recorded three pleasant baths in the James.[31]

Letters from home arrived at irregular intervals. When they did, the prisoners did not attempt to conceal their joy. "Hi ho got a letter from Eva, the first I have received since my capture," Coburn wrote when his wife's letter made it through the lines. "O bless you Eva, ever faithful and true." After hearing from home, Henry Smith of the First Vermont Cavalry wrote back, "It makes me feel a great deal better to hear from home once more and to hear that you are all alive and well and getting along so well with the work." The work of the family farm was a matter of great concern to him. He begged them, "Write to me in your next how you got along haying and harvesting how much corn and potatoes you had how many apples how much stock you keep and so on."[32]

As Smith noted, gambling and fighting were also significant parts of life on Belle Isle. "Card playing and fighting the order of the day," Newell Burch observed in one diary entry. Webb elaborated, "There is a great deal of gambling among the prisoners. Most all have some money, and that is played for also matches, gold-pieces, &c." However, Smith's assertion that the fighters were unable to do much harm was not always true. On September 7 Boudwin wrote that there had been a fight among a group of navy prisoners, "and one of them was very badly punished." The following month Hegeman witnessed a fight between two prisoners, "both plucky." He later wrote that a "crowd of N.Y. roughs" had been involved in a fight with "fists, knives, clubs and stones," which left at least two men dead. January battles, Hegeman wrote, found one man clubbed to death with an ax and another missing a thumb that had been bitten off.[33]

There is little evidence of camp guards interfering with the fighting prisoners. Indeed, prison diaries mention very little interaction with the guards, except for those who smuggled in food to sell. Nathan Webb watched one day in early July as a local outfit replaced regular guards, who were being dispatched to the fighting front. "The 'City Battalion' placed them selves around our pen," he wrote. "Immediately putting on all the airs of three year veterans. It was real amusing to see how military they tried to appear . . . never for an instant relaxing their suddenly put on discipline." When the City Battalion departed, Boudwin wrote, "We have now on guard over us some old soldiers and find them to be a little better & not quite so strick."[34]

The guards could be strict if they felt the deed in question deserved harsh punishment. Both John Boudwin and Horace Smith wrote on August 31 that prisoners who cut into their fellow prisoners' tents had been bucked and gagged. Supper was delayed until the guilty parties were caught, and Boudwin concluded that the punishment "served them right." On December 22 George Hegeman wrote that a prisoner had hoisted an American flag on a small flagstaff, resulting in a "prolonged shout from 10,000 throats." The guards ordered the flag taken down and tied the owner up by the thumbs.[35]

The diarists agreed that the guards seldom hesitated to inflict the ultimate punishment, shooting at the prisoners. Confederate prison records are scant, making corroboration difficult to find, but prison diaries are well garnished with entries concerning shooting incidents. Often the guards' marksmanship was poor, but occasionally the shooters found their mark. Pennsylvania prisoner John A. Porter spent only ten days at Belle Isle in May 1863 before being exchanged. During that time, he wrote, one prisoner was killed and another wounded by the guards.[36]

The number of shootings noted in prison diaries rose as summer headed into fall and the prison population increased. On August 14 a prisoner was shot and killed as he stood near the riverbank. Prison diarists did not agree on whether one or two prisoners standing nearby were wounded. They did agree as to motive. "It was as cold Blooded a Murder as ever witnessed," Boudwin wrote. Horace Smith added, "They were prisoners who came in today and didn't know the rules of the camp. Those cursed Rebs would as soon shoot one of us as they would a snake." On October 25 a Michigan prisoner was shot while walking along the bank. Tippett termed it "a cool *Murder.*" Both he and Smith wrote that the victim had been part of a working squad digging a ditch around the camp.[37]

Mental derangement occasionally led to shootings at Belle Isle. One occurred on September 13. A Massachusetts soldier described by his fellow prisoners as either "crazy" or "a little out of his mind" was the victim. It was after dark, and the man was heading to the sinks when he was shot. On November 19 a man "who was suffering with fever" was shot as he attempted to walk past the guards, explaining to them that he was going home.[38]

Details of a February 11, 1864, shooting are hazy. One diarist wrote that a guard fired at a prisoner who was attempting to steal his blanket. He missed the would-be thief but killed an innocent prisoner standing nearby and wounded three others. Two other prisoners simply recorded that three men had been shot that day.[39]

Occasionally the crack of rifles was a sign that the prisoners were attempting to escape. Newell Burch wrote on October 10 that the guards had fired at a prisoner trying to make his exit. They did not hit him, but the man was captured before he could get away. One week later Smith wrote that two men had been shot during an escape attempt. Neither was killed.[40]

Guards were not the only threat potential escapees faced. The currents of the James River could be equally dangerous. On October 20 the corpse of a soldier from the 154th New York was discovered in the river, brought back to camp, and buried. A comrade who had escaped with him was recaptured and returned the same day.[41]

Often the prisoners offered virtually no details when writing of escapes. On October 3 Tippett simply noted, "Several men escaped last night." Two, he added, had failed when they attempted to bribe a guard. On October 15 Dolphin wrote that twenty men, including a bugler from his regiment, had gotten away the previous night. The next morning, perhaps referring to the same incident, Smith wrote, "Several boys tried to get away from here last night. Some of them succeeded." Perhaps the most unusual escape account was that recorded by Coburn on November 8. Ten prisoners, he wrote, had escaped, accompanied by two of their guards. Unfortunately, none of his fellow prisoners corroborated his account.[42]

As 1863 ended, Confederate officials realized something had to be done to remove the thousands of hungry Yankee mouths from their capital. As reported in the local press, it appeared that their solution would afford those same Yankees a great measure of relief. On December 30 the *Richmond Sentinel* announced that the Confederate government had selected a site near Andersonville, Georgia, for a new prison. This, the paper predicted, would relieve the overcrowding at Belle Isle. Not appreciating the irony of its statement, the *Sentinel* added, "The location is on the Southwestern railroad, between Oglethorpe and Americus, where no difficulty will be encountered in supplying their wants."[43]

7
"500 here died. 600 ran away"
Danville and Beyond, 1864

On October 28, 1863, Gen. Robert E. Lee offered Secretary Seddon some advice. The Federals, Lee had learned, were not likely to resume prisoner exchange. The Confederates, therefore, should make plans to keep a large number of Union captives for the duration of the war. "I would respectfully suggest that the city of Richmond is not a suitable place for the accommodation and safe keeping of these prisoners," Lee went on. Keeping them fed entailed great cost and tied up transportation needed to keep the city's residents supplied. They also posed a security risk. "I have no doubt," Lee wrote, "that even now they add much to the sources of information of the enemy with regard to the movements of troops and the disposition of our forces." To solve these problems he suggested Danville, a Virginia city near the North Carolina border, "where wood is cheap and provisions are in abundance."[1]

Seddon agreed with Lee's analysis. In early November he instructed Gen. Winder to begin sending prisoners to Danville. Winder immediately handed the logistical details over to Capt. Turner. On November 11 some four thousand prisoners clambered into boxcars of the Richmond and Danville Railroad for the 145-mile journey. Before they departed, Winder again urged the secretary to see to it "that a sufficient supply of provisions be insured for their maintenance."[2]

The prisoners were destined for a city that had once prospered from its location in the rich tobacco region of southern Virginia. Although Danville had been spared the ravages of war, the conflict had been bad for business. Most of the town's young men had gone for soldiers, and food and clothing had become scarce. Six tobacco factories were set aside for the reception of the prisoners. One was designated for officers, another for black captives. All were Spartan, lamps and furnishings being removed before the first trains from Richmond arrived.[3]

A second contingent of prisoners left Richmond on the 13th, reaching Danville at about 9:00 P.M. Many did not remain long. There was a small yard outside Prison No. 1 surrounded by a board fence. The night after they arrived a group of captives in Prison No. 1 slipped out and cut a hole in one of the planks. Soon after dark the men began making their exit. Sgt. William McKell of the Eighty-ninth Ohio was one of them. He estimated that between sixty and seventy had gotten away by 11:00 that night. Harlan Howard, another of the escapees, set the number at one hundred.[4]

McKell was quickly recaptured, but Howard eventually made it back to the Union lines. He and two comrades generally traveled at night and hid out in barns and forests during the day. Slaves and free blacks provided food, shelter, and directions along the way. After crossing the Dan River the escapees headed northwest, crossing the Blue Ridge and the New River Valley, passing close to Blacksburg, Virginia. On December 12 they reached Union pickets near Fayetteville, West Virginia. "Happiest hour of my life," Howard wrote. Furloughed, he arrived at his Wisconsin home the day after Christmas.[5]

Meanwhile the prisoners at Danville continued to make escape attempts. In early January they started a tunnel from Prison No. 3. Its terminus was to be the guardhouse, some thirty to forty feet away, where the prisoners apparently planned to emerge when it was unoccupied. The Confederates learned of the project. The prisoners believed a "traitor" from their ranks had betrayed them. Whatever their source of information, the guards herded the two hundred prisoners from the ground floor to an upstairs room, crowding it severely. There they were to remain until the leaders of the escape plan were turned over. Finally the principal planners confessed. They were bucked for an hour on two consecutive mornings, but their comrades were allowed to return downstairs.[6]

Later that month the occupants of Prison No. 5 began a tunnel that one prisoner termed "a masterful piece of work." On the night of the 28th some seventy or eighty men took it to freedom. According to Bergun Brown of the Twenty-ninth Indiana, many more could have gotten away had they been more careful. "All were too eager to get out first & when out did not act cautiously," he observed. The number that made it back to the North is uncertain, but thirteen of the escapees were returned on February 4. Two of those who were successful, members of the Sixth Ohio, later told a Cincinnati newspaper that they reached Union lines at Suffolk on February 13.[7]

Prison No. 5 was the scene of another tunnel escape on February 27. "It seems to be hard work for the Rebs to keep the Yanks together," one prisoner wrote. "They incline to scatter." He added that sixty-nine had gotten away. Another prisoner put the number at seventy.[8]

Despite these successes, a number of attempts failed. "Our tunnel is discovered & closed up," a prisoner in Prison No. 4 wrote on February 26. "A traitor in the house, sure," another wrote. As before the prisoners were driven upstairs to prevent further attempts. After the successful escape the following night, the Confederates launched a thorough search and discovered tunnels under way in Prisons 3 and 6. On other occasions the Confederates could only react. After five prisoners absconded during the night of March 2, the guards boarded up the windows of Prison No. 4.[9]

For prisoners arriving from Belle Isle, Danville at least offered shelter from the elements. Those from Libby and the other Richmond warehouses found little difference. Arriving after dark on December 12, Bergun Brown paid little attention to his surroundings. After looking around the next morning he concluded, "Looks about as usual only dreadful dirty & very closely crowded." He did not identify the prison in which he was housed, but his was likely a universal description of the Danville warehouses. Brown also noted that water was scarce. The entire supply, he wrote, came from pails carried into the prison.[10]

The water situation did not improve with time. "Water is gotten at the river 80 rods off," a prisoner noted in May. James Penfield stayed just a few days at Danville in May 1864 en route to the officers' prison at Macon, Georgia. While there he received a pint of water for washing. Cyrus Heffley, also bound for Macon, wrote from Prison No. 3, "We are hard pressed for water. Men all must thirst." What water the prisoners had, he added, came from the river. Albert Shatzel of the First Vermont Cavalry, en route for Andersonville, also spent a short time at Danville in May. His account of the daily prison routine also indicated that the Dan River was the sole source of water. Shatzel wrote, "Rules of the establishment first Roole call 2d sweep out 3d get watter from the River 4th schermish for Boddy Lice 5th make spoons for soup 6th forward for a wash 7th fall in for Grub & comfort 8th fall in for soup."[11]

Despite Lee's claim that provisions in the Danville area were "in abundance," the prisoners' rations did not immediately improve with their change of base. On January 1, 1864, as a smallpox epidemic raged through the prisons, one prisoner observed, "The Smallpox are very severe among us, but Starvation is the greatest suffering of all." Another wrote that, despite the bitter winter weather, many prisoners were trading their shoes for smuggled rice, salt, and bread. According to Sgt.

McKell, rations during November and December 1863 consisted of "black bread, beef and bean soup." He added, "The soup was nothing more than warm water covered over the top with bugs out of the beans the beans being never washed, but thrown in dirt and all." Rice soup, cabbage soup, or sweet potato soup sometimes offered variety. In January, McKell wrote, cornbread replaced wheat bread. "The beef gave out about the same time and we had pork instead, sometimes very good, and sometimes very poor."[12]

Supplies from the North, from both private and government sources, sometimes made their way to Danville. Brown noted that the December 25 arrival of U.S. government crackers, one pound to the man, made Christmas much happier. McKell charged that only a small percentage of the Federal rations reached the prisoners. "Out of a lot of beans sent, we had soup once or twice," he asserted. "Besides this, we twice received crackers; at one time, ten, and the other five." McKell also accused the Rebel keepers of stealing a good portion of the Federal clothing that arrived in December. So much had been scavenged, he insisted, that the prisoners had to choose between pants or drawers, shoes or socks, and a coat or a blanket. Abram Price of the Sixth Ohio disputed McKell's charges, at least as they applied to the clothing. Price was one of the prisoners selected to help distribute the Union supplies. Soon after the war he wrote, "We went to the different [Danville] prisons and took down the name of every one, and what clothing he needed to make him comfortable. We showed partiality to none. There were but few of the . . . prisoners who were not satisfied."[13]

A large shipment of private boxes reached Danville on January 18. Although the Confederates had opened the boxes for inspection, McKell conceded that nothing had been removed from his. He received clothing, soap, towels, medicine, dried beef, sugar, and tea. He later sold part of the clothing to purchase extra rice and bread. Other prisoners found books to help them overcome the monotony of prison life. Among the unfortunate ones was Bergun Brown. Neither he nor any of his acquaintances received a box. "It is very tantalizing to see so much good eating around and still be confined to prison diet," he wrote.[14]

Another shipment of boxes arrived in mid-March. William Tritt of the Twenty-first Wisconsin set the number at twenty-eight. Tritt did not receive one, but he still benefited, taking in washing and receiving his pay from the bounty of the boxes. On April 11 Tritt's fortune improved when he received a box from his aunt. "Much pleasure and thankfulness," he noted.[15]

As time went on, prison diarists indicated that their rations at Danville improved. "Rations liberally increased, but we suffered many times up to this increase," Tritt wrote on February 1. In March the rations were again reduced, meat disappearing altogether for several days. However, by early May Tritt was again writing of improved fare. Even McKell admitted, "What food we get here, mean and rough as it is, is enough, and all a man should eat of such stuff."[16]

By May Danville had become a temporary stopping point for Virginia prisoners being transferred to Andersonville or Macon. Although less than impressed with the facilities, they, too, noted a distinct improvement in their rations. "We are even more crowded than in Libby," James Love wrote, "but we are much better fed." Another Libby prisoner wrote of Danville, "Very rough place. House dirty and no accommodations." He added, "Our rations are cooked for us and are better than we rec'd at Libby." Arriving from the Lynchburg prison on May 13, Sgt. Edwin T. Marsh of the 140th New York wrote, "We got a plentiful dinner of corn bread rice soup & boiled bacon." For those bound for Andersonville, Danville provided the most filling meals most would enjoy for many months.[17]

Despite their move south from Richmond, the Danville prisoners did not escape the bitter January of 1864. The clothes sent from the North helped, but they did not totally make up for the lack of heating. One captive noted that his building received stoves on December 26. Unfortunately, they could not be set up for lack of pipes. The occupants of his room built a crude fireplace. Some Danville prisoners tried to build fires on pieces of scrap metal they found. Others simply jumped up and down in an attempt to keep warm.[18]

Even if there had been adequate stoves, there was seldom enough wood available to keep them fired. A few details of prisoners were allowed to go out for wood, but they could not supply the demand. Those who went were required to take an oath not to escape. They received extra rations for their efforts. Bergun Brown served several days on one detail, working about four hours each day. He wrote that the parties had to go four miles into the country. The prisoners they were unable to supply resorted to desperate measures in their efforts to secure fuel. Often they tore up the walls or floors of their rooms. One group that was caught doing so was "bucked severely."[19]

On December 13 Brown casually mentioned that smallpox had broken out in the prison. Six days later he was far less casual. "Smallpox is increasing. Dr. has not been to our prison for three days & men lie helpless upon the floor, no medicine or warm food." As the month ended, there were fifteen or more cases in his building. Thirty others had been removed, and the disease was "still on the increase." The death toll is not known, but the unofficial observations of the prisoners suggest that it was substantial. In April McKell observed, "Our prison which was so crowded when I first came to it [in November] that I could scarcely find room to lie down on either of the three floors, now holds all on two floors, with less crowding." At the end of March Tritt wrote simply, "4500 of Sam's boys came to Danville. 500 here died. 600 ran away. 3400 yet remain."[20]

Had the citizens of Danville been calling the shots, none of the Yankee prisoners would have remained. In late January Mayor Thomas P. Atkinson arrived in Richmond with three petitions from Danville residents and a resolution from the city council. All called for the removal of the prisoners from Danville. The dangers of smallpox and "the stench arising from the C.S. prisons" were the main causes of concern. The board of health blamed a "large number of cases of fever" on the presence of the prisons and feared a dramatic increase when summer arrived. As Atkinson waited at a Richmond hotel for a response from Seddon, the January 28 escape occurred. The mayor used that as further ammunition for his cause, asserting that there were "no buildings in the town at all adequate to their safe-keeping."[21]

Capt. Henry McCoy was the first commander of the Danville prison. Price, who worked closely with McCoy and his staff while distributing the Union clothing, termed them "gentlemen in every respect." The Confederate officers did all they could, Price insisted, to see to it that the prisoners did not suffer. In January 1864 Maj. Mason Morfit replaced McCoy. Morfit was universally reviled by postwar memoirists for his alleged cruelty to the prisoners. Prison diarists were more reticent, although McKell noted, "[Morfit] was a man of greater energy and kept the prisoners much closer than the Capt. had before."[22]

McKell was unimpressed with the guards at Danville. Many were conscripts, whom he termed "the most ignorant and surly of all the troops . . . with whom we have had anything to do." He claimed that at least one guard was punished every day for being absent without leave. Usually they were made to stand on the head of a barrel. Like those at Richmond, the Danville sentries were vigilant when it came to prisoners looking out the windows. On December 14 Brown wrote that a guard had shot at a man who threw some water out the window. He missed the guilty party but hit another prisoner in the leg. On February 14 and 16 Tritt wrote that prisoners had been shot for putting their heads outside a window. One was wounded in the hand. Tritt did not record the fate of the other. On May 11 he wrote that yet another prisoner standing at a window had been shot, suffering a broken wrist. In late January both Tritt and fellow prisoner William Haun wrote that a guard was "fooling with a negro wench" in the street, taunting her. He stopped her by charging at her with his bayonet. His gun then discharged, killing her.[23]

Prisoners who arrived in the spring on their way to Georgia reported three more shooting incidents. A prisoner who arrived on May 13 wrote, "The guards fire without warning on any one who puts his head hands or feet out of the window and ere we were here half an hour one was shot but no harm done." Three days later another prisoner reported that a guard fired but missed a man who poked his head out the window. The ball lodged in a beam a foot away from its target. Two diarists recorded yet another shooting on May 21. According to one of them, the victim died.[24]

Diversions were few at Danville. Crowding was one factor. So, too, was the lack of resources. A few prisoners managed to play war with cloth clubs, raising a "dreadful rumpus" in the process. "I have passed the day playing checkers and reading an old magazine of 1857," McKell wrote on April 13. Lice hunting was a twice-daily exercise for many of the prisoners. When a pair of men refused to join in the hunt, the captives who shared their cramped quarters corralled them and shaved their heads. However they spent their time, nothing could overcome the palpable loneliness that was a constant element of prison life. Sometimes all they could do was give in to their despondency. "I sat down by the west windows and looked as far as I can toward home," William Tritt wrote. "It's all I seem to do, touching home."[25]

With the opening of the 1864 spring campaigns between Grant and Lee, the Union Army of the Potomac and the Confederate Army of Northern Virginia became locked in a virtual death grip. It would continue for nearly a year, producing thousands of prisoners. To help handle the deluge, the Confederates began again to send captives to Lynchburg. On June 28 all Richmond prisoners healthy enough to be moved, some twenty-three hundred in number, were also forwarded to the southern Virginia city. Most remained only a few days before being sent on to Danville and then on to Georgia.[26]

The officers were confined in an unidentified building in the city. Maj. Charles Mattocks of the Seventeenth Maine simply described it as the "military prison." The only detail he added was that a stove was the sole piece of furniture in his room. Jacob Heffelfinger of the Thirty-sixth Pennsylvania noted that there was a prison yard where the captives were allowed to go for air and exercise. The commandant he identified as a Lt. Shinn, who treated the prisoners "kindly." By May 12, Mattocks wrote, there were 111 officers in Lynchburg, including two brigadier generals, Alexander Shaler and Truman Seymour.[27]

The officers quickly grasped the realities of prison life. Mattocks wrote that the captives were "living upon a small piece of pork and a small loaf of bread each day, breathing a small amount of genuine fresh air, [and] seeing but a few new faces." Heffelfinger added, "We are fast learning how to do nothing, read nothing and sleep much."[28]

The enlisted prisoners camped in an open field that prison diarists put at anywhere from one to five miles outside the city. Sgt. Marsh arrived May 7. Two days later he placed the prison population at seventeen hundred to eighteen hundred. By the 16th, he wrote, it was "about 2000." Artillery rested on the surrounding hills. According to Marsh, there were "two old guns" staring down at them. Albert Shatzel suggested that there were more than two, writing that the cannon were "placed all around." Marsh observed that the hills were also "crowded with Secesh people gazing at us 'live yankees.'" Shatzel, however, wrote that they were there to do more than just stare. There were, he explained, "some 500 Rebel Citizens guarding us there is no soldiers here."[29]

Both Marsh and Shatzel said the rations were hardtack and a small amount of bacon. Marsh termed the bacon "good," and Shatzel concluded that the rations were "tough but better than none." Both men complained of sleeping on the ground during the cold spring nights. "The wind blowes very hard & it is very cloudy & we are going to have a hard night of it & we have no cover," Shatzel wrote on May 10. That night it rained "just enough to wet us through." Marsh and two fellow prisoners shared a single blanket. "Oh! such nights," he wrote, "so cold to lie on the bare ground with Scarcely anything to cover us."[30]

An anonymous diarist from Indiana arrived at Lynchburg after suffering a shoulder wound during the Wilderness battle. Taken to the rear of the Confederate lines, he was "treated very kindly. I am compelled to form a better opinion of those men since [being] among them," he wrote of his enemies. Still, it was three days before his wound was bandaged. A Confederate surgeon removed the ball from his shoulder on the 12th. The prisoner noted, "He is much of a Gentleman & seems to be verry desirous of alleviating our Sufferings as much as possible." The soldier remained in the field hospital two more days before leaving with five other prisoners and fifteen wounded Confederates.[31]

His group marched to Orange Court House, then traveled by train to Gordonsville. After spending a week at a hospital there, the wounded prisoner arrived in Lynchburg on May 22. He stayed two days in what he described as a "receiving hospital" before going to "Crompton's Hospital." The rations were "but a Scanty diet [of] rice coffee (a miserable Substitute) Corn bread & a verry Small bit of fat bacon once a day." He added to them by paying 50¢ Confederate for an egg. As for the facilities, "We have pretty good beds here but bedbugs are numerous & bold."

He was unimpressed by the treatment he received. On the 31st he noted that the doctor had not visited him for three days.[32]

On June 15 he and thirteen others left the hospital for the "city prison." They were put into an upstairs hall about sixteen by forty-five feet, where some 100 men were crowded together. There were only two small windows at one end. He stayed there four days before being taken to another building a block away, where 147 captives were housed. This facility offered ample room and better ventilation. Rations, issued once a day, consisted of one meal's worth of cornbread, pork, and water.[33]

Far to the south and west, the Confederates reopened the prison at Cahaba, Alabama, during the spring of 1863. Cahaba had been used only as a temporary holding facility the previous year. Now, with the cartel nearing its end, the prisoners arriving there were destined to remain longer. The fifteen-thousand-square-foot prison was also known as Castle Morgan, in honor of Confederate cavalry commander John Hunt Morgan. To convert the warehouse into a prison, the Confederates erected a wooden stockade, with walkways for the guards, around it. They also added wooden bunks.[34]

Capt. Howard A. M. Henderson, a Methodist minister, was in command of the prison. Postwar memoirists, seldom generous in their praise of Confederate prison commanders, were virtually unanimous in their tributes to Henderson's kindness. He worked hard to keep them supplied with clothing, blankets, and medicine. He also endeavored to arrange prisoner exchanges, although circumstances often doomed his efforts to failure. The ex-prisoners were equally unanimous in their condemnation of Lt. Col. Sam Jones, who commanded the post of Cahaba, including the prison guard force. They remembered him as cruel and abusive, a man who looked for any opportunity to inflict severe punishments.[35]

Confederate prison records, scanty for most facilities, are especially so for Cahaba. Those that exist, along with prison diaries, suggest that the prison population fluctuated a great deal during its existence. In January 1864 Henderson reported that there were thirty-five military prisoners, four citizens, and two "Negroes" held at Cahaba. Lt. Edmund E. Ryan of the Seventeenth Illinois, who arrived in mid-February, wrote that he was one of 308 prisoners there. Sgt. David Kennedy of the Ninth Ohio Cavalry put the number at 547 when he entered Cahaba on April 24. In a March 31 report, surgeon R. H. Whitfield indicated that there were 660 prisoners confined, with bunks for only 432. On April 20 Richmond officials ordered that all Cahaba prisoners be sent to Andersonville. On May 3

Lt. Col. Henry Davis, then commanding the post of Cahaba, reported that the transfer was complete. By then, however, the cartel had collapsed and the Confederates were desperate for prison space. Cahaba's respite was temporary. According to an inspection report filed the following October, not only was the prison open for business, but its population had ballooned to 2,151.[36]

Lt. Ryan's opinion of the Cahaba prison was decidedly mixed. The rations, he wrote, consisted of a quart of meal and a quarter pound of meat a day. "Sometimes we receive a few cow peas which are not fit for men to eat," he added. Ryan described the prison as "unclean," so much so that it was impossible for the men to keep clear of vermin. On the positive side, "The officers and Soldiers treat us as officers and true soldiers should be treated as prisoners of war." As for daily activities, "We spend our time in cooking, sleeping, reading, playing cards, singing songs and discussing the various subjects of the day." Ryan concluded, "It is a hard disagreeable life for a human being to live." Although Davis had reported the prison empty of Yankees on May 3, Ryan remained until May 29, when he was sent to the officers' prison at Macon.[37]

Sgt. Kennedy spent only four days at Cahaba before departing for Andersonville. Because construction on the warehouse had never been completed, the roof was unfinished. Kennedy noted, "Nothing to be seen but clear blew Skie while the hot Sun makes us hunt the Shade around our prison wals." He wrote that cornbread and bacon composed the rations, which "just keeps life in the body." On one point he agreed with virtually every military prisoner. "Time is tireson. We Sigh for our liberty."[38]

The most damning condemnation of Cahaba came from surgeon Whitfield. Among his complaints was the lack of bunks, which forced over two hundred prisoners to sleep on the dirt floor of the prison. The bunks themselves were nothing more than rough plank, with no straw or bedding. There were four open windows in the structure and a gap of sixteen hundred feet in the roof. The prison contained only one fireplace. As a result, Whitfield reported, there were some forty fires burning in the poorly ventilated structure. The firewood consisted mainly of green pine and decayed oak. "With such wood and no ventilation, you can well imagine to what a dense smoke these men have been subjected for the past five months," the surgeon complained. The prison water supply came from an artesian well, entering the camp only after passing for two hundred yards through an open gutter in the street. Whitfield noted, "In its course it has been subjected to the washings of the hands, feet, faces, and heads of soldiers, citizens, and negroes, buckets, tubs, and spittoons of groceries, offices and hospital, hogs, dogs, cows, and horses, and filth of all kinds from the streets and other sources." The sinks could accommodate only four prisoners at a time. These conditions, combined with the fact that there was only one wheelbarrow for removing all filth and rubbish, led to "an unavoidable accumulation" of "fruitful sources of disease."[39]

Whitfield wrote that the prisoners received the same rations as Confederate soldiers. That was the only positive note in his report. He exonerated Henderson, who had "exerted himself to the extent of his ability" to address the surgeon's concerns. He concluded by placing the blame where he felt it belonged. "The two quartermasters at this post, with only this prison and one small hospital to supply, have failed to be equal to the task of having this prison supplied with good and sufficient wood, water, and bunks, and putting it in a condition in which it would be moderately comfortable, clean, and healthy."[40]

In at least one area the prisoners were well supplied, thanks to an unlikely benefactor. Cahaba resident Amanda Gardner was a loyal Rebel who had lost a son in the Confederate service. Despite this she proved a Good Samaritan to hundreds of Union prisoners at Cahaba. Amanda supplied them with such food, medicine, and clothing as her limited resources would allow. Jones objected to her humanitarian work, but Henderson championed her cause and made sure she was allowed to continue. For the Union captives this guaranteed a priceless supply of reading material. Mrs. Gardner had a large library, rich in novels and nonfiction works encompassing numerous fields of study. All a bored, lonely prisoner had to do was send a note to Amanda, and she would supply him with a book. Thanks to her good work, Cahaba prisoners had a huge advantage when it came to battling the constant tedium of prison life.[41]

Farther west, a pair of Texas prisons, Camp Groce and Camp Ford, housed the bulk of the Union captives taken in the Trans-Mississippi. Camp Groce was located near Hempstead. It was opened during the spring of 1862 as a training camp, but the Confederates abandoned it nearly a year later because the site was considered unhealthy. They soon reopened the facility as a prison, much to the disgust of the Twentieth Texas. The initial guard outfit had trained there one year earlier, and the men remembered what the conditions had been. The first contingent of 110 prisoners arrived on June 13. More reached Camp Groce as Gen. John B. Magruder, commanding the District of Texas, removed military captives from the Houston jail and the state penitentiary at Huntsville. By the end of October the camp housed 431 prisoners.[42]

Within two months exchange and transfer had emptied Camp Groce. The collapse of the cartel led to the reopening of the prison in June 1864. Soon nearly seven hundred prisoners occupied the tiny camp. Camp officials impressed slaves from nearby plantations to extend the walls. The renovation brought what had been the guard barracks within the limits of the prison. This left the guards to sleep either in tents or under the stars. Meanwhile the health of the prisoners deteriorated, largely due to the poor water. Two wells offered only "a slimy, smelly ooze," and the poorly named Clear Creek "carried a steady stream of human and equine waste" from two nearby cavalry camps.[43]

To the east, Camp Ford, located four miles northeast of Tyler, became the largest Confederate prison west of the Mississippi. Like Camp Groce, Camp Ford had begun as a training camp. On July 21, 1863, Gen. Edmund Kirby Smith, commander of the Department of the Trans-Mississippi, acknowledged a message from Gen. Magruder relative to establishing the prison. Nine days later, Capt. Samuel Richardson arrived at Tyler with forty-eight prisoners and orders to set up the camp. The trainees guaranteed an available guard force. In addition, the surrounding area was rich farm country, so subsistence, it was assumed, would not be a problem.[44]

For its first several months as a prison, Camp Ford had no wall. The number of prisoners was small, and the Confederates provided additional security by doubling the guard details at night. This changed with the arrival of 461 prisoners in early November. Camp officials, playing on the fears of local residents, persuaded them to supply slaves to erect a stockade. According to J. B. Leake of the Twentieth Iowa, the first of them arrived on the 11th. Three days later he reported that there were two hundred slaves hard at work.[45]

Security was one of many concerns the Camp Ford officers had. On November 7 Maj. Thomas Tucker, the camp commander, reported that most of the five hundred prisoners were "perfectly destitute of clothing or shoes." He had been unable to secure lumber for barracks, so the prisoners slept in the open air without blankets. Tucker further complained that the camp had not been supplied with wood. This forced him to detail guards to accompany daily wood-gathering parties. Doing so severely strained his manpower as he had but one company of militia, consisting of seventy-one men fit for duty.[46]

These problems did not remain Tucker's for long. Two days after dispatching his pessimistic report he departed Camp Ford. His successor was Col. Robert T. P. Allen, a West Point graduate and Methodist minister. "[Allen] said he wanted to treat us as he wished to be treated," Leake wrote the day of the new commandant's arrival. According to all accounts, even those published after the war, he strove to do just that. A "kind friend" and "a Christian and a gentleman" were among the descriptions of Allen penned by prisoners. Allen's wife followed his example, visiting the prisoners from time to time and distributing peaches and other provisions.

Not everyone approved of Allen's kindness toward the prisoners. W. W. Heartsill, a Confederate cavalry officer, spent several months at Camp Ford. Seeing Allen deliver dried peaches, butter, and eggs to Yankee officers, he wrote, "This is quite different from the treatment that our officers received at Camp Chase; I think it would do Col Allen good to stay a few months in Fort Delaware."[47]

On May 15, 1864, Col. Thomas Scott Anderson assumed command of the post of Tyler. Allen remained in command of the prison until June, when he was replaced by Lt. Col. John Border. If Allen was the most popular of the Camp Ford commanders, Border was easily the most hated. Prisoners accused him of issuing "arbitrary orders" and of being "surly" and often guilty of "brutal cruelty." Equally despised was Border's adjutant, Lt. B. W. McEachen. Prisoners wrote that McEachen expressed delight at the deaths of captives, and they accused him of stealing from them. Following a July 26 "inspection," prisoner Thomas Evans was without his opera glass. Other prisoners lost pocketknives, spoons, and forks. One of the adjutant's favorite activities was breaking up the prisoners' games of keno. Eventually the Yankees began referring to him as "Keno," which only served to anger him more. "6 or 8 prisoners made to mark time for hallowing Keno at the Adjt," prison diarist William McKinney wrote. Two days later McEachen had two prisoners hung by the thumbs for the same offense. On both occasions the adjutant also cut off rations for a portion of the prisoners.[48]

The spring of 1864 also saw a tremendous increase in Camp Ford's prison population. On April 12 Gen. Smith ordered Allen to prepare for the arrival of between 3,000 and 4,000 captives. Three days later Heartsill noted the arrival of 1,100. More prisoners reached the camp over the next several weeks. When a contingent of 540 entered the gates on May 27 Heartsill placed the prison population at 4,400.[49]

The new arrivals taxed the capacity of the camp, forcing Allen to increase the size of the compound. On April 13 he sent out a group of guards to impress slaves from area planters. According to Heartsill, "a large number" was at work by the 15th. Rather than cutting new posts, the crews simply cut off those already in place. The result was a stockade that was only six feet tall. It occupied about ten acres.[50]

Inside the pen was a hodgepodge of shelters. The early prisoners, arriving when numbers were few, found tools readily available. The Confederates allowed them outside to secure wood, and most built substantial cabins. As time went on, and the prison population increased, both tools and wood became more precious. Eventually messes had to wait hours or even days to secure a drill or an ax.[51]

Arriving in April, Thomas Evans lamented, "Cannot get a tool to do anything with. If we could only get tools & material we could soon make ourselves reasonably comfortable." Eventually they were able to do so. Six weeks later Evans wrote that he had been outside the camp to get wood for shingles. Other messes shared less substantial shelters. Some improvised tents from poles and blankets. Those with even fewer resources simply burrowed into the ground. Some did not even try, sleeping in the open air. As a result the compound presented a haphazard appearance. An Ohio prisoner later recalled the sight of "numberless little huts and caves" as he entered Camp Ford.[52]

"Time passes slowly by in this monotonous place," Evans wrote. "Nothing new or interesting going on." Describing the camp routine, he wrote, "The order of the day being a breakfast of Corn Bread & Beef then a game of ball for exercise & amusement then Beef & Cornbread for Dinner then lounging until evening then prayer meeting in the evening & so time passes away." Checkers, chess, and card games also occupied the prisoners' time. As at all Civil War prisons, books were prized and any that could be found were read and reread.[53]

On June 14 Evans acquired a French book and engaged a lieutenant to give him lessons. He kept at it until he was exchanged at the end of September. Shortly before departing he wrote that the only bright spot of his prison experience was that he had "gained some knowledge of French translation though slight it is." Some prisoners passed the time by carving and whittling, but they often found the raw material scarce. "Four of us went out by the guard for purpose of getting roots to make pipes," a captive wrote on October 30, 1864. "Had poor luck." McKinney and his mess put their time to practical use, planting a garden plot that yielded a "nice mess of sallad."[54]

A large group of Camp Ford prisoners found comfort in faith. Chaplains conducted Sunday morning and afternoon services. Beginning in early May the prisoners gathered beneath an oak tree for nightly prayer services. According to Evans, hundreds turned out for the June 19 service. They sang hymns and listened to a sermon that lasted nearly an hour, "beautifully illustrating the great field of labor open for the christian laborer."[55]

Patriotism was the order of the day on July 4, as about a thousand prisoners gathered to celebrate Independence Day. Lt. Col. Border had given the Yankees permission to conduct the ceremony, but the officer of the day attempted to break it up. The event included speeches, songs by the "glee club," and a reading of the Declaration of Independence. One prisoners concluded, "It was very pleasant, although . . . we are in a very unpleasant condition."[56]

Escape attempts were common at Camp Ford, but they were seldom successful. "Although the prospect of getting away is small yet many are still getting out every night almost," one prisoner observed. One problem was the daunting distance to Union lines. Another was bloodhounds. Originally used to recapture escaped slaves, they were equally adept at tracking down wayward Yankees. "Sergt Sanford is detailed to take charge of a pack of Negro dogs, which are to be kept here to catch escaped prisoners and deserters," a guard wrote on June 19. On another occasion he reported that the dogs had helped bring in nine escapees. "They protest against being caught with dogs, I say 'Fight the devil with fire,' if they do not like it then let them stay in the 'Pen' where no dogs can harm them."[57]

At about 9:30 P.M. on July 2 a group of prisoners boldly attempted to run the guard. The sentries opened fire, but no one was hit. Soon hounds and cavalry were on the trail of the escapees. They returned several over the next few days. The Confederates subjected those who were retaken to a variety of punishments. Most ended up in the guardhouse. At least one was placed in irons and another compelled to stand upon a tree stump for several hours in the hot Texas sun. The next afternoon Col. Border posted the following order: "Hereafter any Fed prisoner being detected in trying to make his escape from the prison either in the act or after he has made his escape will be shot by the one capturing him." The prisoners correctly assumed that the order was a bluff. They nevertheless still risked severe punishment.[58]

Later during the summer of 1864 prisoners began escaping in the "dirt cart," a small wagon that hauled garbage from the camp daily. One of the prisoners had gained the Confederates' confidence, becoming the driver. Two at a time, the would-be escapees allowed themselves to be covered with refuse, the price of being driven through the stockade gate. One prisoner estimated that 125 made their escape in this manner before the Confederates discovered what was happening on August 12. Few, he added, had been returned. The two caught in the act were hung by their thumbs, as was the driver.[59]

Although the Confederates did not carry out their threat to shoot recaptured escapees, there were a number of shootings at Camp Ford during 1864. In at least two cases a Confederate guard joined with the prisoners in condemning the acts. The first occurred on May 22, when a sentry shot and killed Pvt. John J. Calvert of the Seventy-seventh Ohio. Prisoners Thomas Evans and William McKinney both insisted that Calvert had done nothing wrong, terming it a "murder." W. W. Heartsill wrote that Calvert had cursed the guard, but he still did not consider that grounds to fire. The Confederate who had complained of Allen's leniency to the Yankees concluded simply, "[S]hame! shame!! shame!!!"[60]

Heartsill was even more blunt following a shooting on the evening of July 11. This time Heartsill agreed with the prisoners that the victim, Samuel O. Shoemaker of the 130th Illinois, had committed no offense. Another prisoner had been cursing the guard, and the sentry's errant shot claimed the wrong victim. "It is a shame on the officers who will allow such outrite murder to go unpunished," Heartsill wrote, "for it is nothing else, and it is the very cowardliest kind of murder."[61]

Both Evans and McKinney offered sparse entries for a pair of shootings that took place at the end of August. On the 25th a guard shot an Indian soldier from a Kansas regiment. The wound was not serious. Three days later a New York soldier was the victim. As with the previous incidents, Evans asserted that the man was "deliberately shot" and was "violating no rules of the camp offering no provocation." McKinney wrote that the wound was "severe," but if it proved fatal neither diarist mentioned it.[62]

As these shootings occurred at Camp Ford, far to the east a much more famous—and infamous—prison was reaching its peak population. For three years the Confederate government had provided neither planning nor coordination for its prison system. Near a small Georgia community, the fruits of that inaction were manifesting themselves at a prison officially known as Camp Sumter.

8

"I dislike the place"

Andersonville, Plans and Problems

Prisoners arriving at Camp Sumter, better known as Andersonville prison, often recorded their initial impressions of their new surroundings. They varied in detail only. "It is horrid to see," wrote William Peabody of the Fifty-seventh Massachusetts. New York soldier Alonzo Decker described it as "a pen not-fit-for hogs." John Melvin Converse considered it "the hardest plaise I have eaver been in," while James Woodbury simply termed it "a dismal looking place." Alfred Burdick of the Twenty-seventh Massachusetts recorded similar opinions. "Of all places this is the worst I have been in," he wrote, later noting, "A northern farmer would not keep a hog in so filthy a place." To some new prisoners it simply could not be described. "It beggars description," First Vermont soldier George Crosby asserted. "I will not attempt to describe [the prison]," noted George M. Hinkley, "but suffice it to say that it was beyond all description." William H. Haun of the Nineteenth Ohio wrote, "Oh! horror . . . Language can not describe the misery & suffering." With a great deal of understatement, Samuel Foust of the 149th Pennsylvania spoke for all the prisoners at Andersonville when he penned the simple words, "I dislike the place."[1]

The story of Andersonville prison began on November 24, 1863, when Secretary Seddon ordered Capt. William Sidney Winder, son of the provost marshal, to go to Georgia and establish a military prison. The captain was to consult with Governor Joseph Brown and Gen. Howell Cobb. Beyond that, and the suggestion that the prison be located in the vicinity of Americus or Valley Ford, the orders offered no details. That Confederate officials wanted the Richmond prisons emptied is beyond doubt. That they were concerned with the finer points of caring for the departing captives is subject to much doubt.[2]

Many of the factors that would result in over thirteen thousand deaths at Andersonville were apparent from the time Sidney, as the captain was known, arrived in Georgia. President Davis objected to his first choice for a prison site, a location near Albany, because he feared it would be vulnerable to a Union raid. Locals vetoed his second choice, a spot between Americus and Plains. Winder finally was able to lease the area that would become the Andersonville prison from a pair of landowners.[3]

In December Capt. Richard B. Winder, Sidney's cousin, arrived and assumed the post of quartermaster. Both Winders ran up against local intransigence that made it nearly impossible to get anything done. The war had robbed the region of capable white laborers, and slave owners were reluctant to hire out their chattels. At one point Richard Winder considered driving cattle to the post from Florida. He abandoned the plan, in part because the men willing to take on the job were "physically unable." In a rare instance of support, Seddon, desperate to clear the Richmond prisons, empowered the quartermaster to impress slave labor. This got the project moving, but the delay had been such that Andersonville's first prisoners would arrive before their stockade was completed.[4]

The only things in abundance were pine trees, which the impressed laborers were soon felling by the score. The logs were roughly hewn, cut to a length of twenty feet, and sunk five feet into the red Georgia clay. They enclosed a stockade of some fifteen acres. A second, outside wall surrounded the entire stockade. Roofed sentry boxes were placed every eighty-eight feet. Forts at three corners and one on the east side of the prison provided more security. A branch of Sweetwater Creek flowed through the compound.[5]

Richard Winder was able to make arrangements to have corn ground for the prison. Beyond that success, the challenge of supplying the camp was daunting. On February 3, as the War Department was making plans to begin sending prisoners south, the quartermaster explained his plight to Maj. A. M. Allen, the commissary of subsistence at Columbus, Georgia. "I shall want beef, meat, flour, sugar, molasses, rice, soap, candles, &c.," he wrote. Cooking utensils were so scarce that he dispatched a civilian to Cartersville, well north of Atlanta, to secure six one-hundred-gallon iron kettles for boiling. Prisoners had already begun to arrive on the 29th when Richard informed Gen. Winder that he was in desperate need of baking pans. He also called for nails, padlocks, and window glass. Three days later he was forced to impress four four-mule wagons and teams, asking the Lee County sheriff to take them "from plantations from whence they can best be spared."[6]

Andersonville did have a commander. On February 26 Col. Alexander W. Persons of the Fifty-fifth Georgia received the assignment, and Sidney Winder returned to Richmond. Persons arrived without much of a command. The majority of his regiment had been captured a month earlier at Cumberland Gap as Persons enjoyed a fortuitous furlough. Even before assuming command, Persons had informed Capt. Winder that he would have no more than one hundred men. Those who had arrived at Andersonville by February 17 were without weapons.[7]

An unfinished stockade and an unarmed guard force were not enough to discourage Confederate officials. On February 18 the first trainloads of prisoners left Richmond bound for Andersonville. One of the passengers was William H. Smith of the Seventh Michigan Volunteers. Although it has been assumed that the entire detachment left from Belle Isle, Smith wrote, "We leave the building at three A.M. and take the cars." They changed railroads at Petersburg and again at Gaston, North Carolina, where they arrived "at dark." The next morning Smith wrote that the military passengers had slept well despite suffering from cold weather. He estimated that the train was rolling along at only about ten miles per hour. At 3 P.M. it pulled into the Raleigh station. There the men received rations and clambered out of the boxcars. They spent the night in a camp four miles from the city.[8]

The prisoners were up early on the 20th, making coffee before drawing rations and getting back on board the trains at 3:00 A.M. They traveled all day and into the night. At about midnight the engine and three cars of Smith's train ran off the track at Thomasville, North Carolina. Nobody was injured, and the captives took advantage of the unexpected delay to trade with the local citizens for food. They again got under way on the 22nd, passing the prison at Salisbury before arriving at Charlotte at 6:00 in the evening. Once again, the prisoners went into camp.[9]

They resumed their journey at 7:00 A.M. on the 23rd, crossed into South Carolina, and changed cars again at Chester. The trains chugged slowly through the night. At Columbia there was yet another change in lines, along with an issue of four hardtack apiece. On the evening of the 24th they arrived at Augusta, receiving more rations and spending the night. The prisoners were away again at 7:00 the next morning and in Macon at sunset. The guard was changed during the brief stay at Macon. "Citizens guard us," Smith wrote.[10]

The rail convoy continued on that evening, arriving at Anderson Station at 11:00. According to Smith, the men were assigned to squads of one hundred and given their rations. "Go to sleep on the ground," Smith concluded. The Wolverine soldier continued his diary for only three more days before abandoning it for nearly three months. During that time he and some comrades built a "brush house." Smith recorded the arrival of more prisoners on February 28 and 29. He uttered no complaints about his new camp, although he did note on the 29th, "We get no potatoes today."[11]

Prisoner diarists who followed Smith over the next three weeks tended to follow the same route. Two of them, Michael Dougherty and John Kay, wrote that there were sixty men per car. "We are in a pretty fix lying across and on top of each other talking cursing and swearing and fighting," Dougherty observed. Three days into the trip, Kay wrote that the men "almost suffocated in the tight box car, for want of air and water."[12]

Confederate authorities had arranged for the guard to be changed at Branchville, South Carolina. On March 24 Capt. F. T. Miles, commanding the guard detachment there, reported that 6,488 prisoners had passed that point. Twelve had escaped, two had died, and 117 sick had been taken off the cars and delivered to the provost marshal at Augusta. The escapees, two groups of six, had gotten away by cutting holes in their unlit cars. Among the sick were "four well-marked cases" of smallpox who arrived on February 28.[13]

On February 25, shortly before Dougherty and Kay entered the stockade at Andersonville, the editor of the *Macon Telegraph* paid a visit to the prison. He described the stockade as if he were writing a travel brochure, noting the "clear, beautiful stream, with gently sloping hills on either side." Sidney Winder, he continued, "deserves the thanks of the country for the skill and energy displayed." The prisoners impressed him considerably less. "As a general thing, they have very little sense," he wrote. "They are delighted, however, with this change from Richmond."[14]

Dougherty had not yet arrived when the Macon editor visited, but he was not delighted with the change of base. "We were told that this prison was a splendid plase for prisoners," he fumed, "a fine stream of water fine quarters prepared for us . . . but we know better now." The earliest detachments had received buckets and skillets, he added, but the supply had long since run out. By the time Kay arrived on March 13, conditions were already deteriorating. Seven to eight bodies were being taken out every day. "I am afraid this is going to be a bad place in hot weather," he predicted, "in fact it is not any better than Belle Isle to my mind." Kay fashioned a crude shelter for himself by bending small pieces of oak into half circles and spreading a blanket and pine boughs over it. He was not the only one to arrange his own shelter. On March 22, his third day at Andersonville, George Hegeman took a walk around the compound. "Some take their blankets and make shelter tents of them," he wrote. "Others make little houses of sticks, leaves and sod. Some burrough right into the ground. There are hundreds of these burroughs through the prison."[15]

These earliest Andersonville prisoners found their rations, while not abundant, to be usually adequate. A pint of cornmeal and half a pound of beef or pork were the general issue through March, although the amount varied from day to day. On the 16th Kay even noted, "A plenty of meat issued." Peas or beans were occasionally included, and on rare occasions the prisoners received a little salt. Otherwise, there was no variety to the fare. "Dos the people in the Confederacy live altogether on corn meal?" Dougherty wondered. "It appears the[y] must. The kind of meal that we get is the worst quality," he went on. "Corn cobs and all are ground up together. It is regular chop or horse feed." Another prisoner compared it to the chicken feed produced at the mills back home.[16]

Equally annoying to the prisoners was the lack of cooking facilities. "They have miserable arrangements for feeding the prisoners," Kay bemoaned. He pronounced his first experience in cooking cornmeal "a failure." Dougherty observed men baking little cakes on pieces of board held above campfires. Soon he and fellow prisoners were cooking fritters and mush in the same manner and brewing coffee from cornmeal. "We can beat hous Keepers all hallow in inegnuity and inventions," he boasted. Although Smith claimed to have been assigned to a squad of 100, detachments of 270, divided into squads of 90, became the standard units at Andersonville. During March nine men from each squad were permitted to go out for wood. The pine was better than nothing, but it made for smoky fires. Soap was issued rarely, and as Dougherty ungraciously noted, "We look like so many Sweeps or nigers from the smoke of pitch pine."[17]

By the time prison diarists were writing these entries, they had a new stockade commander. Following a furlough and a lengthy trip to Europe, Henry Wirz had returned to the Confederacy. Gen. Winder quickly sent his former subordinate to Andersonville. Col. Persons remained in command of the post and the guard force. Wirz assumed command of the prison. For the thousands of captives confined there, he would become the face of Andersonville prison. As a result, he would eventually become the scapegoat for all the evils of the war.[18]

At Andersonville Wirz again displayed those traits that had made him an alternately popular and hated figure with Union prisoners in 1861 and 1862. His personality was a dichotomy perhaps best described by an inspector sent from Richmond. "Captain Wirz . . . is very firm and rigid in the discipline of the prisoners, and at the same time exercises toward them all proper acts of kindness," Capt. Walter Bowie wrote. As before, he was profane and temperamental. Yet, once again, he worked tirelessly to better the condition of the prisoners. Sadly, circumstances that proved daunting were working against him. A case in point was his plan to improve sanitation in the stockade. Wirz intended to construct twin dams on the stream that bisected the facility. This would create a clean pool of drinking water and a downstream pool for bathing. The sinks would be below the lower dam. From time to time both dams could be opened to flush away the waste. The plan was sound, but the inability to secure tools and lumber doomed it to failure. Indeed, getting implements was so difficult that Persons risked the wrath of his superiors in an attempt to secure a few. In early April he learned tools could be had in Augusta. Nobody was available to send, so Persons left the camp without leave. Seddon demanded a letter of explanation, but Persons returned with the needed items. As for timber, paying military rates, neither Persons nor Richard Winder could compete in the Georgia market. With every available man needed for the guard force, he also had difficulty securing labor.[19]

The prisoners, of course, were not aware of Wirz's efforts. To them, he was simply the "Dutch Captain," the personification of all the suffering within the stockade. Beyond that, he was seldom mentioned in the prisoners' diaries. One of the few to describe him was George Hegeman, who wrote, "He is a thin, nervous looking man and nervous acting, makes a great flourish with his pistol when he calls us d——d Yankee sons of ——hes." According to De Witt Spaulding of the Eighth Michigan, "He is the most curious speciman of humanity I ever saw hump backed round shouldered his legs are three fourths the length of him and one might take him for old satan himself."[20]

Wirz had not been at Andersonville long before he had a "deadline" placed around the interior of the stockade. A feature of virtually every Civil War prison compound in the North or South, it starkly marked the limit of how closely prisoners could approach the wall. Sometimes it was a ditch, sometimes a row of stakes. Andersonville's was a short wall composed of stakes and scrap wood. In addition to this implicit threat, Wirz also soon displayed his previously well-known temper. "The old Dutch captain raising thunder this morning & did not give but part of the men grub," wrote John Whitten of the Fifth Iowa on April 1. John Kay, recently transferred from Belle Isle, said Wirz had kept the men in ranks for four hours and deprived squads of rations because a few men had left the ranks. Hegeman wrote that the tantrum was the result of numerous escape attempts. "The dutch captain says he will starve us if any more escaped," he wrote.[21]

Actual charges of personal misconduct against Wirz are largely absent from prisoner diaries, and those that appear are uncorroborated. On May 12 Hegeman claimed that the commandant had "knocked a poor lame prisoner down sensless with the butt of his pistol." He was the only prisoner to record the incident. On September 4 Samuel Henderson wrote that Wirz had shot a man who was part of a group crowding close to the gate shouting for rations. Not only was this remarkable incident uncorroborated, but Henderson's diary contains evidence of postwar editing.[22]

Indeed, one of the few diaries to mention a personal encounter with the "Dutch captain" does much to moderate his reputation. On June 28 Robert Hale Kellogg of the Sixteenth Connecticut went out as part of a wood detail. On the way back to the stockade, he stopped to dig some red root. The guard hurried him along, and Kellogg left his knife behind. He realized what had happened before returning to the stockade, but the sergeant of the guard would not let him go back. By chance, Wirz rode by at that time. "I called him & told him how it was," Kellogg wrote, "when he told me to come along *with him,* and rode back to the spot with me where I found the knife in the spot I had left it."[23]

By April 1 there were over 7,000 prisoners in the Andersonville stockade. By May 8 the number exceeded 12,000. On June 1 Wirz reported the prison population to be 18,454. Just over 1,000 of that number were in the hospital. As those prisoners began their struggle for survival, Confederate officials struggled to provide a guard force for the prison. At first veteran Confederate regiments composed the camp guard. Many, such as Persons's outfit, were undermanned. Until the stockade was completed, the possibility of a mass escape was real. On April 13 Persons became so concerned over a rumored revolt that he called upon the citizens of nearby Americus to turn out under arms. They remained nine days before a Georgia regiment arrived to relieve them. The editor of the *Sumter Republican* in Americus expressed some doubt about the necessity for the call. He nevertheless supported the commandant's actions. "It will not do for these prisoners to make their escape," he wrote, "for if they do an awful state of affairs throughout South Western Georgia will be the result."[24]

With the spring of 1864 came the campaigns that would eventually end the war. Sherman was heading toward Atlanta, and Grant had his sights set on Richmond. Veteran regiments were desperately needed at the front. None could be spared to guard prisoners. On May 12 and again on May 15 Samuel Cooper ordered regiments at Andersonville to report either to Richmond or to Gen. Joseph Johnston in northern Georgia.[25]

Secretary Seddon called upon Gen. Howell Cobb to fill the void. A native Georgian and veteran politician, Cobb was in charge of the Georgia Reserves. On April 27 the war secretary ordered him to supply as many guards as he deemed necessary for the security of the prison. Ten days later Cobb informed Persons that two regiments of reserves were on their way. Two companies of the Third Georgia Reserves followed on May 23 along with assurances that the rest of the outfit would soon be along. When he sent the Fourth Georgia Reserves on the 28th, Cobb let Persons know that he would not be able to spare any more men for Andersonville. In lieu of more men, Cobb dispatched half a dozen twelve-pound howitzers, "the kind of guns you need for your positions around the stockade."[26]

Cobb also sent a number of suggestions concerning the prison. To Maj. Timothy Furlow, a prominent Americus resident who was about to assume command of a guard battalion, he suggested enlarging the stockade. "If a sufficient force of negroes could be obtained at once to do that work, I should regard the Prison perfectly safe," he wrote. Cobb even offered to send a few of his own slaves. He offered the same advice to Secretary Seddon, along with the recommendation that the prisoners be exchanged. "I need not say to you," he urged the secretary, "that the number accumulating in Georgia is not only eating up our substance [subsistence], but are withdrawing for their safe keeping large forces from the field and from agricultural interests." This, of course, was beyond Seddon's control.[27]

Cobb also sent E. J. Elridge, the chief surgeon of the Georgia Reserves, to Andersonville to conduct an inspection. In his May 6 report, Elridge complained of overcrowding and called for the erection of barracks. He also strongly suggested that the hospital be moved outside the stockade, an action he considered "essential to the proper treatment of the sick." Capt. Bowie, who inspected the prison only a few days later, concurred. Since the prison opened, he reported, 13,218 prisoners had arrived, and 1,026 had died. He did not fault Wirz, Persons, or surgeon Isaiah H. White, all of whom, he believed, had worked tirelessly to better the prisoners' condition. Rather, Bowie cited the hospital accommodations, which he termed "extremely indifferent." Thirty-five worn tent flies composed the hospital. More space was needed, Bowie urged. Mortality was increasing, reaching 131 deaths during the week ending May 8, "and I am of the opinion that this increase will continue unless a decided improvement is made in the hospital accommodations and the comfort of the prisoners."[28]

At least one prisoner shared these professional assessments, expressing his views in much simpler language. On May 12 Samuel Grosvenor of the Sixteenth Connecticut wrote, "I went up & took a look at the hospital & came back feeling sad & disgusted." For William Smith, one of the original Andersonville prisoners, the situation at the hospital had become a part of daily life. In early May Smith was detailed to the hospital's commissary department. Three days after Grosvenor penned his observations, Smith learned that the hospital was to be moved. The process began on the morning of May 21. "It is a very pleasant grove," he wrote of the new location, "but it is tedious moving the sick." The relocation took two days. When it was completed the sick were cared for in a spot southeast of the stockade, 260 by

340 feet. White reported that the hospital could comfortably hold 800 patients. In less than a month, however, 1,020 "of the worst cases" had been crowded in. Many others had to be refused admittance.[29]

It was not the only change taking place at Andersonville. Reading the dire inspection reports, it was obvious to officials in Richmond that the situation at their new prison was spiraling out of control. In May Gen. Winder sent Thomas Turner to conduct yet another inspection. Like those who had gone before him, Turner found the camp to be unhealthy. He noted the poor drainage, the lack of shelter and drinking water, and found much of the camp "in [a] very filthy condition." He did not blame those in charge, noting the shortage of tools. Indeed, Turner strongly commended Wirz for his "good sense and energy." Richmond's response did nothing to address the difficulties directly. Instead, on June 3, President Davis ordered Winder himself to take command at Andersonville. As if that was not enough of a challenge, Secretary Seddon also made him responsible for the officers' prison at Macon. Inspector General Cooper predicted that Winder's very presence "will have a beneficial effect upon the guard and the prisoners." No statement could have provided a clearer indication of the government's lack of understanding of the situation at the Georgia pen.[30]

Meanwhile another danger was threatening the welfare of the Andersonville prisoners. Among the throng of captives heading south from Belle Isle were the "Raiders." In Virginia they had preyed upon their fellow captives, stealing such things as tents and bread. Their change of base did not change their proclivities. Indeed, it was dishonesty that had led most to don the Union blue. Many had entered the army as substitutes, receiving payment to join the service in the place of men who had been drafted. Their intention had been to desert at the first opportunity, pocketing the bounty money and perhaps repeating the process later. The Confederates interrupted these plans, and they found themselves prisoners. Banding together into gangs, they only added to the horrors of prison life.

The constant influx of new prisoners, many of whom arrived with money, guaranteed a steady supply of victims. At first the Raiders tended to strike only under the cover of darkness. One of the first to complain about their activities was surgeon White, who cited their "forays upon the hospital" as a reason for suggesting its removal outside. By May prison diaries were well garnished with accounts of their activities. "A great deal of thieving going on at nights," Michael Dougherty wrote. He termed the Raiders "a mean low set of fellows. They hesitate not to rob the sick the weak and the blind."[31]

The Raiders often provided a rude introduction to life at Andersonville. Such was the case for two members of the Sixteenth Connecticut, part of the garrison that had been captured on April 20 at Plymouth, North Carolina. On their second day at the prison, Samuel Grosvenor and Charles Lee awoke to discover that the Raiders had visited their squad during the night. The haul had been light. One man lost a handkerchief and his diary. Sixteen men agreed to take turns doing guard duty. Grosvenor got up at 2:00 the next morning to take his turn. He braved the stench of the prison and the choking cloud of smoke from waning pine fires, both of which hung low that night. Eventually the prisoners abandoned the guard posting, each man instead sleeping with a club close by.[32]

During the early morning hours of May 22 a group of prisoners caught a Raider in the act. Details of what happened next vary in prison diaries. However, there is no doubt that the man was "roughly handled," as one prisoner noted, once daylight arrived. Most accounts indicate that the man was bucked, half of his head and face were shaved, and he was made to run a gauntlet of hostile captives. Severe as it was, the man's punishment did not deter the Raiders' activities. Five days later another Raider, caught near Robert Kellogg's tent, received the same treatment for his misdeeds. This time the incident culminated in a fight between a group of Raiders and prisoners who had grown sick of them. Clubs and stones were the principal weapons, and one witness observed that "maney a poor cuss got his Head mashed."[33]

In June the Raiders grew bolder, attacking their victims even in the daytime. On June 13 David Kennedy, transferred from Cahaba, wrote that a man had a canteen and a cup stolen from him after the victim "went into a fit." Kennedy concluded, "Steeling is the principle game and many practice it." Samuel Melvin of the First Massachusetts Heavy Artillery wrote that an ill friend was robbed twice within four days. Meanwhile the nighttime raids continued unabated. The situation was such that James Vance of the Fifth United States Cavalry ranked as equal "the Raiders meaness and the unhumanity of the Rebs."[34]

The situation came to a head on June 29. As Capt. Wirz walked along the deadline during the early afternoon a group of prisoners screwed up enough courage to ask for his assistance in dealing with the Raiders. "He said it was no more than right if 26,000 men allowed a band of 50 to run them," one reported. What apparently changed his mind was an incident that occurred that same day. A mob descended upon a new prisoner, robbing him of his watch and a large sum of money. He begged to be allowed to keep the watch, saying it was a gift from his dead brother, but his assailants were unmoved. "More than one of us felt like pitching in to the rescue," one witness admitted, "but the ugly looks of a dozen or more raiders who encircled him cowered us. Perhaps to our shame."[35]

Unable to count on his fellow prisoners, the victim appealed to Wirz. The commandant, in turn, sent in a squad of guards to assist a fledgling police force, termed the Regulators, formed by the prisoners. Together they began rounding up the Raiders, a process that consumed two days. With the tables turned, past victims and their friends took delight in pointing out gang members. "There is lots of men that know these fellows and they are after them with great success," wrote one onlooker. Estimates of the number taken out ranged from sixty to three hundred. Fourteen, those most obviously guilty, remained outside, safely secured in stocks. The rest were returned to the stockade, where their fellow prisoners, armed with clubs, awaited them. As one man described the scene, "Men were stationed along the line with clubs after the old Indian mode of treatment." All received "a beautiful pelting." According to some diarists, one or more were killed.[36]

Searches of the Raiders' shebangs (makeshift huts the prisoners made for shelter) revealed much of their loot. Watches, jewelry, blankets, dishes, and clothing were recovered, along with cash reportedly in the thousands of dollars. The searchers also found knives, clubs, and pistols. According to some accounts, searchers also uncovered the bodies of between one and three victims. Meanwhile Wirz summoned a number of sergeants to his headquarters to choose a jury for the trial of the worst offenders. Winder issued orders authorizing the court. He insisted that charges "be distinctly made with specifications setting forth time and place." Winder was to receive a written record of the proceedings. If all was in order, he would order the sentences carried out. These actions met with the universal approval of the prisoners. "Credit to whom credit is due," one wrote, "and when the Rebs do that which is right I am willing to give them credit."[37]

Still, the prisoners wondered what the fate of the Raiders would be. To make things fair, recent arrivals composed the jury. After considering the evidence, they sentenced six of the worst offenders to death. Winder approved the sentence and sent an account to Richmond officials for their approval. On July 11 workmen began erecting gallows near the south gate of the prison. A notice went up that the condemned would be executed at 4:00 that afternoon. "I thought it was done to give the prisoners a scare," De Witt Spaulding wrote in his diary. Many other captives felt the same way. Still, as prisoner Nehemiah Solon observed, by late afternoon, "The whole camp took their position so as to see the most they could."[38]

At about 4:30 the six were marched in, accompanied by Wirz and some guards. As he neared the gallows Wirz stopped, and as Solon remembered it the next day, said, "At your request I had these men taken out and they have been tried by your own men and now I return them to you in as good condition as when they were taken out. I return them to you to do with as you see fit. May God be merciful to them and you." With that the commandant and the Confederate guards withdrew, turning the condemned men over to the Regulators. Michael Dougherty claimed that in so doing Wirz was "washing his hands of all responsibilities in the execution." It was Dougherty, however, who had termed the Raiders "a mean low set of fellows." He also apparently forgot that the prisoners had appealed to Wirz for his assistance.[39]

"The camp presented a scene of unnatural and solemn quiet," one prisoner wrote. Another observed that one could have heard a pin drop at the moment Wirz withdrew. Excitement abruptly punctured the silence when one of the prisoners broke free. As the nooses were tightened around the other five, he was quickly recaptured. Some protested their innocence, others begged their victims' forgiveness. At least one challenged anyone he had robbed to come forward and say so. Another called out the names of friends to come to his rescue. Few, if any, prisoners were moved by such appeals, and certainly not the Regulators. Soon the traps fell, sending five souls forever beyond Andersonville's walls. The rope of the sixth, considered the worst offender, broke, and he tumbled to the ground. He begged for mercy, but according to one witness, the hangman held a knife to his throat and said, "Shut up you tried to Murder Mee but you did not accomplish it." With that he joined the other five. The bodies dangled from the nooses for about a half hour before they were removed.[40]

The action met with almost universal approval within Andersonville's walls. According to Henry Tisdale of the Thirty-fifth Massachusetts, "With a few exceptions made by their fellow conspirators the judgment has been that it was but their just deserts." Although he termed the execution "a most tuching and sorrowing Inscident," Plymouth prisoner Ransom Chadwick added, "Let this be a warning to all." Solon agreed, feeling it had been necessary to "make an example." John Baer of the Fortieth Indiana philosophized, "This may look hard to [the] civilized and enlightened world but they have been a reign of terror to the camp." William Peabody chose not to watch, noting, "I have no taste for that style." Still, he considered the action "just." Albert Shatzel may have summed up the mood of the entire camp when he concluded, "It was a terrible sight to witness but it had to be done." At 8:00 A.M. the next day he wrote, "Every thing is very quiet in camp this morning."[41]

The Regulators remained, continuing to serve as a prison police force. Their fellow prisoners made few mentions of them in their diaries, perhaps fearing the consequences should the diaries be confiscated. In late August Vance wrote that a prisoner who had stolen some papers from a comrade was turned over to them. The thief was sentenced to wear a ball and a chain. Tisdale believed the Regulators did "good service in keeping order and promoting cleanliness about the camp." Baer was less certain. "They are composed chiefly of the rounders of Brooklin and New York," he wrote, "and in my opinion it would be an impossibility to find an honest man among them." Nevertheless, he concluded, "I presume that under existing circumstances they are a necessary evil used to prevent a greater, and in case of two existing evils it is policy to choose the lesser."[42]

The excitement over the arrest of the Raiders had not yet subsided when another change came to the Andersonville prison. In late May Persons began a project to expand the prison compound, extending the fence to the north. Prisoners provided much of the labor. Although many of their fellow captives sneered at performing any labor for the Rebel keepers, June accessions proved the wisdom of the project. On many days prisoners arrived by the hundreds. Occasionally the number reached over a thousand.[43]

The camp was quite crowded by July 1, the day ten feet of the north wall of the old stockade came down. Detachments forty-nine and above were ordered to move into the ten acres of additional space that had been created. The Confederates gave them two hours to make the move or risk having their blankets confiscated, but logistically the timetable was impossible. "The removal was made in a bungling manner as are all the doings of the rebel officials," one prisoner complained. Rather than sending one detachment at a time, all were herded through the opening at once. As a result, "Everything is excitement and there is very little order about it." One of the participants wrote, "After being most crushed to death I managed to get through [and] find a place with some others of my company."[44]

Many of the prisoners making the move did not feel the change of base improved their condition. "We did not get in [a] much better place than we were in," complained Daniel Hutchins, "for water is so far to carry (also the sink is so far off)." The lack of water was a common grievance. Many prisoners had dug wells that they had to abandon with the move. Henry Stone of the Forty-first Massachusetts wrote that his detachment planned to begin digging the next day. Those left behind were generally more positive about the move. "It makes them very thick in the new part, but in the old part we are much more comfortable," one of them observed. A prisoner who "swapped" into an earlier detachment to avoid the move wrote, "There is much more room now, and the air is much better." Nehemiah Solon was less sanguine about the change. "We hardly miss them," he wrote of the prisoners that moved, "there is so many."[45]

One advantage of the move was a temporarily abundant supply of wood. The work crews had felled all the trees within the extension, and Solon estimated that their efforts resulted in enough fuel for one or two months of cooking. The prison axmen did not stop there. The former north wall of the stockade loomed before them, and it proved a tempting target. "At about dark the boys commenced cutting down the stockade between the two pens and the axes are playing pretty lively now," an observer wrote that night. With a number of projects in mind, the keepers considered the wood as precious as did the kept. "The rebs made quite a blow about it," one prisoner wrote of the nocturnal harvest. Prison officials threatened to withhold rations until the posts were returned. How many they got back is uncertain.[46]

Meanwhile, Gen. Winder was worrying over threats, real and imagined, from within and without. On July 9 he wrote to Gen. Cobb, "Matters have arrived at that point *where I must* have reinforcements." Twelve guards had deserted the previous night, and Winder was convinced that more were about to leave. He implored Cobb to send more reserves and send them quickly. "There is not a moment to spare," he warned, if Cobb did not want "to see Georgia devasted by *the prisoners.*" Cobb had no reinforcements to send, but he went to Andersonville himself to check on the situation. "I found everything quiet," he wrote to his wife. A few men had deserted and more were threatening "merely to scare old Genl Winder out of some more furloughs." Cobb called his reserves out for a pep talk and then departed, "leaving both officers and men perfectly content and satisfied."[47]

As Winder fretted over his guards, a potentially more serious crisis arose. A Union cavalry force under Gen. Lovell Rousseau was charging south through Alabama bound for Georgia—and possibly for Andersonville. Time would prove that the prison was not on Rousseau's itinerary, but Winder was not clairvoyant, and he could not afford to take any chances. He considered moving the prisoners but instead called for volunteers to come to Andersonville's defense. They responded so promptly that the move did not become necessary. In the meantime Rousseau turned north, ending the crisis. Not only did the cavalry raiders fail to liberate any prisoners, they destroyed railroads and foodstuffs needed to sustain those prisoners.[48]

Winder's impromptu militia, and the slave laborers they brought with them, quickly attracted the attention of the prisoners. "The rebs have been building earth works all day and several trains have arrived loaded with . . . malitia," George

Crosby wrote on July 20. He guessed that a raid was the cause of the excitement. Prisoners arriving the next day confirmed his suspicion, according to Charles Lee. "My earnest prayer to the Almighty is that they might be successful and release these 27,000 human beings from such awful suffering," he wrote. Grosvenor noted, "The camp has been alive with reports of a 'raid' by our men. The excitement this evening is intense. The men are wild with mingled hope and fear." David Kennedy was succinct, writing of the potential liberators, "God hurey them through."[49]

As they speculated about their possible liberation, the prisoners watched the slaves work. They built fortifications, dug rifle pits, and transferred commissary stores from the stockade to the new forts. Prison diarists estimated that anywhere from two hundred to six hundred chattel laborers had been pressed into service. One prisoner expressed surprise that the work continued through a Sunday. Another observed, "They appear to be in a hell of a hurrey." As the work went into its fourth day, a third wrote, "The rebbs are getting purtey strong fortifications. Thay work day & night not giving the darkeys an hours rest. They act mighty scart." The excitement did not last long. Soon the prison grapevine brought the discouraging news that the impending raid was a wash. Two days after penning his hopeful entry about the intense anticipation, Grosvenor wrote, "The excitement about being released is pretty much played out & we have settled down into our former style of living."[50]

9
"The Horrors of War"
Andersonville, the Pattern of Life and Death

Just one month before observing that life was back to normal, Samuel Grosvenor had summed up that style of living when he remarked, "I scarcely know what to write. All is monotonous." Another prisoner wrote of one day's itinerary, "Day had been spent in cooking, catching lice and hanging round." Another wrote, "Nothing to do but cook, eat & hunt 'Greybacks' [lice], which the latter there is any amount of." Although he offered more details, John Baer's description of daily life was similar.

> The usual routine of duties in camp are 1st after a poor night's rest to arise and shake off the dirt 2nd to perform the necessary [activities] for cleansing the hands and face and making our toilet. . . . Washing is more from force of habit than any particular good that arises from it as we have to wash in a branch, the water of which passes the Confed. cook house and is uncomfortably greasy. After this our attention is turned to the culinary department. Our cooking utensils consist of two frying pans made of a canteen, two quart cups fournished by our Q. M. to drink coffee out of but they have been converted into mush pots and coffee pots a few knives and spoons. . . . After breakfast we have roll call which as a general thing comes about 10 o'clock A.M. after which it is time to get dinner. After dinner there is nothing more to do until supper time about which time we draw some rations. The interval between dinner and supper is sometimes spent in visiting old chums and as we have a bible in our mess part of the time is put in reading by sòme. Others lie and sleep as for myself it is so hot during the day that I cannot find any pleasure in anything in the shape of sleep I want

all the fresh air I can get and in order to get it I have to circulate around as much as possible owing to the heat.[1]

As at other prisons, loneliness was the twin to boredom. Samuel Melvin felt the combination produced an "agony of mind." John Kay believed hundreds gave up "*and just lay down and die.* Oh! how I have hoped even against myself," he added, "and tried to keep up courage, and battle it through, but it has been a hard, hard struggle." John Pond of the 149th Pennsylvania struggled, too, but he was uncertain of the outcome. "My thoughts are of the loved ones hundreds of miles away," he wrote, "and I ask myself the question will I ever see them again or like thousands of our men will the sands of Ga cover my bones?" One prisoner whose bones did end up beneath the Georgia sands was William Peabody. On at least two occasions he engaged a prison medium to conduct a "spirit communication" between himself and his wife. Peabody claimed the man had adequately described both his wife and the family's furniture. He recorded the details of the encounters in the memoranda section of his diary, hoping to compare notes with his wife at a reunion that never came.[2]

Prison diaries strongly suggest that mail from the North seldom made it to the southern Georgia pen. There are very few entries indicating that prisoners received letters from home; and if letters had come, they certainly would have provided the highlight for those entries. Boxes of supplies arrived in April and May. According to one diarist, "several" reached the prison in early June. Prison records indicate that Wirz forwarded to Richmond letters written by the Andersonville prisoners to their loved ones. One shipment included 1,735 "yankee letters." Of course, there is no way of knowing how many of these were sent on to the North by harried Confederate officials.[3]

Andersonville was no exception to the rule in Civil War prisons that homesickness was most acute on Sundays. Few Sabbath days passed that David Kennedy failed to "heire the chiming bells" and long to be with his family. "A very lonesome sabbath," one prisoner lamented on a hot August day. "Spent the day reading my Bible and thinking [of] home." Another wrote, "It is a beautiful Sabbath morning. What a pleasure and privilege it would be to enjoy it with the loved ones at home." Grosvenor explained, "Sunday in such a place as this is one of the worst days in the week because one spends the time mostly thinking & when he contemplates the misery all around & compares it with the comforts of home the heart grows sick."[4]

At most prisons regular worship services and occasional revivals helped meet the spiritual needs of the captives. Such gatherings took place at Andersonville, but they seem to have been less frequent. Perhaps overcrowding made them difficult to attend. Perhaps the lack of officers left no one to lead religious services. Perhaps their surroundings simply shook the men's faith. Despite the lack of organized worship, Bible reading was very common. A dearth of reading material may have been as much a motivating factor as the desire for divine guidance. "Cant get any thing to read of any kind except the bible which is read a good deal by all," one prisoner explained. William Seeley of the 150th Pennsylvania read the New Testament at least four times during the spring and summer of 1864. There were, of course, prisoners who took comfort from Bible reading. One found himself "deeply interested in reading about Paul's preaching and suffering. I wish I had one fiftieth part of the Christian fortitude he had," he wrote. Another believed the Scriptures lessened the burden of captivity, explaining, "What a consolation though the body can be imprisoned the power of man cannot bind the spirit."[5]

What appears to have been Andersonville's one religious revival occurred in July, lasting much of the month. Prayer meetings became frequent events, and the camp often resounded with the hymns being sung. A number of prisoners reportedly came forward when the invitation was given at the close of the services. According to one prisoner, an organized group was responsible for the services, which were doing "a great deal of good." Another wrote, "A great change in camp. Prayer meeting exhorting every place in camp every night there are prayer metings & without disturbance."[6]

"Notice that those who keep busy stand it best," one man wrote of his fellow prisoners. Even if it was nothing more than digging for roots to be used as fuel or tearing down and rebuilding their crude shanties, the key was to avoid idleness. Many played chess or checkers, often using homemade boards and pieces. Although books were rare, Samuel Gibson managed to secure a biography of William Penn. Guards sometimes smuggled newspapers in to the prisoners, providing not only reading material but highly valued news of the war. In addition to the sounds of the hymns, flute music occasionally wafted through the compound. After spending much of his morning engaged in several games of euchre, one prisoner concluded, "Some think it is a sin to play cards but I do not, especially in this place where a man can find nothing else to do."[7]

According to some prisoners, few of their fellows found gambling so sinful that it discouraged them from participating. "If there are any worse gambling hells this side of Pendemonium than I find here I dont want to find them," one prisoner huffed. Another wrote that the contests were going on "quite lively." Cards and "Chuck luck" games were among the many pastimes available to would-be wagerers. Prisoners arriving with money, such as those captured at Plymouth, provided ready marks.[8]

Fights were also common at Andersonville, particularly during June and early July. "A fight every day sure, and sometimes 2 or 3," one prisoner wrote. It was an observation that made its way into a number of diaries. Some contended that the contests were bloody. At least one wrote that weakness had taken its toll, observing, "Found several fights this morning by the prisoners, poor devils can't fight enough to count." Once the Raiders were rounded up prisoners recorded fewer accounts of fights, suggesting that the incidents may have involved more than simple fisticuffs. Indeed, on July 5, as the Raiders' trial was under way, one prisoner wrote, "Things went on very quiet in camp to-day, only saw one or two fist fights."[9]

Although it appears to have lessened the violence in camp, the trial did not bring an end to it. On August 25 "one of the bullies" struck another man over the head with a club. The victim died the next day. According to the diaries of two prisoners, the assailant was put on trial for murder. One wrote, "I hope they may hang him as he deserves it," but neither recorded the ultimate verdict.[10]

The prisoners also disapproved of comrades who chose to work for the enemy, even if the work benefited the captives. In May, when the Confederates decided to enlarge the stockade, they sought volunteers from among the prisoners. Several stepped forward, gaining extra rations as well as an opportunity to get out of the stockade. Some diarists mentioned the volunteer laborers without comment. One called them "foolish" for assisting the Rebels. James Burton of the 122nd New York wrote, "Hope they will have a good time working for the Confeds in the hot sun, rather *aiding* and *abetting* the Confed Govt taking the place of a Confed soldier & he sent to the front to fight."[11]

Prisoners were also recruited to work in a shoemaking establishment, a furtive project that was the brainchild of Richard Winder. One prisoner estimated that two hundred accepted a parole of honor and signed up. Samuel Melvin volunteered, rationalizing the decision by noting that his enlistment had run out, and "I must try and do something for myself." Other prisoners were less philosophical, especially when the Confederates sent a prisoner into the compound to sign up more would-be shoemakers. He ended up having his head shaved and was forced to sign a parole promising that he would do no more "dirty work for the Rebels."[12]

At least one Rebel objected to the prisoners working outside the stockade. A constituent wrote to Governor Brown that there were some three hundred Yankees on parole from the prison. Some were working on the stockade. Others buried the dead, worked at the bakery, or served as teamsters or carpenters. "They pass about as freely as our own soldiers do," he complained. The man admitted that he could not cite an example of them doing harm. Still, he feared that they might somehow help the other prisoners to escape. He further asserted that they were privy to valuable information that they could pass along to the enemy should they get away.[13]

Seddon asked Winder to reply. In doing so the crusty general complained of individuals who "find fault with everything that does not correspond with their ideas." Winder admitted that he did not like the idea of paroling prisoners, but the lack of labor forced the system upon him. He enclosed a letter from Lt. Col. Furlow, who stated that a sufficient workforce, free or slave, could not be had from the local population. No residents, he further noted, had complained to him about "pillaging or annoyance of any kind by the paroled prisoners." Furlow doubted that there ever would be any such complaints. Those who did misbehave would be returned to the stockade, giving them "every inducement to strictly obey orders and avoid every impropriety."[14]

Those inside the stockade would have agreed that anyone outside its walls would have had "every inducement" to remain. Except for a few tents in the hospital, the Andersonville prisoners received no shelter from their captors. Numerous inspectors called for the erection of barracks. The lack of housing, they argued, not only exposed the prisoners to the elements, but the irregular arrangement of their makeshift shelters made policing nearly impossible. Surgeon White conceded this point, but there was little anyone could do. Wirz had not been able to secure enough lumber to dam the creek that bisected the stockade. Barracks for an eventual thirty thousand prisoners were out of the question.[15]

That left the prisoners to fend for themselves, meaning many had no shelter whatsoever. Arriving in late July, as the prison population neared its peak, Kendrick Howard of the Fourth Vermont estimated that half the prisoners lacked shelter. A spell of wet weather in late May and June prompted a number of observations concerning those prisoners' condition. On one wet, windy morning, a prisoner wrote, "Many of the poor prisoners are standing like horses and cattle, with their backs to the storm, and no shelter." Of a particularly rainy night, another wrote, "Last night was a dreadfull night in prison. It commenced raining at 6 P.M. Continued untill 9 in the evening. It was a verey hard shower. Hundreds had to stay out through it all without a blanket or coat." The rains left the camp extremely muddy, forcing those prisoners without shelter to lie down in the mud for their night's rest. Things were particularly rough for those in the swampy area near the creek. "When it rains it becomes a pittifull state," one prisoner wrote. "The men gets a great dose of filth of every kind."[16]

Any covering the prisoners had they had managed to cobble together from items they brought with them and whatever they could find in the compound. Nehemiah Solon and six comrades paid $16 in Confederate money for a few poles. These they used to support three rubber blankets and two wool blankets, forming a crude tent. M. J. Umstead of the Thirteenth Iowa got a better deal, purchasing his poles for $4. Although blankets were most often used to construct shelter, some prisoners pressed overcoats into service. Alonzo Decker managed to purchase a tent, but it was so leaky that he ended up sleeping in water and mud. Some prisoners who had tents used them for shade during the day and took them down at night and lay beneath them. One prisoner spent a day making fifty bricks from the Georgia clay. He ended up with a shelter constructed of brick walls with a brush and mud roof. Many others simply burrowed into the clay to secure shelter from the elements.[17]

After suffering through wet weather most of June, the prisoners had to endure a brutal sun during the last week of the month. The hot spell continued, with brief respites, through the first three weeks of July before temperatures cooled. The oppressive heat returned in August. "Sutch a scorching sun I never seen before," an Ohio soldier wrote. "It fairley melts our men down to walk around." Another prisoner more succinctly described the weather as "hot as love and twice as hard to handle." By July 7 the "roasting weather" had left Henry Stone and his tentmates "very much tanned." Those without tents were severely sunburned, their feet forming blisters that cracked open. A prisoner who washed his shirt then went for a stroll as it dried found his back so badly burned that he could not lie down.[18]

Securing drinking water was also often a problem for the Andersonville captives. The stream that ran through camp was often fouled by slops from the cookhouse or prisoners who used it to wash. Often they had to haul it a considerable distance to their tents. Anxious to secure fresh water, and perhaps looking for something to do, many of the men dug wells. Success was far from guaranteed. Ransom Chadwick's mess was fortunate, reaching "fine water" at fourteen feet. Usually the task was much more difficult and dangerous. "Came to watter at last. The well is 62 ft deep," one triumphant prisoner wrote in his diary. Daniel Hutchins, who had complained of being forced to abandon his well after moving to the new section on July 1, soon found that his concerns were justified. After seven days he and his comrades had dug sixty feet but were yet to find water. One of the men working on the project had fallen forty feet as he was being lowered into the hole. On at least one occasion a man suffocated when a well he was digging caved in.[19]

Sometimes the prisoners found easier ways of securing water. Vermont soldier Bradford Sparrow wrote that a friend of his purchased a share in a well by trading his knife. New Yorker John Hoster purchased a bucket in the prison and made a strap for it. He allowed the owners of a nearby well to use the bucket in return for water for himself and three friends.[20]

On August 9 a strong storm produced flooding rains that brought down a portion of the prison walls. After the storm abated the prisoners realized it had opened up a spring of pure water. It ran beyond the deadline, but the Confederates put up crude spouting and diverted the flow into barrels. There prisoners gathered daily with cups, tin pails, or whatever else they could find. The wait was long, but the thirsty captives felt it was a small price to pay. "It seems almost a miracle wrought for our welfare," one of them wrote; and indeed the Providence Spring, as it came to be called, has assumed a mythical place in the history of Andersonville prison.[21]

Although not delivered providentially, beer was common in the prison. Most Andersonville brewers soaked meal in water and let it ferment, adding some molasses for flavor. John Kay made beer for his own use, but many prisoners sold at least a portion of what they produced. The going rate was 10¢ to 15¢ a pint. One prisoner wrote that he had sold two "pales" of unknown quantity for a total of $11. Another recorded that "sasafrass beer" could be had at the lower end of the price scale.[22]

If thirst was a frequent problem for the Andersonville prisoners, hunger was a near-constant challenge. Rations at Andersonville represented the efforts of harried prison officials to keep up with the demands of an ever-swelling captive population. Both Wirz and surgeon White reported on different occasions that the prisoners received the same rations as did the guards at the camp. This may have been true, but the guards had many more opportunities to supplement the army issue than did the captives. The claim also addressed only the issue of quantity. As both officers also noted, the quality of rations issued to the prisoners was often poor.[23]

Early on, the standard rations at Andersonville consisted of cornbread and bacon. By June rice and beans were often issued in lieu of cornbread. The following month molasses sometimes replaced meat. On June 22 one prisoner wrote, "Corn bread and cooked rice on alterned [alternate] days with the usual allowance of meat that is to say 3 oz bacon are our rations daily for the last 3 or 4 weeks." Although none were delighted, the prisoners offered few complaints about the amount of food received during the spring months. On June 10 one wrote, "We can live on this very well." The next day another agreed, "Fat as yet, I can live on the rations." Still, the allowance even then varied from day to day, depending upon the ability of the Confederates to procure food. The Southerners seem to have had success toward the end of June. No fewer than five diarists commented on either the 25th or 26th about increased rations, including fresh beef, a welcome change from bacon. One even remarked that the rations were better than the men had received in the Union lines. However, three days later one man wrote, "Fresh beef has 'played out.'" For the remainder of the summer prison diaries would record an inconsistent pattern, with periods of short rations broken by occasional increases in quantity.[24]

Even in these early months, prison officials had difficulties feeding the captives. Securing sufficient supplies was only one part of the problem. Cooking and distributing enough rations for the small city developing in their midst provided an equally daunting challenge for the Confederate keepers. Cooking facilities were primitive, and equipment—like virtually everything else—was scarce. As a result, many of the prisoners received their rations raw. For a time, Wirz allowed details to go out and cut firewood. He ended the practice when a number of prisoners attempted to escape, although it was later resumed.

The processes for preparing cornmeal and cornbread were unappetizing and unhealthy. There was no equipment to sift the cornmeal, and it was distributed cob and all. A frustrated Wirz complained to the post adjutant that if the meal was properly sifted, the resulting ration would be short one-quarter pound. The cornbread, prepared in open troughs, attracted flies, and they quickly became part of the mixture. As for the distribution process, one mess sergeant wrote, "The rations are brought in the afternoon—meat and rice in fifty pound sacks. Cornbread in sheets about 18x24 [inches] and so hard as to endanger our teeth. Bacon sides form our meat ration."[25]

The resulting complaints are well represented in the prisoners' diaries. Some wrote of peas full of dirt, bugs, or worms. When his mess gained a little variety, one prisoner wrote, "Two spoons of rice after three weeks of corn meal, we welcome the change although our rice is wormy." One month later the same prisoner was less sanguine. "Threw my beans [peas] away worms & pods all cooked together." John Kay was one of many prisoners who complained of the "coarse cornbread," which he felt was responsible for the diarrhea from which he suffered. Henry Stone simply considered it "worse than horse food." Sometimes, despite their limited fare, the bread was so bad the prisoners could not bring themselves to eat it. "Evening we got our Rashions there was ½ Loaf of Bread," one man wrote, "& it was so sour & stunk so we had to chuck it over the Dead Line & hear we are with nothing but a dam little piece of meat."[26]

Like everything else, those little pieces of meat were often of poor quality. A portion of the meat received by Solon's detachment on June 22 was "entirely rotten. We took it back to the Quarter master and showed it to him," he wrote. "He said he did not care a damn if it was all rotten he could not help it." Ransom Chadwick's mess celebrated July 4th with beef that was "rather oald all Magetts and stunk enough to knock a man over." Writing on August 5, James Bradd of the Thirteenth Iowa insisted the bacon "would kill a dog if he ever ate it." Six days later he received "a little poor meat an Iowa hog would not eat." Another prisoner wrote that the beef "stinks and [is] green & fly blown." However, the complaints were far from universal. On the 16th Bradd's mess received "the best meal we have had since July 22." Another prisoner expressed satisfaction with the beef issued on the 6th and the 10th, terming it "a rare dish." A more common complaint during the period was a reduction in quantity. As at Belle Isle, not all the prisoners blamed their captors. At least two noted that the Confederates must be "hard up" for provisions.[27]

Prisoners with money were not hard up for anything. As at almost every Civil War prison, Andersonville had its own economy and a thriving business community. The arrival of the Plymouth garrison in early May provided a mighty stimulus. Many of the men had recently received bounty money for reenlisting, and one prisoner claimed they brought with them an influx of $100,000.[28]

Business dealings inside the stockade often involved simple trades or purchases between two individuals. On July 14 Ransom Chadwick sold a one-quart cup for $1. With the dollar he purchased two spoons of soda. Three days later he traded his bacon ration for another cup. Eager to keep as clean as possible, Edwin Marsh swapped a pound of bacon for a hand towel and purchased a half pound of soap for $4.50 Confederate. After his mess located an old tree stump, they rented an ax for a quarter an hour to build up a supply of firewood. Watches, pens, and vests were among the items sold or traded. Highly desired was any container that could be used for cooking, eating, or drawing water. Hoster paid $1 for the bucket that earned him water rights from his neighbors' well. Samuel Gibson did not fare as well, paying $2 for a tin can in which he planned to cook mush. There was even a real estate and housing market in the prison. When Samuel Melvin arrived at Andersonville, crowding forced him to locate near the swamp. Fortunately two of his companions purchased a lot at a higher elevation for $4.50 and invited him to join them. Levi Whitaker of the Eleventh Connecticut benefited from a different kind of transaction. Although most prisoners had to construct whatever shelter they could, Whitaker had a friend who traded his watch and secured the men "a part of a shallow tent."[29]

Tobacco was a frequently traded item. Daniel Hutchins was one of the sellers, obtaining his supply from either a guard or a citizen when going out for wood. Prisoners often traded portions of their rations for tobacco, choosing to feed their habits rather than their stomachs. At least one even traded a precious ration of salt to satisfy his cravings. Buttons and at least one pocketbook also exchanged hands in tobacco deals. Sometimes priorities changed. On July 8 Darius Starr sold his watch key and bought a pair of cotton drawers and a piece of tobacco. Later that month he sold his watch "and had a good supper."[30]

Most Andersonville traders gathered along Market Street, the only real thoroughfare in the haphazardly organized facility. There any variety of prison entrepreneurs could be found. "We have stores oppen in every direction," one prisoner wrote, including "shaving and hair dressing saloons." Soap, tobacco, and cigars were among the many items offered for sale. Like the prisoners' shanties, the businesses generally consisted of a few poles driven in the ground with a blanket put over them.[31]

Although a great variety of products was offered for sale, food stands were by far the most common. According to Solon, who described the process in detail, prisoners with money purchased in bulk from the camp sutler. They then opened up their own stands and "retail out the stuff in small quantities at a large profit." Other prisoners wrote that guards would smuggle items in for prison businessmen. Often the Andersonville captives put their culinary skills to work, selling corncakes or pancakes made in homemade ovens and using the proceeds to purchase salt, soda, or vegetables. Others would buy peas in quantity, cook them, and sell them by the cupful. The variety was described by a prisoner who took a stroll down Market Street: "There was one stand that had cabbages potatoes and turnips tomatoes apples cucumbers squashes beats beans flour bacon salt soda ginger pepper cayenne and Black. Next to him there was a Beer stand next a man selling bean soup next a man with wheat biscuits and butter next wheat slap jacks and molasses next pickled Beets cucumbers and onions cut up in vinegar nice looking cakes and honey and meat next a dish of corn meal doughnuts next a lot of poor gingerbread some corn cakes and molasses and a little Bacon."[32]

Nothing came cheap at the stands. As one prisoner noted, "It requires a huge amount of money to live here." John Kay paid $1.50 for a spoonful and a half of black pepper and wrote that watermelons were selling for $4 apiece, a price confirmed by William Tritt. Potatoes, turnips, beets, and onions reportedly fetched $1, as did three eggs or three peaches. Cabbages went for $3 among prisoners desperate for vegetables. A cup of peanuts could be had for a quarter. Grosvenor wrote that he had gotten a bargain when he purchased six plums for a nickel. Apples, he noted, cost 15¢.[33]

Among the most prudent of Andersonville's consumers was Samuel Gibson, one of the Plymouth prisoners. He arrived with $94, and despite the $2 he shelled out for a tin can, Gibson generally spent wisely. He bought sparingly, spreading his purchases over several months. Those purchases may have had much to do with his survival. Upon arrival he bought poles, which allowed him and three colleagues to make a tent out of their blankets. As time went on he purchased flour, potatoes, and beans, as well as salt and soap. The orange he bought in late May allowed him to delay the onset of scurvy, which afflicted so many of his comrades. When ill and unable to eat the rations issued, he secured biscuits for 35¢. Eventually he survived captivity not only at Andersonville but also at the equally dismal prison in Florence, South Carolina. There he still had enough money to supplement his rations with sweet potatoes, which he purchased as late as November 24.[34]

In August Andersonville's prison population peaked at over thirty-three thousand. The death toll that month neared three thousand. Eventually thirteen thousand Unionists would occupy Andersonville graves, more than one of every three held there. The causes were many, and often they were beyond the control of the Georgia keepers. In the early months the Belle Isle prisoners, who arrived weak after enduring a bitter winter in Richmond, made up a large portion of the death toll.[35]

Facilities for caring for the sick were inadequate in the extreme. As surgeon White noted, the new hospital soon became crowded well beyond its capacity, with far too few tents to accommodate the patients. Straw for bedding could not be had, although White was able to secure pine straw until the hospital population grew beyond the ability to supply even this south Georgia staple. Medicines and other supplies were also difficult to obtain. The military bureaucracy was in part responsible. The needed items came from nearby Macon, but regulations required that requisitions be sent to Atlanta, several miles further. White submitted the requisitions monthly, but the quantities sent often fell far short of what he requested. This, combined with delays in receiving the shipments, often left him "without any medicines whatever." At Winder's instruction, White sent a letter to Confederate surgeon general Samuel P. Moore informing him of the problem. He asked that the medical purveyor at Macon be instructed to issue to the prison on White's requisition. If Moore granted such permission there is no record of it. One month later White was still complaining of the difficulty of receiving medicines. Meanwhile one prisoner observed, "Some of the doctors appear to be kind hearted men but they have no medicine to give that is suitable consequently their examination is nothing but a farce just for show."[36]

On August 2 White reported that he been unable to obtain vegetables for the sick virtually the entire month of July. He added, "Scurvy prevails to a great extent." This disease also afflicted Confederate prisoners in Union camps, but there were far fewer cases in Northern pens. Andersonville diarists first mentioned its appearance in May. On the 3rd Hegeman wrote that scurvy cases were advanced to the point that victims had lost teeth and suffered frightfully swollen limbs. By June 1, according to Kay, many were dying from the disease. Scurvy eventually affected the prison economy. So many men were unable to eat their meat ration that the price for a piece of meat dropped to between 5¢ and 10¢. One prisoner wrote of his afflicted comrades, "The ravages of this disease are terrible. Many going about the camp with bleeding mouths and teeth actually dropping out, legs swollen and turning black and blue." Describing his own case, another despaired, "I for one am nearly helpless. My limbs refuse to support my body and my mouth is so sore that I cannot eat corn bread or any salt meat. I have to eat either meal or Rice gruel."[37]

Diarrhea and dysentery were also common maladies among the Andersonville prisoners. One medical inspector reported that virtually every prisoner in the camp suffered from one or the other. They were caused, he reported, by exposure, the dust, smoke, and filth of the camp, and a "decided irritant effect" of cornbread prepared from unbolted meal. Those inside the compound agreed about the prevalence of the conditions. "Diarrhea still raging to considerable extent," one prisoner wrote in late June. Kay purchased some tea, hoping it might provide a cure in his case. It worked temporarily, but four days later he noted, "Had a very serious sick time last night with diarrhoea—attended with severe cramps in the bowels very painful in deed." The debilitating effects of digestive diseases often led to actions that further threatened the prisoners' health. One wrote, "Diarrhea very bad. John Early dug me a hole [in the] street to use as a sink." Medical inspectors confirmed that it was a common practice.[38]

On August 17 Daniel Hutchins and a friend secured pills for a fellow prisoner suffering from a chronic case of diarrhea and, they believed, typhoid fever. In the days that followed they carried the patient out to sick call but could not get him admitted. The two also failed to get him any more pills "for the Dr is almost a fool." Hutchins gave up his shelter to the man, and he and his friend attempted to keep him clean. "We are willing to do all we can for him to alleviate his sufferings," he explained. On the 27th they performed their final service when they carried the man's body to the prison "dead house."[39]

The experiences of Hutchins and his friends were common scenes at Andersonville. The result of hospital crowding was a pathetic lottery that took place at the gate whenever a sick call was announced. Hundreds or even thousands would show up, some hobbling or crawling on their own, others assisted by friends, and many carried on blankets. There they waited in the broiling sun as the doctors slowly conducted their examinations. Some bore it quietly. Some cried out, begging to be taken to the hospital or at least to someplace where they could get into the shade. A prisoner who witnessed the procession in early August wrote, "The day was mostly spent in getting out the sick. From early morn till past noon there was a constant crowding through the gate. Men in all stages of disease. And not the half of them were taken. Many died in the crowds & many more died afterwards. It was perfectly awful." Writing the same week, a mess sergeant concluded, "Pencil cannot picture the despairing faces nor words describe the sad scenes incident to [the] gatherings of the sick of Andersonville. Especially as the last word came and these who were able hobbled or were borne back to their quarters."[40]

Most of those who made it to the hospital never returned. One such case was Samuel Melvin. In his last diary entry, penned September 15, he pronounced his steward "a good fellow." Melvin lay upon his rubber blanket. Next to him was a man nearly dead with diarrhea. Occupying the next space was a man "most dead with scurvy. And then the tent and blankets are just as full of lice and fleas as ever can be." Melvin concluded, "As things look now, I stand a good chance to lay my bones in old Ga., but I'd hate to as bad as one can, for I want to go home." He died ten days later.[41]

Less typical was the case of George Hegeman. On June 16 he was sent to the smallpox camp. "I am glad to get out in pure air," he wrote. "Am not much afraid of the disease." On July 27, after a gap of nearly a month, Hegeman was able to continue his diary. He had been told that a Confederate surgeon had stayed by his side nearly all of his worst night "and would not leave till satisfied I was through and passed danger. May God bless him and his," Hegeman wrote. "He is one among a thousand."[42]

A number of healthy prisoners received an inside view of the hospital by serving as nurses or in other capacities. "A poor place for them here," John Duff wrote at the end of his first week of duty. "Cannot stand it to live in sutch a plaice as this is," David Kennedy noted. "Theire is more miserey heire than could be emagin." Despite receiving better rations, Kennedy wished to return to the stockade, and he soon did. Neither man was impressed with their fellow prisoners working in the hospital. Kennedy accused them of killing their patients by stealing their rations. Duff wrote on two occasions that prisoners had been punished for selling alcohol or other items from the hospital.[43]

William Smith, one of Andersonville's original prisoners, went to work at the hospital in early May and remained until he was exchanged in February 1865.

Working in the hospital commissary, he recorded numerous frustrations, along with a few victories, in attempting to secure needed supplies. One excursion for buckets and skillets ended in failure. Deliveries of rations were inconsistent. "I have plenty of bread come in again to day but verry little rice," he wrote one day. Five days later, "This morning I get no bread for the sick nothing but pork isshued." Occasionally he was able to get greens or vinegar for some of the men suffering from scurvy but often not enough for all of the cases. In late July he began receiving sporadic supplies of green corn.[44]

As August arrived Smith wrote that crowding was becoming severe. When six hundred patients were admitted on the 3rd, he estimated that there was barely enough room for half of them. The next day he observed, "It is a hard looking sight this morning to see so many sick men laying on the ground. The attendants have to give up their tents for patients." As the month went on, flour was often in short supply, but there was enough cornbread to make up the difference. On the 26th the women of Americus supplemented the patients' rations by sending in "a fine lot of Delicacies."[45]

In early August Lt. Col. Daniel Chandler arrived in Andersonville. He brought with him orders from the inspector general's office in Richmond to report on conditions in the prison. After touring the stockade, Chandler produced a scathing indictment. He conceded the challenge of providing medical care at Andersonville, citing limited facilities and a shortage of commissioned surgeons. Beyond that, Chandler was highly critical of the administration of the camp. He started with the "absence of all regularity in the prison grounds," which made proper policing impossible. The inspecting officer then cited the manner in which sick call was conducted. "The crowd at these times is so great that only the strongest can get access to the doctors," he wrote, "the weaker ones being unable to force their way through the press." He further asserted, "The sanitary condition of the prisoners is as wretched as can be." After reporting the high rates of scurvy and diarrhea, Chandler insisted that camp officials made "little, if any effort . . . to arrest it by procuring proper food."[46]

In an addendum to his report, Chandler praised Wirz for his "untiring energy and devotion to the discharge of the multifarious duties of his position." He termed Capt. Winder "an energetic and efficient officer." Gen. Winder, on the other hand, came in for no such praise. Chandler bluntly called for him to be replaced with someone "who unites both energy and good judgment with some feelings of humanity and consideration for the welfare and comfort" of the prisoners. Chandler claimed Winder had boasted that he had never set foot inside the stockade. He also accused the general of endorsing a policy "deliberately and in cold blood" of letting the prisoners die off until the facility became less crowded. Winder, he concluded, was responsible for making the prison "a place of horrors" and "a disgrace to civilization."[47]

The Confederate War Department, which had done nothing to alleviate conditions at Andersonville, responded with apparent outrage. John A. Campbell, the assistant secretary, insisted that Chandler's report "calls very loudly for the interposition of the Department." That interposition took the form of a message from Assistant Adjutant and Inspector General Robert Chilton to Gen. Winder. Citing portions of Chandler's report, Chilton instructed Winder to "take measures to correct the abuses above mentioned."[48]

Considering the hyperbolic language of Chandler's report, Winder's response was measured. He accused Chandler of conducting only a "superficial" inspection and of being unwilling to listen to any information provided by prison officials. Winder strongly denied the assertion that nothing had been done to provide vegetables for the scurvy patients. All that could be done had been done, he insisted, a claim at least partly sustained by Smith's diary entries. Wirz supported his commander's response, writing that Chandler spent only three hours in the prison and paid little attention to what he, Wirz, had to say. Rather, the inspector had preferred to speak directly to the prisoners, and was "made the plaything of the cute Yankees, who would give him most horrible descriptions of their sufferings."[49]

The following month another medical inspector arrived at Andersonville. In light of the experience with Lt. Col. Chandler, it is perhaps not surprising that Wirz at first denied Dr. Joseph Jones admission to the stockade. A Georgia native, Jones was a graduate of Princeton who received his M.D. from the University of Pennsylvania. His passion was research, and by the time the war began he was well known and respected within his field. Obtaining a major's commission, he investigated medical problems in a number of Confederate hospitals. During the summer of 1864 he received permission from surgeon general Moore to visit Andersonville "with the design of instituting a series of inquiries upon the nature and causes of the prevailing diseases."[50]

The Jones report was largely a rehash of previous inspections. He found overcrowding and the lack of shelter to be important causes of disease in both the stockade and the hospital. Jones also cited the unsanitary practices of the prisoners. It shocked him to see men "urinating and evacuating their bowels at the very tent doors and around the little vessels in which they were cooking their food." He criticized hospital officials for not emptying the boxes used as sinks until they were filled. The result was "a most nauseous and disgusting smell."[51]

As had his predecessors, Dr. Jones listed scurvy, diarrhea, and dysentery as the leading causes of death. Unlike previous inspectors, he gave detailed attention to hospital gangrene, an area of research that especially interested him. Incomplete hospital records made his investigation difficult, but he was able to identify 266 cases, a number he considered "far below the truth." Many cases, Jones concluded, had been entered on the hospital registers under the headings of other ailments. He had no difficulty in determining the causes: "In the depraved and depressed condition of the systems of these prisoners, in the foul atmosphere of the stockade and hospital, reeking with noxious exhalations, the smallest injury, as a splinter running into a hand or foot, the blistering of the arms or hands in the hot sun, or even the abrasions of the skin in scratching a mosquito bite, were often followed by the most extensive and alarming gangrenous ulceration." The gangrene returned "almost invariably" following amputation. Its effects extended "a considerable distance" beyond the hospital and the stockade. To demonstrate that point, Jones cited the case of a sentry who was attacked by hospital gangrene. He had stood guard in a sentry box along the top of the stockade but had never entered the compound itself nor served in the hospital.[52]

Louis Manigault, a Charleston businessman, served as Jones's clerk. The well-traveled Manigault had seen a prison in Shanghai and witnessed the effects of Asiatic cholera in northern China. "But the past is a trifle," he informed his wife on September 18, "and in truth nothing, to what I am now beholding." He had visited the hospital with Jones the previous day, and the smell, he wrote, seemed "quite sufficient to kill at once even a well man." There had been 130 deaths in the hospital the day of his visit. "I was obliged to follow Surgeon Jones, or nothing in the World would have taken me in there," Manigault insisted. "As you stroll along these walks, in the midst of this mass of human suffering, breathing the polluted atmosphere of disease, rendered far more on account of the pestiferous odor arising from the immense number of Gangrenous wounds, I could not but reflect seriously upon the Horrors of War."[53]

Those horrors were no less inside the stockade, and the prisoners' diaries offer ample testimony. Among the most graphic accounts was the scene witnessed by Nehemiah Solon on July 31.

> A man was brought down to the Brook on a stretcher so as that he might be washed. He was quite an old man and his hair was gray. . . . When they took his clothes off a sight that would make one shudder met our view. He was nothing but a breathing skeleton but the worst is to be told. His body . . . was completely covered over with loathsome maggots even his eyes and head were full of them and when they put him in the water he commenced to spit them with blood out of his mouth. I would take my oath that there was not less than two quarts of maggots on him. . . . They washed him and

his clothes and carried him off and without any doubt he is beyond suffering now.[54]

Prisoners beyond suffering at Andersonville went first to the "Dead House." A log structure, it was about twenty-five feet square. A tent cloth roof protected the corpses from the rays of the Georgia sun. "It was as horrible a sight as I have ever witnessed!" Manigault wrote of his visit to the dead house. "I counted thirty dead Yankees, with bodies twisted up in every imaginable form." Michigan prisoner George Hinkley passed the dead house in September as he departed for the Florence prison. He wrote that it "was occupied by about 50 dead bodies that were half petrified. The stanch was worse than a hard fought battle field."[55]

Jones and Manigault also visited the Andersonville cemetery. According to Manigault, paroled prisoners arrived three times a day on four-mule wagons, each bearing thirty to forty corpses. "As the Wagon reached the spot the Corpses were rudely tumbled on the ground," he observed. "A ditch or trench six feet wide, & from four to five feet deep was dug by Yankee paroled-Negroes, who . . . seemed to be perfectly unconcerned; the bodies were placed side by side, and touching each other, with their clothes on." At least one prisoner confirmed Manigault's account of the burial method. Hegeman wrote that the wagon was tilted, and "all the bodies slide down in a confused mass into a long trench." A sharp-pronged rake was then used to arrange the corpses.[56]

Bodies arrived from both the hospital and the stockade. Although one prisoner wrote that the area around the prison gate was "crowded with the dead," it was usually not difficult to find volunteers to carry out the bodies. One reason was the opportunity to enjoy the fresh air outside the camp. Firewood provided a greater incentive. The prisoners were allowed to gather as much as they could carry on the return trip. Although most came back with fuel, some carried pine boughs for bedding. "I have frequently heard men wish that . . . one of their sick comrades would die so that they could get some wood," one prisoner wrote.[57]

Dead comrades also left behind clothing and shoes, which desperate prisoners were eager to obtain. One man wrote with disgust that captives who did nothing to aid sick comrades would eagerly snatch what was left behind after those comrades died. Often the desire to loot the bodies resulted in fights between prisoners. Samuel Melvin candidly noted in his diary that he had secured the shoes of a dead friend. He sold them for $1 and used the money to purchase vinegar and pepper.[58]

Death was about the only way a prisoner could get beyond the confines of the Andersonville stockade. Although quite a few attempted to escape, the vast majority soon found themselves back inside the pen. For one thing, the distances were daunting. A prisoner absconding from Sumter County, Georgia, would have been best advised to head south. Union forces in Florida were actually closer than those approaching Atlanta, but they were still nearly one hundred miles away. However far they had to travel, the escapees would have been viewed with suspicion. Manpower shortages in the Confederacy had reached the point that virtually any male between his teens and fifty years of age not wearing a gray uniform was a strange sight to behold.[59]

If those problems were not enough, bloodhounds pursued escaping Union soldiers. As at Camp Ford and other Confederate prisons, the hounds were transferred from slave patrols to track down Yankee captives. "Roll is called every morning and the moment one is reported missing 15 or 20 thirsty Blood Hounds are let loose upon their tracks," De Witt Spaulding wrote. "They are hunted down like wild beasts and returned to the prison in a torn and mangled condition." When a group of prisoners absconded in early September, William Tritt wrote that the group was overtaken within hearing distance of the camp. One member of the group returned "much bitten by the hounds."[60]

Many of the early escape attempts at Andersonville were made by prisoners outside the stockade on wood details or with other work parties. According to Wirz, forty-seven prisoners escaped during June. All had been beyond the gates when they fled, and all but three were recaptured. The problem, one inspector reported, was that "too great an intimacy" had sprung up between the guards and the small groups of prisoners they supervised. One prisoner even claimed that the guards sometimes accompanied the escapees. In at least one case the sentry did not do so voluntarily. Three prisoners overpowered him, took his musket, and made him exchange clothes with one of their number. One diarist wrote that the men made the guard accompany them for fifteen miles before releasing him. Another claimed that they tied him to a tree five miles away. In any event, all three were soon back at Andersonville, each adorned with a ball and chain. Such incidents became so acute that Wirz ended the wood details for a time.[61]

Several industrious prisoners began tunnels. Few projects were successful because their hungry comrades were too eager to trade information for extra rations. One of the earliest Andersonville excavations began disgorging prisoners on the night of May 4. An alert guard spotted one of the escapees, and the hounds did the rest of the work. All of the men soon found themselves back within the prison walls.[62]

A few weeks later a group of prisoners organized a much more involved plot. On May 21 Grosvenor wrote, "There is much of interest transpiring of which I am not permitted to speak particulars." Despite his stated need for caution, he went on to explain what was transpiring. He also informed Charles Lee, like him a member of the Sixteenth Connecticut. Grosvenor wrote that a "consultation" had taken place the previous night at which the attendees had hatched a plan to escape. The group met the next two nights, planning tactics and discussing possible routes to freedom. The days were spent "in active preparations for the contemplated 'break.'" Grosvenor did not discuss specifics, but by the 24th, the date set for the breakout, he had concluded that the plan was "impracticable." De Witt Spaulding shared his concerns. Approached to lead a group of ten men in the effort, he demurred until he could learn the total strength of the party and decide if the plot had "any chance of . . . succeeding." Meanwhile, Lee determined to wait, hoping Sherman and his host might arrive and save everybody the trouble.[63]

Nothing happened the night of the 24th, perhaps, Lee surmised, because of a heavy rain. If so, the Yankees missed their only opportunity, at least for this particular plot. The next morning a notice from Wirz greeted them. It announced that he was fully aware of the plan. If the attempt was made, he threatened to open up on the stockade with grape and canister. He punctuated the threat by posting lines of sentries on the hill overlooking the compound.[64]

Over the next two days Wirz did what one prisoner dubbed "a cute thing." The commandant had work crews dig trenches around the interior of the stockade to find tunnels. According to Spaulding, they revealed five on the 27th. Lee wrote that some of the ringleaders of the escape attempt were rounded up and escorted out of the camp. Meanwhile the reinforcements—and the guns—scowled down from above. All of this met with the approval of the *Sumter Republican,* published in nearby Americus. Learning of the plot, the editor enumerated the dire consequences that would have resulted had the mass escape succeeded. Destroyed crops and railroad tracks, rifled smokehouses, and "murder and rapine would follow wherever they went. In short, the land would be filled with desolation, wretchedness and mourning."[65]

This setback did not long deter all the prisoners. One group found that it was not just the Rebs that could bring the digging to a halt. Robert Kellogg spent much of the night of May 29 working on a tunnel. He conceded that it was a new form of labor for him, but added, "I'm willing to work hard if I can only get out of this & into 'Uncle Sam's' lines again." He returned to the project the next night, only to dig into the sinks of the old hospital. "That puts an end to that tunnel," he sadly concluded.[66]

In July Capt. Wirz learned of another potential plot. On the 14th he summoned all the mess sergeants and told them he was fully aware of the plan. "In language that was anything but courteous," one wrote, Wirz warned them against gathering together in groups. Should an uprising occur, he added, the artillery would open up with grape and canister, and it would continue as long as a man was seen moving. Later that day, as if to reiterate the point, the big guns fired a couple of blank rounds.[67]

Two days later, with the assistance of a Union "traitor," the Confederates discovered a tunnel that was nearing completion. The following day the prisoners determined the identity of the man who had betrayed the project. They shaved his head, tattooed a "T" on his forehead, and roughed him up a bit. On the 18th prison authorities removed the man from the compound and withheld rations in that portion of the prison until the men who had abused their informant were delivered up or surrendered themselves. The guilty parties confessed the following day. Rations were resumed and, according to one diarist, the men were not punished.[68]

By then, fearing Union cavalry raiders, the Andersonville keepers were more focused on attacks from without than on escapes from within. On the night of July 19–20 a group of prisoners attempted to take advantage of the situation by passing out through a tunnel. Diarists placed the number anywhere from just two to nearly five hundred. As was often the case, overeagerness led them to be spotted, and virtually all were soon back within the confines of the stockade. In the meantime work crews composed of black prisoners filled in the tunnels.[69]

On the night of August 27 a group of prisoners tried an even bolder tactic. On a rainy night, defying the deadline, they sawed out a section of the stockade. The escapade helped conclude a month in which the number of successful escapes spiked. August's consolidated returns showed that thirty prisoners had escaped from Andersonville, and only four had been recaptured. Wirz explained that some twenty-five more had made the attempt but had been returned by the dogs the same day. Eleven, he continued, had escaped from work parties after giving their parole not to escape. Still, he was not pleased. He placed the blame squarely on the guards. Some had been bribed. Others had carelessly allowed prisoners to walk off after depositing implements in the tool shed. "The worthlessness of the guard forces is on the increase day by day," Wirz concluded.[70]

Despite the commandant's assessment, Andersonville's guards appear to have been very diligent in enforcing the camp's deadline. Prison diarists noted that shots rang out at the slightest contact with the aptly named barrier. Still, the sentries were anything but trigger-happy. It seems certain that fewer than twenty prisoners were shot during the camp's existence. Considering the number of youthful, inexperienced, and virtually untrained guards manning the posts, this number was remarkably small.[71]

A brief flurry of shooting incidents marked the arrival of Gen. Winder at the camp. On June 19 a prisoner stepped slightly over the deadline. A sentry fired immediately, missing the guilty party but wounding two men resting nearby in their tent. The next shooting occurred during the night of June 20–21. One prisoner wrote that the victim had "abused the sentinel." Two claimed the man had committed no offense. Three others insisted that he had stepped slightly across the deadline.[72]

Occasionally the desire to quench one's thirst could prove fatal. One such incident occurred on July 13. Three diarists wrote that the man had reached over the deadline to fill his canteen. One added that he did not realize the danger because that section of the railing was broken. Not only was the offender shot, but a bystander was slightly wounded. Another thirsty prisoner was shot through the head and instantly killed on July 27. According to some of the prisoners, the man had recently arrived and may have not been fully cognizant of camp rules. Another wrote simply, "The rebbs kill every healf chance they have." On August 6 a prisoner was killed under nearly identical circumstances. One angry captive wrote, "Shall we not remember this treatment when we meet these cowards on the field or in our own power." Another, who claimed to have witnessed the shooting, observed, "O cruel enemy! your turn may come sooner than you think."[73]

Prisoners did not always blame their guards for shootings. On May 15 a man boldly crossed the deadline and refused to go back, announcing that he wished to die. A sentry finally obliged him. One prisoner believed the victim had been a "traitor" who informed the Confederates of tunneling projects. "If so, shooting was too good for him," he concluded. On July 22 a nervous guard opened fire as the prisoners crowded at the gate during sick call. One prisoner conceded that the men had been "crowding out to fast." Another wrote of the victim, "He was to blame for disobeying."[74]

There was a persistent prison rumor that guards received furloughs of thirty or more days every time they shot a prisoner. That claim was false, but a guard could secure a thirty-day furlough if he supplied a recruit under seventeen years of age or between forty-five and fifty. Among those who tried was Joseph Williams, who sent a form to his wife to show anyone who might be interested. "This would be a good place for them," he wrote, "as their is no fighting to do hear."[75]

According to Williams, the guards got enough to eat, "such as it is." Like the prisoners', their rations consisted of cornmeal and bacon. "I can't eat much of it," he informed his wife. He asked her to send flour, potatoes, onions, and soap. "We have very dul times at this place & very hot weather," he concluded. In a letter to his sister, an unidentified guard added that Andersonville was "a great place for women." They showed up daily with cakes and pies, but the prices were so steep that few guards could afford them. The man noted, "We have verry heavy duty to do down here they have to go on guard every night and day." He avoided most of the duty, however, by serving as a regimental mail carrier.[76]

On September 2, 1864, Atlanta fell to the forces of William Tecumseh Sherman. Three days later Adjutant General Cooper tersely ordered Winder, "Take immediate measures for sending the prisoners at Andersonville and Macon to Charleston and Savannah."[77]

Rumors of Sherman's victory reached the prison compound on the 5th. They were delivered by a batch of new prisoners from the victorious army. In a camp that had learned to view rumors with great suspicion, these personal reports seemed to ring true. "Good," one Andersonville prisoner wrote of the news, "and I think it is true." Another simply wrote, "Sherman Has got Atlanty at last." Looking ahead, a third added, "If he keeps on I think that in time he may relice us from this hole."[78]

The next day prison officials announced that eighteen detachments were to prepare to leave at a moment's notice. They told the men that they were to be exchanged. A Macon newspaper that found its way into the camp contained a report that several released Confederate prisoners had arrived at Atlanta, which seemed to confirm the good news. "There is a good deal of cheering here in camp and the men are pretty well excited," one man wrote. Another observed that most of the prisoners stayed up all night in hopes that the Rebels' claims were true. "All eyes are open at daylight with the greatest anxiety," he added the next morning.[79]

What they beheld that day left most cautiously optimistic. Detachments did indeed begin to leave. "The camp is all in an uproar. Cheers can be heard in every direction," one prisoner noted. Still, he added, "The only fears I have is that they will not go to our lines but to some other prison." Conflicting rumors of the men's destination did battle with each other over the next several days, as more prisoners boarded the cars. Many, feeling that any change had to be an improvement, "flanked" their way into departing detachments, often by bribing their comrades for a place. Anxious prisoners crowded the gate, eagerly awaiting their turn to leave. Those left behind at least had the consolation of a prison that was now far less crowded.[80]

The departures did not empty the Andersonville prison, but they greatly reduced its population. By October 1 there were only 8,218 prisoners remaining. One-fourth of them were in the hospital. At the end of the month the number was down to 4,208. By then those who had left were fully aware of their fate. At least one did not have to wait that long. Arriving in Florence, South Carolina, in mid-September, one prisoner wrote presciently, "See hard times and hungry to i think."[81]

Gen. John H. Winder served the Confederacy in a variety of capacities dealing with Union prisoners. He faced numerous challenges but was seldom given the authority to deal with them. Courtesy Massachusetts MOLLUS Collection, United States Army Military History Institute, Carlisle Barracks, PA

Union prisoners at Castle Pinckney in Charleston Harbor. Prisoners sent from Richmond were housed there in 1861 and 1862. Courtesy Massachusetts MOLLUS Collection, United States Army Military History Institute, Carlisle Barracks, PA.

Richmond's Castle Thunder prison. The majority of inmates held there were civilians facing a variety of charges and Confederate deserters. Courtesy National Archives, Washington, DC.

The interior yard of Castle Thunder. Courtesy Massachusetts MOLLUS Collection, United States Army Military History Institute, Carlisle Barracks, PA.

The military prison at Salisbury, North Carolina. When the facility first opened in 1862, prisoners found the conditions there good. By late 1864 they had deteriorated, and the mortality rate exceeded even that of Andersonville. Courtesy Massachusetts MOLLUS Collection, United States Army Military History Institute, Carlisle Barracks, PA.

Union prisoners playing baseball at Salisbury in 1862. Crowding would eventually put an end to the games. Courtesy National Archives, Washington, DC.

Belle Isle, Richmond, Virginia. The Confederates began using the island in the James River as a prison in the summer of 1862. Union prisoners also stayed there during the bitter fall and winter of 1863–64. Courtesy Massachusetts MOLLUS Collection, United States Army Military History Institute, Carlisle Barracks, PA.

A photo of Libby prison taken at the end of the war. The facility was mainly used to house Union officers. The white paint was reportedly applied to make potential escapees easier to spot after dark. Courtesy National Archives, Washington, DC.

Camp Parole, located near Annapolis, Maryland, held paroled Union prisoners awaiting exchange. At first they were housed in tents. The barracks went up during the spring of 1864. Courtesy Massachusetts MOLLUS Collection, United States Army Military History Institute, Carlisle Barracks, PA.

A flag of truce boat delivers paroled prisoners to Camp Parole. Courtesy Massachusetts MOLLUS Collection, United States Army Military History Institute, Carlisle Barracks, PA.

Prison 3 at Danville, Virginia. The Confederates began sending prisoners to Danville in late 1863 to help relieve overcrowding in Richmond. Courtesy Massachusetts MOLLUS Collection, United States Army Military History Institute, Carlisle Barracks, PA.

Danville's Prison 6. The Confederates used six tobacco warehouses as prisons in the southern Virginia city. Courtesy Massachusetts MOLLUS Collection, United States Army Military History Institute, Carlisle Barracks, PA.

Camp Morgan, located in Cahaba, Alabama, served briefly as a holding camp in 1862. The following year it reopened and eventually housed over two thousand prisoners. Courtesy Massachusetts MOLLUS Collection, United States Army Military History Institute, Carlisle Barracks, PA.

In August 1864 photographer Andrew Jackson Riddle visited Camp Sumter, near Andersonville, Georgia. This view, showing the sinks and the numerous prisoner "shebangs," was taken from the east wall. Courtesy Massachusetts MOLLUS Collection, United States Army Military Institute, Carlisle Barracks, PA.

This Riddle photo shows the Andersonville prisoners crowding near the north gate to receive rations. Courtesy Massachusetts MOLLUS Collection, United States Army Military History Institute, Carlisle Barracks, PA.

Andersonville's burial detail places the body of a Union captive in the long trench that served as a grave. Over thirteen thousand prisoners died at Andersonville. Courtesy Massachusetts MOLLUS Collection, United States Army Military History Institute, Carlisle Barracks, PA.

Camp Oglethorpe, Macon, Georgia. This facility held prisoners captured in the western theater in 1862. In 1864 the Confederates reopened it as a prison for officers only. Courtesy Massachusetts MOLLUS Collection, United States Army Military History Institute, Carlisle Barracks, PA.

During the fall of 1864, Union officers were kept in an open field near Columbia, South Carolina. Because sorghum usually replaced meat in the prisoners' rations, they nicknamed the pen Camp Sorghum. Courtesy Massachusetts MOLLUS Collection, United States Army Military History Institute, Carlisle Barracks, PA.

Christened Camp Asylum, the South Carolina male "lunatic asylum" housed Union officers during the winter of 1864–65. Fortunate captives ended up inside the asylum buildings. Others camped on the grounds. Courtesy Massachusetts MOLLUS Collection, United States Army Military History Institute, Carlisle Barracks, PA.

The execution of Henry Wirz. The Andersonville commandant was hanged outside Old Capitol Prison in Washington, DC, on November 10, 1864. Courtesy American Image Gallery, Gettysburg, PA.

10

"All are glad to go somewhere"

The Officers' Odyssey, 1864–65

Some three months after Union enlisted men and noncommissioned officers began arriving in Andersonville, their officers followed them to Georgia. Their destination was Macon, some forty miles to the north. Officers from the Plymouth garrison arrived as early as May 1. However, it was not until the next day that Adjutant General Cooper informed Howell Cobb that Yankee officers were on their way and ordered him to make preparations for their safekeeping. Cobb responded the same day, informing Cooper that he had ordered barracks erected at Camp Oglethorpe. The prisoners would be kept outside until they were finished.[1]

One week later Macon's mayor received word from the War Department that his city would again be housing Yankee captives. Stockade walls were soon going up at Camp Oglethorpe. In announcing the news to the populace, the *Macon Telegraph* observed, "It is not, in many respects, a good selection, and we are sorry so many prisoners should be quartered in Macon, but perhaps we may as well bear the burden as any other community." On the 18th the paper reported that nearly a thousand prisoners had arrived the previous day. Three more shipments of between five hundred and a thousand reached Macon the following week. Although some remained, the majority appear to have been enlisted men bound for Andersonville.[2]

Among the first contingent of officers to reach Macon were Cyrus Heffley and George Grant, both of whom had spent the previous winter at Libby. Stockade walls with platforms for sentinels were up by the time they arrived on May 17. A second line of guards stood beyond the walls. Although there was a building in the center of the fairgrounds that served as a hospital, the men occupied tents made from their own blankets. Heffley found water to be abundant, and Grant found it to be of good quality. A small stream ran through the compound, and there was also a spring and a well.[3]

The tents proved temporary, although it was not Cobb's forces that put up barracks. On the 20th the officers received lumber to erect their own shelters. Two days later Heffley's mess had its shanty, one hundred feet long by sixteen wide, half under roof. The next day the men added bunks. Arriving on May 25, Charles Mattocks, who had previously spent time at Lynchburg and Danville, wrote, "This is a much better place than any we have had, because we are now out of doors, with sheds built by our own hands to lie under nights." By July 10 one prisoner estimated that two-thirds of the Macon captives had shelter.[4]

On May 25 Capt. George C. Gibbs, who had served at prisons in Richmond and Salisbury, was placed in command of the Macon prison. Capt. W. Kemp Tabb, however, was the officer immediately in charge of the prisoners. Tabb had accompanied the first detachment from Richmond, and he had earned the men's enmity before they ever reached Georgia. One wrote, "He is a dirty low lifed drunken Pig. He was very abusive in language and manner toward us on our way here." Added another, "Capt. Tabbs, who commanded us is a brute and will be remembered by all who saw his actions. He spoke very rough, called officers sons of b——."[5]

Other Macon prisoners soon adopted similar opinions. One termed Tabb "a rascal" and "a most infernal scoundrel." On May 28 the captain threatened to shoot any man who did not fall in line for roll call at the proper time. Two prison diarists dismissed the order as a vain attempt to frighten them. A third considered it nothing more than the ramblings of "a regular drunken fool." The next day James Penfield wrote that Tabb and a guard entered their shed and immediately uncovered a tunnel. He ordered a prisoner to fill it in, and when the officer refused Tabb struck him with a gun and threatened to shoot him. Some two months later Tabb fell into Union hands when a train he was in was captured south of Richmond. Gen. Truman Seymour, who had been a prisoner at Macon, wrote to William Hoffman on behalf of a group of exchanged prisoners. "The prisoners of war very generally desire that steps be taken to visit upon Captain Tabb some of those indignities that he heaped upon them while in his hands," Seymour wrote. He offered few specifics but did claim that he had seen a Macon prisoner bucked and gagged in Tabb's presence.[6]

The Macon captives were no more impressed by their guards. Plymouth prisoner Ira Sampson observed, "Will have conscripts to look after us a mean looking and contemptible appearing organization." Newly minted members of Cobb's reserves, most, estimated James Penfield, were sixteen years old. According to Jacob Heffelfinger, some were only fourteen.[7]

Heffelfinger added that the Confederates mounted two artillery pieces on May 31 to "frown down on us." The deadline also came, with the usual strict orders to stay back or risk being shot. In citing the warning, one prisoner added, "if the sentinel could shoot accurately enough." This was not simply an example of prison humor. During the night of May 18–19 a guard fired at a prisoner who was at least six feet away from the deadline, a fact confirmed by two other sentries. The guard missed, but Tabb informed the prisoners he had nevertheless placed the man under arrest.[8]

Macon diarists recorded only one shooting at the Georgia prison. The victim was Lt. Otto Grearson of the Forty-fifth New York. On the evening of June 11, just after dark, Grearson went to the brook to bathe. He was returning to his quarters when the guard fired a blast of buck and ball. The ball entered his right shoulder, passed through both lungs, and lodged near his left shoulder. His fellow officers took him to the hospital, where he died a few hours later. Diary entries were unanimous in decrying the shooting as unfounded. "I think it is a little less than cold blooded murder," one wrote, "as [Grearson] does not appear to have been violating any regulations of the camp." A friend of the victim, who was with him at the time, insisted that the lieutenant had turned to return when he was shot. Therefore, "It seems almost impossible that the sentinel could have thought him trying to escape."[9]

Unlike at Andersonville, where rations were generally issued daily, the Macon prisoners received four or five days of rations at a time. This meant the officers had to do their own cooking. On May 27 the Confederates issued a skillet and a two-quart tin cooking dish to every squad of ten men. They also received barrels to be used as washtubs.[10]

Although they were not specific, the Macon prisoners generally indicated that Confederates supplied them with enough to eat. The rations most often consisted of cornbread or cornmeal, rice, beans, and pork. Molasses was sometimes issued in lieu of meat. Salt and soap, two items the Andersonville prisoners scarcely received, were often included in the officers' rations. One prisoner estimated that the daily ration per individual included a pint and a fourth of coarse meal, one-quarter gill of molasses and beans, three ounces of bacon, one-sixth gill of rice, and a teaspoonful of salt. Even the officers were not immune to shortages of rations. One occurred in mid-June. Penfield wrote on the 17th that the prisoners had suddenly received half rations. Messmates Templeton Hurst and Jacob Heffelfinger both termed them "scanty."[11]

The Macon officers also had occasional complaints about the quality of their rations. Specifically, diarists wrote of meat that was "stinking" and full of maggots. They also decried the lack of fresh vegetables. By June cases of scurvy were being reported, although they appear to have been fewer and less severe than those at Andersonville. According to one prisoner, many had contracted the disease before leaving Libby.[12]

As at most other military prisons, prisoners with adequate funds could make life more bearable with purchases. Unfortunately, as Cyrus Heffley noted, "Those that have money will live very well, but the majority of us are without that precious article." That was especially true of those who, like Heffley, were sent to Macon after several months in Libby. Captives taken during the spring 1864 campaigns were more likely arrive with funds on hand.[13]

Sutler prices could strain the resources of the most financially solvent captive. Francis Trowbridge Sherman, a staff officer for Gen. Oliver Otis Howard, was captured north of Atlanta on July 7. Three days later he joined what he estimated to be over fifteen hundred officers at Macon. He soon went on a spending spree. Sherman paid $12.50 for a pail, $5.75 for a plate, and $5 for a toothbrush. He secured a knife and a fork for $8.50 and a yard of muslin for $5.75. All of this was purchased his second day in prison. Later he bought a jug for $5 and obtained unknown quantities of tobacco for $6.50 and salt for $4.[14]

Food items fetched equally high prices. After becoming disgusted with a "dry breakfast [of] cornbread without any accompaniments," Heffelfinger invested $3 in a half pound of butter. That must have been close to the going rate, because another prisoner reported that butter was selling for $6.50 a pound. In early July tomatoes were bringing $30 a bushel. At the same time, Mattocks listed the following prices for commodities sold in the yard daily: one quart of blackberries, $1.25; one dozen eggs, $4; a quart of molasses, $6; a peck of potatoes, $5; a pound of flour, $1; and a pound of tobacco, $4.50.[15]

If high prices were a constant of prison life, so, too, was boredom. "All are marred and monotonized by the galling thought that we are and must continue to be prisoners of war," one Macon captive eloquently wrote. Observed another, "The continual wandering of the mind into vague reverie, untill it becomes a burden to itself, is wearisome in the extreme."[16]

The most certain cure for boredom, mail from home, apparently reached Macon only once, on June 14. According to veteran captive Alonzo Keeler, the prisoners had to pay $24 in express fees, but the price was well worth it. Keeler received two letters from his wife, the more recent written May 17. "All well," he noted. Albert Heffley of the 142nd Pennsylvania got one letter from his brother and two from a friend.[17]

The Macon prisoners held occasional religious gatherings, but as at other camps, divine services had to compete with secular activities. Although he attended an evening service on May 29, Heffelfinger complained, "I see no difference here between the Sabbath and the other days of the week." On July 20 Asa Mathews of the First Vermont Cavalry wrote, "In the evening we had a religious service in the moonlight which was an agreeable change." Four days later he wrote that preaching had not been well attended. He added, "In the afternoon I noticed they were playing cards on the same rough table where the minister's Bible lay an hour before. Men known as gentlemen at home do things here which our roughs would almost blush with shame at."[18]

Fights occasionally broke out between the captives confined at Macon. "It is indeed degrading for two officers to settle their troubles by pounding each other," Mattocks wrote, "yet it cannot be denied by the gravest philosophers that it is a more natural than refined method of proceeding." He blamed the resort to fisticuffs, which he termed "quite common," on the "demoralizing influence [of] this manner of life."[19]

Other prisoners engaged in more intellectual pursuits. Keeler took up chess while confined at Macon. Mattocks studied German, even keeping a separate diary in the language. One group of prisoners managed to purchase a set of encyclopedias between Virginia and Macon. The men selected a captain as librarian. When some prisoners found a copy of *Butler's Analogy of Religion,* they appointed a teacher and heard one lesson a day from the treatise. Newspapers were the most prized reading material for prisoners eager to learn about the progress of the war. They were generally allowed at the prison. On days that they were not, the captives speculated that the war news must be good for the Union. Those who could not afford to purchase papers gathered ten deep to hear the latest news read to them.[20]

One advantage the Macon prisoners had over the enlisted men confined at Andersonville was enough space to enjoy a certain amount of outdoor recreation. With some fifteen hundred officers confined in about four acres of ground, space was not abundant. Still, they had sufficient room to engage in fencing, cricket, and the youthful pursuit of "base ball." However, as one Macon prisoner later recalled, "Most of us chose to lie in the shade, wherever it could be found, discussing politics and the situation, at least until we were rested."[21]

On July 4 the prisoners risked the wrath of their captors to celebrate Independence Day. It began during morning roll call when one of the prisoners displayed a small American flag. This attracted a crowd, and soon the captives were singing "Rally 'round the Flag" and "The Star-Spangled Banner," as one prisoner noted, "with a spirit and hearty zeal." Another wrote, "The Reb. officers looked cross but did not disturb us then or attempt to take the flag."[22]

Already thus inspired, the officers called a meeting to be held in the largest barracks in the prison. A Connecticut chaplain offered a prayer to begin the gathering. That was followed by numerous songs and patriotic speeches. All the time the small flag was displayed prominently. The ceremony went on for some time before the Rebels finally put a stop to it. The officer of the day entered and informed the prisoners that Capt. Gibbs had ordered an end to the speechmaking. "The order was complied with," one prisoner wrote, "but not untill rousing cheers had been given for the Flag, for Abraham Lincoln, Gen. Grant, & the Emancipation Proclamation." During the evening hours the prisoners lit improvised fireworks made of pitch pine "and all seemed bent on fun." One officer concluded, "I never so heartily appreciated the '4th of July.'"[23]

A month earlier the Macon prisoners had held an election "to know the choice of the prisoners for the next President." Nine squads cast a total of 612 ballots. Lincoln was the clear choice for reelection, receiving 525 votes. The remaining 87 votes went to a "scattering" of candidates. Andrew Johnson, who became Lincoln's running mate, won the prison vote for vice president.[24]

Despite the results, not all prisoners were pleased with the policies of the Lincoln administration. This was particularly true when it came to the government's position on prisoner exchange. On June 21 a Catholic priest who had been to Andersonville visited the Macon prisoners and described the suffering he had seen. It was a situation, one wrote, "as will forever stigmatize our government."[25]

The next day a group of prisoners called upon the squads to select two men from each one hundred. The men selected were to choose a committee of four to visit Andersonville. From there they would carry a petition to the authorities in Washington demanding a resumption of exchange.

The action met with immediate and vociferous opposition. Heffelfinger felt the petition was "intimating that the rebels are right, and we wrong, in the question of exchange." Hurst added that most officers could not "see it in that light." Penfield simply dismissed the petitioners as "a few Copperheads." The opponents quickly organized a meeting, where a number of prisoners delivered "speeches full of true patriotism." The next day they circulated a counter petition, which reportedly secured "numerous signatures." There, if prison diaries are any indicator, the matter apparently died.[26]

The response of the Macon officers contrasted with the attitude at Andersonville, where the prisoners were somewhat less educated and the suffering was considerably worse. The enlisted prisoners directed much of their bitterness toward black captives, whose fate had doomed the exchange cartel. "We must stay here because they cant aggree [upon] some nigger question," Kendrick Howard complained. "There is a good deal of such talk here in camp." Samuel Gibson was even more vociferous, declaring, "I do not like an Administration that will not protect its citizen Soldiers when unfortunately prisoners of war. The everlasting *Nigger* must be protected and the soldier may take care of himself."[27]

Many prisoners at Andersonville expressed their frustrations without the racial component. "Men are dying verry fast in camp," George Crosby observed. "It seems barbarous for our govmt to let us stay here and die as we are now doing." William Peabody wrote, "If the Government dont get us out they may go to the Devil with Abraham Lincoln and his votes. I will not vote for him again, that is so." David Kennedy expressed a similar view, noting, "I do not think that our goverment can be so bace to hur men. If so my sincere wish is that our rulers was obliged to come heire & stop a while with us." At least one prisoner believed their government harbored more sinister motives. John Baer wrote, "I am not in the habit of complaining of anything the Administration does but I certainly [feel] they are doing wrong in sacrificing as many men as they are doing daily for the sake of keeping an overplus of rebels out of the field."[28]

Even Baer hesitated when some of the Andersonville prisoners, prodded by the Confederates, began circulating their own petition. It was to go to Lincoln and to the governors of all Union states. Baer did not believe that the action "would avail anything." He further believed the prison officials' motive was to "embarrass the [Northern] Government" and "cause them to exchange on rebel terms." Albert Shatzel complained, "Foolish men what the hell did they enlist for onley to serve their country & protect her rights & suffer the consequence, let them be what they will." Samuel Melvin felt differently, writing, "I hope they will send it, for it cannot do harm, & if it will do good, for the sake of humanity send it along." Eventually the petition was sent along, after some originally harsh language toward the Union government was modified. It resulted in the exchange of the six soldiers who delivered it.[29]

With exchange a dead letter, a number of Macon officers determined to escape. At least six made the effort even before Camp Oglethorpe was reopened. Capt. James Wenrick of the 180th Pennsylvania was captured at Cypress Swamp, Tennessee, on April 1, 1864. After a brief stay at Mobile, he and some six hundred other captives were sent away. The men were deposited at Andersonville. Wenrick and the other officers traveled on to Macon and were lodged in a dungeon in the city prison. Wenrick's cell was eight feet square. He shared it with five other officers. "Living not so good," he concluded.[30]

Wenrick's visitors included Gen. Cobb, who provided him with food and money and promised to secure his exchange. Despite this important connection, Wenrick and his cell mates determined to tunnel out. They sawed a hole in the floor on

May 10 and finished the project three days later. Three men made their departure the next night before the tunnel was apparently discovered. In any event, Wenrick wrote the next day, "Great excitement, hundreds come to see the hole." Orders were issued not to feed the officers in the cell. "Jailor pays no attention to it," Wenrick gratefully reported, "says he wishes we had all got out."[31]

More prisoners tried to fulfill the jailer's wish after they reached Camp Oglethorpe. As at other prisons, the tunnels were generally discovered before they could be put into use, "traitors" often receiving the blame. The Confederates found their first Macon tunnel on May 28. Prison diarists made only brief mention of the discovery, focusing instead on Tabb's threat to shoot anyone tardy for roll call.[32]

On the evening of June 26 three or four prisoners crawled under the fence, utilizing a ditch used as a sink. A sentry spotted one of them and fired. The Confederates beat the long roll and released the hounds but were unable to recapture the escapees. The next morning they confined the prisoners to the south side of the camp while they searched the north end for tunnels. They found three, one in a stable and the other two in barracks. According to one prisoner, the Confederates "went directly to them as if they knew all about them." Perhaps they did. "The Rebels say we have traitors among us, and can we think otherwise?" another asked.[33]

"Had a long tour of 'roll call' this evening," Templeton Hurst wrote on July 18. The cause was the discovery of another tunnel by the guards. As annoyed as Hurst may have been by the prolonged roll call, his disappointment paled beside that of Alonzo Keeler. The Wolverine soldier had planned to make his escape through the tunnel "as soon as the nights became dark."[34]

For some prisoners, subterfuge offered a better opportunity for escape than did tunneling. On June 30 a lieutenant went out with a guard detachment wearing a uniform he had fashioned from blankets. It is not clear whether he got away, but one prisoner noted that it was his third attempt. The next day a Confederate fatigue party closed up a failed escape tunnel. Two officers shouldered picks and attempted to walk out with the workers. They were detected before they could make good their escape. On July 6 a prisoner rode out of the yard after sneaking into a box on the sutler's wagon. Less successful was the prisoner who, on July 20, "blacked himself so as to have the appearance of a negro." He was just beyond the prison fence when he was detected and taken to jail.[35]

On June 10 fifty of the highest-ranking Macon prisoners were sent away by the Confederates to parts unknown. Included were all of the generals, colonels, and lieutenant colonels, plus nine majors. Many of those left behind assumed they were being exchanged, but the old Libby prisoners were dubious. "The guesses and rumors are wild and numerous," one prisoner observed. The departing prisoners were optimistic. "They went off in excellent spirits," Mattocks wrote, "and I hope they will not be disappointed in their expectations." Less charitably he added, "These Brigadiers are not a loss to us as they have acted like a set of old women throughout."[36]

Charleston proved to be their destination, but the Macon officers were not going there to be exchanged. Nine days earlier Gen. Samuel Jones, commanding Confederate forces at Charleston, had asked Richmond to send him fifty Yankee prisoners. Union batteries, under command of Gen. John G. Foster, were shelling Charleston from nearby Morris Island. Jones planned to confine the captives "in parts of the city still occupied by citizens, but under the enemy's fire." It was a remarkable request, one that clearly went against the rules of civilized warfare. President Davis approved nevertheless, and Gen. Cobb received orders to send fifty Union officers to Charleston.[37]

On the 13th Jones informed Foster that the prisoners had arrived at Charleston "for safe-keeping." They had been sent to "a part of the city occupied by noncombatants, the majority of whom are women and children." Then, as if an afterthought, Jones added, "It is proper, however, that I should inform you that it is a part of the city which has been for many months exposed day and night to the fire of your guns." Far from being intimidated, Foster responded that he was shipping his own human shields to Morris Island. The incident reflected honor on neither side, but it eventually resulted in the exchange of all the officers.[38]

By July Winder was ready to forward all the Macon prisoners to Charleston. With Sherman approaching Atlanta, he first sought permission on the 13th. Five days later he elaborated. "The prison at Macon is not secure and will take great expense and labor to make it so," he wrote. Furthermore, it was located near factories and railroad depots that would be likely targets of escaping prisoners. Finally, in what was perhaps a telling statement, Winder explained, "It is in an unhealthy locality, to which our troops ought not to be exposed." The War Department apparently gave its approval, because on July 26 Gen. Jones objected to them being sent to Charleston. Their presence, he worried, would complicate the negotiations to exchange those already sent.[39]

On the afternoon of July 27, despite Jones's objections, six hundred Macon prisoners received orders to prepare to leave for Charleston. The trains began pulling out at 4:00 the next morning. Fifty officers and two guards crowded into each boxcar under conditions one prisoner described as "intolerably hot." Some reached Charleston before midnight, others later the following morning.[40]

Cyrus Heffley estimated that seventy-eight prisoners escaped from the trains as they chugged through Georgia and South Carolina. One of them was James Love, who got away just as his train arrived at Charleston. He was free for six days, covering some thirty miles through the South Carolina swamps. Then a farmer who was out raccoon hunting discovered Love's tracks in a cornfield. He put his dogs on the trail and soon had Love in his custody. Francis Sherman and four other officers jumped from the cars between Savannah and Charleston. They were out less than a day before hounds, this time belonging to a slave patrol, overtook them.[41]

Twenty-four hours after the first detachment left Macon, another group boarded the cars, "as anxious as little boys," one of them wrote. This second batch was bound for Savannah, where they were to be confined in a hospital yard. Along the way they were permitted to buy watermelons from citizens. Plenty were available for those who could afford the purchase price of $1. The trains reached the coastal city that evening, attracting a great deal of attention. "A large crowd of men, women, and children, both white and black, are staring at us," Heffelfinger wrote.[42]

After passing under the gazing eyes of the Savannah citizenry, the newly arrived officers entered their new prison yard. Their first impressions were positive. For one, the hospital grounds contained several large shade trees. More important, the rations were more bountiful and of better quality than they had been at Macon. On August 1 the prisoners received hardtack. Although few Civil War soldiers had anything good to say about the tasteless crackers, impervious to the teeth, one of the newly arrived captives termed them "a luxury." The next day the Confederates issued fresh beef, "which was so much of a rarity the whole company was thrown into a perfect jollification meeting," wrote Asa Mathews. The Vermonter further noted that Confederate officials in Savannah were so short of supplies that local citizens were helping to feed the prisoners.[43]

The officers were less pleased with their quarters. One small tent was issued for every six men. In addition, the prisoners complained that the yard itself was less roomy than the compound at Macon. "We are confined in a small enclosure, which had been hastily prepared for our reception," one wrote. Water was also a source of concern. James Wenrick asserted that it was "so bad we can not drink it at all." After the Confederates installed a hydrant it got better but remained muddy. Hurst was less charitable, writing that the water was still "most wretched."[44]

During the night of July 30, the prisoners' second night in Savannah, heavy thunderstorms produced flooding rains that drove several of them out of their tents. Frequent shots and cries for the corporal of the guard also punctuated the night. Morning revealed that a number of Yankees were gone, having taken advantage of the storm to dig under the fence and escape. The Confederates soon adopted a policy of lighting fires just inside the prison walls at night "so the sentinels can see all the deviltry," one prisoner surmised.[45]

The captives' next escape attempt was apparently foiled by a loyal Confederate cow. According to Edward C. Anderson, the Southern officer in charge of Savannah's military prisons, the effort was made during the night of August 7–8. The tunnel, Anderson noted, passed under the enclosure and out to an adjoining street. One prisoner wrote that dozens of his comrades were preparing to make their exit. The mass escape was prevented when the bovine walked over the tunnel, collapsing it with her weight. A Savannah newspaper story matched Anderson's account of the incident. It was also confirmed by the postwar memoirs of Lt. John Ogden of the First Wisconsin Cavalry, who insisted that the cow had been sent "by some evil spirit."[46]

Anderson was even less amused by the incident. He directed that the tents be removed, an action Heffelfinger characterized as "a mean, contemptible trick." The officer of the day also searched the camp for more tunnels. He found two, both nearly completed. This ended the tunneling temporarily, but by the end of the month the prisoners were ready to try again. Once again, fate intervened. The tents were apparently back, because on the evening of the 26th a guard entered one, hoping to sell a shirt to a prisoner. By this means he discovered the latest tunnel. This time two of the leaders soon found themselves in a local jail.[47]

When not digging tunnels, the prisoners passed the time as best they could. Boredom, however, usually prevailed. "This day has passed with nought of interest save one little knock-down between two things known as officers," Asa Mathews wrote on August 4. On Sundays the proximity of local houses of worship added homesickness to the dullness. "This being Sunday I wish more to be at home than any week-day," one sadly noted. "Just now a church bell has started that sounds very much like our Lutheran church bell." Another prisoner on another Sabbath reflected, "This morning, as the sound of church bells struck my ear, my mind wandered afar, to my northern home, and thoughts of pleasant hours in years gone by crowded thick and fast upon me."[48]

Chaplains filled the spiritual void—if not the emotional one—by holding services for their fellow captives. The meetings were not limited to Sundays. "The chaplains held forth with zeal and energy," a prisoner wrote of a Friday evening service. The situation changed on September 2 when both the chaplains and the surgeons, a total of nine prisoners, were sent away for exchange. Officers who had been preachers in civilian life took their place. They proved to be "not very powerful speakers but good enough for our use," one prisoner observed.[49]

During at least one evening a group of prisoners gathered to sing a round of patriotic songs. One of them noted with satisfaction that, when singing "Rally 'round the Flag," the captives put great emphasis on the word "traitor." Although the camp was crowded, the prisoners found room to play a game called "wicket." One mess erected "a gymnasium pole" as a means of exercise. Groups of prisoners also pooled their resources to purchase books and magazines. Mathews first passed the time carving out chess pieces. A shoemaker in civilian life, he then turned his attention to making himself a pair of slippers. Lacking tools, he observed, "Of course I made slow progress, like Grant before Richmond."[50]

On August 20 a different type of diversion broke the monotony. The Confederates sent in a group of female slaves with shovels to fill in an old prison sink. Attracted by curiosity, several prisoners gathered to watch the women work. "Coming by Augusta, Ga, we saw girls ploughing," one wrote. "That amused us but that beat that." Added another, "The sight was quite a novelty to nearly all of the prisoners and did not increase their good opinions of slavery, that 'divine institution.'"[51]

Savannah's role as a military prison changed dramatically on September 8, when fifteen hundred Yankees arrived from Andersonville. It was the first of what would prove to be numerous detachments. Five days later, beginning at 4:00 A.M., the officers boarded trains for Charleston. The prisoners received the announcement of their imminent departure with cheering. As one explained, "Great rejoicing about it all are glad to go somewhere."[52]

The prisoners already sent from Macon to Charleston had spent their first two weeks in the city's jail yard. The yard was crowded, and the water was brackish. Cyrus Heffley described the officers' new companions as "[d]eserters, murderers, horse thieves, public women, in fact all classes of men except gentlemen." Like the fifty high-ranking officers who had arrived from Macon in June, the new arrivals were in the path of Union artillery. None struck their new home, but many fell close. At least one exploded over "the Generals enclosure," but nobody was injured. On August 3 the fifty high-ranking officers left to be exchanged. Before departing, they donated "sundry articles" to those left behind.[53]

The Charleston Confederates issued tents to the arriving prisoners. According to Alonzo Keeler, the rations were also better than those at Macon. The August 1 allotment included fresh beef, flour, and salt, all in sufficient quantities. "Men never felt better over their rations," Keeler wrote. The next day the Confederates issued wheat bread, the first soft bread the prisoners had received in nine months.[54]

The lot of the Charleston prisoners improved considerably on August 13, when detachments began to be moved to two Charleston hospitals. The greater number, some three hundred, went to Roper Hospital. A smaller number occupied the adjacent Marine Hospital. The Confederates required both groups to sign paroles agreeing not to escape. In return the officers acquired better quarters and the freedom to move around the hospital grounds. "It is a fine airy building with a Three Story Piazza all around, with a good yard, built on the center of the lot, and encircled with fine Shade trees," James Love wrote of the Marine Hospital. The rations continued to be acceptable, consisting of fresh beef, cornmeal, flour, rice, and salt. The Confederates also provided camp kettles and pans for cooking. Charles Mattocks, who had spent time at Lynchburg, Macon, and the Charleston jail, wrote that Roper offered "by far the best quarters occupied by any prisoners in the Confederacy."[55]

Indeed, the main drawback to life in the two Charleston hospitals came from the prisoners' own army. Their new quarters were much closer to the targets of Gen. Foster's shells than the jail yard was. The intensity increased during the last week of August. Fragments occasionally fell into the hospitals' yards, and a few found their way into the prison quarters. Nobody was badly injured, although a Roper prisoner suffered a slight wound to the arm. One captive claimed that his comrades viewed the shells in a positive manner. "Every federal officer there felt glad as he heard them growling up town," Nathaniel Rollins wrote soon after being paroled. "He felt that each one screamed in the ears of every rebel *There's no rest for the wicked.*"[56]

It was not merely humanitarian impulses that led the Confederates in Charleston to send the prisoners to improved quarters. It had become a matter of necessity. The Savannah officers were on their way to the city, and there was not enough room in the jail yard. They arrived as Foster's guns were growing more active, delivering their rounds at the rate of about one every fifteen minutes. A shell fragment wounded a prisoner on the 17th.[57]

The newly arrived prisoners also suffered from both the sun and the rain. On a very warm September 22, Hurst wrote, "I am sitting under a shelter of 3 poles forked together, and a blanket thrown over; shade enough for two." This sunny day followed three days of rainy weather. During that period the Confederates allowed the captives to take shelter in the jail during the night. They escaped the rain, but conditions inside were hardly ideal. "Mice, rats, cock-roaches, lice, fleas and 'kindred cattle' infested our beds, while the stench was anything but pleasant," one wrote. "Still it was better than out in the drenching rain." They enjoyed this privilege only at night, however, and all day on the 20th the officers had to remain in a yard flooded with water.[58]

In late September, as the prisoners occupying the hospitals prepared to depart for Columbia, the officers transferred from Savannah left the jail yard. Some went to the two hospitals. Between eighty and ninety ended up in a large, three-story dwelling near the Ashley River. Like those who had come before, the prisoners were happy with the change. One who went to the Roper Hospital wrote, "Transferred from jail Yard to 'Paradise.'" The men in the house were in Foster's line of fire, but they complained more about the omnipresent mosquitoes. Their greatest luxury was a saltwater bathhouse. As Heffelfinger observed, "We can keep neat and clean here, a great item by the way."[59]

In early October these prisoners also left Charleston for Columbia. The South Carolina capital was already housing 239 Union captives, including 132 officers. The officers were in the city jail, along with criminals and Confederate deserters. The enlisted men occupied the jail yard, a "rotten wood fence" providing security. Guards patrolled each side of the fence, but as one inspector noted, "Sentinels, upon examination, exhibit considrable ignorance as to their instructions." Indeed, the entire arrangement reflected the lack of coordination of Confederate prison policy. The same inspector reported, "There is no order establishing a regular military prison for prisoners of war. Prisoners have been turned over, from time to time."[60]

Officials in Columbia felt that enough had been turned over, and they did not want any more. Governor Milledge L. Bonham protested to Secretary Seddon and to Gen. William J. Hardee, commanding the Department of South Carolina, Georgia, and Florida. Eventually he called upon President Davis to order the project stopped. The location, he wrote, was not healthy. He further complained that the prison would increase the probability of enemy raids. Mayor T. J. Goodwin went immediately to the top, forwarding a petition signed by local residents to Davis. The mayor was less concerned about the presence of the Yankees than he was about their ability to purchase food items from the sutler. This, he protested, made it more difficult—and considerably more expensive—for Confederate civilians and soldiers to secure provisions. Confederate captives in Northern prisons, he correctly pointed out, had been denied the privilege of making such purchases. All the protests went for naught. A yellow fever outbreak in Charleston made it impossible to keep the prisoners there any longer. With the Confederacy shrinking, there were fewer options for prison locations. Local concerns notwithstanding, Columbia would have to do.[61]

Gen. Jones sent the Charleston prisoners with no advance warning. Capt. E. A. Semple had been sent from Richmond with orders to establish a prison near Columbia. Instead, he found himself responsible for sixteen hundred Yankee officers despite being "in want of almost everything necessary for their accomodation." The prisoners were painfully aware of Semple's predicament. "At Columbia . . . the rebel authorities were taken entirely by surprise by our coming," one prisoner later wrote. "They kept us at the depot a day and a night trying to determine what should be done with so many yankees." The officers remained in the boxcars overnight, unable to stretch out and secure rest. They got out the next morning, only to be soaked by a heavy rain that lasted all afternoon. The next morning Heffelfinger wrote, "We are a forlorn looking twelve hundred. Rained hard last night soaking blankets, rations and muddling things generally."[62]

Finally the Confederates found a "high piece of waste land" some three miles west of town. Those lucky enough to have blankets improvised shelters with stakes. Others did the best they could with pine boughs. The news was not all bad. Remarkably, boxes from home and clothing from the Sanitary Commission had reached Columbia. "A box, well filled, is a prize indeed in our present situation," one prisoner wrote. James Love may have agreed, but his box was not well filled. Tinware and clothing remained. Expected food and money were missing.[63]

Rations were worse in both quality and quantity than they had been at Charleston. Nathaniel Rollins later wrote, "Five days rations for one man consisted of about two quarts of corn meal usually a little less, one table spoon full of salt, from a pint to a quart of sorghum molasses and sometimes a gill of rice and still more seldom a gill of flour." As at Andersonville, the cornmeal was often ground cob and all. "Sorghum is issued to us plentifully," Hurst wrote. Indeed, the quantities were so great that the prisoners eventually christened the facility Camp Sorghum. Meat was entirely lacking from the prisoners' diets. One insisted that he received none between October 6 and December 9. A Confederate inspector partially confirmed that assertion, reporting on October 26 that no meat had yet been issued. He warned that if the situation was not remedied, escapes were sure to follow. On October 24 the prisoners secured a meat ration on their own when a wild boar made the mistake of wandering into the camp. "He died in a good cause," one prisoner insisted.[64]

Cold weather arrived in Columbia at about the same time as the Yankees. As early as October 9 the prisoners awoke to frost on the ground. Temperatures remained low for the next five nights. Despite the conditions, it was about three weeks before the prisoners were allowed to go out for wood. They fetched not only firewood but pine logs with which to construct crude shelters. The going was slow. Only a few were allowed out at a time. A shortage of axes also limited the amount of work that could get done. Still, the men took a great deal of pride in their projects. "Finished house to-day, chimney draws splendidly," Hurst reported on November 9. Members of a different mess took their chimney building so seriously that a dispute over the project resulted in a fistfight.[65]

The wood details also provided the prisoners with an opportunity to escape. However, security at the camp was such that several attempted to get away well before the details began. Lt. Col. R. Stark Means, a physically disabled soldier, was in command of the camp. An inspecting officer wrote of him, "He is an efficient officer, attentive to his duties." The inspector added, "The guard is composed of very raw recruits both as to the officers and men, and require constant watching and instruction."[66]

The first escape attempt at Columbia occurred on the night of October 12. Among those absconding was a captain who had escaped from the train between Charleston and Columbia. He had been at the camp just one day after being recaptured. It is not known whether he made it this time, but a number of the escapees did not. Several, in fact, returned within forty-eight hours. Six nights later another group of prisoners made a dash for freedom. Four or five shots rang out, as did cries of "Fall in guard" and "Load the cannon." The latter made those remaining more than a bit nervous. "The idea of being blown to atoms by a charge of canister from a gun in the hands of frightened militia is not a pleasant one," a prisoner explained.[67]

The next attempt took place between 7:00 and 8:00 on the evening of the 26th. According to one of the prisoners involved, two got away. However, the commotion attracted the guards' attention, and they opened fire. None of the escapees were hit, but a stray bullet struck and killed a guard occupying a nearby tent.[68]

Once the wood details began, the prisoners realized that they had an excellent opportunity to fool their novice guards. All they had to do was insist that they were paroled as members of work parties. "The guard became negligent where almost anyone could go out without being questioned," a prison diarist wrote. Others claimed that bribery worked equally well, one explaining, "The guard consisted of old men and little boys, none of them seeming to have either knowledge of or sympathy with their cause. Two dollars in greenbacks or a set of brass buttons would buy them." November 3 and 4 witnessed a large number of escapes. One prisoner estimated that 275 got away during those two days. On the 4th Hurst wrote, "About 100 got off [yesterday] it is presumed. Many are going out now (5 P.M.). At least 150 officers have struck out to-day."[69]

Exchange rumors reduced the number of escape attempts for the next two weeks. Then, once again, the disappointed officers came to realize that they were the victims of spurious reports. "Since the exchange rumors have died away, escapes are all the go," one wrote on the 21st. As before, some resorted to bribery while others told the guards they were on parole to get wood. On the 24th a group of prisoners used forged hospital papers to leave the enclosure before officials discovered the ploy. Two days later both Keeler and Heffelfinger estimated that over 100 had walked past the guard, claiming to be on parole. "Quite a number have made their escape since the 3rd and 4th," Cyrus Heffley wrote on November 27, "and but comparatively few have been recaptured, at least not more than are daily escaping." He put the total number of escapees at 550, leaving 1,050 prisoners at Columbia. James Penfield placed the number of escapes at 400 and the prison population at 1,132. On December 6, following an inspection trip to Columbia, Gen. Winder reported that 373 prisoners had escaped from Camp Sorghum. The end of November marked the end of mass escapes. In early December the Confederates secured some sixty slaves to gather wood for the prisoners.[70]

Although the majority of escapees got away unchallenged, there was at least one tragic exception. On the evening of November 26 Lt. Thomas Ekings of the Third New Jersey was shot and killed during an escape attempt. Prison diarists disagreed over details, but according to most accounts, another man was wounded.[71]

Despite the inexperience of the Camp Sorghum guards—or perhaps because of it—shootings were rare at the prison. The first to be noted in prison diaries occurred on October 21. Although some of the captives expressed doubt, most accepted the guard's assertion that the shooting was accidental. The victim died a few minutes later.[72]

The prisoners had a far different opinion of a December 1 shooting. All who wrote of the incident insisted that the guard fired without provocation. The victim was going out for wood, and according to Hurst, "The 'sentinel' halted him and *shot at the same time.*" Other prisoners insisted that the victim had not yet reached the deadline when the guard fired. One simply wrote, "A Lt. of the 66th N.Y. murdered by a guard."[73]

In late November Winder was determined to relocate the prison at Columbia. He sought permission from Richmond to erect a stockade fourteen miles north of the South Carolina capital. Until it was finished he proposed to house the Yankee officers on the grounds of the state's male "lunatic asylum." Governor Bonham, after some initial hesitation, asked the board of regents to allow Winder use of the facility. On December 2 the board gave its approval.[74]

At noon on December 12 the Camp Sorghum prisoners began the march, some two or three miles, to their new quarters. A lucky few, about two hundred in number, ended up inside a two-story building. Among them was Hurst, who was crowded into a room with thirty-four other prisoners. There was barely space to lie down, he complained, but the benefits outweighed the inconveniences. "Here we are beside a good warm fire," he wrote. Hurst acknowledged that he and his comrades were in a "good position." He added, "Oh we will hold on to it at all hazards, this kind of weather."[75]

The rest of the prisoners were outside, surrounded by three brick walls and a plank wall that separated them from the asylum buildings. On the 13th the Confederates began issuing wood to the prisoners, with which they were to build shelters. Plans called for the buildings to be twenty-four feet square, each to house thirty-six. Lumber, however, was hard to come by, and the progress on the shelters was slow. Winder visited the camp on the 22nd, and according to one prisoner, "affected much sympathy for our suffering. Said we must have lumber at once for our buildings." Despite the general's concern, some messes did not get their shanties finished until January. Meanwhile, the Yankees had to endure cold, rainy weather. Conditions often forced them to exercise to keep warm. Others pooled their blankets and slept in reliefs.[76]

As their officers tried to keep warm at Columbia, the enlisted prisoners were enduring even worse conditions in a variety of pens in Georgia, North Carolina, and South Carolina. The Confederacy was contracting, leaving Richmond with fewer options for dealing with its prisoners. As Sherman continued to advance, those options became even fewer. It was a situation that would have taxed the abilities—and the patience—of even the most capable military administrator. In the last summer of the Confederacy there was still no such administrator. In late July Richmond placed Gen. Winder in charge of all prisons in Georgia and Alabama. Gen. William Gardner was to supervise all other prisons east of the Mississippi. The move was a step in the right direction, but a small one. Winder's day-to-day problems at Andersonville left him precious little time to deal with overall prison policy. Soon, he would have to devote almost all his attention to constructing a new pen at Millen, Georgia. Confederate prisons would continue to function on an ad hoc basis, and the prisoners would continue to pay the price.[77]

11
"A disagreeable dilemma"
Black Captives in Blue

In July 1862 the U.S. Congress approved the enlistment of black soldiers into the American armed forces. Two months later President Lincoln announced his intention to enforce his Emancipation Proclamation beginning January 1, 1863. Both changed the nature of the war. Both also had a drastic effect on Union and Confederate prison policies—as well as the captives affected by those policies.

At first, however, Lincoln treaded carefully. Congress had given him the authority "to employ as many persons of African descent as he may deem necessary." The president could "organize and use them in such manner as he may judge best for the public welfare." This left the details clearly in the hands of the executive branch, where many factors had to be considered. High among them were the feelings of the loyal border states, where slavery was still legal. Privately Lincoln also expressed doubts about the capabilities of black soldiers. As a result, blacks entering the Union army were at first limited to garrison duties well behind the lines. His views gradually moderated, however, and by early 1863 the president was ready to allow blacks to help secure the freedom that he had formally proclaimed.[1]

The Confederate response was predictably vociferous. On December 23, 1863, President Davis issued a proclamation declaring that "all negro slaves captured in arms" be delivered to the governors of the states "to which they belong." Their commissioned officers were to meet the same fate. He reiterated those points three weeks later in his annual message to the Confederate Congress. On May 1 the Congress approved a resolution not only sustaining Davis's position but taking Confederate policy even further. The legislators asserted that the Union policies of emancipation and enlisting black soldiers would "bring on a servile war [and] would if successful produce atrocious consequences." Their resolution echoed the

Davis position of returning captured slaves to the states. As for their officers, they would be "deemed as inciting servile insurrection, and shall if captured be put to death or otherwise punished at the discretion of the court." Significantly, the policy applied not only to officers leading ex-slaves but to anyone "employ[ing] negroes in war against the Confederate States."[2]

The Union and Confederate positions in this regard could not be reconciled. If they could have been, there may not have been a war to begin with. Later in the conflict Robert E. Lee and Ulysses S. Grant summed up these positions succinctly in an exchange of messages. Writing on October 19, 1864, Lee stated, "The right to the service or labor of negro slaves in the Confederate States is the same now as when those States were members of the Federal Union. The constitutional relations and obligations of the Confederate Government to the owners of this species of property are the same as those so frequently and so long recognized as appertaining to the Government of the United States with reference to the same class of persons by virtue of its organic law." To this Grant replied, "[I] regard it my duty to protect all persons received into the Army of the United States, regardless of color or nationality. When acknowledged soldiers of the Government are captured they must be treated as prisoners of war." In a strictly legal sense, putting all moral considerations aside, each general presented a strong case. It was simply an issue to which there could be no compromise. That meant the fate of black Union captives would have to depend on the outcome of the war.[3]

Until the war ended the fate of individual black prisoners depended much more upon the attitudes of Confederate officers and men on particular battlefields. This did not bode well for the soldiers of the United States Colored Troops (USCT). In a letter home, famously quoted by historian Bell I. Wiley, one Confederate soldier summed up the feelings of many of his comrades. The soldier wrote, "I hope I may never see a Negro Soldier or I cannot be . . . a Christian Soldier."[4]

Among the first places such feelings were demonstrated was Milliken's Bend, a federal supply base along the Mississippi in Louisiana. Confederates attacked it on June 7, 1863, hoping to disrupt Grant's siege of Vicksburg. The attack failed, but in the aftermath, Adm. David D. Porter found evidence that the Confederates had exacted a measure of vengeance against Union black troops. "The dead negroes lined the ditch inside of the parapet, or levee, and were mostly shot on the top of the head," Porter wrote.[5]

Gen. Richard Taylor, commanding the District of Louisiana, whose troops led the attack, wrote in his after-action report, "A very large number of the negroes were killed and wounded, and, unfortunately, some 50, with 2 of their white officers, were captured." Gen. Edmund Kirby Smith, who commanded the Trans-

Mississippi Department, also considered the capture of the black troops unfortunate. In a message to Taylor he wrote, "I have been unofficially informed that some of your troops have captured negroes in arms. I hope this may not be so, and that your subordinates who may have been in command of capturing parties may have recognized the propriety of giving no quarter to armed negroes and their officers. In this way we may be relieved from a disagreeable dilemma."[6]

The Confederate War Department, at least officially, did not approve of Smith's solution to the "dilemma" posed by black captives. On July 13 Richmond informed him that "a different policy than that suggested by you is recommended. Considering the negroes as deluded victims, they should be received and treated with mercy and returned to their owners." The message concluded, "A few examples might perhaps be made, but to refuse them quarter would only make them, against their tendencies, fight desperately."[7]

Reports soon reached Grant that a few examples had already been made following the fight at Milliken's Bend. In a message to Taylor, Grant reported that "a white man, a citizen of the South" had informed him that "some negroes" and a white sergeant had been hanged after the fight. He hoped that there had been "some mistake in the evidence." However, Grant assured Taylor that if it was the policy of any general "to punish with death prisoners taken in battle, I will accept the issue." In response, Taylor denied any knowledge of such "acts disgraceful alike to humanity and to the reputation of soldiers." He also promised to investigate the matter. Taylor's denial satisfied Grant, and there the matter rested for the time being.[8]

Three weeks later Confederate cavalry, under the command of Col. William Henry Parsons, attacked a small Union fortification not far from Milliken's Bend. Located atop a prehistoric Indian burial mound, the fort was in a strong position. The three white officers agreed to surrender on the condition that they be treated as prisoners of war. They surrendered their force of 113 black soldiers unconditionally. Parsons agreed to the terms. His division commander, Gen. John G. Walker, sustained him in the decision, although he wrote, "I consider it an unfortunate circumstance that any armed negroes were captured." Apparently some of Parsons's men felt the same way. One reported to his family that some twelve to fifteen black soldiers "died" as they were being escorted to the Confederate camp.[9]

In early August 1863, "several eye-witnesses" informed Gen. George Andrews, commanding Union forces at Port Hudson, Louisiana, of another incident involving black prisoners. According to their testimony, Confederates were guilty of hanging black Union soldiers following a skirmish at Jackson, Louisiana. Andrews called upon Col. John L. Logan, Confederate commander at Jackson, to "disavow these acts and punish the perpetrators." Logan denied any knowledge of black prisoners being hanged, although he made no mention of investigating the report.[10]

Logan may have been sincere in his denial. In any event, when he learned later of black prisoners being shot after the same battle, he expressed outrage. Logan demanded reports from Col. John Griffith and Col. Frank Powers, both of whom commanded cavalry regiments in the fight. In remarkably similar responses, Griffith and Powers wrote that the black prisoners had been separated from the "Federal prisoners" after capture. The black captives started out the next morning, under guard, at the front of the column. Somehow the two officers learned that the troopers guarding the prisoners had taken a wrong road. Griffith and Powers rode ahead to put them on the proper route. As they arrived, some of the blacks attempted to escape. "I ordered the guard to shoot them down," Powers wrote. "In the confusion the other negroes attempted to escape likewise. I then ordered every one shot, and with my six shooter assisted in the execution of the order." Logan was skeptical of the reports. He informed Gen. Stephen D. Lee, commanding Confederate cavalry in Mississippi, "My own opinion is that the negroes were summarily disposed of." He added, "The whole transaction was contrary to my wishes and against my own consent." Despite Logan's views, Lee concluded, "Do not consider it to the interest of the service that this matter be further investigated."[11]

The Union defeat at the battle of Poison Spring, Arkansas, on April 18, 1864, led to more reports of racial atrocities. Among the units involved in the fight were the First and Second Kansas Colored Infantry. Both outfits comprised runaway slaves from Missouri and Arkansas. Once again, the Confederates were not inclined to take black prisoners. Maj. R. G. Ward of the First Kansas wrote that "the rebels were seen shooting those that fell into their hands." More evidence of killings based on race was recorded by the victorious Confederates. One bragged that "at least 400 darkies were killed. [N]o black prisoners were captured." Wrote another, "Let me tell you, I never expected to see as many dead Negroes. . . . They were so thick you could walk on them." More evidence was provided by the fact that the First Kansas suffered 117 killed but only sixty-five wounded.[12]

One week later, at the battle of Marks' Mills, Arkansas, Confederate cavalry scooped up thirteen hundred Union soldiers, three hundred escaped slaves, and a number of refugees from Arkansas. After the battle, Lt. Col. Francis M. Drake of the Thirty-sixth Iowa reported that both the slaves and the refugees "were inhumanly butchered by the enemy, and among them my own negro servant." A junior officer from the same regiment wrote, "There was not an armed negro with us &

they shot down our Colored servants & teamsters & others that were following to get from bondage as they would shoot sheep dogs."[13]

In the eastern theater the fall of Plymouth, North Carolina, which produced so many Andersonville prisoners, led to a variety of charges from a surviving black soldier. Sgt. Samuel Johnson of the First U.S. Colored Cavalry quickly removed his blue uniform and put on civilian clothing when he learned that the garrison was to be surrendered. Sent to Richmond, he escaped to Union lines, where he told his story. It was a graphic account. According to Johnson, the Confederates shot, hanged, or beat to death every black man taken wearing a Union uniform. There was no one to corroborate his story, and at least one piece of Confederate correspondence casts some doubt on it. On April 21 Gen. Braxton Bragg informed Governor Zebulon Vance of North Carolina that black prisoners captured at Plymouth would be turned over to the state.[14]

The racial incident best remembered—and most controversial—in Civil War annals is the "Fort Pillow Massacre." Some 570 Union soldiers made up the Tennessee garrison on the Mississippi River. Just under half were black. On April 12, 1864, Gen. Nathan Bedford Forrest's troopers captured the fort. When it was all over, nearly one-third of the fort's blue-clad defenders, most of them black, lay dead. A congressional committee concluded that "at least 300" Union soldiers had been murdered. Although this was clearly an exaggeration, more dispassionate studies leave little doubt that Union soldiers, black and white, were killed after they had surrendered.[15]

Blacks who survived to become prisoners faced the specter of slavery or some form of forced labor at the hands of the Confederates. It had long been a matter of law in the states that formed the Confederacy that blacks lacking papers certifying their freedom were assumed to be slaves. In June 1863 Secretary Seddon also made this the formal policy of the Confederate military.

To at least some Confederates, there was no need to wait for Seddon's announcement. On January 1, 1863, Confederates captured the Union garrison at Galveston, Texas. Among those taken prisoner were Charles Fairfax Revaleon and Charles Gerrish Amos, black residents of Massachusetts. The two young cousins—Amos was sixteen—had been acting as servants to officers of the Forty-second Massachusetts. Their captors took them to Houston, where they were sold. The two came from a prominent family, and when word of their fate reached the Bay State, Governor John Andrew became personally involved. The War Department offered him little satisfaction, reporting that only "success in the war" could secure their freedom. The story had a happy ending, however. Success in the war eventually came, and in June 1865 Revaleon and Amos returned home.[16]

Even in the North, most black families did not have a friend in the governor's mansion. Therefore most cases of Union soldiers returned to masters or sold into slavery did not find their way into government reports. Records that do survive suggest that logistical roadblocks made it very difficult to "restore" slaves taken in battle. In May 1864 Secretary Seddon received word that black prisoners held at Andersonville came from Virginia and North Carolina. With this news came a request that they be sent to Raleigh, making it easier for their former masters to claim them. With both Grant and Sherman in motion against Confederate armies, the demands on the South's rail network were too great, and Seddon denied the request.[17]

Slaves from Andersonville were apparently returned to their masters from time to time. On June 5, 1864, Henry Wirz informed the assistant commissioner of exchange at Cahaba that "the two slaves mentioned are here." He could not return them to Cahaba without an order from the War Department. Instead, Wirz suggested that the owner make an application to the secretary of war stating that the slaves were his. "This has been done often before," Wirz explained. "All the owner will have to procure is an affidavit, sworn & subscribed before a justice of the peace that the negroes in question are his property."[18]

In October 1864 Gen. Dabney H. Maury, commanding the District of the Gulf, placed a circular in the *Mobile Advertiser and Register* listing the names of 575 black prisoners. A similar notice, containing 569 names, appeared a few weeks later. The captives, representing three USCT regiments, had been captured by Forrest in late September and put to work on the defenses of Mobile. Maury's intent was not to return the slaves to their masters. Rather, those masters were invited to "receive the pay due them" for their slaves' labor.[19]

Gen. Gordon Granger, commanding the Union's District of West Florida and South Alabama, informed Gen. Maury that he had "conclusive information" that the prisoners had been put to labor. Maury replied that the captives in question had been "taken away from their homes and their lawful owners by invading parties of U.S. forces." Although they had been put to work, they were "well fed and generally content in their present situation." These slaves, he further asserted, "express an utmost reluctance and indisposition to be restored to the dominion of the United States . . . and are earnest in their desire to return to their lawful owners, from whom they were unwillingly taken away."[20]

This opinion was evidently not unanimous. Joseph Howard of the Tenth USCT escaped from Mobile by stealing a skiff and navigating it to a Federal gunboat in

Mobile Bay. Far from being "generally content," Howard insisted, "We were kept at hard labor and inhumanly treated." Specifically, the prisoners were whipped "for the slightest causes." Often their fellow prisoners were required to inflict the lashes. Howard also contradicted Maury's claim that the laborers were well fed, saying the rations were "corn-meal and mule meat, and occasionally some poor beef."[21]

Black prisoners were also put to work on trenches in the vicinity of Richmond. According to Thomas Turner, eighty-two were sent from prisons under his command. Another sixty-eight went from Castle Thunder. Union officials learned of the practice on October 12, 1864, from four Confederate deserters. Two of them added that the prisoners were so poorly fed that they had traded clothes and shoes for food. Their reports soon reached Gen. Benjamin Butler, who was serving as the Union's commissioner of exchange. Butler informed his Confederate counterpart, Robert Ould, that he was placing a like number of prisoners to hard labor on the Dutch Gap Canal. It was this situation that led to the exchange between Generals Grant and Lee, with Lee insisting that only prisoners who had been identified as slaves were being utilized as laborers.[22]

On July 16, 1863, the black soldiers of the Fifty-fourth Massachusetts had their baptism of fire. In fighting on James Island in Charleston Harbor, the regiment, destined to become the most storied black outfit of the war, fought well. When the day's action ended, the Fifty-fourth had lost fourteen men killed and eighteen wounded. Thirteen had been taken prisoner. Those thirteen posed a problem for Gen. Johnson Hagood, commanding at "Secessionville." "What shall I do with them?" Hagood asked Capt. William F. Nance, the assistant adjutant general. The decision was to send them away from Charleston, "under a strong guard, without their uniform."[23]

The prisoners ended up in Castle Pinckney, beginning an odyssey that tested the meaning of Confederate policy toward black captives. On the 18th, following the failed assault upon Battery Wagner, the Confederates held about a hundred more prisoners from the Fifty-fourth. Meanwhile Gen. P. G. T. Beauregard, commanding the Department of South Carolina, Georgia, and Florida, was trying to determine their proper disposition. On the 17th he informed the War Department that several claimed to be free. "Shall they be turned over to State authorities with the other negroes?" he asked. Four days later he had not received an answer. "What shall be done with the negro prisoners who say they are free? Please answer," he implored.[24]

It was the type of problem that a commissary general of prisoners would have been qualified to handle; and it was yet another example of the difficulties the South encountered by not appointing one. Into the void stepped Governor Milledge I. Bonham of South Carolina. The day after he sent his plea for guidance to Richmond, Beauregard heard from both Seddon and Bonham. The governor insisted that the black prisoners be turned over to him. To bolster his argument, he sent the war secretary a copy of a state law that placed anyone leading a slave insurrection under the jurisdiction of South Carolina. Seddon needed no convincing. He had already told the general that all black prisoners taken in arms were to be turned over to "the authorities of the State where captured." On July 29 Beauregard informed the governor that he was turning the prisoners over to him. Three days later Seddon wrote to the governor, saying he had "no hesitation in complying" with his demand.[25]

Bonham was not finished. On August 8 he further demanded that the white officers taken with the black prisoners be turned over to him. He backed off that point, however, when he learned that the congressional resolution disallowed such deliveries. Bonham then turned his attention to the question of free blacks. While he planned to try immediately the captured former slaves, he proposed that the states and Confederate government agree on a uniform punishment for white officers and free blacks. The governor said he would delay the trials of the latter group until he had received further guidance from Richmond. Seddon referred the matter to Davis, who promptly ducked responsibility. The president contended that "as each case must depend upon its circumstances, and as the two governments will have different classes to deal with, it is not seen how a definite answer can be given."[26]

Left on his own, Bonham ordered an investigation to determine the true status of the prisoners. By then, for reasons not clear, the number of black captives, excluding those who were wounded, was twenty-four. The governor's investigating commission determined that four were slaves. The rest were not only free blacks, but all were from Union states. Bonham concluded to put all twenty-four on trial. The freemen were to be tried for being "found in arms with slaves." Seddon discouraged the trials, fearing Union retaliation. Bonham eventually compromised, putting only the four ex-slaves on trial. He provided them with capable counsel, perhaps too capable, because the court ruled that it lacked proper jurisdiction to rule on the matter. This left the prisoners in a legal limbo, and they returned to the Charleston jail for a long stay.[27]

Bonham was not long daunted by the setback. The following June, learning that black captives had been returned to their owners, he asked Seddon why they were not turned over to the state government. Two months later, more than a year after he had made arrangements to try the four ex-slaves, Bonham again asked for directions concerning the free blacks held by the state. His term of office was about to end, the governor explained, and he hoped to dispose of the matter before departing.[28]

Seddon's response was frank. He urged Bonham to tread lightly, citing the "embarrassments attending this question and the serious consequences which might ensue from the rigid enforcement of the act of Congress." Clearly, the secretary was referring to Union retaliation. He could only suggest that captured slaves be returned to their owners and that free blacks be turned over to the Confederate government. On December 8 Bonham sent all the black prisoners to Gen. Sam Jones. "A few of them, it is supposed, may be slaves, but the State has no means of identifying them or their masters," he wrote, finally washing his hands of the problem.[29]

Bonham was not the only Confederate governor asked to exercise discretion. In April 1864, when he notified Governor Vance that the black Plymouth prisoners were being turned over to him, Braxton Bragg urged caution. He asked Vance to return as many as possible to their former masters in North Carolina. The governor was to notify Bragg if he ascertained that any were slaves of masters in other states. He concluded, "To avoid as far as possible all complications with the military authorities of the United States in regard to the disposition which will be made of this class of prisoners, the President respectfully requests Your Excellency to take the necessary steps to have the matter of such disposition kept out of the newspapers of the State, and in every available way to shun its obtaining any publicity."[30]

Although the exact number cannot be known, a few black captives and some of their white officers reached Confederate prisons. It is a sad irony that this was perhaps the "best" possible outcome. As early as September 1862, the *Richmond Dispatch* reported that there were thirty-one free blacks and sixteen slaves in Libby. The paper said they had been "recently captured with the Yankees," although it did not say whether they had been taken in uniform.[31]

Prison diarists made virtually no mention of their black fellow prisoners. Racism, nearly as rampant in the North as it was in the South, may have played a part in this omission. However, an incident that occurred in July attracted the attention of at least two Libby prisoners, putting their sympathies clearly with the black captives. On the 24th both William Wilson and William Noel wrote that a black prisoner had been whipped the previous night for attempting to escape. Although the number seems incredible, both wrote that the man had received 250 lashes. "Horrible affair," Noel wrote. Wilson agreed, terming the whipping, "A most brutal outrage."[32]

In March 1864 officials at Libby used black prisoners as a means of punishing certain Union officers. They partitioned off a small space, fourteen by twenty feet, from one of the large prison rooms. Into it were put four black privates, along with four of their officers and six officers taken during the Kilpatrick-Dahlgren cavalry raid. They had no stove, nor did they enjoy facilities for washing. A bucket, emptied once a day, served as their sinks. "This was done for mere spite," Noel observed. The *Richmond Whig* agreed. "This is a taste of negro equality, we fancy, the said Yankee officers will not fancy overmuch," the paper gloated. The separate confinement, at least for the USCT officers, apparently proved temporary. On August 26 an officer in the Libby hospital wrote that a lieutenant of a black regiment had been "well treated on the whole, & now in hospital is on the same footing as the rest." He added, "White officers of black troops need not fear in general any longer, that they will be butchered."[33]

On August 10 between twelve and twenty black survivors of the battle of the Crater arrived in Richmond. Many were suffering from "wounds . . . of the worst character." The *Richmond Sentinel* described them as "the most villainous looking black scoundrels we ever set eyes on." According to the paper, a number of "our negroes" watched them arrive, seeing nothing "in their plight or appearance calculated to inspire a desire to go soldiering." The wounded went to the Castle Thunder hospital. The rest were sent on to Salisbury.[34]

They were not the last group of black prisoners transferred from Richmond to the North Carolina prison. On November 28 two Salisbury diarists noted another arrival from Richmond. One set the number at 148, the other at 300. They recorded nothing about their treatment, but at least some survived their captivity. On February 22, 1865, as general exchanges finally resumed, a Salisbury guard wrote that "all the Prisoners, white and Black left here to day."[35]

In January 1864 an inspecting officer visited the Confederate prison at Charleston, where the Morris and James Island prisoners were held. An official told him that all prisoners, black and white, received the same rations. The inspector was skeptical, however. "The negroes look as if they were poorly fed," he wrote. One told him that he got enough to eat by working in the office, but his comrades were not so fortunate. Nine months later Edmund Ryan wrote that all the black captives received as rations were a small piece of cornbread. Those who had been slaves were put to work on fortifications and at neighboring plantations.[36]

On March 14, 1864, Andersonville began receiving shipments of black prisoners and their white officers. They had been captured the previous month in

Florida. John Kay recorded their arrival. He wrote nothing of the treatment the black enlisted men received, but he did note, "The officers were insulted." The officers remained at Camp Sumter because the Confederates refused to recognize anybody leading USCT forces as such. Surgeon White went so far as to refuse to treat a major who had been wounded.[37]

The black prisoners at Andersonville were not sent away to work. There was, however, plenty to do in and around the compound, and the "Negro Squad," as it was termed, was kept busy. As slaves worked on the fortifications, the USCT captives unloaded lumber for proposed barracks. They also served on wood-gathering and burial details. The black prisoners worked under the supervision of "sergeants," who were white fellow prisoners. Those who refused ran the risk of being whipped.[38]

On at least one occasion black prisoners won a victory, much to the approval of their white fellow captives. It happened at Florence on December 20, 1864. A group of Union oath takers was returned to the prison from Charleston, along with a detachment of black prisoners. During the ride the "Galvanized Yanks" had robbed the blacks of clothing and other items. Upon arrival at the Florence compound, as one prisoner observed, "The Negroes went for them and stripped them, under the shout of the crowd of prisoners." It was a rare triumph for a "class of prisoners" who presented their Confederate captors with a "dilemma," one that was often addressed in a tragic manner.[39]

12
"Worse than Camp Sumter"
From Andersonville to Florence

In early September, the Andersonville prisoners followed their officers east. One group began arriving at Savannah on the 8th. Another reached Charleston starting on the 10th. Those sent to Savannah went to a stockade behind the local jail, not far from where the officers were confined. Their imminent arrival threw Gen. Lafayette McLaws, then commanding at Savannah, into a panic. Writing to Gen. Cobb, he protested, "There is no stockade for prisoners here cannot they be kept for a few days where they are. I cannot keep them." With Sherman in Atlanta, such details mattered not. The Andersonville prisoners were headed to the coast, and McLaws would have to make arrangements for them. This seemed impossible. His engineers had been working for six weeks on a stockade but had succeeded only in setting some posts. Desperate, McLaws again placed Edward Anderson in charge of the Savannah prison, agreeing to sustain him in any action he might take. With this authority, Anderson authorized the impressment of slaves and sent out word for all carpenters in the district to report to Savannah. The work began on the afternoon of September 8 and was finished the next evening.[1]

After the initial shipment of fifteen hundred prisoners arrived on September 8, two trains delivered eighteen hundred more the next day, filling the new stockade to its capacity. The sight of the Andersonville captives deeply impressed Anderson. "I visited the stockade this afternoon and was shocked to see the pitiable condition of the prisoners," he wrote on the 9th. "They were dirty & half clad & altogether the most squalid gathering of humanity it had ever been my lot to look upon." Three days later he set crews to work enlarging the stockade. The project was finished on the 17th. As at Andersonville, the old wall came down and the prisoners filed in. The enlargement increased the capacity to ten thousand prisoners.[2]

Under Anderson's orders, a gang of slaves dug a six-foot-deep trench around the stockade to discourage escape attempts. It had not taken the Andersonville prisoners long after reaching Savannah to begin tunneling projects. On the evening of the 10th eight passed out through a tunnel. Within three days Anderson reported that most had been recaptured. One week later another group made the attempt. This time the guards detected them and opened fire, wounding one man in the leg.[3]

This was not the only shooting to take place during the brief tenure of the Savannah military prison. The first occurred on September 8 when one of the Andersonville prisoners stepped across the deadline. The bullet struck him in the hip, and he died two days later. On the 14th a prisoner managed to slip out of the compound. He had made it out of the city and apparently felt he was beyond any danger. It was a fatal error. The moon was shining brightly, and a Confederate soldier from an unidentified outfit shot and killed him.[4]

Escape attempts notwithstanding, the Andersonville prisoners found the Savannah stockade to be a definite improvement. "We have plenty to eat," Charles Knight of the Twenty-second Indiana wrote. According to M. J. Umstead, the rations consisted of one-half pint of cornmeal, three-fourths of a pound of beef, two-thirds of a pint of rice, and a large spoonful of salt. The men also received plenty of wood for cooking. "Our treatment at this place is much better than previous or expected," Umstead concluded. Arriving on September 29, Kendrick Howard wrote, "The boys give a very good account of the place and the rations. Tomorrow will tell." The next day he wrote that the portions could have been greater, but he termed the rations "first rate considering the place we have left." Perhaps the strongest endorsement was the one Howard penned on October 1. "The talk is they are goin to send us to another Stockade," he wrote. "Hope it is not so."[5]

The prisoners also appreciated the favors extended to them by the citizens of Savannah. As early as September 9 Anderson wrote that "a large number of respectably dressed women" gathered around the stockade, throwing bread to the prisoners. After the Andersonville prisoners arrived, one wrote, "Citizens treat the prisoners well." Another reported that "scores" climbed to the top of the stockade and tossed in secondhand clothing, tobacco, and other items.[6]

October brought much cooler temperatures and genuine suffering for the Savannah prisoners. On the 8th one wrote, "12 prisoners chilled to death." The next day another added, "Some of the men Perished with Cold." They were not exaggerated prison rumors. Anderson confirmed the captive's account of the 9th, noting, "Twenty five Yankee prisoners died in the course of the night." He reported that twenty-six died the following night. "This cold weather has been fatal to all those cases of diarrhea which have been lingering for the past fortnight." He added, "Poor devils—It is pitiable to think that it is not in our power to succor them better—yet their Govt refuses to exchange them & by blockading our ports prevents us from receiving those supplies from abroad which would enable us to clothe and care for . . . their prisoners."[7]

Anderson did not have to worry about the prisoners much longer. On October 11 they began to depart for a new prison at Millen, Georgia. By the end of the next day 4,824 had been sent away. Only the sick remained, and on the 18th the Confederates tore down the stockade. McLaws issued the order, hoping to ensure that no more prisoners would be sent. Anderson deplored the move, noting, "A very serviceable garden for the benefit of the poor could readily have been planted within the enclosure."[8]

As had been the case at Savannah, captives transferred from Andersonville to Charleston reached the city soon before the officers departed. The jail yard was still being used when they began to arrive on September 10. They were taken instead to a racetrack that was part of a fairground. Trainloads continued to arrive over the next several days. A count taken on the 19th revealed slightly over five thousand prisoners.[9]

The "prison" was in reality an open field without even a fence around it. The Andersonville captives had been there for nearly three weeks when someone arrived with a plow. The furrows he created became the deadline. "We are not in any prison, but simply under guard," Samuel Gibson wrote. He added, "I like the change of location; & I think this a healthy place." John Hoster observed, "It is a splendid place to encamp, but difficult to get water." The Andersonville veterans solved that problem by digging wells. One group struck water at six feet. Hoster secured a share in it by "furnishing a strap."[10]

Rations at Charleston were scant for the arriving enlisted men. "I gues I shall starve yet," Ransom Chadwick bleakly predicted on September 16. One day earlier Samuel Gibson wrote, "Our 'grub' is of the best quality, but a little short in quantity." The situation proved temporary. By the 21st Gibson was acknowledging, "Our grub is of a *first rate* quality and gaining in quantity." By the end of the month, the rations included beans, rice, wheat flour, hominy, salt, and soap. "We draw a small quantity of fresh beef daily," Gibson added. On the 29th Chadwick penned the rare entry, "Had 3 Big Meales Shure." Samuel Grosvenor considered the Charleston rations "the best we have ever drawn in the Confederacy."[11]

Belying their city's reputation as the cradle of secession, the women of Charleston showed up in large numbers to succor the prisoners. "The ladies here are kind and generous—The Irish women in particular," one prisoner wrote. "They come up to the dead line and throw loaves of bread, tobacco, rice, etc. notwithstanding the threats of the guard to bayonet them." Another captive watched as a local woman tossed a loaf of bread to the prisoners when a guard briefly looked away. It landed close to the deadline, and the guard cocked his weapon as a warning. The standoff ended when a captive arrived with a pole and safely retrieved the gift.[12]

The guards apparently did not interfere when local residents brought goods in for the hospitalized captives. On September 14, the enlisted prisoners' fourth day at Charleston, Hoster wrote, "Citizens are coming in hourly with pails, baskets, pitchers, etc. filled with luxuries for the sick." The women were still providing for the sick on the 29th. Chagrined over the exchange issue, an angry Daniel Hutchins wrote, "We still are in this muddy hole & no one seems to care for us, only the ladies of Charleston."[13]

Hutchins was not the only prisoner who held that opinion. Beginning in mid-September a number of captives agreed to help the Confederates work on fortifications around Charleston. Edmund Pope of the First Vermont Cavalry wrote that four hundred prisoners accepted the Rebels' initial offer. Gibson, who was "chagrined" at the men's decision, set the number at 350. At least a few prisoners went a step further. On the 25th Hoster wrote that 156 members of the work squads had taken the oath of allegiance to the Confederate government.[14] They would not be the last Union prisoners to take the oath of allegiance.

On October 1 fifteen hundred captives left Charleston. Prison rumors, which proved to be correct, had them bound for Florence, South Carolina. More would depart over the next few days, and Charleston's tenure as a major Confederate prison would be over. Florence would prove to be a far worse facility than Charleston. Indeed, many prisoners would compare it unfavorably with Andersonville.[15]

Such was not the case with the Savannah prisoners who were transferred to Millen, Georgia. On July 28, as Andersonville's prisoner population neared its peak, Gen. Winder dispatched Capt. D. W. Vowles and Sidney Winder to eastern Georgia to locate a site for a new prison. Howell Cobb objected to any new prison within the borders of Georgia, but the situation was desperate and Winder prevailed.[16]

On August 5 the two junior officers informed Winder that they had chosen a site along the Augusta Railroad five miles from the village of Millen. Winder requested, and Secretary Seddon granted, permission to impress slaves, teams and wagons, lumber, and sawmills to rush the project forward. Meanwhile Inspector General Cooper once again reflected Richmond's ignorance of the challenges Winder faced in Georgia. On September 5 he urged the general to hurry the work, going as far as to ask, "Cannot part be at once prepared before completion of the whole prison grounds?" Two days later Winder seemed to allay Cooper's concerns, announcing, "Prison very nearly complete and admirably adapted to the purpose."[17]

That announcement proved a bit premature. Winder himself did not arrive at Millen until September 17. He was soon complaining to Cooper that a lack of money and labor were delaying the work. The latter concern he addressed by calling upon Anderson at Savannah to send fifty mechanics from among the Yankee prisoners. On the 24th he predicted that the prison would be ready within a week. The facility covered forty-two acres, he reported, and was "the largest prison in the world." Once again Winder was too optimistic. On October 8 he informed Richmond that the stockade was enclosed, but because of a lack of transportation, there were no facilities for baking and cooking. The prison also lacked a hospital.[18]

Such details never seemed to matter to the Confederate War Department, and on October 11 Anderson began the transfer from Savannah. By then the prison had been christened Camp Lawton, in honor of Alexander R. Lawton, the Confederate quartermaster general. Although it now had a name, it was still lacking capable guards. On the 12th Winder put out a desperate plea to Cobb for two regiments of the Georgia Reserves. The guards he had were "the most unreliable and disorganized set I have ever seen. They plunder in every direction," Winder insisted. He also urged that sawmill workers ordered to the front be allowed to remain so work could continue on the hospitals and other buildings. Seven hundred sick prisoners had arrived by October 15, and there were no facilities to care for them.[19]

Despite Winder's concerns, the prisoners arriving at Millen considered it an improvement over their former pens. "The camp looks better than any [other] prison," wrote James Vance, who had been in Libby, Andersonville, and Savannah. Henry Tisdale wrote that the rations were double what the men had received at Andersonville, although he complained of beans that were "buggy." The camp had a "fine stream running through it," Tisdale continued. The Confederates had constructed sinks over the lower end. As a result, sanitary facilities were "in glad contrast to the horribly filthy arrangements of Andersonville." Charles Knight, writing succinctly, noted, "This is a good camp."[20]

On November 1 prisoners from Andersonville began arriving at Millen. Over the next several days a number of detachments arrived, pushing the prison population over ten thousand. They, too, found Millen to be decidedly better than Andersonville. "We have a very nice camp for a prison," Sheldon R. Curtiss wrote.

"We live first rate out here." Chester T. Hart of the Fifteenth Illinois wrote, "Paradise compound [compared] to Sumpter. Good water. Trees. Better fixings. More rations & better." One of the most important advantages Millen had to offer was abundant space. There was enough room that the prisoners were able to set aside an unoccupied portion of the camp for a recreation area, where ball games allowed them to pass the time.[21]

Indeed, Winder reported that Camp Lawton could easily accommodate thirty-two thousand prisoners. It is a sad irony, and telling of the Confederacy's lack of a coherent prison policy, that Union captives spent a deadly summer at Andersonville. There they endured the season's heat, not far from the Florida border, crowded into a prison far too small to hold them comfortably. Nothing is certain, but it seems very likely that the summer of 1864 would have been far more comfortable for the Yankees at Millen. It seems equally likely that the death toll would have been much lower. Now, with winter on the way, prisoners were again being sent northward.[22]

Winter set in early in northern Georgia in 1864. By the end of October, the nights had become very cold, and many of the prisoners were virtually without clothing. The night of October 22–23 was especially bitter. Charles Knight reported that some thirty prisoners "chilled to death" during the night. After looking around the following morning, Amos Ames of the Fourth Iowa wrote, "It was an awful sight, more like a hard fought battle field with the dead and wounded where they have fallen, than anything else I ever saw." With the hospital not yet completed and no shelter planned, the sick lay upon the ground. By November 486 of the 10,229 prisoners sent to Millen had died, and many cold nights were yet to come.[23]

The deteriorating weather, along with diminishing rations, combined by the end of October to produce more anger among the prisoners over the failure of the government to resume exchange. "We hear nothing of exchange and many bitter words are spoken against our government," Tisdale wrote.[24]

The Confederates were quick to take advantage of the captives' dissatisfaction. On the 25th they began seeking out men whose terms of enlistment had run out. Three days later they removed those men from the camp and offered them the opportunity to take an oath of allegiance to the Confederacy and join the Southern army. They also called for shoemakers and mechanics to volunteer their services. According to Umstead, the Confederate recruiters were able to enlist 375 prisoners. Ames insisted that all who departed were "foreigners." Umstead called for their hanging, but Amos Yeakle candidly wrote, "If our Government leaves me here until New Years I will take the oath of allegiance."[25]

Despite their anger over the Union's exchange policy, a majority of the Millen prisoners apparently supported the Lincoln administration. On November 8, election day in the United States, some twenty-six hundred captives marked their own ballots. Prison diaries varied in reporting the results, but Lincoln was clearly the winner, most diarists putting his majority at over nine hundred. One added the next day, "The McClellanites keep very cool and do not say a word about the election of yesterday since they were beaten so bad at the ballot box."[26]

Thanks to Sherman and his approaching army, Millen did not remain home to Union prisoners very long. On November 19 Gen. Hardee ordered Winder to remove the Camp Lawton prisoners to Savannah. Six days later Winder reported that all prisoners had left Millen. Savannah was equally threatened, however, and most went to camps at Blackshear and Thomasville, deep in southern Georgia, before ending up back at Andersonville.[27]

Meanwhile large detachments of Andersonville prisoners had left Camp Sumter. They were headed to Florence, South Carolina, and a prison stockade that was destined to be one of the South's worst. The prison grew out of the strong desire of Gen. Jones, commanding at Charleston, no longer to be a jail keeper. With Federal forces "exhibiting unusual activity" in the area, and with only eight hundred men, mainly home guards, to guard the prisoners, Jones was understandably nervous. He first appealed to Gen. James Chesnut, commanding the South Carolina militia, for men. Chesnut demurred, explaining that he already had orders from Richmond to provide guards for prisoners en route for Charleston. Indeed, learning on September 11 that twenty-four thousand were coming from Georgia, Chesnut actually asked Jones for a battalion of men. This was all Jones needed to hear. Fearing he was about to be overwhelmed with Yankee captives, the general sent a staff officer to Florence to locate a site for a stockade. Although he informed Seddon of the action, Jones did not consult with Gen. Gardner, who had been placed in charge of prison matters in South Carolina.[28]

The first of the Andersonville prisoners arrived at Florence on September 14, only three days after Jones had dispatched the officer to scout out the site. More detachments followed over the next several days. Many of the new arrivals were weak with hunger, having received virtually no rations since leaving Andersonville. The Union diarists were not the only ones upset by the poor treatment. Pvt. H. L. Ravenel, a South Carolina militiaman who accompanied the prisoners through his home state, wrote, "I heard that our prisoners were treated badly but I never thought that our government would allow men to suffer as these do." In a letter to his mother, Ravenel explained that the men received no rations as they passed through South Carolina. Upon arrival the Confederates issued cornbread "as hard as a brick." The men suffering from scurvy were unable to chew it. Ravenel predicted that the scurvy victims would soon all die if they were not given vegetables. "To show you how much they suffer for the want of them," he added, "they have barked every sasafrass tree in their incampment." Ravenel concluded, "I can't believe our Confederacy will prosper as long as the prisoners are allowed to suffer as much as they do at present."[29]

The stockade was nothing more than an open field with a guard line, a picket line, and a few artillery pieces around it. It was located about a mile and a half east of Florence. Trains brought the prisoners almost to their new home, although they had to walk through a woods the remaining several feet. Edwin Marsh, one of the first prisoners to arrive at Florence, wrote that the light guard force offered the opportunity to escape "but we were tame from hunger."[30]

Despite their weakness, some of the Yankees made a break for it as they approached their new prison. Others escaped from wood details or simply charged through the guard lines. The majority of them were soon back at Florence. "A number of men are risking their lives to run the guard, but the most are brought back," one prisoner observed. Another explained, "Our men run away every day but are brought back in a day or two. The country is full of swamps and full of rebel scouts and pickets picking up their own deserters." Among those learning that lesson was John Pond. The Pennsylvania soldier bolted into the woods with a group of comrades after debarking from their boxcar on September 15. "Traveling is very difficult," Pond noted as the men navigated the swamps. Desperate for food, the prisoners approached a plantation on the 20th and were retaken. "Was treated kindly by the men who took me," Pond noted. Seven days later the group was back at Florence prison. Getting his first good look at the facility, Pond wrote, "The situation of our men is deplorable in this place worse if any thing than Anderson Ga."[31]

Not all prisoners shared Pond's assessment, at least during their first few weeks at Florence. David Kennedy wrote that the guards were kinder there than they had been at Andersonville. The officers, he added, "apeer to [be] gentleman if thay are rebbs." William Tritt was grateful when the Confederates allowed the prisoners out to tear down a rail fence for fuel. "It seemed singular to see a fence picked up in a minute and carted off," he remarked.[32]

As at most Civil War military prisons, the subject of rations dominated the diaries of the Florence captives. Most observations were negative. Kennedy believed the only food the prisoners got was what local farmers "fetch in." Tritt asserted that the Florence rations contained "less nutriment" than did those at Andersonville.

"Leaves us very hungry," he added. After receiving only a pint of rice on September 18, George Hinkley wrote, "Starvation stares us in the face here." Those with money fared better. Confederates sold sweet potatoes for $25 a bushel Confederate or $5 in greenbacks. George Crosby wrote, "Starvation drove me to sell the ring that my wife gave me." He used the money to buy sweet potatoes and cornmeal. Crosby also watched as his fellow destitute prisoners sold their clothing to acquire food.[33]

The conditions led many men to take the oath of allegiance to the Confederacy and join the Southern army or navy. By October 12 the Confederates had recruited 807 into their service. The number might have been higher had not Secretary Seddon ordered that only foreign-born men be accepted. "The Yankees are not to be trusted so far, or at all," he explained. "Curses upon them," Crosby wrote of the oath takers. Other prisoners were more understanding of the prodigals. "Starvation is driving a great many to take the oath," Pond explained. Marsh also sympathized with the oath takers, but he added, "I don't think they can Starve me to it 'Union forever.' "[34]

By October 2 the slave laborers had completed the stockade, and the guards herded the prisoners into the compound. Their new prison was 1,400 by 725 feet, enclosing twenty-three and one-half acres. About six acres were uninhabitable swamp. A ditch, 5 feet deep and 7 feet wide, surrounded the stockade. The catwalk for the guards was dirt thrown up against the wall. A stream ran through the camp. As at Andersonville, the intent of the Confederates was to use the upper portion for drinking water and washing and for the lower part to carry off the filth from the sinks.[35]

"It was quite a sight to see 500 men on the move, loaded with their traps, tents and kettles," Tritt wrote of the relocation. Other diarists only complained that the transfer delayed the issuing of the day's "middling" rations. Marsh and a comrade saw the move as an opportunity to escape. The pair bored into a cave they had dug, hoping to get away after everyone else was gone. The Confederates discovered them, however, and drove them away at the point of a bayonet. Six days after the prisoners entered the stockade the Confederates laid out streets and formed the men into detachments.[36]

October 2 was also the day the Charleston prisoners began arriving at Florence. By November 5 they would push the prison population to 12,362. Some had left Charleston holding on to the slim hope that this trip might lead to exchange. Upon viewing their new stockade, one wrote, "Our hearts sank within us but remembering that we had been in such a life & got safely out we thanked God & took courage." Samuel Gibson found consolation in the fact that his detachment was the first to enter. This circumstance enabled them to "get the advantage of position" as well as access to wood for fuel and shelter. Gibson believed he had secured enough wood to last two months "if used with care." Still, Gibson's overall impression of his new prison was not positive. On his fourth day at Florence the Pennsylvania soldier wrote, "This morning pleasant but not so our condition, there is already a great deal of misery in this camp & as the season advances suffering must increase."[37]

The Charleston prisoners who followed Gibson to Florence shared his opinion. One termed it a "hard sight." Another wrote, "A pretty tough looking place." Most troubling were the inevitable comparisons with Andersonville. "The Bull Pen presents a horrible aspect it is worse than camp Sumter in all respects," Daniel Hutchins wrote. John Converse wrote simply, "It looks worse than Camp Sumter."[38]

The improvised, haphazard nature of the prisoners' shanties at Florence only strengthened the comparisons with Andersonville. Oscar Wood of the Fifth Michigan Cavalry was able to purchase a tent for $2. "We are agoing to build a hutt out of slats & dirt so that we can have our blanket that we use for a tent to cover us at night," Hutchins wrote. It took him and his comrades two days to complete it. In November they added a fireplace and a chimney. James Bradd and four other prisoners followed a similar pattern. They finished their log and blanket shanty on October 3, adding a clay and stick fireplace at the end of the month. Gibson used his surplus of wood to construct a shelter soon after his arrival. Two weeks later, fearing that his stay could extend through the winter, he determined to build more substantial quarters, "half cave & half tent," for four men. Their beds consisted of "the soft side of a number of rails," covered by pine boughs and overcoats.[39]

By October 17, one prisoner reported, the majority had either a cave or a shanty for shelter. Some, however, were still exposed to the elements. More were left without cover in November, when a spell of rainy weather collapsed a number of the caves.[40]

Florence also had four "police companies" composed of fifty prisoners each. Although they performed duties similar to Andersonville's Regulators, prison diaries suggest that different personnel made up the companies. Each company was on duty every fourth day, receiving double rations for their services. Those duties varied widely. John Hoster spent part of one day searching for prisoners selling salt above the approved price. He then joined in a search for a man who had been accused of robbing his tent mate. The suspect was apprehended, found guilty, and sentenced to receive fifty lashes, although the chief of police quit after twenty-four. "Committing nuisances in the street" was also a whipping offense, frequently enforced after night had fallen. The companies also performed humanitarian services, such as distributing axes to men without wood and going out to get beef for prisoners in the hospital. Although few prisoners made mention of the police, Henry Tisdale concluded, "A squad of police formed from our own men is on duty and good order, and a good measure of cleanliness in the streets and bye-ways prevails quite in contrast to that which prevailed at Andersonville."[41]

The stockade had been opened about a week when the severe cold snap that also plagued Savannah and Millen hit. "We have had a very cold night and the men have suffered beyond my discription," Edmund Pope wrote on October 8. "It doesn't seem as though men could live long in this condition." By the 22nd Bradd was writing of "a great deal of suffering and deaths because of the cold." One week later Gibson graphically observed, "There is considerable frost this morning & many a poor miserable wretch lies stark & stiff in death, having perished for want of shelter and proper clothing." Although somewhat less dramatic, at least one Confederate inspecting officer agreed that the cold exacerbated a bad situation at Florence. On October 12 Lt. Col. W. D. Pickett reported that three-fourths of the prisoners lacked adequate clothing. "As a consequence, there is a great deal of suffering these cool nights and much additional sickness must follow."[42]

Pickett urged that Federal authorities be apprised of the condition of their prisoners and asked to send clothing and blankets. Although there is no evidence that Pickett's report prompted the action, blankets from the U.S. Sanitary Commission arrived at Florence one week later. There were far too few to supply the need. The Confederates issued five to every one hundred men. They were to go to the most needy. The policy was the same when clothing from the North arrived a few days later. "The Heaven sent sanitary commission is doing a great deal of good," Gibson observed, "but cannot relieve 1/10 part of the sufferers." The Confederates distributed another shipment of clothing in mid-November, but even this was not enough to supply all the prisoners.[43]

Cold weather returned with a vengeance in mid-December. Writing on the 18th, Henry Tisdale noted that scores of prisoners were without hats or shoes, "and the past week has seen a dozen or more poor fellows numbered with the dead the verdict being 'frozen to death.'" The wood that was issued was green, he added, "and almost defeats our attempts to get heat from it." On December 15, George Hegeman described this poignant scene: "A cold, raw Northeast storm, so cold last night that in trying to keep warm burned the knees out of my pants, blistered my face and hands and I almost perished with cold. Cleared off at 8 A.M. Still cold. Several died last night, the weather being too severe for their delicate health. Four young men lay down by the fire last night right on the cold wet ground and one thin blanket to cover them. About 8 o'clock, as none of them stirred, a man tried to awake them and found them all dead. The man cried like a child, as did many others who viewed them."[44]

Col. George P. Harrison was at first placed in command of the Florence prison. Lt. Col. John F. Iverson of the Fifth Georgia became commandant of the prison in October or early November. Iverson was also put in charge of the guard force. On December 6 Iverson assumed overall command of the prison. Winder, who had finally been named commissary general of prisoners for the Confederacy, issued the order.[45]

Prison diarists paid little attention to Harrison and Iverson. There are occasional references, however, to Lt. Thomas Barrett, one of two officers responsible for roll calls and the enforcement of prison regulations. Postwar memoirs labeled Barrett a "brutal fool" and "the most cruel man we ever came in contact with." Samuel Henderson, whose diary shows signs of postwar editing, made two references to Barrett. On October 9 he wrote that the lieutenant ordered that a prisoner be given thirty lashes, a punishment that proved fatal. Early the following month Henderson claimed that Barrett struck a prisoner over the head with a club and killed him. According to John Hoster, all the prisoners were "routed out" of their places on November 25 and sent to the other side of the camp for a roll call. During the process, "I saw Barrett hit a man over the shoulders with a club." The prisoners eventually forwarded their concerns to Gen. Winder. He was at Florence preparing to investigate their claims when he died of a heart attack on February 6, 1865.[46]

On November 12 both William Tritt and John Pond recorded an incident of hanging by the thumbs, one of the cruelest punishments meted out in Civil War prisons. Pond wrote that one man received the punishment. According to Tritt, it was three or four. Both diarists agreed that an escape attempt prompted the action. Neither explained who had handed down the sentence, but it certainly fell within Barrett's responsibilities.[47]

The Fifth Georgia was the only veteran outfit acting as a guard at Florence. Five reserve battalions served with them. On November 5 the Georgia regiment reported an aggregate of 284 men. By late January that number was down to 90. One inspecting officer briefly summed up the capabilities of the Florence guards: "Sentinels are inexperienced—seem to be well instructed, but poorly understand their instructions." Added another, "The guard force inefficient and without proper discipline."[48]

One of the inspectors reported, "The dead-line is about ten or twelve feet from the palisades, and marked by a small ditch, for the most part, and in some places by a pole-fence, in the swamp by an imaginary line." As at Andersonville, the guards tended to enforce its limits strictly. Florence's first shooting incident occurred on October 5. One prisoner wrote, "One man shot at the watering place on account of a blunder." He added, "It wants fixing all blame to the managers of the place, for some guards have no judgment."[49]

On December 4 a "sick man" was shot after he "blundered near the deadline." Four days later, two diarists wrote that a prisoner suffered a gunshot wound to his upper arm. One said the victim had "tumbled in the ditch called the deadline." More troubling was the shooting that occurred on January 4, 1865. Two prisoners recorded similar accounts of the incident. One wrote that a guard shot and wounded a prisoner "for speaking to him." The other penned the simple entry, "A man gets shot for asking for a chew of tabacco."[50]

These incidents notwithstanding, guards did not pose the greatest threat to the prisoners at Florence. By December rations were down to a pint and a half of either rice or meal. Some days the prisoners also got a few beans or some salt. Sweet potatoes were a rare treat. No meat was issued the entire month. John Hoster fared better for some time, thanks to money and a tent mate who earned an extra ration, beef included, carrying wood. Still, by late January he was writing, "We suffer terribly with hunger every day and the principal topic of conversation is of having something good to eat and plenty of it."[51]

Iverson also realized that the rations at Florence were inadequate. On January 31 he informed Winder, "I have the honor to state that the ration being issued to the prisoners at this prison is totally insufficient for their sustenance, as large numbers are dying daily, and I am satisfied it is from not being properly fed." The daily allotment, he explained, consisted of a pound of meal and a pound of peas per man, plus three pounds of salt per one hundred. Winder forwarded the message to Cooper, "and most earnestly request[ed] that a remedy be immediately applied." Cooper, in turn, referred both communications to Lucius C. Northrup, the Confederacy's commissary general of subsistence. The prickly Northrup, who had clashed previously with Winder, offered a brusque reply. "The state of the commissariat will not allow the issue of a full ration to our own troops in the field, much less to prisoners of war." More ominously, he added, "It is just that the men who caused the scarcity shall be the first to suffer from it." Remarkably, Cooper offered no response to this tacit endorsement of a policy of starving prisoners. Instead he weakly predicted that future exchanges should relieve the problem.[52]

As winter wore on, hunger combined with bitter temperatures to make the plight of the Florence prisoners nearly unbearable. On January 27 the normally optimistic Hoster wrote, "Have to remain in the tent as usual. It is freezing cold all the time and the moment we step outside the tent the cold wind penetrates our threadbare garments." Edwin Marsh added, "I had to be up twice through the night and almost perished from the cold." According to Marsh, four or five prisoners had frozen to death two nights earlier.[53]

In February the death rate increased even more when an unnamed fever swept through the camp. "Can get no medicine & So must let it run its course," Marsh wrote after becoming ill. On the 13th he wrote that one-half of the prisoners were too sick to leave their tents. He was apparently not exaggerating. The same day Iverson offered the following bleak assessment: "Seven thousand prisoners—about 3,000 sick—very destitute of clothing." Four days later a Florence guard informed his sister that Yankees were "dying off rapidly from a dangerous kind of fever." They pushed the prison's death count to 2,802 out of the 12,000 sent there, a rate comparable to Andersonville's.[54]

By February 1 Amos Yeakle again decided that he had had his fill of prison life. The Pennsylvanian, who had been a prisoner nearly eight months, wrote, "If I am not soon released I will take the oath." This time, to Yeakle's relief, his threat was not put to the test. On the 18th he headed north to be exchanged. He was among the last to leave Florence. On the 23rd Florence guard Charles Young informed his family, "We have nothing at all to do now, as the prisoners have nearly all been sent off." Meanwhile, with Sherman in South Carolina, "Florence is being fortified with a view to holding the place."[55]

Exchange, of course, brought relief beyond imagination to the Florence prisoners; but the South Carolina hamlet was not the only place where emaciated Yankees celebrated. By late 1864 virtually every facility ever utilized as a major Confederate prison was back in business. This included Andersonville, which had never entirely ceased operation. Richmond's prisons, despite the threat of Gen. Grant's forces, resumed housing captives. Simply put, the Confederacy finally resorted to putting prisoners any place they could. Often these prisoners ended up being chased away by their own armies. Sadly, their stories demonstrate that the horrors of Florence were not atypical.

13
"Will not God deliver us from this hell?"
The Downward Spiral

On November 21, 1864, Gen. Winder was finally named commissary general of prisoners for the Confederacy. All officers and men at Confederate prisons east of the Mississippi were now officially under his authority. More important, "Commandants of posts in the vicinity of these military prisons are made subordinate to Brigadier General Winder in all matters necessary for the security of the prisoners. Department, army and other commanders are required not to interfere with the prisoners, the prison guard, or the administration of the prisons."[1]

The order addressed a situation that had long frustrated Gen. Gardner. Although the War Department had placed him in charge of prisons in Virginia and the Carolinas, he was seldom informed of the movements of prisoners. On October 14 he complained to officials in Richmond that the officers held at Columbia had been sent there "without my knowledge or consent." He had "heard unofficially" about the prison at Florence. "Local commanders will move prisoners about and interfere in various ways, so as to baffle all efforts to secure harmony and method," he complained.[2]

The orders left no question as to Winder's authority. Unfortunately they came three years too late. By the time the appointment came, careful planning was out of the question. The Confederacy was on its last legs, and all the commissary general could do was react to a deteriorating situation. Advancing Union armies were drastically reducing the options available for prison location. Strained resources added to the problem. With no commissary general of prisoners in place, Confederate prison policy had been haphazard since 1861. Now, even with a capable officer in place, circumstances dictated that it would continue to be haphazard.

Virtually any location that could be utilized as a prison soon was—at least temporarily. Even Richmond, despite the nearby presence of the Army of the Potomac, again housed prisoners during the late summer and fall of 1864. Libby served as a holding facility for newly captured Yankees. For most the stay was brief before they could be sent on to prisons farther south. However, at least a few captured in late August remained for several weeks before being either exchanged or transferred.[3]

Some things had not changed at the former warehouse. On his first morning at Libby, Julius F. Ramsdell of the Thirty-ninth Massachusetts approached a window for a breath of fresh air. "The guard on the sidewalk below seeing me, leveled his gun and threatened to fire," Ramsdell wrote. "I drew back quickly, for the balls in the beams overhead were proof enough for me that he would have kept his word if I had not done so." George Albee of the Thirty-sixth Wisconsin reported that the guards were "a parcel of old men & Boys in citizen dress." Albee and his fellow prisoners found their attempts at guard mounting "quite interesting." As Ramsdell indicated, they had to watch carefully to avoid hearing "the clicking of one of their old Rusty muskets."[4]

As before, the Libby rations were a source of complaint among the prisoners. "Got some stuff called bean soup about 5 P.M.," Maj. Byron Parsons of the Ninety-fourth New York wrote. "The meat had the appearance of having been boiled without washing." The next day brought an issue of "stinking ham & corn bread" for breakfast and "more of the celebrated bean soup" in the evening. Later rations of beans were filled with bugs. The quantity of rations was no better than the quality. On September 16 Albee wrote, "To day my Ration was a little bigger than yesterday & I *am not quite as hungry,* for it had grown to be a settled fact that I am to be more or less hungry as long as I am in Rebel hands."[5]

Another settled fact of prison life was the presence of lice. On September 9 Albee wrote that he "'skirmished' [and] found the 'Graybacks' thicker than I have before since I have been here." Six days later Parsons observed, "Had a good time looking for lice this morning found three very large ones and plenty of nitts."[6]

Although life at Libby was less than desirable, Albee realized that things could have been worse. On a cold and rainy September 6 he wrote, "Our condition seems bad enough but I can't help but think of & pity our poor boys over on Belle Island who have less to eat than us & have no shelter, Blankets or Rubbers & are wholly exposed to the peltings of the merciless storm, while we at least have a dry place to sleep."[7]

The Confederates pressed Belle Isle back into service when three thousand prisoners from Petersburg reached Richmond on June 24, 25, and 26. At the end of August one prison diarist placed the number of captives there at fifty-nine hundred. In mid-September another estimated that there were five thousand Yankees on the island. Confederate officials in Richmond put the total at six thousand. Whatever the exact number was, when fifteen hundred arrived on August 29, Patrick Henry Campbell of the 107th Pennsylvania wrote, "It makes it so crowded that we have scarcly room to lie down."[8]

It also posed familiar problems for Confederate officials. On September 24 Maj. Garnett Andrews, assistant adjutant general for the Richmond prisons, reported that there were only nine officers and 327 men for a guard force. All were convalescent soldiers. Meanwhile, Clarence Morfit, the assistant quartermaster, informed Andrews that he could scrounge only twenty-five tents for the island; nor was lumber available for shelters. Andrews was able to get "a few old tents from the hospital department," but they fell far short of supplying the need. He predicted, "The sufferings of the prisoners of war on Belle Island for want of protection from the weather are so great that they may lead to serious consequences."[9]

"We have no blankets nor tents," one prisoner wrote on September 3. "We lay on the ground like cattle night & day." One week later Fred Shelton of the Fourth New York Heavy Artillery lamented, "For two weeks I have slept on the naked ground with a blanket for only the two nights past and passed through some hard rain storms all on half rations!" He suffered for another two weeks before he and ten comrades received a Sibley tent, "as good a tent as the island affords." As the month ended both Shelton and Thomas Springer of the 191st Pennsylvania wrote that the prisoners were receiving tents, nine to every group of one hundred.[10]

Rations were also in short supply when Belle Isle reopened. The Confederates issued them twice a day, usually at 10:00 or 11:00 in the morning, then at 3:00 or 4:00 in the afternoon. Ramsdell wrote that the prisoners received half what they had at Libby. The rations consisted of a quarter loaf of cornbread and either bean soup or "a small piece of fat smoked bacon." When the prisoners received bacon, the Rebels allowed them to dip their cornbread in the grease that collected in the bottom of the pail. There was not enough for everybody, so half the squad received it on alternating days. Occasionally the captives received a double ration of the bean soup, but this was a rare occurrence. Prison thieves were again at work, leaving many of the men without cups for their soup. As a result, many received their rations in their shoes.[11]

The prisoners were not alone in their hunger. As had been the case the previous summer, the Confederates had to guard carefully the bread intended for the Yankees "to protect it from the women in the city who are in all most a starving condition." Still, those same guards found enough bread to conduct a brisk trade with the prisoners. When the camp first reopened a loaf was going for $5 Confederate or $1 in Union money. The market was such that by early September the price was down to 25¢ or 50¢ a loaf. By then the currency had to be Northern. The guards had quit accepting their own money. Prisoners also traded pens, rings, and even shirts for food or tobacco.[12]

The guards apparently traded more out of a sense of necessity than they did from a profit motive. As the nights grew cooler, one prisoner observed that most of the sentries lacked overcoats. Those on duty had blankets over their shoulders. Those not at a post huddled around a fire. According to Fred Shelton, the youngest among them were ten or eleven years old, the oldest between sixty-five and seventy. Shelton added that they were extremely nervous. "They seem afraid we will escape in broad daylight over a fence of tight boards built 12 feet high with a strong guard constantly patrolling around it."[13]

At least five shootings occurred during Belle Isle's last incarnation as a Confederate prison. The first was during the evening of August 25. Two Richmond newspapers reported that the shots rang out twice that night, each time thwarting attempts of prisoners to escape by diving into the river. In each instance, the papers claimed, one prisoner was killed and another was wounded. Two prison diarists wrote that two men had been killed during the night. They failed to mention any attempt to escape, claiming that the prisoners were shot for "getting into the ditch," a reference to the deadline. One of them insisted that one of the victims had fallen into the river.[14]

A Confederate guard, "a boy no more than ten years old," shot and killed another prisoner the following night. The Confederates allowed a few men at a time to go down to the river to wash and drink. The victim, who was ill, was slowly making his way back to the center of the enclosure. The sentry shouted, "You damned Yank if you do not move faster I will shoot you," then immediately fired. The officer of the guard removed the shooter from his post. As further punishment he was required to carry water to his fellow guards for an undisclosed period.[15]

Following over a month of quiet, the crack of muskets was again heard at Belle Isle on the nights of October 1 and 2. Prisoners offered few details of the shootings, but they conceded that both victims had approached too close to the deadline. The first man suffered a wound to the arm. The second was killed. The prison claimed its last shooting victim during the morning of October 16. Most of the prisoners had been transferred to other depots by that time, but Shelton remained. He wrote that the prisoner died for the offense of "coming in step to near the fence."[16]

The vigilance of the youthful guards combined with the location of the prison to make escape from Belle Isle nearly impossible. About a dozen captives found this out on September 9 when they attempted to swim their way to freedom. They made it only as far as a small adjoining island, where the Confederates spotted them and brought them back.[17]

Another prisoner apparently got away by taking advantage of the daily trips to the river and enlisting the aid of fellow captives. On September 27 the resourceful man had a few comrades bury him in the sand. He placed his head under the roots of a tree, allowing him to breathe. The next morning the prisoners found his boots, which he had removed for a nocturnal swim, at the riverbank. His success inspired two other prisoners, who attempted the same trick the next day. Another pair of prisoners informed on them, and soon Rebel guards were jabbing swords and bayonets into the sand until they found the wayward Yanks. The Confederates forced them to remain there for about twenty-four hours.[18]

A small number of prisoners made it out of camp by working for the Confederates. "Over 50 went to the city as shoemakers and coopers to day on Paroll of Honor," Shelton noted on September 25. "Happy to say none of our Regiment have as yet dishonored themselves by such conduct." Extra rations were the incentive, but the Confederates found it difficult to supply the need. "The enormous appetites of the Yankee mechanics are not satisfied by the regular ration," Morfit complained. He sought permission from Richmond's quartermaster to purchase "one or two barrels of meat" every day to keep them fed.[19]

On October 4 Thomas Springer and Fred Shelton recorded the departure of eleven hundred prisoners from Belle Isle. A thousand more followed the next day. "They went south on the Danville road probably for Salsbury in North Carolina," Shelton correctly guessed. He and Springer soon joined them. They traveled in stock cars, fifty to sixty men crowded into each car. Soon Belle Isle was again vacant, except for a few prisoners left behind to maintain the site.[20]

The fighting on the Virginia front also swelled the prison population at Danville. Many captives went directly there from the battlefield. In September Richmond officials sent six hundred more from Belle Isle. The move eased a crisis on the island but filled Danville "to its utmost capacity."[21]

The influx of prisoners from Richmond strained the resources at Danville. On October 5 Arthur Wyman of the Fifty-ninth Massachusetts wrote that three cabbage leaves and a piece of cornbread made up that day's ration. "I give this as a pretty fair specimen of our living here," he added. "Occasionally we receive a peice of meat about an inch square." Byron Parsons of the Ninety-fourth New York offered a similar description. "Rations corn bread of a very coarse quality were issued at 9 A.M. and beef at 1 P.M. small ration and bean soup which we would not eat at 5 P.M. No nourishment in it. Tasted flat like dishwater," he explained. In August Samuel Foster, a recently exchanged prisoner, wrote to a relative of a fellow captive he had left behind. His account of the rations at Danville could not have encouraged the family.

> As to our treatment and fare it was as bad fully as has been represented, although it could with a little washing and cleansing have been made much better. The meat was generally very fat Bacon, and sometimes very badly cured it was cooked in very large pieces & never washed much. The Beans was the common field Bean of the South, generally black and were cooked after the meat in the same kettle & same water (without washing) and just in the condition they were brought from the field. . . . Our bread was corn mostly and that very inferior. It was never sifted, and I have frequently thought it had been ground up cob & corn all together as I have picked out pieces of cob an inch in length very frequently.[22]

In November the fare at Danville improved for a short time. Large rations of beef, combined with potatoes purchased from the guard, allowed Parsons and his mess to enjoy a number of good meals. After receiving a large issue of wheat bread, meat, and cabbage, Wyman wrote, "Verily the Confederacy is getting quite generous." By the end of the year he was again listing the rations as "corn bread and starvation."[23]

A bitter fall and winter also contributed to the prisoners' misery. As early as October 9 one captive was writing of ice forming in the prison yard. Within a few weeks the cold temperatures were sending men to the hospital. Lt. Col. Robert C. Smith, who assumed command of the prison on October 12, allowed groups of prisoners to run around on the bottom floors of the warehouses to avoid freezing to death. At least one inspecting officer believed Smith could have done more. "The prisons at this post are in a very bad condition, dirty, filled with vermin, little or no ventilation, and there is an insufficiency of fireplaces," Lt. Col. Arthur S. Cunningham reported on January 27, 1865. Most prisoners had neither clothing nor blankets. The mortality rate was about five men a day. Cunningham was amazed that the number was so low. "It is a matter of surprise," he wrote, "that the prisoners can exist in the close and crowded rooms, the gas from the coal rendering the air fetid and impure." He concluded, "This could be easily remedied by a proper attention on the part of the officers in charge and dictated by a sense of common humanity."[24]

Yankees at Danville and other Southern prisons enjoyed some relief in early 1865 after Union and Confederate officials agreed to send clothing and blankets through the lines. During the first week in January, twenty-five hundred prisoners confined at Libby and Pemberton in Richmond received blankets. One month later another shipment reached Danville and Salisbury. Shirts, trousers, and blankets were issued, and according to one prisoner, "They were very welcome as the weather is quite cold."[25]

As Fred Shelton had predicted, the prisoners who left Belle Isle in October ended up in Salisbury. Since the signing of the exchange cartel, the North Carolina depot had mainly housed Confederate soldiers serving sentences of courts-martial and Southern civilians of questionable loyalty. In July the *Carolina Watchman* reported that Salisbury housed fewer than ten prisoners of war. On October 4 the paper informed its readers that "a large number of yankee prisoners" was on its way. The *Watchman* noted that there had been "some talk" of relocating the prison, adding the opinion that "it would be wise to do so."[26]

Upon their arrival from Belle Isle, a few prisoners expressed satisfaction with the change. "This is a pleasant camp situated in a Red Oak grove on high ground," Samuel McClain wrote. Thomas Springer agreed, observing, "The camp is a very pleasant one. One half is shaded by tall oak." Byron Parsons, who arrived from Libby, appreciated the fact that there was a yard for exercise. He termed the rations "very good and quite plenty." According to Springer, they were double what the men had received at Belle Isle.[27]

These views changed quickly. After two cold nights without shelter, McClain wrote, "We paud a nest in the dirt like 2 dogs & slept like hogs." On October 9 Shelton noted, "It was awful cold last night they gave us two loads of wood to several thousand of us but many suffered terribly." There were eight thousand prisoners there, he explained, "full double the number that they have accommodations for." Arriving from Danville ten days later, Harvey Henderson was appalled at the sight. "Was put in a yard where was confined about 7000 of our men without any shelter," he wrote. "Not many of them have any blankets. Their sufferings are unparrilled."[28]

It took only a week for mortality figures to creep into the prisoners' diary entries. Not long after that they became a dominant item. On October 12 Patrick Campbell noted that three men had died during the night. On the 16th he wrote that five to eight was the daily toll. Two other prisoners placed the mortality figure at twelve. From there the number increased dramatically. Two prisoners reported that twenty-seven bodies were removed from the camp on the 28th. Another solemnly observed, "It keeps a nigger and a team in business continualy hawling dead Yankees off from the ground."[29]

It was not just the prisoners who were appalled by the death toll at Salisbury. In a letter to his wife, a guard wrote, "I feeal a touch of sorrow when I Lok of my stand on the Garrison and see the Amount of suffering and wretchedness in the space alloted to the yanky prisoners there are from 10 to 25 prisoners Buried here Every Day." Chaplain Mangum was back at Salisbury following an absence of a year. "I can't tell you how miserable the condition of the prisoners is in the garrison here," he wrote home. "They are dying very rapidly. They throw them in the graves like dogs. I saw five hauled out just so in the wagon & thrown in the trench this morning." He added, "I suppose we cannot do much better—we are so 'hard run.'" One guard, writing to his family, was more blunt: "Now i will in form you that the por yankes is dying fast her tha throw them 4 or 5 in a wagen at a time and hall them in a old field and throw them in a trench with their eyes and mouth wide open and throw the dirt rite in their eyes and mouth."[30]

In late October the Confederates issued tents, but they could supply only two for every hundred prisoners. One captive complained that it was enough for about one-fourth of the prisoners. A few more were distributed on November 9, but most remained without shelter. Following a particularly miserable night, one prisoner wrote, "It rained all night last night drove many of the poor boys out of their holes in the ground then they had no place to go for shelter would paddle around in the mud wet thru to the skin it would seem by times as tho there was no God to permit these (Devils) to keep men in such a place."[31]

A lack of food also contributed to the mortality at Salisbury. Maj. Abram Myers, the commissary officer at Salisbury, engaged mills for several miles around to grind meal. He also sent out agents with strict instructions to buy, borrow, or impress supplies for the thirteen thousand individuals that made up the prison and the post. Myers even visited the depot at Salisbury to impress trainloads of passing provisions. Despite his efforts, the near failure of the wheat crop in 1864 and the sheer numbers of prisoners combined to thwart him.[32]

The prisoners' diary entries poignantly reflected the resulting anger, desperation, and despair. "A good many men around hungry and stealing everything that will sell to get something to eat," noted one. Another pleaded, "Nothing to eat vary Hungery o my god deliver mee out of this plase for I am tired of living this way o my god deliver mee." Others saw sinister motives at play. One wrote, "They starve us to try to get us to take the oath and enlist." Another observed, "During the dark hours when grub and shelter are skarce they take to obtain recruits."[33]

Not all the prisoners blamed their captors for their plight. "They *can't get the flour,*" Shelton explained. "It comes in in little loads of six and eight barrells all along through the day. I should judge they scoured the country for it." Springer agreed, noting, "They cannot begin to feed what is here now." Campbell believed the lack of personnel and equipment was also to blame, writing, "They can not bake fast enough to supply the whole of us so some has to waite."[34]

On rare occasions the Salisbury prisoners ate well. Thirty barrels of cornmeal reached the camp on November 9, and for the next three days the Yankees enjoyed "the best rations the Confederacy ever treated us to." In addition to cornbread, there were large servings of beef, at least by prison standards, and "very good" rice soup. There was another brief period of "full rations" in early December.[35]

Even water proved difficult to obtain at Salisbury. "We have to guard the yankies in squads to the creek about half a mile to get watter like Cattle," one guard wrote on October 17. The prisoners soon began digging wells, but they were shallow and generally exhausted by 7:00 A.M. Another problem was the fact that the soil at Salisbury was what one inspector termed "a stiff, tenacious red clay" that would not drain. As a result, a great deal of filthy surface water went down the wells. That same inspector concluded that the wells and the creek combined barely met the need for cooking and drinking water.[36]

The prisoners also faced a threat from their fellow captives. Upon their arrival on October 6, Byron Parsons and his comrades were greeted by a gang of Union deserters who attempted to rob them of their clothing. "They were handsomely repulsed with sore heads," Parsons proudly reported. The Confederates separated the two classes of prisoners the next day, but the Salisbury captives still faced a threat from prisoners they christened the "Muggers." They seem to have been somewhat less active than Andersonville's Raiders. Still, prison diarists frequently mentioned that bread, salt, tin cups, and other items had been stolen. One wrote, "There is roben and stealing all the time." During the night of December 7–8, one prisoner heard the cry "Murder" two or three times. The next morning he was told that a prisoner had been killed for a "paltry little sum of money." An inspector who visited the camp in early 1865 reported that the Muggers had murdered a black prisoner in the prison hospital. Guard David McRaven wrote to his wife, "I often see things to amuse me among the yankies they steal from Each Other and it is very common to see them fight Each other like Dogs."[37]

Although there is no direct evidence to support prisoners' assertions that their captors starved prisoners to obtain recruits, the Confederates did enlist a number of desperate Salisbury captives. Between October 1 and February 5, 1,737 joined the Southern ranks. The Confederates began recruiting in early November, seeking volunteers to perform garrison duty. "A good many foreigners took the oath this morning," Shelton pointed out on the 23rd, "but the real *blue bellied* Yanks can't see it." Later he conceded that at least five members of his company had taken the oath.[38]

Escape attempts were rare at Salisbury, but on November 25, 1864, a large group of prisoners made one of the most desperate efforts of the war to break out. At 2:00 P.M. the Confederates changed the interior guard force of nine men. As the sentries who had been relieved were leaving the compound, two squads of about one hundred men each attacked them and secured their weapons. They then opened fire on the parapet.

At that point poor organization on each side manifested itself. Maj. John H. Gee, commander of the camp, later wrote, "The guard, consisting of reserves, were with difficulty got to fire upon them, some of them throwing down their arms and running off." However, the prisoners were unable to take advantage of the confusion because many of them were equally confused. Those camped nearest to the gate had no prior knowledge of the uprising. Instead of securing the gate, most ran toward the attacking prisoners. Others, unaware of what was happening, saw to their own safety. "After one or two balls had been fired through our tent we were all flat on the ground," one of them explained.[39]

"By great exertions," Gee wrote of his guards, "a few were induced to fire." It was a pair of six-pounder guns that won the day for the Confederates. One was manned by a convict lodged there, who took over after a sentinel fled. The first shell fired failed to explode, bouncing harmlessly into the town of Salisbury. The Rebels than loaded canister. Two rounds were all it took to quell the uprising. When it was all over, three guards were dead and some ten wounded. The prisoners lost sixteen killed and sixty wounded. The *Carolina Watchman* gloated, "Almost certain destruction is the best that [the prisoners] may expect should they make a serious effort to brake out, and if they are so fool hardy as to attempt it in defiance of the guard we of course cannot be responsible for the great loss of life they must sustain." Its bravado notwithstanding, the paper urged all citizens to "thoroughly organize" in case they might be needed.[40]

Despite the violence of November 25 and the inexperience of the guards, there were few shootings at Salisbury. On October 16 a sentry shot an officer of the 155th New York after he approached too close to the fence. One prisoner claimed that the guard in question was only twelve years old. Three nights later a number of prisoners attempted to escape by crawling through a hole under the fence. Between five and ten got away, but at least three were later recaptured. A guard shot a prisoner the same night, although prison diarists suggested that the victim was not part of the group trying to escape.[41]

As time wore on, the mortality rate at Salisbury reached frightful levels. By the middle of November cold weather had definitely set in. "I believe it is the coldest day I ever saw!" one prisoner wrote on the 22nd. "We all suffered a terrible night with the cold." The next day he added, "Froze hard last night. A good many died from the cold." Soon prison diarists were recording between forty and sixty deaths every day. "The Men are dying off faster than ever," one prisoner wrote on the 14th. Eleven days later he added, "Fearfull here now from 40 to 50 [dead] a day how long will we last?" The same day, prisoner Henry Ladd summed up the despair of many, writing, "Only got four ounces of bread today. Suffering with cold. Nearly naked. Covered with lice. Oh, what a fate! Must we die? Will not God deliver us from this hell?" On January 4, 1865, James Canon of the Thirty-sixth Wisconsin penned an equally blunt assessment. "This is the ofleast plase I ever Saw it is nothing but mud and Shit and they Hall dead men out by the wagon load the dead men looks like hogs pulled out of the Straw."[42]

Although less graphic, Gen. Winder agreed with Sgt. Canon. After inspecting the camp on December 13, Winder offered six reasons why it should be abandoned. Two dealt with security issues, but the commissary general also cited the lack of water and wood. With no stream close by, the sinks produced a "stench that is insupportable both to the prisoners and the people of the vicinity." The soil was "entirely unfit for a prison, being a stiff, sticky clay, and after a slight rain is over shoe-tops in mud, without a dry spot within the inclosure." Winder recommended that the government sell the Salisbury facility and use the proceeds to establish a new prison between Columbia and Charlotte.[43]

Another Confederate offering a bleak assessment of conditions at Salisbury was Dr. Richard O. Currey, who was in charge of the prison hospital. On December 22 he sent a report to Isaiah White. The former Andersonville surgeon had been named chief surgeon of prison hospitals east of the Mississippi. What he heard from Currey likely sounded all too familiar. The crowding in the compound and the "subterranean chambers" that the prisoners dug for shelter prevented proper policing. "Such is the nature of this soil, and so crowded are these grounds, and so scant are the supplies of fuel and provisions, that it is not strange that the bill of mortality should be heavy," Currey insisted.[44]

The surgeon listed pneumonia, diarrhea, and typhoid fever as the most prevalent diseases in the camp. Hospital gangrene had broken out in the wound ward, in part because of the crowding there. Indeed, the entire hospital was crowded and facilities fell far short of the demand. When the influx of prisoners occurred in October, the surgeon had requested 450 bunks. He eventually received 100. By the time he reported to White, the average number under treatment was 700. Straw had to make do as bedding for the majority of prisoners. Currey made sure his patients had warm fires and sufficient food. A lack of guards made it imprudent to supply them with more, because when they did, the items "were nearly all stolen in a short time." Like Winder, Currey recommended that the prison be abandoned. "If the prisoners are not removed," he concluded, "the good of the service imperatively demands that the Hospitals should be."[45]

Privately, Salisbury's guards added their voices to the discussion. "I have ben working near the gate where the yankies are hauled out to Bury," McRaven informed his wife in January. "There was 4 Loads went out to Day 8 at a Load. . . . It looks bad to see humanity so carelessly Delt with it would shock any one not used to sutch sights but we see it Every Day and it has lost its Effect on us." Still, he did not want his wife to visit the prison. "I Do not [want] you Ever to attempt to come here I want to see you as bad as it is possible for any one But *not here, not here.*" The state of things was such that some guards were deserting. McRaven wrote, "Some of Our men are very Easy to give up there still are some of them runing away I hate to see it." Another guard was more sympathetic to the deserters, telling his wife, "i can not get a thing to eat here." He added that about half the guards were barefoot, and many were "al most naked," and he predicted, "You need not bee surprised if we break up here Saturday in a general run and go home."[46]

Guards—and even surgeons—held little sway with officials in Richmond, but in early 1865 Secretary Seddon heard from two people who did. The first was Lucius Northrup. The commissary general of subsistence was no more sympathetic to the prisoners' plight than he had ever been. Rather, he was concerned that thirteen thousand captives were consuming food that could be sent to Lee's army at Petersburg. Seddon referred the matter to Winder, who replied that events in the field had severely curtailed his options. "I know of no place south and west of the Savannah River that could be considered safe," Winder concluded.[47]

The second message came from Governor Vance of North Carolina. "Accounts reach me of the most distressing character in regard to [the Salisbury prisoners'] suffering and destitution," he wrote. The governor expressed not only a humanitarian concern but also a fear that such conditions "would lay us open to a severe retaliation."[48]

By the time Vance's message arrived in Richmond, John Breckinridge had replaced Seddon as secretary of war. He immediately demonstrated that he shared his predecessor's desire to do as little as possible to address the problems of Confederate prisons. Orders quickly emanated from the War Department stating, "Cause an inspection to be made of the prison at Salisbury, and have such directions given to the inspection officer as will enable him to correct the evils complained of."[49]

Thomas W. Hall conducted the inspection, visiting the prison on three occasions. Hall reported that the prisoners had not received sufficient wood for a harsh winter, and he blamed that on "a want of energy on the part of the post quartermaster." He also faulted prison officers for not erecting log cabins for shelter. Pine logs were available in abundance, he explained, and prisoners could have provided the labor. Hall further cited a lack of policing. "All sorts of filth are allowed to be deposited and to remain anywhere and everywhere," he wrote, "unsightly to the eye and generating offensive odors and in time, doubtless, disease." Gee attempted to explain away the lack of proper policing by suggesting that it was too dangerous to let prisoners work with tools. "The excuse cannot be considered sufficient," Hall concluded. Despite these human shortcomings, Hall put most of the blame for the suffering at Salisbury on "the unfortunate location of the prison." Like Winder before him, he noted that the soil made drainage virtually impossible. "In warm weather or in a season of drought," Hall predicted, "the sinks would not fail to prove a source of great annoyance, and possibly pestilence, not only to the prison, but in the town of Salisbury."[50]

By the time Hall penned his report, the resumption of the exchange cartel was beginning to empty Salisbury of its prison population. It was military necessity that finally shut it down. The Confederates needed the facility's buildings as ordinance workshops. This need, unlike the previous humanitarian concerns, finally led to the removal of the prisoners. By March 19 Salisbury prison was virtually empty.[51]

Salisbury closed with a frightful mortality rate. Between October 5, 1864, and February 1, 1865, 10,321 Union prisoners arrived there. According to the prison's burial sergeant, a total of 3,406 died, a figure that includes deaths through February 13. This 33 percent rate of mortality exceeded even Andersonville's.[52]

To the west, the Cahaba prison again began to fill in late 1864. Sherman was marching to the sea, making Andersonville vulnerable to Union raids. Meanwhile Gen. John Bell Hood was moving north from Atlanta, hoping to disrupt the Union warrior's supply line. A number of Hood's prisoners ended up at Castle Morgan, as the Alabama prison had been christened.[53]

Among them was Henry Mahler of the Sixth Iowa, captured in Tennessee by members of Gen. Joseph Wheeler's cavalry on October 25, 1864. "Our prison is crowded with Yanks of every description," he wrote upon reaching Cahaba. He found his fellow prisoners to be "as selfish as they possibly can be." Cooking and eating utensils were in short supply, and those who had them refused to share. Rations included rice, beef, flour, salt, and pumpkins. Mahler termed the rations "sufficient" and occasionally "abundant."[54]

Francis Hall of the Eighteenth Michigan arrived at Cahaba on October 4. One week later he informed his family that there were eighteen hundred prisoners there. "I am very comfortably situated," he wrote. "I am happy to say more so than many others whose clothes are nearly worn out my own are good yet." Writing from a parole camp at Vicksburg the following March, he told of spending a cold winter with little or no firewood. "It was not extremely severe though enough to make me feel badly at times." Hall, too, wrote that the rations had been sufficient, concluding, "If we had been allowed as good accomodations as Fathers horses my health would undoubtedly have been as good as when in the Regiment."[55]

Ironically, a Confederate inspector was more critical of the Cahaba rations than were the two prisoners. Lt. Col. Chandler, who had produced the scathing report of conditions at Andersonville in August, complained in an October 16 report that bread and meat were virtually the only rations the prisoners received. Vinegar, needed to prevent scurvy, had not been issued to either the prisoners or the guard for several months. Chandler agreed with Mahler that the prisoners did not have enough cooking utensils. He also shared Hall's concern over a lack of firewood, adding that the majority of the 2,151 prisoners were without sufficient clothing or blankets.[56]

Like Salisbury, Cahaba had a major escape attempt that involved the capture of the interior guard. The circumstances surrounding the effort, however, were quite different. The plot originated with Capt. Hiram Hanchett of the Sixteenth Illinois Cavalry. Captured near Nashville on December 3, 1864, Hanchett had removed his clothing and put on civilian clothes before being taken and gave his name as George Schellar. He later claimed that a superior officer had told him that captured civilians would be immediately passed through the lines. That did not happen, and as the days passed at Cahaba he apparently grew increasingly nervous that he might be found out. Captured in civilian clothes, he might have been charged with being a spy.

A desperate man, Hanchett hatched a desperate scheme. Before daylight on the morning of January 20, 1865, he and a group of selected prisoners rushed the interior guards, took their weapons, and placed them under guard. Two sentinels got away, however, and they sounded the alarm. Meanwhile, Hanchett was shouting for one hundred men to follow him and take the camp, along with its three pieces of artillery. "The guards have all been mugged—and my God, boys, ain't you going to stand by me?" one prisoner heard him yell. He found no volunteers. Soon one of the guns was brought to bear upon the prisoners, ending the uprising.[57]

Some prisoners were arrested, but all claimed to have had no knowledge of the escape plot. H. A. M. Henderson was still in command of the prison, and Sam Jones remained in command of the guard force. Both agreed that the prisoners would receive no rations until the leader of the uprising was turned over to them. After two or three days, Hanchett voluntarily surrendered. He remained in the Cahaba jail until exchange freed all the prisoners. At that time four men from Jones's command took him away under the pretext that Hanchett was to be exchanged. He was not seen again, and Union officials concluded that Jones had murdered him. However, evidence to prove the charge was lacking.[58]

On March 1 flooding rains sent the Cahaba and the Alabama rivers out of their banks. Soon two to four feet of water covered the compound. Henderson had gone to a new assignment, leaving the far less sympathetic Jones in total charge of the prison. One postwar memoirist claimed that the guards appealed to Jones to allow the prisoners to move to higher ground. His reported reply was, "No! Not if every damned Yankee drowns." The most he would do was supply lumber to allow the prisoners to build makeshift platforms. There they remained for five or six days before exchange began to empty the prison.[59]

For the majority of prisoners who left Millen, Georgia, in November, that departure marked the start of a circuitous odyssey characterized by cold weather and hunger. Gen. Winder placed the detachments under the command of Col. Henry Forno, Camp Lawton's commanding officer, and dispatched them south along the Savannah, Albany, & Gulf Railroad. Surmounting numerous difficulties, including having three trains broken down at one time, Forno established a camp at Blackshear, in southeastern Georgia.[60]

Bitter cold weather followed the prisoners south. "Never suffered so much from cold in my life," an Illinois soldier wrote. According to M. J. Umstead, a few prisoners froze to death during their first night at the new prison. They were camped in a thick pinewoods, however, and axes were apparently plentiful. Soon the prisoners not only had ample firewood but substantial log shelters as well. They also expressed satisfaction with the rations, which included large issues of beef. As for the guards, one prisoner termed them "obliging," and another wrote, "Most of the guard are very good, and try to use us well."[61]

One prisoner termed those same guards "very vigilant," a trait that a sentry seems to have taken too far on November 30. Blackshear had no stockade, only a line of guards. Two stakes marked the "gate," and prisoners going out for wood or water were required to pass between them. When one carelessly walked to the side, the guard fired without warning, killing the prisoner. Another prisoner suffered a wounded arm during the night of December 2. He was part of a group that attempted to escape by running past the guard line. Similar attempts were made almost every night. Many got away, but almost all were soon back, the victims of swamps and Confederate patrols.[62]

The Yankees remained at Blackshear for just over two weeks. Sherman was fast approaching Savannah, threatening to sever the camp's connection with Winder and most of the Confederacy. On December 5 the commissary general ordered Forno to send the prisoners to Thomasville, in southwestern Georgia, only some fifteen miles from the Florida border. The pattern was the same as before. Following a bitterly cold trip by rail, the prisoners marched into a pinewoods that served as their camp. Wood was again abundant, but axes were harder to come by, even for 50¢ an hour. One prisoner traded a day's rations for one hour's use of an ax. Also, the Confederates allowed fewer men out at a time to secure wood.[63]

Diversions were few, and not always pleasant. A few prisoners got out on parole as drummers and fifers. The Confederates needed them to drill their men. The captives also noted that a number of citizens from Thomasville came out to see the real live Yankees. "They hated us they seemed to enjoy seeing us suffer," one wrote. Still, another one noted, "Good to see ladies—even Rebs." On December 15 M. J. Umstead recorded a much sadder scene, writing, "A horrible sight today, three men brought in the camp almost torn to pieces by the bloodhounds." The trio had attempted to escape en route from Blackshear.[64]

The prisoners' stay at Thomasville also proved brief. On December 17 Gen. Beauregard informed Howell Cobb that the five thousand Yankees should be returned to Andersonville. Gen. Hardee repeated the message in the form of a direct order five days later, explaining that enemy forces were nearby. By then the prisoners were already on their way back to Camp Sumter. They departed early on the morning of December 19, as the Confederates burned what little there was of their camp.[65]

A difficult four-day march followed, through swamps and over muddy roads. It rained part of the way, and one prisoner wrote, "A good many yanks and guards gave out." They reached Albany, Georgia, on the 23rd. Over the next two days, the prisoners again boarded freight cars for the journey back to Andersonville. There, George Clarkson wrote, a familiar face greeted them, "Old Capt Wirtz, cursing flourishing revolver and threatening to shoot the men." Writing after the war, Henry Sauer of the Fifth Iowa Cavalry recalled, "Old dutch Capt Wirts was glad to see us come back again, for he had been loansome while we were gone, he said the prison looked forsaken without us." Sauer also credited Wirz with allowing the men to go out and gather firewood and pine boughs for bedding. He may have been the only postwar memoirist who ever had anything kind to say about the Andersonville commandant.[66]

The first challenge Andersonville's returning prisoners faced was avoiding the cold. The Confederates had erected a few hospital sheds in their absence, but there were far too few to meet the demand of five thousand captives. In a few cases, the efforts of those left outside ended in tragedy. Christmas night brought not only bitter temperatures but rain as well. Like the prisoners attempting to escape the heat the previous summer, many burrowed into the ground. One of their caves collapsed during the night, suffocating between two and four. On New Year's Eve a prisoner reached across the deadline to snatch a piece of lumber with which to build a fire. A guard spotted him and shot him dead.[67]

Cold weather plagued the prisoners nearly the entire month of January and into early February. When temperatures moderated for short periods, rain often fell. Guards told them that the winter was unusually harsh, and the snow that fell on February 8 punctuated that point. Diarists wrote frequently of the severe suffering endured by men with insufficient shelter. Those without shoes found it difficult to walk on the frozen ground. In a few cases prisoners wrote that their comrades had frozen to death.[68]

Security concerns on the part of the Confederates made it more difficult for the prisoners to battle the elements. On February 8 prisoners with axes received orders to report to the gate for a wood-chopping detail. When they assembled, however, camp officials confiscated the axes. They had heard a rumor that a plot was afoot to chop down the stockade and escape. Five days later they returned to the stockade prisoners who had been paroled to cook for their fellow captives. The result was rations issued raw with no means to cook them.[69]

The Rebels did devise a creative plan to help the prisoners battle scurvy. On March 8 they sent in barrels, corn, and molasses. At the same time they called out division sergeants to give them "instructions about beer for the camp." The news led one to predict, "A good time must be coming."[70]

It was, but it was not because of beer. Almost since the camp had opened, periodic rumors of exchange had floated around the Andersonville stockade, only to come crashing down again. Ten days after the barrels arrived, the latest round of Camp Sumter rumors finally proved true. Before that, Yankee prisoners had already begun heading north from other stockades. Not all would make it home, but for the thousands who did, the happiest day of their lives was not far away.

14
"I am getting ready to feel quite happy"
Exchange and Release

On February 6, 1865, Gen. John H. Winder entered the prison compound at Florence to begin an inspection. He had taken only a few steps inside when he collapsed, dead of a heart attack. His tenure as commissary general of prisoners had been just over two months.[1]

Word of Winder's death reached the officers at Columbia the same day. The news did not exact sympathy from the Yankee captives. "No prisoner expressed regret at the demise of this cruel and tyranical old man," one wrote. Added another, "Great rejoicing among the prisoners over the confirmation of his death." One diarist even insisted, "His last words were give the prisoners no meat cut their sorghum down and give them the siftings of corn-meal."[2]

Had those same prisoners read some of Winder's messages to Richmond, they might have moderated their views. They show an exasperated officer begging an unresponsive Confederate bureaucracy to ameliorate the condition of the prisoners. "I most respectfully ask the attention of the Department to the destitute condition of the prisoners of war at all prisons in regard to clothing and blankets," he had written on December 15. "They are suffering very much for want of them. I hope some measures may be immediately taken to supply the want." When nothing was done, he repeated virtually the same message on January 26.[3]

Winder also refused to lend thirty prisoners to Gen. Beauregard, who wanted to use them to remove torpedoes, primitive land mines, from a Confederate railroad line. Beauregard huffed that Union generals had utilized Confederate captives for the same purpose, but Winder was not moved. "I don't think this is legitimate work for prisoners of war," he wrote, and Richmond sustained him.[4]

Winder's greatest effort on behalf of the prisoners was his attempt to get the

Confederate government to begin paroling the Yankees unilaterally. He first proposed it on December 31, suggesting that there was no safe place to keep them in a shrinking Confederacy. Those whose terms of service had expired should go first, he suggested. Winder repeated the request on January 20. "I am at a loss to know where to send prisoners from Florence," he informed Inspector General Samuel Cooper. "In one direction the enemy are in the way. In the other the question of supplies presents an insuperable barrier."[5]

Limited exchanges had actually begun in early November. Butler and Ould, commissioners of exchange, had reached an agreement to begin exchanging sick prisoners who would likely be unfit for duty for at least sixty days. On November 4 Ould instructed Winder, then still at Millen, to begin forwarding prisoners for exchange.[6]

News of the impending exchange reached Florence on November 26. The next day Samuel Grosvenor wrote, "At an early hour . . . the exchange excitement became intense. The first thousand went out for examination & the sick & convalescents were taken for exchange." A number of prisoners tried to "flank" their way out, he added, but received nothing more than a set of handcuffs for their trouble. By the 28th the Confederates were shipping out prisoners from the second group of one thousand, and Samuel Gibson reported, "The hospital is nearly cleaned out."[7]

Because of the inability to secure transportation, many of the men who left Florence soon found themselves back inside the stockade. By December 5 the Confederates were again sending prisoners away. Despite Grosvenor's earlier claims, both James Bradd, who left on the 8th, and George Hegeman, who was paroled on the 13th, "flanked" their way into groups of departing prisoners. Grosvenor received his parole on the 8th and "went out with a broad grin on my countenance." He and his contingent had to wait four days for transportation. As they lay outside the compound, bitter cold and winds descended upon them. "I never suffered so much in one night in my life," he wrote on the 12th. A number of parolees died of exposure while awaiting the trains.[8]

The departing Florence prisoners all took the trains to Charleston, where they boarded Confederate transports, which delivered them to Union steamers. "The sight of the dear old flag revived our weak lungs and such a shout went up that was heard for many a mile around on the still bay," George Hegeman wrote. He added that he was so excited that he fainted for the first time in his life as he boarded the ship. More men died as the ships headed north, but one prisoner remarked, "Whiskey the chief cause of the deaths."[9]

The transports delivered the men to Camp Parole. Two years earlier paroled prisoners had offered few kind words about the Maryland facility. But to men who had spent months in Andersonville or Florence, it was a paradise. They received clean clothes, hearty meals and, perhaps most important, a certain freedom of movement. "A splendid Camp good quarters and plenty of grub," one wrote. Added another, "This is a nice camp—something like living." Four days before Christmas Samuel Gibson succinctly summed up his situation: "Arrive at Annapolis md. at 7 A.M. this morn; soon we are taken ashore, the sick to the hospital, the well to the bath house where after a warm bath, we are each presented with an entire suit of new clothes. Then muster for pay & Furlough. *God be thanked.*"[10]

Florence was not the only prison from which jubilant Yankee captives departed. Confederate surgeons began examining the Millen prisoners on November 13, and detachments were soon leaving the Georgia pen. According to one prisoner, a thousand left five days later. George Hichborn of the Twentieth Maine, who had been captured at the Wilderness and held at Lynchburg and Andersonville, went with a detachment that was sent out on the 21st. He reached Annapolis on December 1 and received new clothes and "had A wash all over." Joseph Hodgkins of the Nineteenth Massachusetts received his parole on November 25. As he left Millen, he came across a group of men who were "laughing in their sleeves" after fooling the Confederate doctors. Two days later he arrived on a Union transport off Savannah. "I feel very thankful to God," he wrote, "that he has spared my life and health through all that I have passed, and permitted me once more to look upon the dear old flag."[11]

A small number of prisoners even left Andersonville. Among them was John Kay, who had been captured on October 11, 1863, and had been at the Georgia pen since March 13. Kay had faithfully made entries in his diary until November 9. There was then a gap until December 6, when he wrote, "Thanks to the Lord for his mercies endure forever. this day landed in our own boats—in our own lines,—very weak indeed." Charles Ross of the Eleventh Vermont left Andersonville on November 15. "I am one of the luckey or unluckey ones," he wrote, not sure what his fate would be. At first his luck seemed to be bad, as the trains took him only as far as Millen. However, on the 19th he left Camp Lawton, and the next day he was aboard a Union transport, concluding, "The boys feel some different from what they did in the Stoccade."[12]

In February the issue of exchange suddenly reemerged. The last days of the Confederacy were clearly approaching, and Gen. Grant, who had long opposed exchange on military grounds, began to relent. On February 2 he reported that he was arranging to exchange three thousand prisoners a week. The Confederates, in desperate straits, believed they could do even better. On the 11th Ould offered to deliver one thousand a day to Wilmington and a like number to the James River. "I can have even a larger number in readiness at any named day," he informed Grant. Five days later Cooper informed commandants at Florence, Salisbury, and Charlotte, "A general exchange of prisoners has been agreed upon, and the entire exchange will be effected in as short a time as possible." The prisoners, he added, could be given the news.[13]

By then the prisoners at Danville had already received the news and had begun the celebration. "Some of the officers were nigh going crazy," wrote John Beck of the Forty-fifth Pennsylvania on February 15. "Some sent out and got applejack & got drunk." According to Byron Parsons, the next day was a long one as the prisoners waited for orders to depart. "Sit up until late had every thing packed up ready for a start." They left on the 17th but were soon back at Danville because one of the lead trains ran off the track. Things went more smoothly the next day, and by late afternoon a large contingent of prisoners had reached Richmond. More arrived the next day. All were taken to Libby prison, where they signed their paroles and soon departed for Camp Parole.[14]

At Florence, the prisoners were not sure if the orders they received to move meant exchange or transfer to yet another pen. The early detachments went to Wilmington, which was intended to be the point of exchange. However, Gen. John Schofield, commanding there, refused to receive them, forcing the Confederates to remove them to Goldsboro, some eighty miles away. A flurry of telegrams followed, including one from Lee to Grant. Noting that "adequate provision for their subsistence or comfort" was not available, Lee implored, "On the score of humanity I would ask that General Schofield be instructed to receive them." A message from Grant to Schofield quickly resolved the problem.[15]

The captives, of course, were unaware of the high-level confusion. All Oscar Wood knew was that he had left Florence on February 17, arrived at Wilmington the next day, then boarded a train that same evening for Goldsboro. On the 22nd he wrote, "We are still in the field. We hear that [there] is certainly an exchange but believe very little." Fortunately for Wood's sick comrades, the women of Goldsboro were "very kind" in supplying food and clothing. Amos Yeakle was part of a detachment sent from Florence on the 18th. They reached Wilmington the next morning, where some Confederates said they were to be exchanged and others said they were bound for Salisbury. Yeakle remained in Wilmington until the 21st, when he climbed aboard a train for Goldsboro. Both eventually returned to Wilmington. Wood boarded a boat for Annapolis on March 1, Yeakle two days later.[16]

For the prisoners confined at Salisbury, the journey to freedom was even more difficult. It began on the morning of February 22, when the prisoners were called into line to hear their paroles read to them. Soon after that, the Yankees marched out of the camp. One guard witnessing the departure observed, "There was a string of Yankee prisoners & negroes about 2½ or 3 miles long they were cheerful and glad to leave and I think more of us are glad they are gone."[17]

The column made about eight miles that afternoon before making camp along the Yadkin River. Soon after the men settled down into their pine straw beds, the rain began. It continued off and on for the next four days as the prisoners marched fifty miles to Greensboro. Rations were few, and the rains made it virtually impossible to kindle fires with which to cook them. According to David McRaven, who accompanied the contingent as a guard, the Confederates had sent ahead for rations, but a train wreck prevented them from arriving. As a result, neither guards nor prisoners had received much to eat. On the 24th James Canon summed up the march, writing, "[R]aining very hard very mudy nothing to Eat But corne Bread all wet and cold and traveling."[18]

At Greensboro trains were waiting to deliver the prisoners to the point of exchange near Wilmington. Although they spent only about twenty-four hours at Greensboro, their presence prompted complaints from local residents. "Prominent citizens" asserted that there was a "looseness of discipline exerted over the prisoners." An inspector who looked into the complaints concluded, "Prisoners were allowed to straggle over the country and town, to purchase liquor, and to annoy the citizens."[19]

From Greensboro the prisoners passed through Raleigh and continued on to Goldsboro, where they signed their paroles. About ten miles from Wilmington, the weary captives entered Union lines. Coffee, hardtack, and beef were waiting for them. "Plenty to Eat and lots of friends," was one prisoner's succinct assessment. There were not enough transports for all the parolees, leading to a wait of a few days for some. Most, however, reached Camp Parole by March 10. There they enjoyed "a good hot water bath" and received a clean, new uniform. It was, wrote one relieved soldier, "the first time we could cry free from *lise*."[20]

On February 12, with Sherman fast approaching, the Confederate War Department ordered that the prisoners at Columbia be quickly removed. Charlotte was to be their destination, and the post commander there, Col. William J. Hoke, received orders to make ready for eighteen hundred Yankee officers. The transfer began two days later. It was slowed when one of the trains carrying the captives hit three cows en route, but the prisoners benefited when the resulting meat ration was issued to them.[21]

Col. Hoke protested the decision to send the Columbia prisoners to him. "It is very unsafe to let the 1,200 Federal officers remain here," he informed Richmond on the 14th. "The guard is small and no enclosure." The next day he added, "Guard broke down." Soon prison diarists were recording numerous escapes from the makeshift pen. "Lots & lots escaped last night & to day," Alonzo Keeler wrote on the 17th. The next day Templeton Hurst estimated that 250 had absconded since leaving Columbia, "not having any belief in 'Exchange,' & [having] a splendid opportunity to escape." The attempts were not limited to Union prisoners. One escape saw thirty Yankees and two Confederate guards leave Charlotte together.[22]

For all prisoners, the stay in Charlotte was brief. Early on the morning of February 20 they boarded trains for Wilmington to be exchanged. Their seats proved precious for panicky Confederate citizens. "People at every station flocked to the cars to get passage north out of Sherman's way," one prisoner wrote on the 20th. He added, "All is confusion. The Confederacy is trembling to its center." As was the case with the enlisted men, the officers enjoyed "liberty and hospitality" at Wilmington. A trip to Camp Parole followed. Upon his arrival in early March one of the officers wrote, "I am in God's Country again. A new, clean suit of clothing, plenty to eat and plenty to wear."[23]

By then the parolees were pouring into Annapolis, so much so that they were straining the capacity of the facility. On March 10 Col. F. D. Sewall, Camp Parole's commanding officer, ordered battalion commanders to "give their personal attention to the mustering and furloughing of men as fast as they arrive." The Union, however, was not receiving as many captives as it was returning to the South. Learning on March 27 that the Union had received only 16,700 prisoners while delivering 24,200 to the Confederates, Gen. Grant directed that shipments of Confederate captives be slowed.[24]

To the west, exchange reached Andersonville on March 18 when a thousand prisoners left. Those left behind were dubious. "I do not know but the Rebs all say [it is] for exchange," one wrote. "I hope it is not another prison." After so many disappointments, the skepticism was understandable. This time, however, the trains were destined for Vicksburg and Union lines.[25]

The next departure took place on the 24th. By then the Confederate camp sutler had come to see exchange as a moneymaking opportunity. He began by offering to move prisoners up on the list for a fee of $50. The price quickly plummeted, reaching as low as $1, according to one prison diarist. Eventually he accepted rings, buttons, blankets, "or almost any little trinket" for the chance to get out of the pen. Wirz threatened that prisoners paying bribes would be kept at Andersonville until the camp was broken up, but the order failed to discourage the transactions. John Ely of the 115th Ohio admitted in his diary that he and a group of friends paid $80 in greenbacks, $80 in Confederate money, and Ely's watch to the sutler. They left the same evening.[26]

Ely's group left on the evening of the 24th, part of a contingent of approximately five hundred. Similar numbers headed west over the next several days, although some had to return because of insufficient transportation. On April 14 Gen. Napoleon Dana reported that some forty-seven hundred prisoners had reached Vicksburg from Andersonville and Cahaba. The number would have been closer to eleven thousand, he added, had it not been for Union general James H. Wilson's cavalry raid across Alabama. According to Dana, some eleven hundred of the returned prisoners, mostly those from Andersonville, were sick.[27]

The paroled prisoners were stationed at Camp Fisk, a piece of neutral ground that was the brainchild of Union colonel A. C. Fisk and Lt. Col. H. A. M. Henderson, the former Cahaba commander. In February the two officers agreed to keep paroled prisoners from both sides at the camp near Vicksburg. Their superiors, Gen. Morgan L. Smith of the Union army and the Confederate Col. N. G. Watts, ratified the agreement on the 21st. Under its terms, no hostile action was to occur upon the grounds. The Union agreed to lay a pontoon bridge across the Big Black River. Confederate guards were to occupy the left bank. Union guards were stationed on the right bank. The Union was to provide food for parolees from both armies. Henderson insisted that the camp be named in honor of his opposite number in the negotiations.[28]

D. A. Johnston, a Union soldier stationed at the reception point, was more graphic than Dana had been concerning the prisoners' condition. "A more dejected set of men it has never been my lot to look upon," he wrote. Many of the Andersonville prisoners were "nothing but walking skelitons." A large number of the parolees, he feared, "will never get to see their Dear old homes again." Indeed, many had already died by the time he penned his remarks on April 9. One ambulance, he noted, had arrived from Jackson with four men in it—all dead.[29]

For the healthier men, the parole camp seemed like an oasis. "Oh how different from Andersonville," John Ely wrote. He added, "Looks like being among humans again." As George Clarkson crossed the pontoon bridge leading into Camp Fisk, friendly hands offered coffee and hardtack. "How good it tasted," he wrote. "My feelings I will not try to describe for I can not." After receiving a nice tent and abundant rations the next day, Clarkson concluded, "Uncle Sam is a great man."[30]

News of the war's closing days—both good and bad—also caught up with the parolees. On April 6, three days after the actual event, a hundred guns in Vicksburg celebrated the fall of Richmond. "War news glorious. Lee has caved to Grant, bully, bully, glorious bully." Again the guns fired in celebration. Ten days later another news bulletin, this one five days old, reached Camp Fisk. "Had news of the assassination of President Lincoln, cannot believe it to be true," Clarkson wrote. "It cast gloom over the entire camp, nothing doing." Believing Secretary of State Seward had also been killed, Ely termed the victims "[t]he greatest men of the day and the best friends of the South."[31]

On April 23 Clarkson received orders to "pack up and start North." That evening he boarded the steamer *Sultana.* "Boat very crowded," he wrote in his diary.[32]

Indeed it was. The *Sultana,* a two-year-old Mississippi River packet boat, was rated for 376 passengers. This day, however, in excess of 2,000, mostly prisoners from Cahaba and Andersonville, clambered aboard at Vicksburg. At about 1:00 A.M. on the 24th the boat started north. "Decks so crowded that there is hardly room to lay down or stir," Clarkson noted. The vessel had made it a few miles beyond Memphis when, in the early morning hours of April 27, a boiler exploded. Two more quickly blew. Wreckage and passengers were thrown violently into the river as the boat began to burn.[33]

Adam Russell of the Fifth Michigan Cavalry, a survivor of Andersonville, later recalled being awakened by the noise of the explosion. He stripped to his shirt and drawers, and when it was "so hot I could stand it no longer," he stripped off a section of railing and dived into the river. The steamer *Bostonia* later picked him up, along with several other passengers. Another Michigan soldier, Alonzo Van Vlack of the Eighteenth Infantry, also stripped down to his shirt and drawers. A strong swimmer, he jumped overboard and swam away. "I was soon out of the throng of the drownding ones," he later wrote. He eventually reached a tree limb and clung to it until rescued by another steamer.[34]

"The scene was awful, all was confusion," Clarkson wrote. "Hundreds were caught in crashed timbers, scalded, the river was full of struggling men and a few women . . . in a few minutes the boat took fire, some were praying, some cursing, some in the burning ruins were screaming in there agony." An alligator on board was freed, he added, and a passenger grabbed its cage as a floatation device. Clarkson remained on board "till the fire got too hot for comfort," then dived into the river. He swam for the shore and "hitched myself to some little trees." He remained for several hours before being rescued. Clarkson spent the next three days at a Memphis hospital, then caught another northbound steamer. He eventually reached Camp Chase, where he was mustered out of the service. From there he headed to Pontiac, Michigan, where he arrived at home on May 21, writing, "I am almost dead riding but my troubles are ended now I will live in peace."[35]

Clarkson was among the lucky few. Although the death toll will never be known, there is no doubt that a majority of the passengers aboard the *Sultana* perished. William Hoffman, the Union commissary general of prisoners, reported that there had been 1,866 soldiers on board. Of those only 765 were saved, leaving 1,101 killed. Including crew and civilian passengers, he placed the total loss at 1,238. Historians of the disaster believe Hoffman's estimate to be low, one suggesting that "the true number may well have been more than 1,600."[36]

Not all the Andersonville parolees headed toward Vicksburg. Several started out for Jacksonville, Florida. On March 24 Gen. Gideon Pillow, who had succeeded Winder as commissary general of prisoners, sent a message to the "Officer Commanding Federal Forces" at Jacksonville. He proposed to deliver a portion of the Andersonville prisoners there, terming the route "less fatiguing . . . than any other at present open." Gen. E. P. Scammon replied that he would receive the prisoners, "although I have received no instructions in reference to exchanges."[37]

On April 4 the first detachment of southbound prisoners, "a happy set," one wrote, left Andersonville. Trains delivered them to Albany, Georgia, that afternoon. From there they marched to Blue Springs. By the 7th they had reached Thomasville. The next day word came that the prisoners would have to return to Andersonville. Gen. Quincy Gillmore, commanding the Department of the South, had informed Scammon that the prisoners could not be received until definite instructions had arrived from Gen. Grant. Wrote one disappointed prisoner, "We are all kind of down in the mouth."[38]

The disappointment proved short lived. The first group of prisoners that had left reentered the Andersonville stockade on April 13. Detachments that had followed them out of the compound had already completed the round trip. News of the fall of Richmond served as a consolation prize. The prisoners also received Wirz's promise that they would soon be on their way again. This proved to be true. On the evening of the 17th the trains again began to bear their human cargo out of the camp, this time for good. Over the next several days more shipments followed. Once again the prisoners went to Albany and then on to Thomasville. "The rebs say they are determined to put us through to our lines," one hopeful Yank wrote.[39]

The prisoners were detained at a camp near Lake City, Florida. There, surrounded by alligators and rattlesnakes, they were paroled. The prisoners also learned of Lee's surrender and of the assassination of President Lincoln. Then they moved on to Jacksonville, where transports were waiting to deliver them to Annapolis. "It filled my heart so much with joy," one former prisoner wrote as he arrived at the Maryland parole camp. "Everyone trying to make us comfortable," he added. Viewing Annapolis, another wrote, "This is a beautiful town."[40]

As eastern prisoners were starting north, Union captives in the Trans-Mississippi continued to arrive at Confederate prison pens. On March 18, 1865, Arthur E. Gilligan, a Massachusetts native serving with the Third Rhode Island Cavalry, entered the compound at Camp Ford with a detachment of prisoners from Shreveport. He had been captured in Louisiana on January 24 and spent a month at Shreveport before being sent on to Camp Ford. There he met former comrades and "talked over old time with the boys." After getting settled in, he noted, "We live as though we were somewhat at home now. We are in a house which doesn't leak."[41]

By April 13 Gilligan was reporting, "There are a good many sick." That day a friend went to the hospital, suffering from scurvy. Although his health remained good, Gilligan suffered from loneliness and boredom. "I am getting very lonesome and hardly know what to do with myself," he wrote. "If I could only improve my time some way I should get along quite well." He spent some of his time playing chess, reading the Bible, and practicing both the guitar and the flute. The Massachusetts native also watched his fellow prisoners play baseball. His favorite diversion was going out on wood detail. "While we were out I enjoyed myself first rate," he wrote of one excursion. "The day was so pleasant." Gilligan returned with a good supply of "scurvy root to be chewing and keep off the scurvy."[42]

On April 19 rumors of the fall of Richmond reached the Tyler, Texas, compound. News of Lee's surrender followed four days later. "I don't believe a word of it," Gilligan wrote. Meaningful confirmation did not arrive until May 13, when a parole officer came in and announced that he was going to "parole the whole camp." The work got under way the following day, and the skeptical Gilligan wrote, "I am getting ready to feel quite happy." On the 15th he reported that most of the guard force had deserted, and those that remained were drunk. That evening a prisoner band got together and serenaded the Confederate officers. "The whiskey was passed around and I partook freely," Gilligan admitted.[43]

By the time Gilligan and his comrades celebrated with their keepers, a number of Trans-Mississippi prisoners had reentered Union lines. On May 4 a Confederate official reported that 5,901 captive Yankees had been delivered. The Confederates had received 5,844 prisoners from Northern pens in return. Gilligan's trip home began at about 9:00 A.M. on May 17. The next evening, as the men camped following their second day of marching, a number of Confederate parolees stopped by on their way home.[44]

On May 23 Gilligan and his comrades went aboard a steamer near Shreveport. Two days later they passed a Confederate ram. The crew members shouted that they were waiting for the Yankees to come and surrender. On the 28th Gilligan arrived at New Orleans and was taken to a military hospital with "the itch." He remained until June 9, when he boarded a steamer for the trip along the Gulf and up the Atlantic coast. The boat put in at Philadelphia on the 16th. Gilligan remained in the City of Brotherly Love until July 28, when he was transferred to New York. Three days later he was mustered out of the service, and on August 1 he arrived at his home near Springfield.[45]

By then the war was long over, and the tables had been turned on a number of Confederate prison keepers. Most prominent among them was Henry Wirz, against whom vengeful Union leaders—civilian and military—seemed determined to direct their wrath. Arrested near Andersonville in May, he was taken to Washington, DC, for a three-month trial that one historian of Andersonville has termed a "legal lynching." Wirz was charged with "maliciously, willfully, and traitorously" conspiring to "injure the health and destroy the lives" of prisoners. The military commission conducting the trial blocked potential defense witnesses from testifying while allowing the prosecution to present sensational and inaccurate evidence. For example, witnesses swore that they had seen Wirz kick and shoot prisoners at a time he was away on sick leave. As one writer noted, Wirz was "a dead man from the start." He was found guilty, and on November 10 he was hanged in the yard of Washington's Old Capitol Prison.[46]

John H. Gee, who had commanded at Salisbury, was tried before a military commission in Raleigh in February 1866. The main charge against him was "murder, in violation of the laws of war." One specification asserted that he had ordered guards to open fire with artillery during the "slight disturbance," actually a serious escape attempt, on November 25, 1864. Six other specifications were based on shootings that had occurred at Salisbury. Gee was also charged with "willful and malicious failure and neglect," resulting in the deaths of thousands of prisoners. Although conditions at Salisbury were as bad or worse than those at Andersonville, Gee was found not guilty on all charges.[47]

Dick Turner was apprehended soon after Richmond fell and placed in Libby prison. Taking advantage of his knowledge of the facility, he escaped on May 11 by removing a wooden bar from a window during a storm. According to a Union soldier stationed in Richmond, it had been painted to resemble the iron bars and inserted by a Union prisoner hoping to find an opportune time to escape. Turner, he believed, had discovered it by accident. Turner was later recaptured and held in the city penitentiary. In June 1866 Union officials determined that there were no grounds for charging him.[48]

Sidney Winder escaped to Canada, later returning to Baltimore after passions had cooled. His cousin Richard was arrested in August 1865. For a time he was lodged with Wirz in the Old Capitol Prison. Gen. Grant ordered his release following the execution of Wirz, but President Andrew Johnson had him sent to Richmond to face charges concerning his involvement with Andersonville prison. The following March Joseph Holt, the judge advocate general, informed the War Department that there was not sufficient evidence to put him on trial.[49]

By then Union officials had lost their taste for high-profile trials. Talk of trying Jefferson Davis for treason gradually abated, and the Confederate president, held at Fortress Monroe, was released on May 13, 1867. Henry Wirz, it appeared, had paid for the sins of many. Those sins were more of omission than of commission. They rested mainly with officials of a Confederate War Department fighting for the very existence of its country. That department never bothered to develop a coherent policy involving prisoners; nor did it vest anyone with sufficient authority to organize its prison system. The result was a disaster, and the victims were Wirz and thousands of captives in blue.

Notes

Abbreviations

ADAH—Alabama Department of Archives and History, Montgomery

ALPL—Abraham Lincoln Presidential Library, Springfield, IL

ANHS—Andersonville National Historic Site, Andersonville, GA

CHL, CM—Clarke Historical Library, Central Michigan University, Mt. Pleasant

CHS—Connecticut Historical Society, Hartford

CWMC—Civil War Miscellaneous Collection, United States Army Military History Institute, Carlisle Barracks, PA

CWTI—*Civil War Times Illustrated* Collection, United States Army Military History Institute, Carlisle Barracks, PA

DU—Rare Book, Manuscript, and Special Collections Library, Duke University, Durham, NC

FHS—FHS Historical Society, Louisville, KY

HSP—Historical Society of Pennsylvania, Philadelphia

LC—Library of Congress, Washington, DC

MARBL, Emory—Manuscript, Archives, and Rare Book Library, Emory University, Atlanta

MHS—Massachusetts Historical Society, Boston

MNHS—Minnesota Historical Society Library, St. Paul

NA—National Archives and Records Administration, Washington, DC

NYHS—New York Historical Society, New York

OHS—Ohio Historical Society, Columbus

OR—U.S. War Department, *The War of the Rebellion: A Compilation of the Official Records of the Union and Confederate Armies,* 128 vols. (Washington, DC: Government Printing Office, 1880–1901). Unless otherwise noted, all references will be to series 2.

PM, NC—Pearce Museum, Navarro College, Corsicana, TX

PRCPC—Papers relating to Confederate Prison Camps and Other Places Where Federal Prisoners Were Confined during the Period 1861–1865, National Archives and Records Administration, Washington, DC

PSA—Pennsylvania State Archives, Harrisburg

RG—Record Group

RPL—Rowan Public Library, Salisbury, NC

SAF—State Archives of Florida, Tallahassee

SCHS—South Carolina Historical Society, Charleston

SHC, UNC—Southern Historical Collection, University of North Carolina Library, Chapel Hill

SHSI—State Historical Society of Iowa, Iowa City

UGA—Hargrett Library, University of Georgia, Athens

UM, BHL—Bentley Historical Library, University of Michigan, Ann Arbor

UM, WLCL—William L. Clements Library, University of Michigan, Ann Arbor

USAMHI—United States Army Military History Institute, Carlisle Barracks, PA

UVA—Special Collections, University of Virginia Library, Charlottesville

VHS—Virginia Historical Society, Richmond

VTHS—Vermont Historical Society, Barre

WHMC—Western Historical Manuscript Collection, University of Missouri, Columbia

WHS—Wisconsin Historical Society, Madison

Chapter 1

1. *Richmond Dispatch,* June 13, July 1, 1861; *Richmond Enquirer,* June 15, July 16, 1861; *Richmond Whig,* July 17, 1861.

2. *Richmond Dispatch,* July 2, 1861; Emory M. Thomas, *The Confederate Nation: 1861–1865* (New York: Harper Colophon, 1979), 99–104.

3. Sandra V. Parker, *Richmond's Civil War Prisons* (Lynchburg, VA: H. E. Howard, 1990), 1–2; Headquarters, Richmond, Special Orders 202, June 25, 1861, PRCPC, RG 109, NA.

4. Parker, *Richmond's Civil War Prisons,* 3–4.

5. Arch Frederic Blakely, *General John H. Winder, C.S.A.* (Gainesville: University of Florida Press, 1990), 9–10, 50–52; Parker, *Richmond's Civil War Prisons,* 2.

6. *Richmond Dispatch,* July 24, 1861; William H. Jeffrey, *Richmond Prisons, 1861–1862, Compiled from the Original Records Kept by the Confederate Government; Journals Kept by Union Prisoners of War, Together with the Name, Rank, Company, Regiment, and State of the Four Thousand Who Were Confined There* (St. Johnsbury, VT: *Republican* Press, 1895), 9–10; Parker, *Richmond's Civil War Prisons,* 4.

7. *Richmond Dispatch,* June 25, July 27, August 2, 1861; *Richmond Whig,* August 2, 1861.

8. *Richmond Examiner,* October 24, 1861; *Richmond Dispatch,* October 25, 1861; *Richmond Whig,* October 25, 1861.

9. *Richmond Whig,* August 5, 10, 1861.

10. *Richmond Enquirer,* September 20, 1861; *Charleston Mercury,* October 29, 1861.

11. Blakely, *General John H. Winder,* 54–55; *Richmond Examiner,* August 9, 12, 28, 1861.

12. *Richmond Whig,* July 31, 1861; *Richmond Examiner,* July 31, August 2, 1861.

13. Jeffrey, *Richmond Prisons,* 21–22; *Richmond Enquirer,* September 24, 1861.

14. *Richmond Dispatch,* November 21, 1861; *Richmond Enquirer,* November 21, 1861; Jeffrey, *Richmond Prisons,* 22.

15. *Richmond Enquirer,* September 5, 10, 13, October 4, 1861; *Richmond Whig,* September 16, 1861; *Richmond Examiner,* September 20, 23, 1861.

16. *OR,* 3:718–19; Jeffrey, *Richmond Prisons,* 86.

17. *Richmond Enquirer,* September 17, November 18, 1861.

18. *OR,* 3:694.

19. Stephen Berry, *House of Abraham: Lincoln and the Todds, a Family Divided by War* (Boston: Houghton Mifflin, 2007), 61–63; *OR,* 3:687.

20. Berry, *House of Abraham,* 20, 85–86; Jeffrey, *Richmond Prisons,* 111–12, 131.

21. Entry for August 20, 1861, Charles Carroll Gray Diary, SHC, UNC.

22. *OR,* 3:711; Blakely, *General John H. Winder,* 60, 157; William C. Harris, *Prison-Life in the Tobacco Warehouse at Richmond. By a Ball's Bluff Prisoner* (Philadelphia: George W. Childs, 1862), 135; *New York Herald,* January 6, 1862.

23. Entries for September 2, 3, 1861, Willard W. Wheeler Diary, UM, WLCL.

24. Entry for September 4, 1861, Wheeler Diary, UM, WLCL.

25. Entries for October 24, 25, 26, 28, 29, 31, November 21, 28, 1861, Jonathan P. Stowe Diary, *CWTI* Collection, USAMHI.

26. Hiram Eddy to wife, August 27, 1861, Hiram Eddy Papers, CHS; entry for November 7, 1861, Stowe Diary, *CWTI* Collection, USAMHI; entries for September 5, 6, 1861, Wheeler Diary, UM, WLCL.

27. Entry for September 5, 1861, Wheeler Diary, UM, WLCL; entry for November 3, 1861, Stowe Diary, *CWTI* Collection, USAMHI.

28. Entry for January 5, 1862, Elisha Rice Reed Diary, WHS. Reed did not acquire his diary until 1862. He first used it to record his memories of the previous six months.

29. Entry for January 5, 1862, Reed Diary, WHS.

30. *OR,* 3:698, 700, 701.

31. Entries for August 2, 3, 5, 8, 13, 1861, Gray Diary, SHC, UNC.

32. Entries for August 31, September 9, 1861, Gray Diary, SHC, UNC.

33. Philip Shaw Paludan, *The Presidency of Abraham Lincoln* (Lawrence: University Press of Kansas, 1994), 53.

34. Charles W. Sanders Jr., *While in the Hands of Enemy: Military Prisons of the Civil War* (Baton Rouge: Louisiana State University Press, 2005), 33–34; *OR,* 3:11–20.

35. *OR,* 3:4–6.

36. Ibid., 3:689–90, 692, 710, 714.

37. Sanders, *While in the Hands of the Enemy,* 77–78; *OR,* 3:20, 738–39.

38. Sanders, *While in the Hands of the Enemy,* 77–78; entries for November 12, 20, 1861, Gray Diary, SHC, UNC.

39. George W. Kenney to parents, November 12, 1861, to "Dear Lizzie," November 21, 1861, to father, December 27, 1861, George W. Kenney Papers, DU; Paul Joseph Revere to "Dear John," November 11, 1861, Revere Family Papers, LC.

40. James Jenkins Gillette to parents, August 8, 1861, to father, August 18, 1861, to parents, October 2, 1861, James Jenkins Gillette Papers, LC.

41. Sanders, *While in the Hands of the Enemy,* 37.

42. *OR,* 3:183, 191, 217, 242, 429, 539, 568, 604, 4:394, 395, 400, 437; Maj. Gen. John E. Wool to ?, January 18, 1862, Schedule of Papers in the Archive Office Referring to the Exchange and Treatment of Prisoners in Southern Prisons, RG 109, NA.

Chapter 2

1. *Richmond Whig,* August 5, 1861; *Richmond Examiner,* September 7, 1861; *OR,* 3:726.

2. Entries for September 10–12, 1861, Gray Diary, SHC, UNC.

3. *Charleston Courier,* September 11, 1861; *Charleston Mercury,* September 12, 14, 1861.

4. Entries for September 13, 15, 1861, Gray Diary, SHC, UNC.

5. Lonnie Speer, *Portals to Hell: Military Prisons of the Civil War* (Mechanicsburg, PA: Stackpole Books, 1997), 26; *Charleston Mercury,* September 19, 1861; Eddy to wife, October 3, 1861, Eddy Papers, CHS; entries for September 18, October 20, 1861, Gray Diary, SHC, UNC.

6. Entries for October 30, November 25, 17, 1861, Gray Diary, SHC, UNC; Eddy to wife, December 4, 1861, Eddy Papers, CHS.

7. Entries for December 6, 8, 24, 25, 1861, Gray Diary, SHC, UNC.

8. Entry for January 1, 1862, Eddy Diary, Eddy Papers, CHS; entry for January 1, 1862, Gray Diary, SHC, UNC; entry for March 18, 1862, Frank T. Bennett Diary, DU.

9. Entries for March 18, 19, 22, 1862, Bennett Diary, DU.

10. *OR,* 3:730, 733–34; F. W. Pickens to Judah Benjamin, November 26, 1861, Benjamin to Pickens, November 28, 1861, PRCPC, RG 109, NA; *Charleston Courier,* November 5, 1861.

11. Entry for January 1, 1862, Gray Diary, SHC, UNC; entry for January 1, 1862, Eddy Diary, Eddy Papers, CHS.

12. Entries for January 2, 4, 12, 15, 17, 1862, Gray Diary, SHC, UNC.

13. *Charleston Mercury,* November 8, 1861, February 24, March 3, 1862; entry for February 22, 1862, Eddy Diary, Eddy Papers, CHS.

14. Entries for May 6, 8, 9, 14, 19, 20, 1862, Bennett Diary, DU.

15. Entries for May 9, 16, 21, 1862, Bennett Diary, DU.

16. Entries for September 21, 22, 23, 24, 25, 26, 28, 29, 1861, Wheeler Diary, UM, WLCL.

17. *OR,* 3:772, 781, 791.

18. Entries for September 30, October 6, 11, December 12, 1861, January 6, 7, 1862, Wheeler Diary, UM, WLCL.

19. Entries for October 6, 20, November 2, 10, December 8, 25, 1861, January 2, 1862, Wheeler Diary, UM, WLCL.

20. *OR,* 3:730–32.

21. Ibid., 3:734, 745, 751–52, 757–58.

22. Entries for January 5, 8, 10, 16, 1862, Reed Diary, WHS.

23. *OR,* 3:754, 803, 814, 815; Capt. John Adams to Lt. Col. L. Jordan, March 9, 1862, PRCPC, RG 109, NA; entry for March 4, 1862, Nathaniel Kenyon Diary, W. S. Hoole Special Collections Library, University of Alabama, Tuscaloosa.

24. Entries for March 9, 11, 12, 14, 15, 16, 17, 26, 27, 1862, Kenyon Diary, W. S. Hoole Special Collections Library, University of Alabama, Tuscaloosa.

25. Entries for January 5, 16, 28, February 4, 1862, Reed Diary, WHS; entries for March 17, 19, 30, 1862, Kenyon Diary, W. S. Hoole Special Collections Library, University of Alabama, Tuscaloosa.

26. Entries for March 18, 30, April 1, 1862, Kenyon Diary, W. S. Hoole Special Collections Library, University of Alabama, Tuscaloosa; entry for May 17, 1862, Frank Hughes Diary, in Norman Niccum, ed., "Diary of Lieutenant Frank Hughes," *Indiana Magazine of History* 45 (September 1949): 277.

27. Entry for April 15, 1862, Kenyon Diary, W. S. Hoole Special Collections Library, University of Alabama, Tuscaloosa; Elias Perry to Nanny Perry, n.d., Elias Perry Letter, Missouri Historical Society, St. Louis; *OR,* 4:230–31; Isaac Morgan to Thomas Morgan, May 22, 1862, Isaac Morgan Civil War Letter, 1862, ADAH.

28. *OR,* series 1, 10, pt. 1, 105; entries for April 7, 8, 11, 12, 16, 1862, Willard W. Felton Diary, WHS; entries for April 7, 8, 9, 13, 15, 1862, Levi Minkler Diary, Wisconsin Veterans Museum, Madison.

29. Entries for April 16, 18, 19, 22, 23, May 1, 16, 17, 1862, Felton Diary, WHS; entries for May 6, 22, 23, 26, 27, 1862, Minkler Diary, Wisconsin Veterans Museum, Madison.

30. Entries for May 14, 15, 21, 23, 24, 25, 27, 28, 1862, Kenyon Diary, W. S. Hoole Special Collections Library, University of Alabama, Tuscaloosa; entry for May 27, 1862, Hughes Diary, in Niccum, "Diary of Hughes," 278; entry for July 10, 1862, Moses T. Anderson Diary, Special Collections, Dartmouth College Library, Hanover, NH.

31. Undated entry, Madison Miller Diary, Missouri Historical Society, St. Louis; entries for April 9, 12, 13, 16, 17, 18, 1862, Charles Whipple Hadley Diary, SHSI; *Mobile Tribune,* n.d., quoted in *Macon Telegraph,* April 21, 1862.

32. Entries for April 21, 22, 24, 25, 28, 1862, Hadley Diary, SHSI; William O. Bryant, *Cahaba Prison and the* Sultana *Disaster* (Tuscaloosa: University of Alabama Press, 1990), 17–19.

33. Entries for May 4, 5, 6, 7, 1862, Hadley Diary, SHSI; *Macon Telegraph,* May 3, 13, 1862.

34. *Macon Telegraph,* May 7, 10, 29, 1862.

35. Entries for May 15, 16, 1862, Hadley Diary, SHSI.

36. Entry for May 22, 1862, Hadley Diary, SHSI; *Macon Telegraph,* May 21, June 2, 1862.

37. Entry for May 31, 1862, Charles Van Riper Diary, UM, BHL; entry for May 31, 1862, Kenyon Diary, W. S. Hoole Special Collections Library, University of Alabama, Tuscaloosa; entries for May 31, June 1, 2, 5, 1862, Hughes Diary, in Niccum, "Diary of Hughes," 279; Perry to Nanny Perry, n.d., Perry Letter, Missouri Historical Society, St. Louis.

38. Entry for June 19, 1862, Hughes Diary, in Niccum, "Diary of Hughes," 281; entries for June 5, 15, 23, 25, 1862, Kenyon Diary, W. S. Hoole Special Collections Library, University of Alabama, Tuscaloosa; entry for June 19, 1862, Van Riper Diary, UM, BHL; entries for July 11, 13, 1862, Anderson Diary, Special Collections, Dartmouth College Library, Hanover, NH.

39. Entries for May 9, 11, 1862, Hadley Diary, SHSI; entries for June 16, 17, 18, 19, 29, July 1, 1862, Hughes Diary, in Niccum, "Diary of Hughes," 280–82.

40. Entries for July 1, 3, 1862, Kenyon Diary, W. S. Hoole Special Collections Library, University of Alabama, Tuscaloosa; entries for June 26, 29, July 2, 4, 1862, Hughes Diary, in Niccum, "Diary of Hughes," 281–83; *Macon Telegraph,* June 21, 1862.

41. *Macon Telegraph,* July 10, 1862; entries for July 9, 10, 1862, Kenyon Diary, W. S. Hoole Special Collections Library, University of Alabama, Tuscaloosa; entry for July 9, 1862, Hughes Diary, in Niccum, "Diary of Hughes," 284.

42. Entries for July 10, September 30, 1862, Kenyon Diary, W. S. Hoole Special Collections Library, University of Alabama, Tuscaloosa.

43. Entries for September 14, 20, October 3, 1862, Kenyon Diary, W. S. Hoole Special Collections Library, University of Alabama, Tuscaloosa; entries for September 15, 19, 20, 24, 25, 1862, Van Riper Diary, UM, BHL.

44. *OR,* 3:682–83; Henry T. Clark to Walker, July 10, 1861, PRCPC, RG 109, NA.

45. Louis Brown, *The Salisbury Prison: A Case Study of Confederate Military Prisons, 1861–1865* (Wendell, NC: Avera, 1980), 15, 19; *OR,* 3:693–94.

46. *OR,* 3:732–34, 736–37; Requisition for $15,000.00 for the Purchase of Chambers' Factory Property at Salisbury, North Carolina, PRCPC, RG 109, NA.

47. *OR,* 3:738, 748; (Salisbury, NC) *Carolina Watchman,* November 11, December 9, 1861.

48. Brown, *The Salisbury Prison,* 40–41; (Salisbury, NC) *Carolina Watchman,* December 9, 16, 1861.

49. A. W. Mangum to sister, January 10, 1862, Mangum Family Papers, SHC, UNC.

50. *OR,* 3:770, 855, 861–62; Braxton Craven to Benjamin, January 7, 1862, PRCPC, RG 109, NA; Mangum to sister, January 10, 1862, Mangum Family Papers, SHC, UNC.

51. (Salisbury, NC) *Carolina Watchman,* March 24, 1862.

52. Entries for February 14, 15, 1862, Wheeler Diary, UM, WLCL; entry for April 3, 1862, Reed Diary, WHS.

53. Budd Walcer to brother, April 21, 1862, Budd Walcer Letters, CWMC, USAMHI; John S. Crocker to wife, May 17, 1862, Frank S. Brockett Collection, #381, Division of Rare Books and Manuscript Collections, Cornell University Library, Ithaca, NY; entries for June 9, 17, 1862, Eddy Diary, CHS; Thomas S. Montgomery Memoir, CHL, CM; (Salisbury, NC) *Carolina Watchman,* May 12, 1862.

54. Programme of Fourth of July Celebration, at Confederate Prison, Salisbury, North Carolina, Willis Peck Clarke Papers, WHS; entry for July 4, 1862, Eddy Diary, CHS.

55. *OR,* 3:895; entry for May 17, 1862, Gray Diary, SHC, UNC; Crocker to wife, May 20, 1862, Frank S. Brockett Collection, Division of Rare Books and Manuscript Collections, Cornell University Library, Ithaca, NY.

56. Entry for June 22, 1862, Gray Diary, SHC, UNC; entry for June 30, 1862, Eddy Diary, CHS; (Salisbury, NC) *Carolina Watchman,* June 30, July 31, 1862.

Chapter 3

1. Parker, *Richmond's Civil War Prisons,* 9–10; *Richmond Dispatch,* March 7, 27, 1862.

2. Parker, *Richmond's Civil War Prisons,* 9–10; *Richmond Dispatch,* March 27, 31, 1862.

3. Entry for March 26, 1862, Gray Diary, SHC, UNC; entries for March 26, 30, April 9, 1862, Eddy Diary, CHS.

4. Eddy to wife, April 30, 1862, Eddy Papers, CHS; John S. Crocker to wife, May 20, 1862, Frank S. Brockett Collection, Division of Rare Books and Manuscript Collections, Cornell University Library, Ithaca, NY; entry for August 12, 1862, William D. Wilkins Diary, LC; James A. Bell to brother, September 30, 1862, Bell Collection, Small Manuscripts Collection, Delaware Public Archives, Dover.

5. Entry for August 12, 1862, Wilkins Diary, LC; Bell to brother, September 30, 1862, Bell Collection, Small Manuscripts Collection, Delaware Public Archives, Dover; Crocker to wife, May 24, 1862, Brockett Collection, Division of Rare Books and Manuscript Collect-

ions, Cornell University Library, Ithaca, NY; Eddy to wife, April 30, 1862, Eddy Papers, CHS; George C. Parker to mother, October 17, 1862, George C. Parker Letters, *CWTI* Collection, USAMHI.

6. Parker to mother, October 16, 1862, Parker Letters, *CWTI* Collection, USAMHI; Bell to brother, September 30, 1862, Bell Collection, Small Manuscripts Collection, Delaware Public Archives, Dover; entry for July 20, 1862, Daniel F. Cooledge Diary, VTHS.

7. Crocker to wife, May 20, 1862, Brockett Collection, Division of Rare Books and Manuscript Collections, Cornell University Library, Ithaca, NY.

8. Eddy to wife, May 2, 1862, Eddy Papers, CtHS; Crocker to wife, May 20, 1862, Brockett Collection, Division of Rare Books and Manuscript Collections, Cornell University Library, Ithaca, NY; entry for August 12, 1862, Wilkins Diary, LC.

9. Blakely, *General John H. Winder,* 52–53; *OR,* 2:1373–74.

10. Eddy to wife, May 1, 1862, Eddy Papers, CHS; Bell to brother, September 30, 1862, Bell Collection, Small Manuscripts Collection, Delaware Public Archives, Dover.

11. *Richmond Enquirer,* March 3, 1862; Blakely, *General John H. Winder,* 121, 132; *Richmond Dispatch,* March 3, June 11, August 14, 1862.

12. Parker, *Richmond's Civil War Prisons,* 17; *Richmond Enquirer,* August 21, 1862.

13. *Richmond Dispatch,* March 20, April 3, 10, 11, 22, May 31, September 5, 1862; *Richmond Examiner,* March 6, 1862.

14. Blakely, *General John H. Winder,* 136–37; *Richmond Dispatch,* July 7, September 18, 1862.

15. *Richmond Dispatch,* May 15, 1862; *Richmond Examiner,* July 2, 1862; *OR,* 4:821.

16. Blakely, *General John H. Winder,* 156; Parker, *Richmond's Civil War Prisons,* 14; *Richmond Dispatch,* July 5, 1862.

17. Entries for August 16, 18, 19, 1862, Wilkins Diary, LC.

18. Entries for May 25, June 11, 17, 18, 1862, Ziba Roberts Diary, UM, WLCL.

19. Entries for June 11, 17, 1862, Charles Blinn Diary, Special Collections, University of Vermont Libraries, Burlington; *OR,* 4:779.

20. *OR,* 4:779–80, 788–89.

21. Entries for June 18, 20, 21, 24, 25, 1862, Blinn Diary, Special Collections, University of Vermont Libraries, Burlington; entries for June 24, 26, 30, July 1, 4, 16, 17, 1862, Roberts Diary, UM, WLCL.

22. Entries for June 24, July 1, 4, 14, 30, 31, August 1, 1862, Roberts Diary, UM, WLCL.

23. *Richmond Dispatch,* July 9, 12, 14, 19, 1862; *Richmond Enquirer,* July 11, 1862; *Richmond Examiner,* July 22, 1862.

24. *Richmond Dispatch,* July 14, 1862; entries for July 14, 29, 1862, William M. Collin Diary, LC; entry for August 17, 1862, Simon Hulbert Diary, MS 1578, NYHS; Albert Irwin to Bernard John Dowling Irwin, September 21, 1862, Bernard John Dowling Irwin Papers, LC.

25. Parker, *Richmond's Civil War Prisons,* 15; Charles Gardner Reminiscences, *CWTI* Collection, USAMHI; *Richmond Dispatch,* September 1, 1862; entries for August 22, 29, 1862, Hulbert Diary, NYHS; Irwin to Bernard John Dowling Irwin, Irwin Papers, LC.

26. *Richmond Dispatch,* July 19, September 1, 1862; entry for August 16, 18, 1862, Collin Diary, LC; Irwin to Bernard John Dowling Irwin, September 21, 1862, Irwin Papers, LC; entries for August 18, 20, 1862, Hulbert Diary, NYHS.

27. Entries for August 22, 23, 24, 25, 1862, Collin Diary, LC.

28. *Richmond Dispatch,* June 21, 1862; *OR,* 4:865, 868, 871, 928; Wirz to Winder, August 28, 1862, Letters and Orders Issued, Military Prison at Richmond, January 1862–December 1863, RG 109, NA.

29. *OR,* 4:901, 928; Blakely, *General John H. Winder,* 144, 157–58; Frank L. Byrne, "Libby Prison: A Study in Emotions," *Journal of Southern History* 24, no. 4 (1958): 431.

30. Blakely, *General John H. Winder,* 144–45; *Richmond Dispatch,* November 3, 1862.

31. *Richmond Dispatch,* October 17, 1862; *Richmond Enquirer,* October 21, December 13, 29, 1862.

32. *Richmond Dispatch,* December 27, 1862; *Richmond Enquirer,* November 19, 1862.

33. *OR,* 5:872–73, 887–88.

34. *Richmond Enquirer,* November 27, 1862; *Richmond Dispatch,* November 28, 1862.

35. A transcript of the committee's investigation can be found in *OR,* 5:871–924.

36. Ibid., 5:920–24.

37. Eugene Marvin Thomas III, "Prisoner of War Exchange during the American Civil War" (PhD diss., Auburn University, 1976), 50–51; *OR,* 3:51–52, 155, 158, 165, 167, 171, 175–77, 181, 183–84.

38. Thomas, "Prisoner of War Exchange," 27–32; *OR,* series 1, 7:161, series 2, 3:271–72.

39. *OR,* 3:778–79, 792, 794.

40. Ibid., 3:785–88.

41. Ibid., 3:222–23.

42. Ibid., 3:248, 253, 790–91.

43. Roger Pickenpaugh, *Captives in Gray: The Civil War Prisons of the Union* (Tuscaloosa: University of Alabama Press, 2009), 46–48; *OR,* 3:254.

44. *OR,* 3:301, 322, 800–801, 803, 812–13.

45. Ibid., 4:169–70, 797–98, 800–801, 807.

46. Ibid., 4:174, 176–77, 266–68, 807, 815–16; Hal Bridges, *Lee's Maverick General: Daniel Harvey Hill* (New York: McGraw Hill, 1961), 87.

47. Entries for July 24, August 4, 1862, Bennett Diary, DU; entries for July 25, 30, 1862, Samuel M. Jackson Diary, Harrisburg Civil War Roundtable Collection, USAMHI; entries for July 14, August 10, 1862, Hulbert Diary, NYHS; James Lowry to mother, July 21, 1862, James Addison Lowry Letters, SHC, UNC.

48. Blakely, *General John H. Winder,* 154–59; *Richmond Dispatch,* August 6, 11, 14, 18, 1862.

49. *Richmond Dispatch,* September 1, 5, 1862; Gardner Reminiscences, *CWTI* Collection, USAMHI.

50. *Richmond Dispatch,* July 26, 28, 1862.

51. *Richmond Dispatch,* August 4, 6, 1862; entry for August 5, 1862, Jackson Diary, Harrisburg Civil War Roundtable Collection, USAMHI.

52. *OR,* series 1, 12, pt. 3: 435, 473–74, series 2, 4:271.

53. Ibid., 4:830–31, 836–37.

54. *Richmond Enquirer,* August 12, 1862; *Richmond Whig,* August 12, 1862; *Richmond Dispatch,* August 12, 1862.

55. Parker to mother, October 16, 1862, Parker Letters, *CWTI* Collection, USAMHI.

56. Entries for August 12, 13, 1862, William D. Wilkins Diary, CHL, CM.

57. Entries for August 15, 16, 17, 24, 1862, Wilkins Diary, CHL, CM.

58. Entry for August 28, 1862, Wilkins Diary, CHL, CM; *OR,* 4:865.

59. Entries for August 31, September 6, 7, 18, 1862, Wilkins Diary, CHL, CM.

60. Entries for August 26, 27, September 11, 1862, Wilkins Diary, CHL, CM.

61. Entries for September 6, 15, 1862, Wilkins Diary, CHL, CM. For one such petition, see *OR,* 4:873.

62. *OR,* 4:938–39; entries for August 23, 24, 1862, Wilkins Diary, CHL, CM.

63. *Richmond Dispatch,* September 15, November 5, 1862; *Richmond Examiner,* September 24, 1862.

64. *Macon Telegraph,* May 21, June 2, 1862; entry for May 22, 1862, Hadley Diary, SHSI; entries for October 7, 9, 10, 12, 1862, Kenyon Diary, W. S. Hoole Special Collections Library, University of Alabama, Tuscaloosa.

65. Entries for October 4, 7, 8, 1862, Bennett Diary, DU.

66. Entries for August 14, 16, 26, September 12, 15, 1862, Hulbert Diary, NYHS.

Chapter 4

1. *OR,* 4:94; William Best Hesseltine, *Civil War Prisons: A Study in War Psychology* (1930; repr., Columbus: Ohio State University Press, 1998), 74–75.

2. *OR,* 4:94.

3. Ibid., 4:191.

4. Entry for July 12, 1862, Hadley Diary, SHSI.

5. Entries for July 13, 14, 15, 16, 1862, Hadley Diary, SHSI; Amos N. Currier, W. F. McCarren, and seven other captains of detachments, Petition, July 14, 1862, Benton Barracks, St. Louis, Missouri, Abstracts and Copies of Orders, Letters, and Telegrams relating to Paroled and Exchanged Federal Prisoners of War, RG 249, NA.

6. *OR,* 4:246.

7. Ibid., 4:250–51, 257–66, 295.

8. Headquarters, Department of the Mississippi, Circular, July 19, 1862, Benton Barracks, St. Louis, Missouri, Headquarters, Paroled Men, General and Special Orders Issued and Received, RG 393, NA; *OR,* 4:242.

9. *OR,* 4:299.

10. Entries for July 29, August 6, 10, 1862, Hadley Diary, SHSI; General Orders 2, July 31, 1862, Special Orders 25, August 30, 1862, General Orders 15, September 11, 1862, General Orders 19, September 22, 1862, General Orders 21, October 1, 1862, Benton Barracks, St. Louis, Missouri, Headquarters, Paroled Men, General and Special Orders Issued and Received, RG 393, NA.

11. *OR,* 5:128, 231, 288, 378, 414, 617, 668.

12. Entries for January 8, 10, 11, 13, 1863, Jackson Thompson Diary, WHS.

13. Entries for January 30, February 6, 26, 28, March 1, 11, 12, 26, 28, 29, April 1, 3, 4, 7, 1863, Thompson Diary, WHS.

14. Entries for April 14, 16, 1863, Thompson Diary, WHS.

15. Entries for April 22, May 4, 17, June 16, 28, July 4, 1863, Thompson Diary, WHS.

16. Entries for July 29, August 19, 28, 1863, Thompson Diary, WHS; E. L. Phillips to Ira Russell, March 18, 1863, Ira Russell Papers, SHC, UNC.

17. *OR,* 8:987–88.

18. Ibid., 4:499, 522, 529.

19. Lew Wallace, *Lew Wallace: An Autobiography* (New York: Harper & Brothers, 1906), 2:632–34; Lew Wallace to Gen. Lorenzo Thomas, September 30, 1862, Headquarters, United States Paroled Forces, Columbus, Ohio, Letters Sent, RG 393, NA.

20. *OR,* 4:545–46, 563, 569–71; Roger Pickenpaugh, *Camp Chase and the Evolution of Union Prison Policy* (Tuscaloosa: University of Alabama Press, 2007), 49–50.

21. Pickenpaugh, *Camp Chase,* 52.

22. Entries for August 19, 22, 1862, William L. Curry Diary, William L. Curry Letters and Journals, UM, WLCL; Alfred G. Ryder to mother, September 15, 1862, Ryder Family Papers, UM, BHL.

23. Ryder to mother, October 1, 1862, Ryder to "Dear Friends," October 8, 1862, Ryder Family Papers, UM, BHL; entries for October 16, 30, November 6, 15, 19, 1862, Curry Diary, Curry Letters and Journals, UM, WLCL.

24. Wallace to Thomas, October 18, 1862, Headquarters, United States Paroled Forces, Columbus, Ohio, Letters Sent, RG 393, NA.

25. Special Orders No. 9, October 19, 1862, Special Orders No. 54, November 4, 1862, Camp Lew Wallace, Columbus, Ohio, General and Special Orders Issued and Received, RG 393, NA; General Orders No. 9, December 30, 1862, Camp Chase, Ohio, General Orders, RG 393, NA; Col. W. L. McMullen to "Captain," November 22, 1862, United States Paroled Forces, Columbus, Ohio, Correspondence relating to Imprisoned, Paroled, and Disabled Union Veterans, RG 249, NA.

26. Pickenpaugh, *Camp Chase,* 53–54; Special Orders No. 203, December 20, 1862, Camp Lew Wallace, Columbus, Ohio, General and Special Orders Issued and Received, RG 393, NA; Gen. James Cooper to "Major Pearce," December 29, 1862, United States Paroled Forces, Columbus, Ohio, Correspondence relating to Imprisoned, Paroled, and Disabled Union Soldiers, RG 249, NA.

27. The special orders for exchange can be found in United States Paroled Forces, Columbus, Ohio, General and Special Orders Issued and Received, RG 393, NA; United States Paroled Forces, Columbus, Ohio, Journal of Costs of Arrest and Transportation of Paroled Federal Prisoners of War Who Failed to Return from Furloughs, RG 249, NA.

28. Entries for April 14, 15, 20, 22, 23, 1862, Hiram F. Penland Diary, UM, BHL; entries for April 1, 4, 9, May 4, 5, 25, June 1, July 2, 1862, Fernando E. Pomeroy Diary, in Randolph C. Downes, ed., "The Civil War Diary of Fernando E. Pomeroy," *Northwest Ohio Quarterly* 19 (July 1947): 140–42.

29. Valentine G. Barney to wife, September 22, 1862, Valentine G. Barney Letters, VTHS; Charles Kline to mother and sisters, September 23, 1862, Charles Kline Civil War Letters, SCHS; entry for September 16, 1862, Nicholas De Graff Diary, *CWTI* Collection, USAMHI; Calvin A. Haynes to wife, September 18, 1862, Calvin A. Haynes Letters, Manuscripts and Special Collections, New York State Library, Albany; for Camp Douglas, see George Levy, *To Die in Chicago: Confederate Prisoners at Camp Douglas, 1862–65* (Gretna, LA: Pelican, 1999).

30. Kline to mother and sisters, September 23, 1862, Kline Letters, SCHS; Barney to wife,

September 22, 1862, Barney Letters, VTHS; entries for September 21, 22, 1862, Charles E. Smith Diary, in George R. Cryder and Stanley R. Miller, eds., *A View from the Ranks: The Civil War Diaries of Corporal Charles E. Smith* (Delaware, OH: Delaware County Historical Society, 1999), 75.

31. *OR,* 4:546–47.

32. Levy, *To Die in Chicago,* 109–10.

33. Ibid.; Kline to mother and sisters, October 1, 7, 1862, Kline Letters, SCHS.

34. Entry for September 29, 1862, De Graff Diary, *CWTI* Collection, USAMHI; Barney to wife, October 1, 12, November 7, 9, 1862, Barney Letters, VTHS.

35. Entry for September 28, 1862, Smith Diary, in Cryder and Miller, *A View from the Ranks,* 79; Barney to wife, October 1, 1862, Barney Letters, VTHS.

36. *OR,* 4:596, 600.

37. Entries for October 1, 2, 3, 4, 1862, Smith Diary, in Cryder and Miller, *A View from the Ranks,* 81–84; Benjamin Thompson Reminiscences, *CWTI* Collection, USAMHI.

38. Haynes to wife, October 20, 1862, Haynes Letters, Manuscripts and Special Collections, New York State Library, Albany.

39. Entries for October 16, 21, 1862, Smith Diary, in Cryder and Miller, *A View from the Ranks,* 88–90; entries for October 17, 21, 1862, Charles Wesley Belknap Diary, CWMC, USAMHI.

40. Entry for October 22, 1862, Smith Diary, in Cryder and Miller, *A View from the Ranks,* 90.

41. *OR,* 4:644–45.

42. Entries for October 23, 24, 25, 1862, Smith Diary, in Cryder and Miller, *A View from the Ranks,* 90–91; entry for October 25, 1862, Belknap Diary, CWMC, USAMHI; entry for October 26, 1862, De Graff Diary, *CWTI* Collection, USAMHI; Barney to wife, December 2, 1862, Barney Letters, VTHS.

43. Entry for November 20, 1862, De Graff Diary, *CWTI* Collection, USAMHI.

44. Entries for July 19, 22, 24, 1862, Henry N. Bemis Diaries, Musselman Library, Gettysburg College, Gettysburg, PA; entry for July 26, 1862, Jerome J. Robbins Diary, UM, BHL.

45. Milton Mozart Woodford to sister, October 28, 1862, Churchill-Woodford Family Papers, CHS; entry for August 18, 1862, Robbins Diary, UM, BHL.

46. Entries for September 17, 20, 1862, Hulbert Diary, NYHS; entries for August 17, 21, 1862, Roberts Diary, UM, WLCL; entry for July 27, 1862, Bemis Diary, Musselman Library, Gettysburg College, Gettysburg, PA.

47. Entry for September 22, 1862, Robbins Diary, UM, BHL; entry for September 22, 1862, Hulbert Diary, NYHS.

48. William N. Harrison to "Cousin Frank," November 29, 1862, William H. Harrison Letter, accession 40494, Personal Papers Collection, Library of Virginia, Richmond; Lt. Col. George Sangster to Keeper of the Jail, Annapolis, September 10 (2 messages), 11, 15, 16, 18, October 5, 10, 1862, Sangster to Provost Marshall, Annapolis, October 21, 1862, Sangster to Lt. Col. William Hoffman, May 29, 1863, Camp Parole, Maryland, Letters and Telegrams Sent, RG 249, NA; entry for October 20, 1862, Robbins Diary, UM, BHL.

49. Frederick Schmalsriedt to brother, March 4, 1863, Schmalsriedt Family Papers, UM, BHL; entries for August 15, September 24, October 24, 1862, Robbins Diary, UM, BHL.

50. Entries for September 29, November 13, 1862, Robbins Diary, UM, BHL; entry for February 8, 1863, Woodford Diary, Churchill-Woodford Family Papers, CHS.

51. Sangster to Col. William D. Whipple, October 21, 1862, Sangster to Capt. F. J. Keffer, April 25, 1863, Camp Parole, Maryland, Letters and Telegrams Sent, RG 249, NA.

52. Col. Adrian Root to Col. Carlos A. Waite, July 25, 1863, Root to Hoffman, July 29, 1863, Camp Parole, Maryland, Letters and Telegrams Sent, RG 249, NA.

53. *OR,* 4:345–46.

54. Ibid., 4:727.

55. Ibid., 4:749.

56. Ibid., 4:771, 5:6.

57. Ibid., 5:38, 58–69.

58. Ibid., 5:348–49.

59. Ibid., 5:395; Hoffman to Col. John C. Kelton, March 7, 1863, Office of the Commissary General of Prisoners, Letters and Telegrams Sent, RG 249, NA.

60. Hoffman to Capt. Gardner S. Blodgett, April 23, July 6, 24, 1863, Hoffman to Col. Adrian Root, August 19, 28, 1863, Office of the Commissary General of Prisoners, Letters and Telegrams Sent, RG 249, NA; Root to Hoffman, August 26, September 2, 1863, Camp Parole, Maryland, Letters and Telegrams Sent, RG 249, NA.

61. Entry for September 30, 1862, Hulbert Diary, NYHS; entry for May 23, 1863, William L. Aughinbaugh Diary, UM, WLCL; Charles D. Grannis Reminiscences, WHS.

62. Capt. W. M. Gwynne to Col. Gabriel De Korponay, October 29, 1862, De Korponay to Capt. R. C. Gale, November 10, 1862, A. A. G. Rollin to De Korponay, November 22, 1862, Camp Banks, Alexandria, Virginia, Letters Received, RG 393, NA; Special Order 26, October 21, 1862, Special Order 1, January 8, 1863, Camp Banks, Alexandria, Virginia, Orders Issued, RG 393, NA.

63. *OR,* 4:359, 588–89, 620, 5:124.

64. Ibid., 4:562, 638, 641, 5:86–87, 289, 699, 719.

65. Pickenpaugh, *Captives in Gray,* 62–67.

Chapter 5

1. *Richmond Dispatch,* December 18, 19, 31, 1862, January 17, 1863; *OR,* 5:813.

2. *Richmond Whig,* March 10, 1863; Blakely, *General John H. Winder,* 161; Ernest B. Furgurson, *Ashes of Glory: Richmond at War* (New York: Alfred A. Knopf, 1996), 193–94.

3. Entries for January 16, 18, 22, 23, 24, 1863, George F. Gill Diary, FHS.

4. Entries for February 20, 21, 22, 1863, Charles B. Stone Diary, Special Collections, University of Vermont Libraries, Burlington.

5. Entry for February 25, 1863, Stone Diary, Special Collections, University of Vermont Libraries, Burlington.

6. Entries for February 16, 17, 18, 19, 20, 1863, Stone Diary, Special Collections, University of Vermont Libraries, Burlington.

7. Entries for January 4, 5, 7, 8, 9, 10, 14, 15, 1863, Gill Diary, FHS.

8. Entries for March 5, 6, 9, 10, 11, 14, 16, 18, 22, 1863, Penland Diary, UM, BHL; entries for March 25, 26, 30, April 1, 2, 4, 9, 1863, John Edwin Holmes Diary, WHS.

9. *OR,* 5:696–97; Parker, *Richmond's Civil War Prisons,* 50.

10. Entries for June 22, 23, 1863, William T. Wilson Diary, vol. 1006, OHS; entry for Au-

gust 17, 1863, Louis R. Fortescue Diary, SHS, UNC; entry for October 3, 1863, Harlan Smith Howard Diary, in Warren A. Jennings, ed., "Prisoner of the Confederacy: Diary of a Union Artilleryman," *West Virginia History* 36 (July 1975): 314.

11. Henry Clay Taylor to parents, March 21, 1864, Henry Clay Taylor Papers, WHS; entries for July 20, 21, 1863 Fortescue Diary, SHC, UNC; entries for July 19, 20, 22, 1863, George W. Grant Diary, DU.

12. Entries for October 27, 28, 30, 1863, Nathaniel Rollins Diary, WHS; entry for October 28, 1863, Alonzo Merrill Keeler Diary, Keeler Family Papers, UM, BHL; entry for October 29, 1863, John B. Kay Diary, UM, BHL; James Higginson to father, November 12, 1863, Higginson Family Papers, MHS; entry for November 12, 1863, in James A. Penfield, *The 1863–1864 Diary of Captain James Penfield, 5th New York Volunteer Cavalry, Company H* (Ticonderoga, NY: Press of America, 1999).

13. *OR,* 6:439–40, 498.

14. Entries for July 22, August 11, 1863, William A. Noel Diary, Rare Book Department, Boston Public Library; entries for June 27, July 21, 1863, Wilson Diary, OHS; entries for July 23, September 4, 1863, in Penfield, *Diary of Penfield,* 78, 97; entry for October 1, 1863, Keeler Diary, Keeler Family Papers, UM, BHL.

15. Entries for August 1, September 2, 1863, Grant Diary, DU; entry for July 28, 1863, George R. Lodge Diary, in Roger Tusken, ed., "In the Bastile of the Rebels," *Journal of the Illinois State Historical Society* 56 (Summer 1963): 322–23; entry for August 19, 1863, Fortescue Diary, SHC, UNC; entries for October 9, 12, 15, 1863, Nelson Purdum Diary, vol. 938, OHS; entries for October 15, 17, 26, 27, 28, 1863, Howard Diary, in Jennings, "Prisoner of the Confederacy," 316–17.

16. Entries for November 28, December 10, 1863, Noel Diary, Rare Book Department, Boston Public Library; entry for February 24, 1863, Wilson Diary, OHS; entries for October 29, 30, 1863, Fortescue Diary, SHC, UNC; entries for November 16, December 12, 1863, Keeler Diary, Keeler Family Papers, UM, BHL.

17. Entry for December 9, 1863, Noel Diary, Rare Book Department, Boston Public Library; Frank L. Byrne, ed., "A General Behind Bars: Neal Dow in Libby Prison," in *Civil War Prisons,* ed. William B. Hesseltine (Kent, OH: Kent State University Press, 1962), 61–62.

18. *OR,* 6:457–58, 459, 482–83, 485, 510.

19. Ibid., 6:515, 537, 570–71, 659, 686.

20. Entries for December 14, 16, 1863, Wilson Diary, OHS; entry for December 14, 1863, Noel Diary, Rare Book Department, Boston Public Library; entries for December 14, 25, 1863, Keeler Diary, Keeler Family Papers, UM, BHL; entry for December 25, 1863, Lodge Diary, in Tusken, "In the Bastile of the Rebels," 329.

21. Entries for July 28, September 2, December 6, 1863, Noel Diary, Rare Book Department, Boston Public Library; entries for September 10, December 25, 26, 1863, in Penfield, *Diary of Penfield,* 100, 144; entries for July 26, September 20, 26, 1863, Fortescue Diary, SHC, UNC; entry for November 17, 1863, Lodge Diary, in Tusken, "In the Bastile of the Rebels," 327–28; entry for October 6, 1863, Keeler Diary, Keeler Family Papers, UM, BHL; entry for November 10, 1863, Rollins Diary, WHS.

22. Entries for July 8, September 20, 1863, Noel Diary, Rare Book Department, Boston Public Library; entry for July 24, 1863, in Penfield, *Diary of Penfield,* 79; entry for September

20, 1863, Wilson Diary, OHS; entry for September 20, 1863, Fortescue Diary, SHC, UNC; entries for September 3, 9, 1863, William Henry Powell Diary, Chicago Historical Society.

23. Entry for August 30, 1863, Fortescue Diary, SHC, UNC; entry for February 9, 1864, Robert T. Cornwall Diary, in Thomas M. Boaz, ed., *Libby Prison and Beyond: A Union Staff Officer in the East, 1862–1865* (Shippensburg, PA: Burd Street, 1999), 103; entry for January 26, 1864, Wilson Diary, OHS.

24. Entry for August 4, 1863, Noel Diary, Rare Book Department, Boston Public Library; entry for December 24, 1863, Kay Diary, UM, BHL; entry for January 19, 1864, Wilson Diary, OHS; entry for January 20, 1864, Cornwall Diary, in Boaz, *Libby Prison and Beyond,* 70; Wilson N. Paxton to "Cousin Ella," October 28, 1863, Thomas and Wilson N. Paxton Letters, 1861–1863, PM, NC.

25. Entry for November 1, 1863, Purdum Diary, OHS; entry for October 18, 1863, Keeler Diary, Keeler Family Papers, UM, BHL; James E. Love to "Mollie," January 4, 1864, James Edwin Love Papers, Missouri Historical Society, St. Louis.

26. Entries for October 7, 11, November 16, 1863, Fortescue Diary, SHC, UNC; entries for November 11, 16, 1863, Keeler Diary, Keeler Family Papers, UM, BHL; entry for November 17, 1863, Lodge Diary, in Tusken, "In the Bastile of the Rebels," 328.

27. Entries for October 9, 31, 1863, Purdum Diary, OHS; entry for December 9, 1863, Rollins Diary, WHS; entry for October 23, 1863, Keeler Diary, Keeler Family Papers, UM, BHL.

28. Entries for July 5, 8, 1863, Noel Diary, Rare Book Department, Boston Public Library; entries for July 5, 8, 1863, Wilson Diary, OHS; entries for September 22, 23, 24, 1863, in Penfield, *Diary of Penfield,* 105–6.

29. Entries for November 7, 10, December 21, 1863, Keeler Diary, Keeler Family Papers, UM, BHL; entries for December 17, 26, 1863, Wilson Diary, OHS.

30. Entry for October 16, 1863, Fortescue Diary, SHC, UNC; entry for October 1, 1863, Keeler Diary, Keeler Family Papers, UM, BHL; entry for November 21, 1863, Kay Diary, UM, BHL; entry for April 10, 1864, Cornwall Diary, in Boaz, *Libby Prison and Beyond,* 130; entry for February 4, 1864, Wilson Diary, OHS.

31. Entry for September 14, 1863, Noel Diary, Rare Book Department, Boston Public Library; entry for October 3, 1863, Keeler Diary, Keeler Family Papers, UM, BHL; entry for December 29, 1863, Kay Diary, UM, BHL; entries for September 14–16, 1863, Fortescue Diary, SHC, UNC; entries for January 12, 24, 1864, Cornwall Diary, in Boaz, *Libby Prison and Beyond,* 65, 71.

32. Entries for July 13, October 12, 1863, Wilson Diary, OHS; entry for October 12, 1863, Keeler Diary, Keeler Family Papers, UM, BHL; entries for August 22, September 5, 1863, in Penfield, *Diary of Penfield,* 91, 97; entry for February 3, 1863, Cornwall Diary, in Boaz, *Libby Prison and Beyond,* 101; entry for September 5, 1863, Grant Diary, DU.

33. Entries for July 29, August 4, 11, September 8, 1863, Grant Diary, DU; entry for September 6, 1863, Fortescue Diary, SHC, UNC; entries for March 25, 26, 28, 30, 31, April 1, 2, 5, 1864, Cornwall Diary, in Boaz, *Libby Prison and Beyond,* 125–29.

34. Entry for November 20, 1863, Kay Diary, UM, BHL; entry for July 30, 1863, Lodge Diary, in Tusken, "In the Bastile of the Rebels," 323.

35. Entries for October 12, December 24, 1862, Wilson Diary, OHS; entries for October 13, 17, 1863, Fortescue Diary, SHC, UNC; entries for October 13, December 25, 1863, Lodge

Diary, in Tusken, "In the Bastile of the Rebels," 326, 329; entry for December 24, 1863, Noel Diary, Rare Book Department, Boston Public Library; entry for December 24, 1863, Keeler Diary, Keeler Family Papers, UM, BHL.

36. Entries for July 4, 5, 1863, Noel Diary, Rare Book Department, Boston Public Library; entries for July 4, 5, 1863, Wilson Diary, OHS.

37. Entry for September 12, 1863, in Penfield, *Diary of Penfield,* 101; Love to "Mollie," December 5, 1863, Love Papers, Missouri Historical Society, St. Louis; entries for April 18, May 4, 1864, Grant Diary, DU; entry for December 14, 1863, Wilson Diary, OHS; entry for March 31, 1864, Rollins Diary, WHS.

38. Entry for August 11, 1863, Noel Diary, Rare Book Department, Boston Public Library; entry for September 9, 1863, Fortescue Diary, SHC, UNC; entry for August 14, 1863, Lodge Diary, in Tusken, "In the Bastile of the Rebels," 324.

39. Entry for September 29, 1863, Noel Diary, Rare Book Department, Boston Public Library; entry for September 1, 1863, Fortescue Diary, SHC, UNC.

40. Entry for February 28, 1864, Wilson Diary, OHS; entry for September 12, 1863, Grant Diary, DU; entry for September 15, 1863, in Penfield, *Diary of Penfield,* 102.

41. Entry for December 29, 1863, Noel Diary, Rare Book Department, Boston Public Library; entries for December 29, 31, 1863, Wilson Diary, OHS.

42. Entry for December 25, 1863, Kay Diary, UM, BHL; Higginson to father, November 12, 1863, Higginson Family Papers, MHS; entry for January 7, 1864, Cornwall Diary, in Boaz, *Libby Prison and Beyond,* 63.

43. Entry for July 15, 1863, Noel Diary, Rare Book Department, Boston Public Library; entries for July 15, 1863, January 23, 1864, Wilson Diary, OHS; entry for January 23, 1864, Cornwall Diary, in Boaz, *Libby Prison and Beyond,* 71; entry for January 24, 1864, Lodge Diary, in Tusken, "In the Bastile of the Rebels," 331–32; entries for August 4–5, 1863, in Penfield, *Diary of Penfield,* 85.

44. Entry for August 11, 1863, Fortescue Diary, SHC, UNC; entry for November 23, 1863, Keeler Diary, Keeler Family Papers, UM, BHL; entries for September 9, October 10, 13, 1863, January 31, 1864, Lodge Diary, in Tusken, "In the Bastile of the Rebels," 325, 326, 332.

45. Entry for July 18, 1863, in Penfield, *Diary of Penfield,* 75; entry for November 19, 1863, Kay Diary, UM, BHL; entry for October 27, 1863, Purdum Diary, OHS.

46. Entry for June 27, 1863, Noel Diary, Rare Book Department, Boston Public Library.

47. Entry for October 1, 1863, Noel Diary, Rare Book Department, Boston Public Library; entry for October 2, 1863, Wilson Diary, OHS; entry for October 2, 1863, in Penfield, *Diary of Penfield,* 110; *Richmond Examiner,* October 5, 1863.

48. Entry for March 1, 1864, Noel Diary, Rare Book Department, Boston Public Library; entry for March 1, 1864, Wilson Diary, OHS; entries for March 1, 11, 1864, Lodge Diary, in Tusken, "In the Bastile of the Rebels," 335, 336; entry for March 1, 1863, Dow Diary, in Byrne, "A General Behind Bars," 73–74; Furgurson, *Ashes of Glory,* 249–55.

49. Entry for March 5, 1864, Wilson Diary, OHS; entries for March 5, 21, 1864, Lodge Diary, in Tusken, "In the Bastile of the Rebels," 335, 337; entry for March 5, 1864, Rollins Diary, WHS; entries for March 6, 20, 1864, Cornwall Diary, in Boaz, *Libby Prison and Beyond,* 117, 123; entries for March 5, 20, 28, 1864, Cyrus P. Heffley Diary, in Earl E. Boyer, ed., *Civil War Diaries of Capt. Albert Heffley and Lt. Cyrus P. Heffley* (Apollo, PA: Clossen, 2000), 103,

105, 106; entries for March 20, 28, 1864, Keeler Diary, Keeler Family Papers, UM, BHL; *OR,* 6:1110–11.

50. Blakely, *General John H. Winder,* 173; entry for March 3, 1864, Noel Diary, Rare Book Department, Boston Public Library.

51. Entry for March 2, 1864, Dow Diary, in Byrne, "A General Behind Bars," 74; entry for March 2, 1864, Lodge Diary, in Tusken, "In the Bastile of the Rebels," 335; entry for March 3, 1864, Wilson Diary, OHS; entry for March 2, 1864, Cyrus P. Heffley Diary, in Boyer, *Civil War Diaries,* 103; entry for March 3, 1864, Cornwall Diary, in Boaz, *Libby Prison and Beyond,* 116.

52. Entry for October 24, 1863, Fortescue Diary, SHC, UNC; entries for October 25, December 12, 1863, Wilson Diary, OHS; entries for October 25, November 24, 1863, Keeler Diary, Keeler Family Papers, UM, BHL; entries for October 25, November 24, 1863, Rollins Diary, WHS; entry for December 11, 1863, in Penfield, *Diary of Penfield.*

53. Entry for January 29, 1864, Noel Diary, Rare Book Department, Boston Public Library; entry for January 30, 1864, Grant Diary, DU; entries for January 29, 30, 31, February 1, 2, 1864, Wilson Diary, OHS; entries for January 29, 30, 31, February 1, 2, 1864, Cyrus P. Heffley Diary, in Boyer, *Civil War Diaries,* 98–99; entries for January 29, 30, 31, February 1, 1864, Cornwall Diary, in Boaz, *Libby Prison and Beyond,* 72, 100.

54. Frank E. Moran, "Colonel Rose's Tunnel at Libby Prison," *Century Magazine,* March 1888, 770, 772.

55. Ibid., 772.

56. Ibid., 772–75.

57. Ibid., 775–78; William S. Long Reminiscences, Breckinridge-Long Papers, LC; Morton Tower Memoirs, VHS.

58. Moran, "Colonel Rose's Tunnel," 778–83.

59. Ibid., 783–84; entry for February 10, 1864, Noel Diary, Rare Book Department, Boston Public Library; entry for February 10. 1864, Wilson Diary, OHS; entry for February 10, 1864, Cyrus P. Heffley Diary, in Boyer, *Civil War Diaries,* 100.

60. Entries for February 10, 11, 12, 1864, Grant Diary, DU; entries for February 11, 12, 13, 14, 1864, Noel Diary, Rare Book Department, Boston Public Library; entries for February 11, 13, 17, 1864, Wilson Diary, OHS; entries for February 11, 12, 13, 14, 16, 18, 1864, Cyrus P. Heffley Diary, in Boyer, *Civil War Diaries,* 101–2; entries for February 11, 12, 14, 14, 15, 16, 1864, Cornwall Diary, in Boaz, *Libby Prison and Beyond,* 104–6.

61. Moran, "Colonel Rose's Tunnel," 789–90; Furgurson, *Ashes of Glory,* 244–47; *OR,* series 1, 33:559–66.

Chapter 6

1. *Richmond Dispatch,* January 17, May 14, 1863; *Richmond Examiner,* May 14, 16, 1863.

2. Entries for June 25, July 1, 1863, Henry G. Tracy Diary, CHS; entry for June 27, 1863, Nathan B. Webb Diary, ALPL; *Richmond Examiner,* July 21, September 1, 1863; *Richmond Sentinel,* October 23, 1863; *OR,* 6:545.

3. Entry for June 23, 1863, Tracy Diary, CHS; entry for June 26, 1863, Webb Diary, ALPL; entries for July 23, 24, 1863, Horace Smith Diary, WHS; entry for July 24, 1863, Newell Burch Diary, WHS.

4. Entries for July 24, August 10, 1863, Smith Diary, WHS; entry for June 27, 1863, Webb Diary, ALPL; entry for August 23, 1863, John A. Boudwin Diary, John A. Boudwin Papers, 1863–1864, PM, NC; entry for September 18, 1863, William S. Tippett Diary, Library of Virginia, Richmond; entry for September 25, 1863, William Dolphin Diary, in C. M. Crisfield, ed., *William Dolphin's Civil War Diary, August 15, 1863 through April 14, 1864* (Ossining, NY: Ossining Historical Society, 1991), 20.

5. Parker, *Richmond's Civil War Prisons,* 33–34.

6. Entry for July 26, 1863, Smith Diary, WHS; entry for October 20, 1863, George Hegeman Diary, in James J. Heslin, ed., "The Diary of a Union Soldier in Confederate Prisons," *New York Historical Society Quarterly* 41 (July 1957): 240–41; entry for June 28, 1863, Webb Diary, ALPL; entry for June 22, 1863, Anonymous Diary (Eighteenth Connecticut Infantry), CHS.

7. Entries for June 24–30, 1863, Tracy Diary, CHS; entries for August 8–13, 25, 1863, Boudwin Diary, PM, NC; entry for November 3, 1863, Dolphin Diary, in Crisfield, *Dolphin's Diary,* 32; entry for November 12, 1863, Jacob Osburn Coburn Diary, in Don Allison, ed., *Hell on Belle Isle: Diary of a Civil War POW* (Bryan, OH: Faded Banner, 1997), 86; entry for December 8, 1863, John Whitten Diary, LC; entries for November 12, 26, 1863, Burch Diary, WHS; entry for November 27, 1863, Tippett Diary, Library of Virginia, Richmond.

8. Entries for December 9, 12, 1863, Whitten Diary, LC; entries for September 20, October 1, November 6, 1863, Tippett Diary, Library of Virginia, Richmond; entry for July 25, 1863, Smith Diary, WHS; entry for July 7, 1863, Webb Diary, ALPL.

9. Entry for November 12, 1863, Tippett Diary, Library of Virginia, Richmond; entry for November 15, 1863, Coburn Diary, in Allison, *Hell on Belle Isle,* 88; entry for October 31, 1863, Dolphin Diary, in Crisfield, *Dolphin's Diary,* 32.

10. *OR,* 6:439, 456, 821–22; Blakely, *General John H. Winder,* 167–68; Sanders, *While in the Hands of the Enemy,* 186–87.

11. Entry for October 19, 1863, Smith Diary, WHS; entries for November 10, 1863, February 21, 1864, Hegeman Diary, in Heslin, "Diary of a Union Soldier," 244, 253; entry for July 16, 1863, Webb Diary, ALPL.

12. Aaron E. Bachman Memoirs, Harrisburg Civil War Roundtable Collection, USAMHI; entry for January 29, 1864, Michael Dougherty Diary, ANHS; entry for July 10, 1863, Webb Diary, ALPL; entry for March 5, 1864, Kay Diary, UM, BHL; entry for December 26, 1863, Hegeman Diary, in Heslin, "Diary of a Union Soldier," 247.

13. Entry for November 29, 1863, Dolphin Diary, in Crisfield, *Dolphin's Diary,* 41, 88.

14. Entry for December 30, 1863, Tippett Diary, Library of Virginia, Richmond; entries for August 28, 29, 30, 31, September 2, 3, 10, 1863, Boudwin Diary, PM, NC; entry for November 2, 1863, Coburn Diary, in Allison, *Hell on Belle Isle,* 64.

15. Entry for September 30, 1863, Smith Diary, WHS; entry for July 12, 1863, Webb Diary, ALPL.

16. Entries for September 7, 10, 1863, Smith Diary, WHS; entries for September 1, 3, 10, 1863, Boudwin Diary, PM, NC; entries for July 3, 16, 1863, Webb Diary, ALPL; *Richmond Examiner,* October 5, 1863.

17. Entries for October 20, 23, 26, 1863, Hegeman Diary, in Heslin, "Diary of a Union Soldier," 241–43; entries for January 14, 15, 25, 27, 28, 1864, Coburn Diary, in Allison, *Hell on Belle Isle,* 122–25; entry for December 29, 1863, Dolphin Diary, in Crisfield, *Dolphin's Diary,*

51; entry for January 14, 1863, Tippett Diary, Library of Virginia, Richmond; entries for October 26, 27, 1863, Smith Diary, WHS.

18. Entry for July 30, 1863, Burch Diary, WHS; Jonathan Boynton Memoir, CWMC, USAMHI; entries for July 24, August 4, 6, 7, 1863, Smith Diary, WHS.

19. Entries for August 6, 9, September 19, 1863, Boudwin Diary, PM, NC; entry for July 2, 1863, Webb Diary, ALPL; entries for November 1, 9, 1863, William Culbertson Robinson Diary, ALPL; entry for December 11, 1863, Whitten Diary, LC; entry for January 21, 1864, Kay Diary, UM, BHL.

20. Entries for November 15, December 31, 1863, January 4, 1864, Coburn Diary, in Allison, *Hell on Belle Isle,* 88, 118, 120; entry for December 19, 1863, Hegeman Diary, in Heslin, "Diary of a Union Soldier," 247; entry for January 22, 1864, Dougherty Diary, ANHS; entry for February 15, 1864, Kay Diary, UM, BHL.

21. Entries for November 5, 24, 27, 1863, Tippett Diary, Library of Virginia; entry for November 23, 1863, Dolphin Diary, in Crisfield, *Dolphin's Diary,* 39; entries for November 5, 23, 1863, Coburn Diary, in Allison, *Hell on Belle Isle,* 78, 99.

22. *OR,* 6:482–83.

23. Sanders, *While in the Hands of the Enemy,* 193–94; Blakely, *General John H. Winder,* 171; Frank Wilkeson, *Turned Inside Out: Recollections of a Private Soldier in the Army of the Potomac* (1887; repr., Lincoln: University of Nebraska Press, 1997), 224; *OR,* 7:111.

24. *OR,* 6:545; Blakely, *General John H. Winder,* 170–71.

25. *OR,* 6:587–88.

26. Ibid., 6:1087–90.

27. Entry for December 10, 1863, Whitten Diary, LC; entry for January 6, 1864, Hegeman Diary, in Heslin, "Diary of a Union Soldier," 248; entry for January 25, 1864, Kay Diary, UM, BHL.

28. Entries for August 13, 26, 1863, Boudwin Diary, PM, NC; entry for December 11, 1863, Coburn Diary, in Allison, *Hell on Belle Isle,* 111.

29. Entry for August 11, 1863, Boudwin Diary, PM, NC; entries for October 4, December 31, 1863, Tippett Diary, Library of Virginia, Richmond; entry for July 9, 1863, Webb Diary, ALPL.

30. Entry for August 15, 1863, Smith Diary, WHS.

31. Entries for July 3, 15, 1863, Webb Diary, ALPL; entries for July 5, 7, 12, 1863, Tracy Diary, CHS.

32. Entry for January 26, 1864, Coburn Diary, in Allison, *Hell on Belle Isle,* 127; Henry A. Smith to family, October 23, 1863, Henry A. Smith Letters, VTHS.

33. Entry for August 23, 1863, Burch Diary, WHS; entry for July 3, 1863, Webb Diary, ALPL; entry for September 7, 1863, Boudwin Diary, PM, NC; entries for October 31, December 15, 18, 1863, January 24, 1864, Hegeman Diary, in Heslin, "Diary of a Union Soldier," 250.

34. Entry for July 2, 1863, Webb Diary, ALPL; entry for September 14, 1863, Boudwin Diary, PM, NC.

35. Entry for August 31, 1863, Smith Diary, WHS; entry for August 31, 1863, Boudwin Diary, PM, NC; entry for December 22, 1863, Hegeman Diary, in Heslin, "Diary of a Union Soldier," 247.

36. Entry for May 13, 1863, John A. Porter Diary, PSA.

37. Entry for August 14, 1863, Boudwin Diary, PM, NC; entries for August 14, October 5, 1863, Smith Diary, WHS; entry for October 25, 1863, Tippett Diary, Library of Virginia, Richmond; entry for October 25, 1863, Dolphin Diary, in Crisfield, *Dolphin's Diary,* 30.

38. Entry for September 13, 1863, Smith Diary, WHS; entries for September 13, November 19, 1863, Burch Diary, WHS; entry for September 13, 1863, Boudwin Diary, PM, NC; entry for November 19, 1863, Robinson Diary, ALPL.

39. Entry for February 11, 1864, Tippett Diary, Library of Virginia, Richmond; entry for February 11, 1864, Dolphin Diary, in Crisfield, *Dolphin's Diary,* 66; entry for February 12, 1864, Whitten Diary, LC.

40. Entry for October 10, 1863, Burch Diary, WHS; entry for October 17, 1863, Smith Diary, WHS.

41. Entry for October 20, 1863, Burch Diary, WHS; entry for October 20, 1863, Smith Diary, WHS.

42. Entry for October 3, 1863, Tippett Diary, Library of Virginia; entry for October 15, 1863, Dolphin Diary, in Crisfield, *Dolphin's Diary,* 26; entry for October 16, 1863, Smith Diary, WHS; entry for November 8, 1863, Coburn Diary, in Allison, *Hell on Belle Isle,* 80.

43. *Richmond Sentinel,* December 30, 1863.

Chapter 7

1. *OR,* 6:438–39.

2. Ibid., 6:455, 502; James I. Robertson Jr., "Houses of Horror: Danville's Civil War Prisons," *Virginia Magazine of History and Biography* 69 (July 1961): 329.

3. Robertson, "Houses of Horror," 329–31.

4. Entry for April 11, 1864, William J. McKell Diary, in Watt P. Marchman, ed., "The Journal of Sgt. Wm. J. McKell," *Civil War History* 3 (September 1957): 320–21; entries for November 13–14, 1863, Howard Diary, in Jennings, "Prisoner of the Confederacy," 319–20. McKell did not secure his diary until April 1864. He used his first entry to recount events of the previous five months.

5. Entries for November 15–December 26, 1863, Howard Diary, in Jennings, "Prisoner of the Confederacy," 320–23.

6. Entry for April 11, 1864, McKell Diary, in Marchman, "Journal of McKell," 326–27.

7. Entries for January 29, February 4, 1864, Bergun H. Brown Diary, Bergun H. Brown Papers, 1861–1872 (C3798), WHMC; entry for April 11, 1864, McKell Diary, in Marchman, "Journal of McKell, 327; entry for January 29, 1864, William L. Tritt Diary, WHS; *Cincinnati Commercial,* February 26, 1864, in *New York Times,* February 28, 1864.

8. Entry for February 28, 1864, Tritt Diary, WHS; entry for February 27, 1864, William H. Haun Diary, Missouri Historical Society, St. Louis; entry for February 28, 1864, Brown Diary, WHMC.

9. Entries for February 26, 28, 1864, Haun Diary, Missouri Historical Society, St. Louis; entries for February 26, 27, March 3, 1864, Tritt Diary, WHS.

10. Entries for December 12, 13, 1863, Brown Diary, WHMC.

11. Entry for May 7, 1864, Tritt Diary, WHS; entry for May 9, 1864, in Penfield, *Diary of Penfield,* 157; entry for May 8, 1864, Cyrus P. Heffley Diary, in Boyer, *Civil War Diaries,* 109;

entry for May 14, 1864, Albert Harry Shatzel Diary, in Donald F. Danker, ed., "Imprisoned at Andersonville: The Diary of Albert Harry Shatzel, May 5, 1864–September 12, 1864," *Nebraska History* 38 (June 1957): 88.

12. Entry for January 1, 1864, Haun Diary, Missouri Historical Society, St. Louis; entry for January 7, 1864, Tritt Diary, WHS; entry for April 11, 1864, McKell Diary, in Marchman, "Journal of McKell," 328.

13. Entry for December 25, 1863, Brown Diary, WHMC; entry for April 11, 1864, McKell Diary, in Marchman, "Journal of McKell," 326, 328; Ann N. Hansen, ed., "A Southern Odyssey: The Narrative of Abram Price," *Timeline* 6 (October–November 1989): 25.

14. Entry for April 11, 1864, McKell Diary, in Marchman, "Journal of McKell," 326; entries for January 18, 19, 1864, Brown Diary, WHMC.

15. Entries for March 17, 19, April 11, 1864, Tritt Diary, WHS; entry for March 18, 1864, Haun Diary, Missouri Historical Society, St. Louis.

16. Entries for February 1, March 16, 17, 26, 27, May 4, 1864, Tritt Diary, WHS; entry for May 3, 1864, McKell Diary, in Marchman, "Journal of McKell," 333.

17. Love to wife, May 10, 1864, Love Papers, Missouri Historical Society, St. Louis; entry for May 8, 1864, Cyrus P. Heffley Diary, in Boyer, *Civil War Diaries,* 109; entry for May 13, 1864, Edwin T. Marsh Diary, Edwin T. Marsh Papers, 1863–1917, PM, NC.

18. Entry for April 11, 1864, McKell Diary, in Marchman, "Journal of McKell," 326; entries for December 26, 1863, January 13, 24, 1864, Brown Diary, WHMC; entry for February 17, 1864, Tritt Diary, WHS.

19. Entries for January 13, 24, 1864, Brown Diary, WHMC; entries for February 17, April 6, 1864, Tritt Diary, WHS; Robertson, "Houses of Horror," 331–32.

20. Entries for December 13, 19, 30, 31, 1863, Brown Diary, WHMC; entry for April 11, 1864, McKell Diary, in Marchman, "Journal of McKell," 327; entry for March 28, 1864, Tritt Diary, WHS.

21. *OR,* 6:888–90, 895.

22. Hansen, "A Southern Odyssey," 25; Robertson, "Houses of Horror," 339; entry for April 11, 1864, McKell Diary, in Marchman, "Journal of McKell," 326.

23. Entries for April 13, May 3, 1864, McKell Diary, in Marchman, "Journal of McKell," 329, 333; entries for December 14, 1863, February 2, 1864, Brown Diary, WHMC; entries for January 28, February 14, 16, May 11, 1864, Tritt Diary, WHS; entry for January 27, 1864, Haun Diary, Missouri Historical Society, St. Louis.

24. Entry for May 13, 1864, Marsh Diary, PM, NC; entry for May 16, 1864, Shatzel Diary, in Danker, "Imprisoned at Andersonville," 89; entry for May 21, 1864, William T. Peabody Diary, ANHS; entry for May 21, 1864, Henry H. Stone Diary, ANHS.

25. Entries for February 16, April 10, May 5, 11, 1864, Tritt Diary, WHS; entry for April 13, 1864, McKell Diary, in Marchman, "Journal of McKell," 329.

26. *OR,* 6:422–23.

27. Entries for May 9, 12, 16, 1864, Charles Mattocks Diary, in Philip N. Racine, ed., "*Unspoiled Heart": The Journal of Charles Mattocks of the 17th Maine* (Knoxville: University of Tennessee Press, 1994), 141–45; entries for May 10, 17, 1864, Jacob Heffelfinger Diary, *CWTI* Collection, USAMHI.

28. Entry for May 15, 1864, Mattocks Diary, in Racine, "*Unspoiled Heart,*" 142; entry for May 10, 1864, Heffelfinger Diary, *CWTI* Collection, USAMHI.

29. Entries for May 7, 8, 9, 16, 1864, Marsh Diary, PM, NC; entry for May 10, 1864, Shatzel Diary, in Danker, "Imprisoned at Andersonville," 87.

30. Entries for May 7, 8, 10, 1864, Marsh Diary, PM, NC; entries for May 9, 10, 1864, Shatzel Diary, in Danker, "Imprisoned at Andersonville," 86–87.

31. Entries for May 6, 7, 9, 12, 14, 31, 1864, Diary of anonymous Indiana soldier, William Smith Diary, UVA. The unknown soldier shared Smith's diary.

32. Entries for May 14, 16, 22, 25, 1864, Anonymous Diary, in Smith Diary, UVA.

33. Entries for June 15, 19, 1864, Anonymous Diary, in Smith Diary, UVA.

34. Bryant, *Cahaba Prison and the* Sultana *Disaster,* 20–24.

35. Ibid., 37–38, 44–48.

36. Capt. H. A. M. Henderson to ?, January 1864, PRCPC, RG 109, NA; undated entry, ca. February 21, 1864, Edmund E. Ryan Diary, Peoria Historical Society Collection, Bradley University Library, Peoria, IL; entry for April 25, 1864, David Kennedy Diary, MNHS; *OR,* 6:1124, 7:76, 110, 1001.

37. Undated entries, February–May, 1864, Ryan Diary, Peoria Historical Society Collection, Bradley University Library, Peoria, IL.

38. Entries for April 25, 26, 1864, Kennedy Diary, MNHS.

39. *OR,* 6:1124.

40. Ibid.

41. Bryant, *Cahaba Prison and the* Sultana *Disaster,* 79–86.

42. Amy L. Klemm, "A Shared Captivity: Inmates and Guards in the Texas Military Prison System, 1863–1865" (MA thesis, University of Houston, 1997), 7–10.

43. Ibid., 11–16.

44. William R. Boggs to John B. Magruder, July 21, 1863, PRCPC, RG 109, NA; Klemm, "A Shared Captivity," 20–21.

45. Klemm, "A Shared Captivity," 23; entries for November 9, 11, 14, 1863, J. B. Leake Diary, in Roger Davis, ed., "The Camp Ford Diary of J. B. Leake," *Chronicles of Smith County, Texas* 42 (2003): 49.

46. *OR,* 6:484.

47. Entry for November 9, 1863, Leake Diary, in Davis, "Diary of Leake," 49; Leon Mitchell Jr., "Camp Ford Confederate Military Prison," *Southwestern Historical Quarterly* 66 (July 1962): 13–14; Klemm, "A Shared Captivity," 98–99; entries for April 24, May 7, 16, June 6, 1864, William Fortunatus McKinney Diary, in Howard O. Pollan, ed., "The Camp Ford Diary of Captain William Fortunatus McKinney," *Chronicles of Smith County, Texas* 25 (Summer 1996): 17–19; entry for March 13, 1864, W. W. Heartsill Diary, in Bell Irvin Wiley, ed., *Fourteen Hundred and 91 Days in the Confederate Army* (Wilmington, NC: Broadfoot, 1987), 198.

48. Klemm, "A Shared Captivity," 99; Mitchell, "Camp Ford," 14; entry for July 26, 1864, Thomas L. Evans Diary, Thomas L. Evans Papers, SPC 972-0007, Archives and Special Collections Department, Eastern Washington University Library, Cheney, WA; entries for August 9, 11, 1864, McKinney Diary, in Pollan, "Diary of McKinney," 21.

49. Edmund Kirby Smith to Robert T. P. Allen, April 12, 1864, PRCPC, RG 109, NA; en-

tries for April 15, 17, 18, May 15, 21, 27, 1864, Heartsill Diary, in Wiley, *Fourteen Hundred and 91 Days,* 200, 204–6.

50. Klemm, "A Shared Captivity," 25; entry for April 15, 1864, Heartsill Diary, in Wiley, *Fourteen Hundred and 91 Days,* 200.

51. Mitchell, "Camp Ford," 3.

52. Entries for April 19, June 3, 1864, Evans Diary, Archives and Special Collections Department, Eastern Washington University Library, Cheney, WA; Klemm, "A Shared Captivity," 29; Samuel Fulton Reminiscences, *CWTI* Collection, USAMHI.

53. Entry for May 7, 1864, Evans Diary, Archives and Special Collections Department, Eastern Washington University Library, Cheney, WA.

54. Entries for June 14, September 3, 1864, Evans Diary, Archives and Special Collections Department, Eastern Washington University Library, Cheney, WA; entry for October 30, 1864, James M. Sampson Diary, MHS; entry for May 25, 1864, McKinney Diary, in Pollan, "Diary of McKinney," 18.

55. Entries for April 24, May 1, 8, June 18, 19, 1864, Evans Diary, Archives and Special Collections Department, Eastern Washington University Library, Cheney, WA; entry for July 3, 1864, Anonymous Diary, R. H. Porter Civil War Collection, University of Texas at San Antonio Libraries, Special Collections.

56. Entry for July 4, 1864, Evans Diary, Archives and Special Collections Department, Eastern Washington University Library, Cheney, WA; entry for July 4, 1864, Anonymous Diary, R. H. Porter Civil War Collection, University of Texas at San Antonio Libraries, Special Collections; entry for July 4, 1864, McKinney Diary, in Pollan, "Diary of McKinney," 20.

57. Entry for July 3, 1864, Anonymous Diary, R. H. Porter Civil War Collection, University of Texas at San Antonio Libraries, Special Collections; entries for March 27, June 19, 1864, Heartsill Diary, in Wiley, *Fourteen Hundred and 91 Days,* 198, 208.

58. Entries for July 2, 3, 25, August 4, 19, 1864, Evans Diary, Archives and Special Collections Department, Eastern Washington University Library, Cheney, WA; entries for July 2, 3, 1864, 1864, Anonymous Diary, R. H. Porter Civil War Collection, University of Texas at San Antonio Libraries, Special Collections; entries for July 2, 3, 26, August 4, 1864, McKinney Diary, in Pollan, "Diary of McKinney," 20.

59. Fulton Reminiscences, *CWTI* Collection, USAMHI; entries for August 1, 12, 1864, McKinney Diary, in Pollan, "Diary of McKinney," 21; entries for August 12–13, 1864, Evans Diary, Archives and Special Collections Department, Eastern Washington University Library, Cheney, WA.

60. Leon Mitchell Jr., "Prisoners of War in the Confederate Trans-Mississippi," (MA thesis, University of Texas, 1961), 91–92; entry for May 22, 1864, McKinney Diary, in Pollan, "Diary of McKinney," 18; entry for May 22, 1864, Heartsill Diary, in Wiley, *Fourteen Hundred and 91 Days,* 205.

61. Mitchell, "Prisoners of War," 92; entry for July 12, 1864, Evans Diary, Archives and Special Collections Department, Eastern Washington University Library, Cheney, WA; entry for July 11, 1864, McKinney Diary, in Pollan, "Diary of McKinney," 20; entry for July 12, 1864, Heartsill Diary, in Wiley, *Fourteen Hundred and 91 Days,* 210.

62. Entries for August 25, 28, 1864, Evans Diary, Archives and Special Collections Department, Eastern Washington University Library, Cheney, WA; entries for August 25, 28, 1864, McKinney Diary, in Pollan, "Diary of McKinney," 21–22.

Chapter 8

1. Entry for May 29, 1864, Peabody Diary, ANHS; entry for June 15, 1864, Alonzo Tuttle Decker Diary, ANHS; entry for June 8, 1864, John Melvin Converse Diary, Kansas State Historical Society, Topeka; entry for June 25, 1864, James Woodbury Diary, MNHS; entry for May 30, 1864, Alfred D. Burdick Diary, WHS; entry for May 23, 1864, George R. Crosby Diary, VTHS; entry for June 28, 1864, George M. Hinkley Diary, WHS; entry for May 21, 1864, Haun Diary, Missouri Historical Society, St. Louis; entry for June 7, 1864, Samuel L. Foust Diary, ANHS.

2. *OR,* 6:558.

3. William Marvel, *Andersonville: The Last Depot* (Chapel Hill: University of North Carolina Press, 1994), 14–16.

4. Ibid., 17–18; Blakely, *General John H. Winder,* 176–77; *OR,* 6:965–66.

5. Ovid Futch, *History of Andersonville Prison* (Gainesville: University of Florida Press, 1968), 5; Blakely, *General John H. Winder,* 176–77.

6. Blakely, *General John H. Winder,* 176; *OR,* 6:914, 962, 972, 1000, 1015.

7. *OR,* 6:965–66, 993; Marvel, *Andersonville,* 21.

8. Entries for February 18–19, 1864, Smith Diary, UVA.

9. Entries for February 20–22, 1864, Smith Diary, UVA.

10. Entries for February 23–25, 1864, Smith Diary, UVA.

11. Entries for February 26–29, 1864, Smith Diary, UVA.

12. Entries for March 3–10, 1864, Dougherty Diary, ANHS; entries for March 8–13, 1864, Kay Diary, UM, BHL; entries for March 16–22, 1864, Whitten Diary, LC.

13. *OR,* 7:1091–92; Capt. F. T. Miles to Gen. Thomas Jordan, March 6, 1864, PRCPC, RG 109, NA.

14. *Macon Telegraph,* February 27, 1864.

15. Entry for March 13, 1864, Dougherty Diary, ANHS; entries for March 16, 20, 1864, Kay Diary, UM, BHL; entry for March 22, 1864, Hegeman Diary, in Heslin, "Diary of a Union Soldier," 256.

16. Entries for March 14, 16, 1864, Kay Diary, UM, BHL; entries for March 18–23, 28–30, 1864, Dougherty Diary, ANHS; entry for March 21, 1864, Hegeman Diary, in Heslin, "Diary of a Union Soldier," 256.

17. Entries for March 20, 21, 1864, Kay Diary, UM, BHL; entries for March 11, 13, 16, 1864, Dougherty Diary, ANHS; entry for March 24, 1864, Hegeman Diary, in Heslin, "Diary of a Union Soldier," 256.

18. Marvel, *Andersonville,* 38.

19. Blakely, *General John H. Winder,* 181–82; Futch, *History of Andersonville Prison,* 19; Marvel, *Andersonville,* 45; *OR,* 7:63, 136.

20. Entry for March 22, 1864, Hegeman Diary, in Heslin, "Diary of a Union Soldier," 257; entry for June 25, 1864, De Witt Spaulding Diary, UM, BHL.

21. Marvel, *Andersonville,* 38; entry for April 1, 1864, Whitten Diary, LC; entry for April 1, 1864, Kay Diary, UM, BHL; entry for April 1, 1864, Hegeman Diary, in Heslin, "Diary of a Union Soldier," 258.

22. Entry for May 12, 1864, Hegeman Diary, in Heslin, "Diary of a Union Soldier," 262; entry for September 4, 1864, Samuel Henderson Diary, DU.

23. Entry for June 28, 1864, Robert Hale Kellogg Diary, CHS.

24. Futch, *History of Andersonville Prison,* 17; *OR,* 7:438; (Americus, GA) *Sumter Republican,* April 22, 1864.

25. *OR,* series 1, 36, pt. 2: 1011; 38, pt. 4: 704.

26. Ibid., series 2, 7:92; Braxton Bragg to Howell Cobb, May 3, 1864, box 68, folder 1, Howell Cobb Papers, UGA; Howell Cobb to Alexander Persons, May 9, June 3, 1864, Lamar Cobb to Persons, May 23, 24, 28, 1864, box 39, Cobb-Erwin-Lamar Papers, UGA.

27. Cobb to Timothy Furlow, May 26, 1864, Cobb to Seddon, June 6, 1864, box 39, Cobb-Erwin-Lamar Papers, UGA.

28. *OR,* 7:120–21, 135–39.

29. Entry for May 12, 1864, Samuel E. Grosvenor Diary, CHS; entries for May 15, 20, 21, 1864, Smith Diary, UVA; *OR,* 7:386–87.

30. *OR,* 7:167–70, 192, 213–14; Blakely, *General John H. Winder,* 183–84.

31. *OR,* 7:125; entry for May 20, 1864, Dougherty Diary, ANHS.

32. Entries for May 5, 6, 1864, Grosvenor Diary, CHS; entries for May 4, 20, 1864, Charles G. Lee Diary, in Paul C. Helmreich, ed., "The Diary of Charles G. Lee in Andersonville and Florence Prison Camps, 1864," *Connecticut Historical Society Bulletin* 41 (January 1976): 15, 17.

33. Entry for May 22, 1864, S. J. Gibson Diary, LC; entry for May 22, 1864, James Burton Diary, MARBL, Emory; entry for May 27, 1864, Shatzel Diary, in Danker, "Imprisoned at Andersonville," 94; entry for May 22, 1864, John Duff Diary, ANHS; entries for May 21, 27, 1864, Kellogg Diary, CHS; entries for May 27, 28, 1864, Nehemiah Solon Diary, CHS; entries for May 22, 27, 1864, Gibson Diary, LC.

34. Entry for June 13, 1864, Kennedy Diary, MNHS; entries for June 16, 19, 1864, Samuel Melvin Diary, in Alfred S. Roe, ed., *The Melvin Memorial* (Cambridge, MA: Riverside, 1910), 109, 110; entry for June 17, 1864, James W. Vance Diary, James W. Vance Papers, VFM 1834, OHS.

35. Entry for June 29, 1864, John L. Hoster Diary, MARBL, Emory; entry for June 28, 1864, Henry W. Tisdale Diary, ANHS; entry for June 30, 1864, Solon Diary, CHS; entry for June 29, 1864, Lee Diary, in Helmreich, "Diary of Lee," 20; entry for June 29, 1864, Kellogg Diary, CHS.

36. Entry for June 30, 1864, Solon Diary, CHS; entry for June 30, 1864, Hinkley Diary, WHS; entry for July 4, 1864, John A. Baer Diary, ANHS; entry for June 29, 1864, Spaulding Diary, UM, BHL; entry for June 28, 1864, Hoster Diary, MARBL, Emory; entry for June 28, 1864, Tisdale Diary, ANHS.

37. Entry for June 30, 1864, Hinkley Diary, WHS; entry for June 30, 1864, Kellogg Diary, CHS; entry for June 28, 1864, Tisdale Diary, ANHS; entry for June 30, 1864, Solon Diary, CHS; entry for June 30, 1864, Vance Diary, OHS; entry for June 30, 1864, John Pond Diary, SAF; entry for June 30, 1864, Kennedy Diary, MNHS; entry for June 30, 1864, Grosvenor Diary, CHS; entry for June 30, 1864, Gibson Diary, LC; *OR,* 7:426.

38. *OR,* 7:527; entry for July 11, 1864, Spaulding Diary, UM, BHL; entry for July 12, 1864, Solon Diary, CHS.

39. Entry for July 12, 1864, Solon Diary, CHS; entry for July 11, 1864, Dougherty Diary, ANHS.

40. Entry for July 12, 1864, Tisdale Diary, ANHS; entry for July 11, 1864, Dougherty Diary, ANHS; entry for July 12, 1864, Solon Diary, CHS; entry for July 11, 1864, Baer Diary, ANHS; entry for July 11, 1864, Spaulding Diary, UM, BHL; entry for July 11, 1864, Marsh Diary, PM, NC; entry for July 11, 1864, James Buckley Diary, ALPL.

41. Entry for July 12, 1864, Tisdale Diary, ANHS; entry for July 11, 1864, Ransom Chadwick Diary, MNHS; entry for July 12, 1864, Solon Diary, CHS; entry for July 11, 1864, Baer Diary, ANHS; entry for July 11, 1864, Peabody Diary, ANHS; entries for July 11, 12, 1864, Shatzel Diary, in Danker, "Imprisoned at Andersonville," 111.

42. Entries for August 29, September 1, 1864, Vance Diary, OHS; entry for July 12, 1864, Tisdale Diary, ANHS; entry for August 9, 1864, Baer Diary, ANHS.

43. Marvel, *Andersonville,* 82–83, 91.

44. *OR,* 7:427; entry for July 1, 1864, Kellogg Diary, CHS; entry for July 3, 1864, Tisdale Diary, ANHS; entry for July 1, 1864, Spaulding Diary, UM, BHL; entry for July 1, 1864, George Clarkson Diary, ANHS.

45. Entry for July 1, 1864, Daniel Hutchins Diary, UM, WLCL; entry for July 1, 1864, Stone Diary, ANHS; entry for July 1, 1864, Shatzel Diary, in Danker, "Imprisoned at Andersonville," 107; entry for July 1, 1864, Lee Diary, in Helmreich, "Diary of Lee," 21; entry for July 1, 1864, Darius Starr Diary, in E. Merton Coulter, ed., "From Spotsylvania Courthouse to Andersonville: A Diary of Darius Starr," *Georgia Historical Quarterly* 41 (June 1957): 187–88; entry for July 2, 1864, Solon Diary, CHS.

46. Entry for July 2, 1864, Solon Diary, CHS; entry for July 1, 1864, Lee Diary, in Helmreich, "Diary of Lee," 20; entry for July 2, 1864, Decker Diary, ANHS; entry for July 2, 1864, Kellogg Diary, CHS; entry for June 30, 1864, Dougherty Diary, ANHS.

47. Winder to Cobb, July 9, 1864, box 68, folder 7, Cobb to wife, July 11, 1864, box 68, folder 8, Cobb Papers, UGA.

48. Marvel, *Andersonville,* 151–52; *OR,* 7:483.

49. Entry for July 20, 1864, Crosby Diary, VTHS; entry for July 21, 1864, Lee Diary, in Helmreich, "Diary of Lee," 22; entry for July 20, 1864, Grosvenor Diary, CHS; entry for July 20, 1864, Kennedy Diary, MNHS.

50. Entries for July 20, 23, 1864, Baer Diary, ANHS; entries for July 20, 22, 1864, Edmund Pope Diary, VTHS; entries for July 21, 22, 1864, Shatzel Diary, in Danker, "Imprisoned at Andersonville," 114; entry for July, 31, 1864, Decker Diary, ANHS; entry for July 31, 1864, Pond Diary, SAF; entry for July 21, 1864, Francis Wilbur Goodyear Diary, box 2, folder 32, Beinecke Rare Book and Manuscript Library, Yale University, New Haven, CT; entry for July 23, 1864, Kennedy Diary, MNHS; entry for July 22, 1864, Grosvenor Diary, CHS.

Chapter 9

1. Entry for June 22, 1864, Grosvenor Diary, CHS; entry for June 1, 1864, Peabody Diary, ANHS; entry for July 12, 1864, Baer Diary, ANHS.

2. Entry for July 18, 1864, Melvin Diary, in Roe, *Melvin Memorial,* 110; entry for June 9, 1864, Kay Diary, UM, BHL; entry for July 6, 1864, Pond Diary, SAF; entries for June 7, 26, 1864, Peabody Diary, ANHS.

3. Entry for April 25, 1864, Whitten Diary, LC; entry for May 25, 1864, Dougherty Diary,

ANHS; entry for June 17, 1864, Marsh Diary, PM, NC; entry for September 1, 1864, Goodyear Diary, Beinecke Rare Book and Manuscript Library, Yale University, New Haven, CT; entry for July 9, 1864, Clarkson Diary, ANHS; Wirz to Capt. W. S. Winder, May 18, 1864, Wirz to Robert Ould, October 6, 1864, Wirz to Ould, January 30, 1865, Andersonville Prison, Georgia, Letters Sent, May 1864–March 1865 RG 109, NA.

4. Entries for June 5, 12, 26, July 3, 10, 24, 31, 1864, Kennedy Diary, MNHS; entry for August 7, 1864, Goodyear Diary, Beinecke Rare Book and Manuscript Library, Yale University, New Haven, CT; entry for October 2, 1864, J. E. Hodgkins Diary, in Kenneth C. Turino, ed., *The Civil War Diary of Lieut. J. E. Hodgkins, 19th Massachusetts Volunteers, from August 11, 1862 to June 3, 1865* (Camden, ME: Picton, 1994), 105; entry for May 8, 1864, Grosvenor Diary, CHS.

5. Entry for July 31, 1864, Kendrick R. Howard Diary, VTHS; entries for June 2, July 19, 27, September 9, 1864, William Seeley Diary, #1073, HSP; entry for August 19, 1864, Lee Diary, in Helmreich, "Diary of Lee," 22–23; entry for July 10, 1864, Goodyear Diary, Beinecke Rare Book and Manuscript Library, Yale University, New Haven, CT.

6. Entry for July 22, 1864, Baer Diary, ANHS; entry for July 16, 1864, Haun Diary, Missouri Historical Society, St. Louis; entries for July 5, 13, 1864, Lee Diary, in Helmreich, "Diary of Lee," 21; entry for July 24, 1864, Foust Diary, ANHS; entry for July 21, 1864, Hodgkins Diary, in Turino, *Diary of Hodgkins,* 101.

7. Entry for August 14, 1864, Tisdale Diary, ANHS; entry for August 8, 1864, Gibson Diary, LC; entry for June 26, 1864, Converse Diary, Kansas State Historical Society, Topeka; entries for July 16, 18, 30, 31, 1864, Baer Diary, ANHS; entry for June 2, 1864, Solon Diary, CHS; entries for June 6, 24, 1864, Lee Diary, in Helmreich, "Diary of Lee," 19–20.

8. Entry for June 21, 1864, Gibson Diary, LC; entry for May 17, 1864, Burton Diary, MARBL, Emory; entry for May 30, 1864, Tritt Diary, WHS; entry for September 3, 1864, Burdick Diary, WHS.

9. Entry for July 2, 1864, Tritt Diary, WHS; entry for June 10, 1864, Peabody Diary, ANHS; entry for June 9, 1864, Chadwick Diary, MNHS; entry for June 16, 1864, Kellogg Diary, CHS; entry for June 9, 1864, Crosby Diary, VTHS; entry for June 9, 1864, Solon Diary, CHS; entry for July 5, 1864, Hinkley Diary, WHS.

10. Entry for August 26, 1864, Yeakle Diary, ANHS; entry for August 27, 1864, Tritt Diary, WHS.

11. Entry for May 22, 1864, Dougherty Diary, ANHS; entry for May 31, 1864, Chadwick Diary, MNHS; entry for May 23, 1864, Kellogg Diary, CHS; entry for May 24, 1864, Burton Diary, MARBL, Emory.

12. Marvel, *Andersonville,* 46–47; entry for July 27, 1864, Goodyear Diary, Beinecke Rare Book and Manuscript Library, Yale University, New Haven, CT; entry for July 26, 1864, Melvin Diary, in Roe, *Melvin Memorial,* 123; entry for June 15, 1864, Tritt Diary, WHS; entry for June 9, 1864, Dougherty Diary, ANHS.

13. *OR,* 7:436–37.

14. Ibid., 7:601–2, 623–24.

15. Ibid., 7:168, 541–42, 547, 557.

16. Entry for July 27, 1864, Howard Diary, VTHS; entry for June 17, 1864, Kay Diary, UM, BHL; entry for June 3, 1864, Kennedy Diary, MNHS; entry for June 15, 1864, Lee Diary, in Helmreich, "Diary of Lee," 19; entries for May 26, 27, 1864, Dougherty Diary, ANHS.

17. Undated entry, ca. May 25, 1864, Solon Diary, CHS; entry for July 30, 1864, M. J. Umstead Diary, ANHS; entry for June 17, 1864, Decker Diary, ANHS; entry for June 12, 1864, Tisdale Diary, ANHS; entries for June 13, 15, 1864, Foust Diary, ANHS; entries for July 21, 24, 1864, Goodyear Diary, Beinecke Rare Book and Manuscript Library, Yale University, New Haven, CT; entry for June 28, 1864, Hinkley Diary, WHS.

18. Entry for July 16, 1864, Kennedy Diary, MNHS; entry for August 4, 1864, Chadwick Diary, MNHS; entries for July 7–8, 1864, Stone Diary, ANHS; entries for June 26, July 13, 1864, Lee Diary, in Helmreich, "Diary of Lee," 20, 21.

19. Entry for June 23, 1864, Henderson Diary, DU; entry for July 2, 1864, Burdick Diary, WHS; entries for June 27, August 9, 1864, Chadwick Diary, MNHS; entries for July 1, 8, 1864, Hutchins Diary, UM, WLCL; entries for June 19, July 16, 1864, Vance Diary, OHS; entry for July 19, 1864, Clarkson Diary, ANHS.

20. Entry for July 16, 1864, Bradford Sparrow Diary, Special Collections, University of Vermont Libraries, Burlington; entry for July 12, 1864, Hoster Diary, MARBL, Emory.

21. Marvel, *Andersonville,* 179–80; entries for August 9, 16, 1864, Clarkson Diary, ANHS; entry for August 21, 1864, Tisdale Diary, ANHS.

22. Entry for June 27, 1864, Kay Diary, UM, BHL; entry for June 22, 1864, Solon Diary, CHS; entry for June 10, 1864, Chadwick Diary, MNHS; entry for June 16, 1864, Dougherty Diary, ANHS.

23. *OR,* 7:207, 427, 522, 525, 558.

24. Entries for May 16, June 22, 1864, Dougherty Diary, ANHS; entries for June 10, 25, 28, 1864, Hutchins Diary, UM, WLCL; entry for June 11, 1864, Stone Diary, ANHS; entry for June 25, 1864, Lee Diary, in Helmreich, "Diary of Lee," 20; entry for June 25, 1864, Gibson Diary, LC; entry for June 26, 1864, Solon Diary, CHS; entry for June 26, 1864, Starr Diary, in Coulter, "From Spotsylvania Courthouse to Andersonville," 187.

25. Marvel, *Andersonville,* 52–53, 58, 79–80; *OR,* 7:207; entry for June 12, 1864, Tisdale Diary, ANHS.

26. Entry for May 19, 1864, Grosvenor Diary, CHS; entries for June 20, August 20, 1864, Stone Diary, ANHS; entry for August 24, 1864, Kennedy Diary, MNHS; entries for July 13, August 11, 1864, Goodyear Diary, Beinecke Rare Book and Manuscript Library, Yale University, New Haven, CT; entries for July 8, 10, 1864, Kay Diary, UM, BHL; entry for June 20, 1864, Shatzel Diary, in Danker, "Imprisoned at Andersonville," 104.

27. Entry for June 22, 1864, Solon Diary, CHS; entry for July 4, 1864, Chadwick Diary, MNHS; entries for August 5, 11, 16, 1864, James Bradd Diary, SHSI; entry for August 13, 1864, Yeakle Diary, ANHS; entries for August 6, 10, 1864, Foust Diary, ANHS; entry for August 12, 1864, Shatzel Diary, in Danker, "Imprisoned at Andersonville," 119.

28. Marvel, *Andersonville,* 57.

29. Entries for May 22, July 14, 17, 1864, Chadwick Diary, MNHS; entries for May 25, 27, July 4, 1864, Marsh Diary, PM, NC; entries for June 3, 4, 14, 1864, Melvin Diary, in Roe, *Melvin Memorial,* 104, 106; entry for May 30, 1864, John B. Gallison Diary, MHS; entry for July 12, 1864, Hoster Diary, MARBL, Emory; entry for June 20, 1864, Gibson Diary, LC; entry for May 31, 1864, Levi Whitaker Diary, ANHS.

30. Entry for June 28, 1864, Hutchins Diary, UM, WLCL; entry for July 18, 1864, Sparrow Diary, Special Collections, University of Vermont Libraries, Burlington; entries for July 12, 18, August 19, 1864, Whitaker Diary, ANHS; entry for August 28, 1864, Charles A. Knight

Diary, Charles A. Knight Papers, accn. 1665, Manuscripts Division, J. Willard Marriott Library, University of Utah, Salt Lake City; entry for October 3, 1864, Foust Diary, ANHS; entries for July 8, 26, 1864, Starr Diary, in Coulter, "From Spotsylvania Courthouse to Andersonville," 188, 189.

31. Entries for June 1, 2, 16, 18, 1864, Dougherty Diary, ANHS; entries for June 22, July 8, 1864, Solon Diary, CHS; entry for July 7, 1864, Baer Diary, ANHS.

32. Entries for June 22, July 8, 31, 1864, Solon Diary, CHS; entry for June 1, 1864, Dougherty Diary, ANHS; entry for June 27, 1864, Kellogg Diary, CHS; entry for July 11, 1864, Goodyear Diary, Beinecke Rare Book and Manuscript Library, Yale University, New Haven, CT.

33. Entry for June 2, 1864, Dougherty Diary, ANHS; entries for June 4, July 12, 1864, Kay Diary, UM, BHL; entry for July 13, 1864, Tritt Diary, WHS; entry for July 12, 1864, Seeley Diary, HSP; entries for June 11, 24, 1864, Grosvenor Diary, CHS.

34. Entries for May 27, June 20, July 22, August 2, 17, November 24, 1864, Gibson Diary, LC.

35. Marvel, *Andersonville,* 180, 238; entry for May 31, 1864, Seeley Diary, HSP.

36. *OR,* 7:386–87, 427, 430, 525, 558; entry for June 21, 1864, Solon Diary, CHS.

37. *OR,* 7:525; entry for May 3, 1864, Hegeman Diary, in Heslin, "Diary of a Union Soldier," 261; entries for May 16, June 1, 1864, Kay Diary, UM, BHL; entries for July 19, August 12, 1864, Solon Diary, CHS; entry for August 14, 1864, Tisdale Diary, ANHS.

38. James O. Breedon, "Andersonville—A Southern Surgeon's Story," *Bulletin of the History of Medicine* 47, no. 4 (1973): 337–39; entry for June 24, 1864, Tritt Diary, WHS; entries for July 4, 5, 8, 1864, Kay Diary, UM, BHL; entry for July 22, 1864, Foust Diary, ANHS.

39. Entries for August 17, 18, 18, 21, 22, 23, 26, 27, 1864, Hutchins Diary, UM, WLCL.

40. Entry for August 3, 1864, Grosvenor Diary, CHS; entries for June 12, July 10, August 7, 1864, Tisdale Diary, ANHS; entry for August 12, 1864, Henderson Diary, DU; entries for August 11, 16, 1864, Chadwick Diary, MNHS.

41. Entry for September 15, 1864, Melvin Diary, in Roe, *Melvin Memorial,* 133.

42. Entries for June 16, 28, July 27, 1864, Hegeman Diary, in Heslin, "Diary of a Union Soldier," 265.

43. Entries for June 13, August 10, September 1, 1864, Duff Diary, ANHS; entries for August 8, 9, 11, 1864, Kennedy Diary, MNHS.

44. Entries for May 5, June 7, 8, 11, 13, 24, 25, 27, July 9, 25, 1864, Smith Diary, UVA.

45. Entries for August 3, 4, 21, 27, 28, September 1, 1864, Smith Diary, UVA.

46. *OR,* 7:546–48.

47. Ibid., 7:551–52.

48. Ibid., 7:551, 755.

49. Ibid., 7:755–56, 758–59.

50. Breeden, "Andersonville—A Southern Surgeon's Story," 318–19.

51. Ibid., 324–26.

52. Ibid., 336–38; *OR,* 8:618–20.

53. Louis Manigault to wife, September 18, 1864, Manigault Family Record, SCHS.

54. Entry for July 31, 1864, Solon Diary, CHS.

55. Manigault to wife, September 18, 1864, Manigault Family Record, SCHS; entry for September 13, 1864, Hinkley Diary, WHS.

56. Manigault, Confederate States Military Prison of Andersonville, Manigault Family Record, SCHS; entry for September 12, 1864, Hegeman Diary, in Heslin, "Diary of a Union Soldier," 168.

57. Entry for September 2, 1864, Goodyear Diary, Beinecke Rare Book and Manuscript Library, Yale University, New Haven, CT; entry for August 22, 1864, Baer Diary, ANHS; entry for August 14, 1864, Yeakle Diary, ANHS; entries for August 14, 20, September 3, 1864, Lee Diary, in Helmreich, "Diary of Lee," 22–24.

58. Entry for July 15, 1864, Marsh Diary, PM, NC; entry for August 14, 1864, Decker Diary, ANHS; entry for August 22, 1864, Baer Diary, ANHS; entry for September 4, 1864, Melvin Diary, in Roe, *Melvin Memorial,* 130.

59. *OR,* 7:168.

60. Entry for May 27, 1864, Spaulding Diary, UM, BHL; entry for September 4, 1864, Tritt Diary, WHS.

61. *OR,* 7:137, 438; entry for June 14, 1864, Hegeman Diary, in Heslin, "Diary of a Union Soldier," 264; entries for April 6–7, 1864, Dougherty Diary, ANHS; entry for April 15, 1864, Kay Diary, UM, BHL. The dates of the Dougherty Diary are not always reliable. Kay likely cites the accurate date of the incident.

62. Marvel, *Andersonville,* 63–64; entry for May 5, 1864, Whitten Diary, LC; entry for May 5, 1864, Burton Diary, MARBL, Emory.

63. Entries for May 21–24, 1864, Grosvenor Diary, CHS; entries for May 21–25, 1864, Lee Diary, in Helmreich, "Diary of Lee," 17–18; entry for May 25, 1864, Spaulding Diary, UM, BHL.

64. Entry for May 25, 1864, Kellogg Diary, CHS; entry for May 25, 1864, Lee Diary, in Helmreich, "Diary of Lee," 18; entry for May 25, 1864, Grosvenor Diary, CHS; entry for May 27, 1864, Shatzel Diary, in Danker, "Imprisoned at Andersonville," 94–95.

65. Entry for May 26, 1864, Kellogg Diary, CHS; entry for May 27, 1864, Spaulding Diary, UM, BHL; entry for May 27, 1864, Crosby Diary, VTHS; entry for May 27, 1864, Whitten Diary, LC; entry for May 27, 1864, Lee Diary, in Helmreich, "Diary of Lee," 18; (Americus, GA) *Sumter Republican,* May 28, 1864.

66. Entries for May 30–31, 1864, Kellogg Diary, CHS.

67. Entry for July 17, 1864, Tisdale Diary, ANHS; entry for July 14, 1864, Grosvenor Diary, CHS; entry for July 14, 1864, Hoster Diary, MARBL, Emory; entry for July 15, 1864, Shatzel Diary, in Danker, "Imprisoned at Andersonville," 112; entry for July 14, 1864, Goodyear Diary, Beinecke Rare Book and Manuscript Library, Yale University, New Haven, CT.

68. Entry for July 16, 1864, J. M. Burdick Diary, in Ovid Futch, ed., "The Andersonville Diary of Sergeant J. M. Burdick," *Georgia Historical Quarterly* 45 (September 1961): 289; entries for July 16–17, 1864, Decker Diary, ANHS; entry for July 17, 1864, Hinkley Diary, WHS; entry for July 17, 1864, Baer Diary, ANHS; entry for July 18, 1864, Kay Diary, UM, BHL; entries for July 18–19, 1864, Lee Diary, in Helmreich, "Diary of Lee," 21.

69. Entry for July 20, 1864, Goodyear Diary, Beinecke Rare Book and Manuscript Library, Yale University, New Haven, CT; entry for July 20, 1864, Hinkley Diary, WHS; entry for July 20, 1864, Decker Diary, ANHS; entry for July 20, 1864, Crosby Diary, VTHS; entry for July 20, 1864, Shatzel Diary, in Danker, "Imprisoned at Andersonville," 113; Marvel, *Andersonville,* 153.

70. Entry for August 28, 1864, Vance Diary, OHS; entry for August 28, 1864, Gallison Diary, MHS; entry for August 28, 1864, Goodyear Diary, Beinecke Rare Book and Manuscript Library, Yale University, New Haven, CT; *OR,* 7:708.

71. Marvel, *Andersonville,* 172.

72. Entry for June 19, 1864, Solon Diary, CHS; entry for June 19, 1864, Kellogg Diary, CHS; entries for June 19, 22, 1864, Gibson Diary, LC; entry for June 21, 1864, Dougherty Diary, ANHS; entry for June 21, 1864, Grosvenor Diary, CHS; entry for June 21, 1864, Pond Diary, SAF; entry for June 21, 1864, Lee Diary, in Helmreich, "Diary of Lee," 19; entry for June 21, 1864, Marsh Diary, PM, NC; entry for June 21, 1864, Melvin Diary, in Roe, *Melvin Memorial,* 111.

73. Entries for July 13, 27, August 6, 1864, Tritt Diary, WHS; entries for July 14, August 7, 1864, Gates Diary, CHS; entries for July 13, August 6, 1864, Hinkley Diary, WHS; entries for July 16, August 6, 1864, Grosvenor Diary, CHS; entry for July 27, 1864, Kay Diary, UM, BHL; entry for July 27, 1864, Kennedy Diary, MNHS; entry for July 27, 1864, Gallison Diary, MHS; entry for August 6, 1864, Pond Diary, SAF; entry for August 7, 1864, Hegeman Diary, in Heslin, "Diary of a Union Soldier," 267; entry for August 6, 1864, Gibson Diary, LC.

74. Entry for May 15, 1864, Kellogg Diary, CHS; entries for May 15, July 22, 1864, Gibson Diary, LC; entry for July 22, 1864, Stone Diary, ANHS.

75. Joseph Williams to family, July 12, 1864, Williams to wife, July 24, 1864, box 1, folder 4, Williams Family Papers, UGA; for rumors of guards receiving furloughs for shooting prisoners, see entry for June 22, 1864, Kennedy Diary, MNHS; entry for July 14, 1864, Yeakle Diary, ANHS; entry for July 27, 1864, Shatzel Diary, in Danker, "Imprisoned at Andersonville," 115.

76. Williams to wife, July 24, 1864, Williams to family, August 6, 1864, box 1, folder 4, Williams Family Papers, UGA; unknown soldier to Patience Everett, June ?, 1864, Patience Everett Papers, DU.

77. *OR,* 7:773.

78. Entry for September 5, 1864, Pope Diary, VTHS; entry for September 5, 1864, Joseph B. Felton Diary, ANHS; entry for September 5, 1864, Kennedy Diary, MNHS; entry for September 5, 1864, Vance Diary, OHS.

79. Entry for September 6, 1864, Pope Diary, VTHS; entries for September 6–7, 1864, Tritt Diary, WHS; entry for September 4, 1864, Pond Diary, SAF.

80. Entry for September 6, 1864, Howard Diary, VTHS; entries for September 7–11, 1864, Marsh Diary, PM, NC; entry for September 10, 1864, Pond Diary, SAF; entry for September 10, 1864, Tritt Diary, WHS.

81. *OR,* 7:1082–83; entry for September 16, 1864, Woodbury Diary, MNHS.

Chapter 10

1. Entry for May 1, 1864, Ira B. Sampson Diary, SHC, UNC; Cooper to Cobb, May 2, 1864, box 68, folder 1, Cobb Papers, UGA; *OR,* 7:106.

2. *Macon Telegraph,* May 11, 18, 21, 24, 25, 1864.

3. Entry for May 17, 1864, Cyrus Heffley Diary, in Boyer, *Civil War Diaries,* 109–10; entry for May 17, 1864, Grant Diary, DU.

4. Entries for May 20, 22, 23, 1864, Cyrus Heffley Diary, in Boyer, *Civil War Diaries,* 110;

entry for May 25, 1864, Mattocks Diary, in Racine, "*Unspoiled Heart,*" 148; entry for July 10, 1864, Asa D. Mathews Diary, VTHS.

5. *OR*, 7:372; entries for May 18, 25, 1864, Cyrus Heffley Diary, in Boyer, *Civil War Diaries,* 110–11; entry for May 17, 1864, Grant Diary, DU.

6. Entry for May 26, 1864, Sampson Diary, SHC, UNC; entry for May 28, 1864, Heffelfinger Diary, *CWTI* Collection, USAMHI; entry for May 28, 1864, Templeton B. Hurst Diary, manuscript 6, PSA; entry for May 28, 1864, Cyrus Heffley Diary, in Boyer, *Civil War Diaries,* 111; entry for May 29, 1864, in Penfield, *Diary of Penfield,* 164; *OR*, 7:582.

7. Entry for May 8, 1864, Sampson Diary, SHC, UNC; entry for May 19, 1864, in Penfield, *Diary of Penfield,* 160–61; entry for May 24, 1864, Heffelfinger Diary, *CWTI* Collection, USAMHI.

8. Entry for May 31, 1864, Heffelfinger Diary, *CWTI* Collection, USAMHI; entry for June 28, 1864, James E. Wenrick Diary, AM 6695, HSP; entry for July 28, 1864, Mathews Diary, VTHS; entry for May 19, 1864, Grant Diary, DU.

9. Entry for June 12, 1864, Hurst Diary, PSA; entry for June 12, 1864, Mattocks Diary, in Racine, "*Unspoiled Heart,*" 155–56; entries for June 11–12, 1864, in Penfield, *Diary of Penfield,* 168; entry for June 11, 1864, Keeler Diary, Keeler Family Papers, UM, BHL; entry for June 11, 1864, Cyrus Heffley Diary, in Boyer, *Civil War Diaries,* 111.

10. Entry for May 27, 1864, Heffelfinger Diary, *CWTI* Collection, USAMHI; entry for May 27, 1864, Hurst Diary, PSA; entry for May 27, 1864, in Penfield, *Diary of Penfield,* 163.

11. Entry for June 17, 1864, Mattocks Diary, in Racine, "*Unspoiled Heart,*" 157; entries for May 28, June 1, 4, 9, 17, 1864, in Penfield, *Diary of Penfield,* 163, 165–69; entries for June 9, 16, 1864, Hurst Diary, PSA; entry for June 16, 1864, Heffelfinger Diary, *CWTI* Collection, USAMHI.

12. Entries for May 23, July 6, 1864, Keeler Diary, Keeler Family Papers, UM, BHL; entry for July 1, 1864, Wenrick Diary, HSP; entries for June 17, 19, 1864, Mattocks Diary, in Racine, "*Unspoiled Heart,*" 158–59; entry for July 21, 1864, Mathews Diary, VTHS.

13. Entry for May 18, 1864, Cyrus Heffley Diary, in Boyer, *Civil War Diaries,* 110.

14. Entries for July 12, 19, 1864, Francis Trowbridge Sherman Diary, UVA.

15. Entry for July 5, 1864, Heffelfinger Diary, *CWTI* Collection, USAMHI; entry for July 2, 1864, Keeler Diary, Keeler Family Papers, UM, BHL; entry for July 4, 1864, Mattocks Diary, in Racine, "*Unspoiled Heart,*" 165.

16. Charles Mattocks to mother, June 5, 1864, in Racine, "*Unspoiled Heart,*" 154; entry for June 21, 1864, Heffelfinger Diary, *CWTI* Collection, USAMHI.

17. Entry for June 14, 1864, Keeler Diary, Keeler Family Papers, UM, BHL; entry for June 14, 1864, Albert Heffley Diary, in Boyer, *Civil War Diaries,* 82; entry for June 14, 1864, Hurst Diary, PSA.

18. Entry for May 29, 1864, Heffelfinger Diary, *CWTI* Collection, USAMHI; entries for July 20, 24, 1864, Mathews Diary, VTHS.

19. Entry for July 6, 1864, Mattocks Diary, in Racine, "*Unspoiled Heart,*" 167.

20. Entry for June 15, 1864, Keeler Diary, Keeler Family Papers, UM, BHL; entries for May 25, July 14, 1864, Mattocks Diary, in Racine, "*Unspoiled Heart,*" 149, 169; John Ogden Reminiscences, Wisconsin Veterans Museum, Madison; entries for July 21, 22, 1864, Mathews Diary, VTHS.

21. Love to "Mollie," June 2, 1864, Love Papers, Missouri Historical Society, St. Louis; en-

tries for June 5, July 6, 1864, Mattocks Diary, in Racine, "*Unspoiled Heart,*" 151, 167; Ogden Reminiscences, Wisconsin Veterans Museum, Madison.

22. Entry for July 4, 1864, Hurst Diary, PSA; entry for July 4, 1864, Heffelfinger Diary, *CWTI* Collection, USAMHI; entry for July 4, 1864, Mattocks Diary, in Racine, "*Unspoiled Heart,*" 163.

23. Entry for July 4, 1864, Hurst Diary, PSA; entry for July 4, 1864, Heffelfinger Diary, *CWTI* Collection, USAMHI; entry for July 4, 1864, Mattocks Diary, in Racine, "*Unspoiled Heart,*" 163–64; entry for July 4, 1864, Albert Heffley Diary, in Boyer, *Civil War Diaries,* 83.

24. Entry for June 7, 1864, Heffelfinger Diary, *CWTI* Collection, USAMHI; entry for June 7, 1864, Hurst Diary, PSA.

25. Entry for June 21, 1864, Keeler Diary, Keeler Family Papers, UM, BHL.

26. Entries for June 22–23, 1864, Heffelfinger Diary, *CWTI* Collection, USAMHI; entries for June 22–23, 1864, Hurst Diary, PSA; entries for June 22–23, 1864, in Penfield, *Diary of Penfield,* 169–70; entry for July 22, 1864, Mattocks Diary, in Racine, "*Unspoiled Heart,*" 160–61.

27. Entry for August 3, 1864, Howard Diary, VTHS; entry for July 16, 1864, Gibson Diary, LC.

28. Entry for July 23, 1864, Crosby Diary, VTHS; entry for July 16, 1864, Peabody Diary, ANHS; entry for July 8, 1864, Kennedy Diary, MNHS; entry for August 15, 1864, Baer Diary, ANHS.

29. Entry for July 26, 1864, Baer Diary, ANHS; entry for July 15, 1864, Shatzel Diary, in Danker, "Imprisoned at Andersonville," 112; entry for July 15, 1864, Melvin Diary, in Roe, *Melvin Memorial,* 120. See also Marvel, *Andersonville,* 145–49, 165.

30. Entries for April 21, 30, 1864, Wenrick Diary, HSP.

31. Entries for May 10–15, 1864, Wenrick Diary, HSP.

32. Entry for May 28, 1864, Cyrus Heffley Diary, in Boyer, *Civil War Diaries,* 111; entry for May 28, 1864, in Penfield, *Diary of Penfield,* 163.

33. Entry for June 27, 1864, Heffelfinger Diary, *CWTI* Collection, USAMHI; entries for June 26–27, 1864, in Penfield, *Diary of Penfield,* 173; entries for June 26–27, 1864, Keeler Diary, Keeler Family Papers, UM, BHL; entries for June 26–27, 1864, Cyrus Heffley Diary, in Boyer, *Civil War Diaries,* 112.

34. Entry for July 18, 1864, Hurst Diary, PSA; entry for July 18, 1864, Keeler Diary, Keeler Family Papers, UM, BHL.

35. Entries for June 30, July 1, 1864, Keeler Diary, Keeler Family Papers, UM, BHL; entries for July 1, 6, 20, 1864, Hurst Diary, PSA; entries for July 1, 6, 20, 1864, Heffelfinger Diary, *CWTI* Collection, USAMHI.

36. Entry for June 10, 1864, Keeler Diary, Keeler Family Papers, UM, BHL; entry for June 10, 1864, Heffelfinger Diary, *CWTI* Collection, USAMHI; entry for June 10, 1864, Mattocks Diary, in Racine, "*Unspoiled Heart,*" 155.

37. *OR,* 7:185, 216–17.

38. *OR,* series 1, 35, pt. 2: 132–35; Sanders, *While in the Hands of the Enemy,* 227.

39. *OR,* 7:463, 472, 502.

40. Entries for July 27–28, 1864, Sherman Diary, UVA; entries for July 27–28, 1864, Keeler Diary, Keeler Family Papers, UM, BHL; entry for August 1, 1864, Cyrus Heffley Diary, in Boyer, *Civil War Diaries,* 112.

41. Entry for August 1, 1864, Cyrus Heffley Diary, in Boyer, *Civil War Diaries,* 112; Love to "Mollie," August 3, 1864, Love Papers, Missouri Historical Society, St. Louis; entries for July 28–29, 1864, Sherman Diary, UVA.

42. Entries for July 28–29, 1864, Mathews Diary, VTHS; entry for July 29, 1864, Edward C. Anderson Diary, SHC, UNC; entry for July 29, 1864, Wenrick Diary, HSP; entries for July 28–29, 1864, Heffelfinger Diary, *CWTI* Collection, USAMHI.

43. Entries for July 30, August 1, 2, 1864, Heffelfinger Diary, *CWTI* Collection, USAMHI; entries for July 30, August 1, 2, 1864, Hurst Diary, PSA; entries for August 1, 2, 1864, Mathews Diary, VTHS.

44. Entry for July 30, 1864, Heffelfinger Diary, *CWTI* Collection, USAMHI; entry for July 29, 1864, Mathews Diary, VTHS; entries for August 18, 19, 1864, Wenrick Diary, HSP; entry for August 24, 1864, Hurst Diary, PSA.

45. Entry for July 31, 1864, Heffelfinger Diary, *CWTI* Collection, USAMHI; entry for July 31, 1864, Hurst Diary, PSA; entry for August 3, 1864, Mathews Diary, VTHS.

46. Entry for August 8, 1864, Anderson Diary, SHC, UNC; entry for August 8, 1864, Heffelfinger Diary, *CWTI* Collection, USAMHI; *Savannah News,* quoted in *Macon Telegraph,* August 15, 1864; Ogden Reminiscences, Wisconsin Veterans Museum, Madison.

47. Entry for August 8, 1864, Anderson Diary, SHC, UNC; entry for August 8, 1864, Mathews Diary, VTHS; entries for August 8, 27, 1864, Heffelfinger Diary, *CWTI* Collection, USAMHI; entry for August 27, 1864, Hurst Diary, PSA.

48. Entry for August 4, 1864, Mathews Diary, VTHS; entry for August 21, 1864, Hurst Diary, PSA; entry for August 7, 1864, Heffelfinger Diary, *CWTI* Collection, USAMHI.

49. Entries for July 31, August 4, 14, September 2, 1864, Heffelfinger Diary, *CWTI* Collection, USAMHI; entries for July 31, August 7, 14, 28, 1864, Wenrick Diary, HSP; entries for July 31, August 12, September 2, 1864, Mathews Diary, VTHS.

50. Entries for August 3, 11, 15, 19, 22, 25, 26, 31, 1864, Mathews Diary, VTHS; entry for August 23, 1864, Wenrick Diary, HSP; entry for August 20, 1864, Hurst Diary, PSA.

51. Entry for August 20, 1864, Mathews Diary, VTHS; entry for August 20, 1864, Hurst Diary, PSA; entry for August 20, 1864, Heffelfinger Diary, *CWTI* Collection, USAMHI.

52. Entry for September 8, 1864, Anderson Diary, SHC, UNC; entry for September 12, 1864, Mathews Diary, VTHS; entries for September 12–13, 1864, Hurst Diary, PSA.

53. Entry for August 1, 1864, Cyrus Heffley Diary, in Boyer, *Civil War Diaries,* 112; entries for July 31, August 2–4, 1864, Keeler Diary, Keeler Family Papers, UM, BHL; entries for July 31, August 2, 1864, Sherman Diary, UVA.

54. Entry for July 30, 1864, Sherman Diary, UVA; entries for August 1, 2, 1864, Keeler Diary, Keeler Family Papers, UM, BHL; entry for July 31, 1864, in Penfield, *Diary of Penfield,* 182.

55. Love to "Mollie," August 20, 1864, Love Papers, Missouri Historical Society, St. Louis; entries for August 16, 17, 18, 19, 22, 23, 1864, Keeler Diary, UM, BHL; entry for August 17, 1864, in Penfield, *Diary of Penfield,* 186; entry for September 7, 1864, Mattocks Diary, in Racine, "*Unspoiled Heart,*" 197.

56. Entries for August 28, September 2, 17, 1864, Sherman Diary, UVA; entry for August 31, 1864, Mattocks Diary, in Racine, "*Unspoiled Heart,*" 187; entry for September 17, 1864, Keeler Diary, Keeler Family Papers, UM, BHL; Rollins to Timothy O. Howe, January 26, 1865, Rollins Diary, WHS.

57. Entry for August 13, 1864, Sherman Diary, UVA; entry for August 15, 1864, Mattocks Diary, in Racine, "*Unspoiled Heart,*" 187–88; entry for September 16, 1864, Hurst Diary, PSA; entry for September 18, 1864, Wenrick Diary, HSP.

58. Entries for September 21, 22, 1864, Hurst Diary, PSA; entries for September 18–21, 1864, Heffelfinger Diary, *CWTI* Collection, USAMHI.

59. Entry for September 22, 1864, Wenrick Diary, HSP; entries for September 27–30, 1864, Hurst Diary, PSA; entries for September 26–28, 1864, Heffelfinger Diary, *CWTI* Collection, USAMHI.

60. *OR,* 7:611.

61. Ibid., 7:894, 930, 975, 1030–31, 1060–62; M. L. Bonham to Seddon, October 6, 1864, PRCPC, RG 109, NA.

62. *OR,* 7:986; Rollins to Howe, January 26, 1865, Rollins Diary, WHS; entry for October 6, 1864, Hurst Diary, PSA; entries for October 6–7, 1864, Heffelfinger Diary, *CWTI* Collection, USAMHI.

63. Rollins to Howe, January 26, 1865, Rollins Diary, WHS; entries for October 8, 9, 1864, Heffelfinger Diary, *CWTI* Collection, USAMHI; Love to "Mollie," October 10, 1864, Love Papers, Missouri Historical Society, St. Louis.

64. Rollins to Howe, January 26, 1865, Rollins Diary, WHS; entry for October 18, 1864, Hurst Diary, PSA; *OR,* 7:1046; entry for October 24, 1864, Thomas W. Rathbone Diary, in Louis Bartlett, ed., "Captain T. W. Rathbone's 'Brief Diary of Imprisonment,' July 1–November 21, 1864," *Ohio History* 71 (January 1962): 49; entry for October 24, 1864, Heffelfinger Diary, *CWTI* Collection, USAMHI.

65. Entries for October 9–14, 28, 1864, Keeler Diary, Keeler Family Papers, UM, BHL; entries for October 9, 11, 30, 1864, Heffelfinger Diary, *CWTI* Collection, USAMHI; Rollins to Howe, January 26, 1865, Rollins Diary, WHS; entry for October 28, 1864, Rathbone Diary, in Bartlett, "Rathbone's Diary," 50; entry for November 9, 1864, Hurst Diary, PSA.

66. *OR,* 7:1046.

67. Entry for October 13, 1864, Hurst Diary, PSA; entry for October 13, 1864, Rathbone Diary, in Bartlett, "Rathbone's Diary," 47; entries for October 13, 19, 1864, Heffelfinger Diary, *CWTI* Collection, USAMHI; entry for October 19, 1864, in Penfield, *Diary of Penfield,* 201.

68. Entry for October 26, 1864, Rathbone Diary, in Bartlett, "Diary of Rathbone," 50; entry for October 26, 1864, Keeler Diary, Keeler Family Papers, UM, BHL; entry for October 26, 1864, Heffelfinger Diary, *CWTI* Collection, USAMHI.

69. Entry for November 5, 1864, Cyrus Heffley Diary, in Boyer, *Civil War Diaries,* 114–15; Rollins to Howe, January 26, 1865, Rollins Diary, WHS; entry for November 4, 1864, Hurst Diary, PSA.

70. Entries for November 21, 26, 1864, Heffelfinger Diary, *CWTI* Collection, USAMHI; entries for November 24, 26, 29, 1864, Keeler Diary, Keeler Family Papers, UM, BHL; entries for November 28, 29, 1864, Hurst Diary, PSA; entries for November 27, December 4, 1864, Cyrus Heffley Diary, in Boyer, *Civil War Diaries,* 115; entry for November 27, 1864, in Penfield, *Diary of Penfield; OR,* 7:1196.

71. Entry for November 27, 1864, in Penfield, *Diary of Penfield,* 207; entry for November 27, 1864, Heffelfinger Diary, *CWTI* Collection, USAMHI; entry for November 26, 1864, Hurst Diary, PSA; entry for November 27, 1864, Keeler Diary, Keeler Family Papers, UM, BHL.

72. Entry for October 21, 1864, Rathbone Diary, in Bartlett, "Rathbone's Diary," 49; entry for October 22, 1864, Hurst Diary, PSA; entry for October 21, 1864, Heffelfinger Diary, *CWTI* Collection, USAMHI; entry for October 22, 1864, Rollins Diary, WHS.

73. Entry for December 1, 1864, Hurst Diary, PSA; entry for December 1, 1864, in Penfield, *Diary of Penfield,* 209; entry for December 1, 1864, Heffelfinger Diary, *CWTI* Collection, USAMHI; entry for December 1, 1864, Albert Heffley Diary, in Boyer, *Civil War Diaries,* 81; entry for December 1, 1864, Keeler Diary, Keeler Family Papers, UM, BHL.

74. *OR,* 7:1179–80, 1184, 1196–97; Blakely, *General John H. Winder,* 200.

75. Entries for December 12–13, 1864, Hurst Diary, PSA.

76. Entries for December 12, 18, 1864, January 8, 1865, Cyrus Heffley Diary, in Boyer, *Civil War Diaries,* 116; entries for December 13, 15, 21, 22, 1864, January 2, 1865, Heffelfinger Diary, *CWTI* Collection, USAMHI; entries for December 13, 14, 16, 22, 24, 27, 29, 1864, Keeler Diary, Keeler Family Papers, UM, BHL.

77. *OR,* 7:501–2.

Chapter 11

1. Dudley Taylor Cornish, *The Sable Arm: Black Troops in the Union Army, 1861–1865* (Lawrence: University Press of Kansas, 1956), 46–47, 95–96; James M. McPherson, *The Negro's Civil War: How American Negroes Felt and Acted during the War for Union* (Urbana: University of Illinois Press, 1965), 164, 169.

2. *OR,* 5:797, 807–8, 940–41.

3. Ibid., 7:1010–11, 1018.

4. Bell Irvin Wiley, *The Life of Johnny Reb: The Common Soldier of the Confederacy* (Baton Rouge: Louisiana State University Press, 1987), 314.

5. *OR,* series 1, 24, pt. 2: 454.

6. Ibid., series 1, 24, pt. 2: 459, series 2, 6:21–22.

7. Ibid., 6:113.

8. Ibid., series 1, 24, pt. 3: 425–26, 443–44, 469.

9. Anne J. Bailey, "A Texas Cavalry Raid: Reaction to Black Soldiers and Contrabands," *Civil War History* 35, no. 2 (1989): 138–45; *OR,* series 1, 24, pt. 2: 466.

10. Ibid., series 2, 6:177–78, 189.

11. Ibid., 6:258–59.

12. Gregory J. Urwin, "'We Cannot Treat Negroes as Prisoners of War': Racial Atrocities and Reprisals in Civil War Arkansas," *Civil War History* 42, no. 3 (1996): 193–97; *OR,* series 1, 34, pt. 1: 754.

13. Urwin, "'We Cannot Treat Negroes as Prisoners of War,'" 204–5; *OR,* series 1, 34, pt. 1: 714–15.

14. *OR,* 7:78–79, 459–60.

15. McPherson, *The Negro's Civil War,* 216–17.

16. *OR,* 5:455–56, 469–70, 484, 8:703.

17. Ibid., 7:174.

18. Wirz to H. A. M. Henderson, June 5, 1864, Andersonville Prison, Georgia, Letters Sent, May 1864–March 1865, RG 109, NA.

19. *OR,* 7:26–27, 109.

20. Ibid., 7:354–55.

21. Ibid., 7:153

22. Ibid., 7:967–69, 987–88, 1010–11.

23. Cornish, *The Sable Arm,* 151; *OR,* 7:123.

24. *OR,* 7:125, 132, 135; Cornish, *The Sable Arm,* 153–55.

25. *OR,* 7:139–40, 145–46, 159, 169; Howard C. Westwood, "Captive Black Union Soldiers in Charleston—What to Do?" *Civil War History* 28, no. 1 (1982): 32–33.

26. *OR,* 7:190, 193–94.

27. Westwood, "Captive Black Union Soldiers in Charleston," 34–35, 38–39; *OR,* 6:245–46.

28. *OR,* 7:409, 463.

29. Ibid., 7:703–4, 1206.

30. Ibid., 7:78.

31. *Richmond Dispatch,* September 12, 1862.

32. Entry for July 24, 1863, Noel Diary, Rare Book Department, Boston Public Library; entry for July 24, 1863, Wilson Diary, OHS.

33. Entry for March 11, 1864, Lodge Diary, in Tusken, "In the Bastile of the Rebels," 336; entry for March 17, 1864, Noel Diary, Rare Book Department, Boston Public Library; *Richmond Whig,* March 8, 1864; entry for August 26, 1864, Arthur G. Sedgwick Diary, in William M. Armstrong, ed., "Libby Prison: The Civil War Diary of Arthur G. Sedgwick," *Virginia Magazine of History and Biography* 71 (October 1963): 456.

34. *Richmond Sentinel,* August 10, 1864; *Richmond Dispatch,* August 10, 1864.

35. Entry for November 28, 1864, Fred T. Shelton Diary, Fred T. Shelton Papers, 1861–1865, PM, NC; entry for November 28, 1864, James Canon Diary, WHS; Elbert L. Sherrill to Amanda McRaven, February 22, 1865, in Louis A. Brown, ed., "The Correspondence of David Orlando McRaven and Amanda Nantz McRaven, 1864–1865," *North Carolina Historical Review* 26 (January 1949): 92.

36. *OR,* 6:843; entry for September 13, 1864, Ryan Diary, Peoria Historical Society Collection, Bradley University Library, Peoria, IL.

37. Entry for March 14, 1864, Kay Diary, UM, BHL; Marvel, *Andersonville,* 41–42.

38. Marvel, *Andersonville,* 105, 154–55, 175, 203.

39. Entry for December 20, 1864, Tritt Diary, WHS.

Chapter 12

1. Lafayette McLaws to Howell Cobb, September 9, 1864, box 68, folder 19, Cobb Papers, UGA; entries for September 7–8, 1864, Anderson Diary, SHC, UNC.

2. Entries for September 8–9, 12–17, 1864, Anderson Diary, SHC, UNC.

3. Entries for September 11, 12, 13, 18, 1864, Anderson Diary, SHC, UNC; entry for September 11, 1864, Knight Diary, J. Willard Marriott Library, University of Utah, Salt Lake City.

4. Entries for September 10, 14, 1864, Anderson Diary, SHC, UNC.

5. Entry for September 12, 1864, Knight Diary, J. Willard Marriott Library, University of Utah, Salt Lake City; entry for September 12, 1864, Umstead Diary, ANHS; entries for September 29–30, October 1, 1864, Howard Diary, VTHS.

6. Entry for September 9, 1864, Anderson Diary, SHC, UNC; entry for October 10, 1864, Umstead Diary, ANHS; entry for October 11, 1864, Tisdale Diary, ANHS.

7. Entry for October 8, 1864, Knight Diary, J. Willard Marriott Library, University of Utah, Salt Lake City; entries for October 9–10, 1864, Anderson Diary, SHC, UNC.

8. Entries for October 11–13, 18, 1864, Anderson Diary, SHC, UNC.

9. Entry for September 12, 1864, Hoster Diary, MARBL, Emory; entry for September 12, 1864, Gibson Diary, LC; entry for September 12, 1864, Pope Diary, VTHS; entries for September 15, 19, 1864, Stone Diary, ANHS.

10. Entry for September 15, 1864, Stone Diary, ANHS; entry for September 29, 1864, Hegeman Diary, in Heslin, "Diary of a Union Soldier," 269; entries for September 14–15, 1864, Gibson Diary, LC; entry for September 12, 1864, Hoster Diary, MARBL, Emory.

11. Entries for September 14–16, 25, 29, 1864, Chadwick Diary, MNHS; entries for September 14–15, 21, 26, 28, 1864, Gibson Diary, LC; entry for September 28, 1864, Grosvenor Diary, CtHS.

12. Entry for September 29, 1864, Hegeman Diary, in Heslin, "Diary of a Union Soldier," 269; entry for September 17, 1864, Hoster Diary, MARBL, Emory; entry for September 13, 1864, Grosvenor Diary, CHS.

13. Entry for September 14, 1864, Hoster Diary, MARBL, Emory; entry for September 29, 1864, Hutchins Diary, UM, WLCL.

14. Entry for September 14, 1864, Pope Diary, VTHS; entry for September 15, 1864, Gibson Diary, LC; entry for September 14, 1864, Chadwick Diary, MNHS; entry for September 25, 1864, Hoster Diary, MARBL, Emory.

15. Entry for October 1, 1864, Pope Diary, VTHS; entry for October 1, 1864, Hutchins Diary, UM, WLCL.

16. *OR,* 7:509; Blakely, *General John H. Winder,* 193–94.

17. *OR,* 7:546, 565, 593, 773, 783.

18. Ibid., 7:841, 854, 869–70, 955, 993.

19. Entry for October 11, 1864, Anderson Diary, SHC, UNC; Speer, *Portals to Hell,* 378; Winder to Cobb, October 12, 1864, box 68, folder 20, Winder to Cobb, November 11, 1864, box 69, folder 3, Cobb Papers, UGA; *OR,* 7:993.

20. Entry for October 10, 1864, Vance Diary, OHS; entry for October 17, 1864, Tisdale Diary, ANHS; entry for October 12, 1864, Knight Diary, Manuscripts Division, J. Willard Marriott Library, University of Utah, Salt Lake City.

21. Entries for November 7, 18, 1864, Sheldon Curtiss Diary, CHL, CM; entries for November 15, 17, 1864, Chester Townsend Hart Diary, ANHS; entry for October 30, 1864, Tisdale Diary, ANHS.

22. *OR,* 7:993.

23. Entry for November 5, 1864, Curtiss Diary, CHL, CM; entry for October 23, 1864, Knight Diary, Manuscripts Division, J. Willard Marriott Library, University of Utah, Salt Lake City; entry for October 23, 1864, Amos W. Ames Diary, in Dorothy Carlson, ed., "A Diary of Prison Life in Southern Prisons," *Annals of Iowa* 40 (Summer 1969): 6; entry for October 15, 1864, Felton Diary, ANHS; *OR,* 7:1113.

24. Entry for October 30, 1864, Tisdale Diary, ANHS.

25. Entries for October 25, 27, 18, 1864, Felton Diary, ANHS; entries for October 26–29,

1864, Umstead Diary, ANHS; entry for October 28, 1864, Ames Diary, in Carlson, "Diary of Prison Life," 6; entry for November 4, 1864, Yeakle Diary, ANHS.

26. Entry for November 8, 1864, Ames Diary, in Carlson, "Diary of Prison Life," 7; entry for November 9, 1864, Yeakle Diary, ANHS; entries for November 8–9, 1864, Umstead Diary, ANHS.

27. *OR,* 7:1145, 1160.

28. Ibid., 7:817, 1086; Gen. James Chesnut to Gen. Sam Jones, September 10, 11, 1864, James Chesnut Letterbook, 1864–1865, MARBL, Emory.

29. Entry for September 15, 1864, Tritt Diary, WHS; entry for September 15, 1864, Crosby Diary, VTHS; entry for September 17, 1864, Hinkley Diary, WHS; H. L. Ravenel to mother, September 17, 1864, Ravenel Family Papers, SCHS.

30. Entry for September 16, 1864, Henderson Diary, DU; entry for September 15, 1864, Marsh Diary, PM, NC.

31. Entry for September 20, 1864, Hinkley Diary, WHS; entry for September 22, 1864, Crosby Diary, VTHS; entries for September 15–27, 1864, Pond Diary, SAF.

32. Entry for September 17, 1864, Kennedy Diary, MNHS; entry for September 17, 1864, Tritt Diary, WHS.

33. Entry for September 16, 1864, Kennedy Diary, MNHS; entry for September 24, 1864, Tritt Diary, WHS; entry for September 18, 1864, Hinkley Diary, WHS; entries for September 16, 25, October 2, 1864, Crosby Diary, VTHS.

34. *OR,* 7:822, 972–73; entry for September 30, 1864, Crosby Diary, VTHS; entry for September 30, 1864, Pond Diary, SAF; entry for September 30, 1864, Marsh Diary, PM, NC.

35. *OR,* 7:1098.

36. Entries for October 2, 6, 7, 1864, Tritt Diary, WHS; entry for October 2, 1864, Marsh Diary, PM, NC; entries for October 2, 6, 1864, Hinkley Diary, WHS; entries for October 2, 6, 1864, Bradd Diary, SHSI.

37. *OR,* 7:972; entry for October 2, 1864, Grosvenor Diary, CHS; entries for October 2, 3, 6, 1864, Gibson Diary, LC.

38. Entry for October 7, 1864, Chadwick Diary, MNHS; entry for October 4, 1864, Pope Diary, VTHS; entry for October 5, 1864, Hutchins Diary, UM, WLCL; entry for October 7, 1864, Converse Diary, Kansas State Historical Society, Topeka.

39. Entry for January 5, 1865, Oscar C. Wood Diary, ANHS; entries for October 9–11, November 19, 1864, Hutchins Diary, UM, WLCL; entries for October 3, 27, 1864, Bradd Diary, SHSI; entries for October 3, 19, 23, 1864, Gibson Diary, LC.

40. Entries for October 17, November 22, 1864, Tritt Diary, WHS.

41. Entry for October 4, 1864, Bradd Diary, SHSI; entries for October 9, 11, 13, 15, November 1, 1864, Hoster Diary, MARBL, Emory; entry for November 28, 1864, Tisdale Diary, ANHS.

42. Entry for October 8, 1864, Pope Diary, VTHS; entry for October 22, 1864, Bradd Diary, SHSI; entry for October 29, 1864, Gibson Diary, LC; *OR,* 7:973.

43. Entry for October 19, 1864, Pond Diary, SAF; entries for October 20, 26, November 15, 19, 1864, Tritt Diary, WHS; entry for October 26, 1864, Gibson Diary, LC; entry for November 16, 1864, Stone Diary, ANHS.

44. Entry for December 18, 1864, Tisdale Diary, ANHS; entry for December 15, 1864, Hegeman Diary, in Heslin, "Diary of a Union Soldier," 278.

45. *OR,* 7:972, 1097–99, 1150, 1197.

46. Ibid., 7:1099, 8:765–66; Speer, *Portals to Hell,* 274–75; entries for October 9, November 3, 1864, Henderson Diary, DU; entry for November 25, 1864, Hoster Diary, MARBL, Emory.

47. Entry for November 12, 1864, Tritt Diary, WHS; entry for November 12, 1864, Pond Diary, SAF.

48. *OR,* 7:1099, 8:137.

49. Ibid., 7:1098; entry for October 5, 1864, Gibson Diary, LC; entry for October 5, 1864, Tritt Diary, WHS.

50. Entries for December 4, 8, 1864, Tritt Diary, WHS; entry for December 4, 1864, Gibson Diary, LC; entry for December 8, 1864, Hoster Diary, MARBL, Emory; entry for January 4, 1865, Yeakle Diary, ANHS; entry for January 4, 1865, Wood Diary, ANHS.

51. Accounts of December rations come mostly from the Yeakle Diary (ANHS) and the Tritt Diary (WHS); entries for December 28, 1864, January 26, 1865, Hoster Diary, MARBL, Emory.

52. *OR,* 8:160–61.

53. Entry for January 27, 1865, Hoster Diary, MARBL, Emory; entry for January 27, 1865, Marsh Diary, PM, NC.

54. Entry for February 13, 1865, Marsh Diary, PM, NC; *OR,* 8:218; Charles S. Young to sister, February 17, 1865, Young Family Papers, SCHS; Blakely, *General John H. Winder,* 197.

55. Entries for February 1, 18, 1865, Yeakle Diary, ANHS; Young to sister, February 23, 1865, Young Family Papers, SCHS.

Chapter 13

1. *OR,* 7:1, 150.

2. Ibid., 7:986–87.

3. Byrne, "Libby Prison," 441.

4. Entry for August 23, 1864, Julius Frederic Ramsdell Diary, SHC, UNC; entry for August 28, 1864, George E. Albee Diary, Library of Virginia, Richmond.

5. Entries for August 20–21, 29, September 15, 1864, Byron Parsons Diary, LC; entry for September 16, 1864, Albee Diary, Library of Virginia, Richmond.

6. Entry for September 9, 1864, Albee Diary, Library of Virginia, Richmond; entry for September 15, 1864, Parsons Diary, LC.

7. Entry for September 6, 1864, Albee Diary, Library of Virginia, Richmond.

8. *Richmond Examiner,* June 27, July 1, 1864; entry for August 29, 1864, Thomas W. Springer Diary, UVA; *OR,* 7:870; entries for August 29, September 17, 1864, Patrick Henry Campbell Diary, RPL.

9. *OR,* 7:870–72.

10. Entry for September 3, 1864, Samuel McClain Diary, MS 640, Center for Archival Collections, Bowling Green State University, Bowling Green, OH; entries for September 10,

25, 30, 1864, Shelton Diary, Shelton Papers, 1861–1865, PM, NC; entry for September 29, 1864, Springer Diary, UVA.

11. Entries for August 24, 30, 1864, Ramsdell Diary, SHC, UNC; entries for August 25, September 19, 1864, Campbell Diary, RPL; entries for August 31, September 18, 1864, McClain Diary, Center for Archival Collections, Bowling Green State University, Bowling Green, OH; entries for September 16, 19, 20, 21, 22, 23, 24, 1864, Springer Diary, UVA; entry for September 15, 1864, Shelton Diary, Shelton Papers, 1861–1865, PM, NC; entry for August 30, 1864, James W. Eberhart Diary, in Florence C. McLaughlin, ed., "Diary of Sailsbury [*sic*] Prison by James W. Eberhart," *Western Pennsylvania Historical Magazine* 56 (July 1973): 220.

12. Entry for September 3, 1864, Shelton Diary, Shelton Papers, 1861–1865, PM, NC; entry for August 31, 1864, Ramsdell Diary, SHC, UNC; entries for August 28, September 4, 8, 1864, Springer Diary, UVA; entry for August 31, 1864, Eberhart Diary, in McLaughlin, "Diary of Eberhart," 220; entries for September 3, 8, 1864, Campbell Diary, RPL.

13. Entry for September 12, 1864, Ramsdell Diary, SHC, UNC; entries for September 11, October 16, 1864, Shelton Diary, Shelton Papers, 1861–1865, PM, NC.

14. *Richmond Sentinel,* August 27, 1864; *Richmond Whig,* August 27, 1864; entry for August 25, 1864, Campbell Diary, RPL; entry for August 26, 1864, Ramsdell Diary, SHC, UNC; entry for August 26, 1864, Eberhart Diary, in McLaughlin, "Diary of Eberhart," 217.

15. Entry for August 27, 1864, Ramsdell Diary, SHC, UNC; entry for August 27, 1864, Campbell Diary, RPL.

16. Entries for October 2, 3, 1864, Campbell Diary, RPL; entries for October 2, 3, 1864, Springer Diary, UVA; entries for October 2, 3, 1864, McClain Diary, Center for Archival Collections, Bowling Green State University, Bowling Green, OH; entries for October 3, 16, 1864, Shelton Diary, Shelton Papers, 1861–1865, PM, NC.

17. Entry for September 9, 1864, Eberhart Diary, in McLaughlin, "Diary of Eberhart," 223; entry for September 9, 1864, McClain Diary, Center for Archival Collections, Bowling Green State University, Bowling Green, OH; entry for September 9, 1864, Springer Diary, UVA.

18. Entries for September 28, 29, 1864, Eberhart Diary, in McLaughlin, "Diary of Eberhart," 225; entries for September 28–29, 1864, Shelton Diary, PM, NC; entry for September 29, 1864, Campbell Diary, RPL.

19. Entry for September 25, 1864, Shelton Diary, Shelton Papers, 1861–1865, PM, NC; Clarence Morfit to W. B. Gross, November 16, 1864, Letters Sent by Capt. C. Morfit, Assistant Quartermaster at Richmond, 1863–1865, RG 109, NA.

20. Entries for October 4–6, 1864, Shelton Diary, Shelton Papers, 1861–1865, PM, NC; entries for October 4–6, 1864, Springer Diary, UVA; entry for October 7, 1864, Campbell Diary, RPL; Parker, *Richmond's Civil War Prisons,* 65.

21. *OR,* 7:840.

22. Entry for October 5, 1864, Arthur Wyman Diary, CWMC, USAMHI; entry for October 21, 1864, Parsons Diary, LC; Samuel D. Foster to William Johnston, August 17, 1864, Samuel D. Foster Letter, MS 1990-01, Special Collections, Virginia Polytechnic Institute and State University Library, Blacksburg.

23. Entries for November 2, 3, 10, 20, 1864, Parsons Diary, LC; entries for November 20, December 30, 1864, Wyman Diary, CWMC, USAMHI.

24. Entries for October 9, December 1, 1864, Wyman Diary, CWMC, USAMHI; entry

for November 22, 1864, Parsons Diary, LC; Robertson, "Houses of Horror," 339–41; *OR,* series 1, 46, pt. 2: 1051.

25. *OR,* 7:926, 929, 1008–9, 1018, 1281, 8:71–73, 220–21; entry for February 11, 1865, John Beck Diary, courtesy of Clark Beck, Seattle, WA; entries for February 12, 16, 1865, Wyman Diary, CWMC, USAMHI.

26. (Salisbury, NC) *Carolina Watchman,* July 18, October 4, 1864.

27. Entry for October 7, 1864, McClain Diary, Center for Archival Collections, Bowling Green State University, Bowling Green, OH; entries for October 8, 9, 1864, Springer Diary, UVA; entry for October 9, 1864, Parsons Diary, LC.

28. Entry for October 10, 1864, McClain Diary, Center for Archival Collections, Bowling Green State University, Bowling Green, OH; entries for October 9, 11, 1864, Shelton Diary, Shelton Papers, 1861–1865, PM, NC; entry for October 19, 1864, Harvey Henderson Diary, SC1737, Manuscripts and Special Collections, New York State Library, Albany.

29. Entries for October 12, 16, 28, 1864, Campbell Diary, RPL; entries for October 16, 28, 1864, Springer Diary, UVA; entry for October 16, 1864, Eberhart Diary, in McLaughlin, "Diary of Eberhart," 230; entry for October 27, 1864, Shelton Diary, Shelton Papers, 1861–1865, PM, NC.

30. David Orlando McRaven to wife, October 29, 1864, in Brown, "Correspondence of McRavens," 57; Mangum to sister, November 8, 1864, Mangum Family Papers, SHC, UNC; B. White to family, November 15, 1864, B. White Letter, RPL.

31. Entry for October 24, 1864, Shelton Diary, Shelton Papers, 1861–1865, PM, NC; entry for October 26, 1864, Campbell Diary, RPL; entry for October 26, 1864, Henderson Diary, Manuscripts and Special Collections, New York State Library, Albany; entry for November 9, 1864, Oscar D. Morhaus Diary, RPL; entry for December 26, 1864, Francis A. Dawes Diary, *CWTI* Collection, USAMHI.

32. Brown, *Salisbury Prison,* 96–97.

33. Entry for November 24, 1864, Morhaus Diary, RPL; entry for November 10, 1864, Canon Diary, WHS; entry for November 6, 1864, Campbell Diary, RPL; entry for November 9, 1864, Shelton Diary, Shelton Papers, 1861–1865, PM, NC.

34. Entry for October 25, 1864, Shelton Diary, Shelton Papers, 1861–1865, PM, NC; entry for November 4, 1864, Springer Diary, UVA; entry for October 13, 1864, Campbell Diary, RPL.

35. Entries for October 9–12, 1864, Springer Diary, UVA; entries for October 9–11, 1864, Eberhart Diary, in McLaughlin, "Diary of Eberhart," 223–24; entries for November 9–11, December 2–6, 1864, Shelton Diary, Shelton Papers, 1861–1865, PM, NC; entries for November 12, December 2–4, 1864, Campbell Diary, RPL.

36. McRaven to wife, October 17, 1864, in Brown, "Correspondence of McRavens," 53; entry for October 16, 1864, Shelton Diary, Shelton Papers, 1861–1865, PM, NC; entry for November 26, 1864, Eberhart Diary, in McLaughlin, "Diary of Eberhart," 236; *OR,* 8:246; Brown, *Salisbury Prison,* 117.

37. Entry for October 6, 1864, Parsons Diary, LC; entries for October 14, 18, 1864, Springer Diary, UVA; entries for November 6, December 8, 1864, Eberhart Diary, in McLaughlin, "Diary of Eberhart," 233, 241; entry for November 25, 1864, Canon Diary, WHS; McRaven to wife, December 25, 1864, in Brown, "Correspondence of McRavens," 74.

38. *OR,* 8:254; entry for November 5, 1864, Springer Diary, UVA; entry for November 5,

1864, Eberhart Diary, in McLaughlin, "Diary of Eberhart," 233; entries for November 9, 23, December 6, 14, 1864, Shelton Diary, Shelton Papers, 1861–1865, PM, NC.

39. *OR,* 8:1163, 1230; entry for November 25, 1864, Springer Diary, UVA; entry for November 25, 1864, Eberhart Diary, in McLaughlin, "Diary of Eberhart," 236; entry for November 26, 1864, Shelton Diary, Shelton Papers, 1861–1865, PM, NC; entry for November 25, 1864, Henderson Diary, Manuscripts and Special Collections, New York State Library, Albany.

40. *OR,* 8:1230; R. C. Craven to wife, November 27, 1864, R. C. Craven Letter, RPL; (Salisbury, NC) *Carolina Watchman,* November 28, 1864.

41. Entry for October 16, 1864, Parsons Diary, LC; entries for October 16, 20, 1864, Campbell Diary, RPL; entries for October 16, 20, 1864, Shelton Diary, Shelton Papers, 1861–1865, PM, NC; entries for October 16, 20, 1864, Springer Diary, UVA.

42. Entries for November 22–23, 1864, Morhaus Diary, RPL; entry for November 23, 1864, Shelton Diary, Shelton Papers, 1861–1865, PM, NC; entry for November 14, 25, 1864, Springer Diary, UVA; entry for November 25, 1864, Henry H. Ladd Diary, RPL; entries for November 24, December 7, 1864, January 4, 1865, Canon Diary, WHS.

43. *OR,* 7:1219–21.

44. Ibid., 7:1169; Richard O. Currey to Isaiah H. White, December 22, 1864, Isaiah H. White Papers, DU.

45. Currey to White, December 22, 1864, White Papers, DU.

46. McRaven to wife, January 18, 22, February 3, 1865, in Brown, "Correspondence of McRavens," 81, 84, 87; N. Alexander to "Dear Sarah," January 4, 1865, N. Alexander Letter, RPL.

47. *OR,* 8:11–12.

48. Ibid., 8:167.

49. Ibid., 8:167–68.

50. Ibid., 8:245–49.

51. Ibid., 8:403, 411.

52. Ibid., 8:254.

53. Bryant, *Cahaba Prison and the* Sultana *Disaster,* 92–93.

54. Entries for November 5, 9, 12, 17, 1864, Henry Mahler Diary, SHSI.

55. Francis Everett Hall to family, October 11, 1864, March 18, 1865, Francis Everett Hall Papers, UM, BHL.

56. *OR,* 7:998–1001, 1088.

57. Ibid., 8:117–21; Bryant, *Cahaba Prison and the* Sultana *Disaster,* 101–6; Alonzo Van Vlack Reminiscences, Van Vlack Family Papers, UM, BHL.

58. *OR,* 8:118–21, 794–95, 951.

59. Van Vlack Reminiscences, John Leonard Myer Reminiscences, Van Vlack Family Papers UM, BHL; Daniel B. Walker to family, April 10, 1865, Daniel B. Walker Letters, FHS; Bryant, *Cahaba Prison and the* Sultana *Disaster,* 108–13.

60. *OR,* 7:1204.

61. Entries for November 23, 26, 27, 1864, Hart Diary, ANHS; entry for November 23, 1864, Umstead Diary, ANHS; entries for November 27, 30, 1864, Clarkson Diary, ANHS; Henry Sauer Reminiscences, Henry Sauer Papers, 1866, PM, NC.

62. Entries for November 30, December 3, 7, 1864, Hart Diary, ANHS; entries for No-

vember 30, December 3, 1864, Ames Diary, in Carlson, "Diary of Prison Life," 10; entries for November 30, December 1, 1864, Clarkson Diary, ANHS.

63. *OR*, 7:1204; entries for December 12, 13, 1864, Hart Diary, ANHS; entries for December 12, 14, 15, 1864, Umstead Diary, ANHS; entries for December 11, 13, 14, 1864, Clarkson Diary, ANHS.

64. Entries for December 15, 18, 1864, Hart Diary, ANHS; Sauer Reminiscences, Sauer Papers, 1866, PM, NC; entry for December 15, 1864, Umstead Diary, ANHS.

65. Beauregard to Cobb, December 17, 1864, Hardee to Cobb, December 22, 1864, box 69, folder 9, Cobb Papers, UGA; undated entry, ca. December 20, 1864, James Appleton Blackshear Diary, MARBL, Emory.

66. Entries for December 19–24, 1864, Ames Diary, in Carlson, "Diary of Prison Life," 11; entries for December 19–24, 1864, Umstead Diary, ANHS; entries for December 19–25, Clarkson Diary, ANHS; Sauer Reminiscences, Sauer Papers, 1866, PM, NC.

67. Marvel, *Andersonville,* 228–29; entries for December 25, 26, 1864, Umstead Diary, ANHS; entry for December 25, 1864, Clarkson Diary, ANHS; entries for December 26, 31, 1864, George M. Shearer Diary, ANHS; entries for December 25, 31, 1864, Knight Diary, Manuscripts Division, J. Willard Marriott Library, University of Utah, Salt Lake City.

68. Entries for January 8, 24, February 6, 1865, Umstead Diary, ANHS; entries for January 14, 19, 24, 1865, Shearer Diary, ANHS; entry for January 26, 1865, John C. Ely Diary, John C. Ely Papers, VFM 408, OHS; entries for December 26, 29, 1864, January 2, 15, 26, 1865, Clarkson Diary, ANHS.

69. Entries for February 8, 13, 1865, Shearer Diary, ANHS; entries for February 8, 13, 1865, Ames Diary, in Carlson, "Diary of Prison Life," 14, 15; entries for February 9, 13, 1865, Ely Diary, Ely Papers, OHS; entry for February 13, 1865, Clarkson Diary, ANHS; entry for February 13, 1865, Duff Diary, ANHS.

70. Entry for March 8, 1865, Ely Diary, Ely Papers, OHS; entry for March 8, 1865, Ames Diary, in Carlson, "Diary of Prison Life," 16; entry for March 8, 1865, Clarkson Diary, ANHS.

Chapter 14

1. Blakely, *General John H. Winder,* 4–5.

2. Entry for February 9, 1865, Heffelfinger Diary, *CWTI* Collection, USAMHI; entry for February 8, 1865, Keeler Diary, Keeler Family Papers, UM, BHL; entry for February 8, 1865, Albert Heffley Diary, in Boyer, *Civil War Diary,* 89.

3. *OR*, 7:1229, 8:135.

4. Ibid., 8:49–50.

5. Ibid., 7:1304, 96.

6. Ibid., 7:793, 818, 1090.

7. Entries for November 26–27, 1864, Hutchins Diary, UM, WLCL; entry for November 26, 1864, Hegeman Diary, in Heslin, "Diary of a Union Soldier," 276; entry for November 27, 1864, Grosvenor Diary, CHS; entries for November 27–28, 1864, Gibson Diary, LC.

8. Entry for November 28, 1864, Hinkley Diary, WHS; entry for December 3, 1864, Hutchins Diary, UM, WLCL; entry for December 5, 1864, Seeley Diary, HSP; entry for De-

cember 8, 1864, Bradd Diary, SHSI; entry for December 14, 1864, Hegeman Diary, in Heslin, "Diary of a Union Soldier," 277; entries for December 8, 11, 12, 1864, Grosvenor Diary, CHS.

9. Entries for December 16, 18, 1864, Hegeman Diary, in Heslin, "Diary of a Union Soldier," 178; entries for December 11–14, 1864, Bradd Diary, SHSI; entries for December 10–14, 1864, Stone Diary, ANHS.

10. Entry for December 18, 1864, Bradd Diary, SHSI; entry for December 17, 1864, Stone Diary, ANHS; entry for December 21, 1864, Gibson Diary, LC.

11. Entries for November 15, 18, 24, December 1, 2, 1864, George W. Hichborn Diary, UVA; entries for November 21, 22, 25, 26, 27, 1864, Hodgkins Diary, in Turino, *Diary of Hodgkins,* 109–11.

12. Entry for December 6, 1864, Kay Diary, UM, BHL; entries for November 15, 16, 20, 22, 1864, Charles Ross Diary, in C. M. Destler, ed., "A Vermonter in Andersonville: Diary of Charles Ross, 1864," *Vermont History* 25 (July 1957): 244–45.

13. *OR,* 8:170, 206, 238.

14. Entries for February 15–20, 1865, Beck Diary, courtesy of Clark Beck, Seattle, WA; entries for February 16–20, 1865, Parsons Diary, LC; entries for February 17–19, 1865, Wyman Diary, CWMC, USAMHI; entries for February 16–18, 1865, Mattocks Diary, in Racine, "*Unspoiled Heart,*" 258–59.

15. *OR,* 8:276, 285–89.

16. Entries for February 17–March 1, 1865, Wood Diary, ANHS; entries for February 18–March 3, 1865, Yeakle Diary, ANHS.

17. Entry for February 22, 1865, Henderson Diary, Manuscripts and Special Collections, New York State Library, Albany; Elbert L. Sherill to Amanda McRaven, February 22, 1865, in Brown, "Correspondence of McRavens," 92.

18. Entries for February 22–26, 1865, Henderson Diary, Manuscripts and Special Collections, New York State Library, Albany; entries for February 22–26, 1865, Dawes Diary, *CWTI* Collection, USAMHI; entries for February 22–26, 1865, Canon Diary, WHS; entries for February 22–26, 1865, Shelton Diary, Shelton Papers, 1861–1865, PM, NC; David McRaven to wife, February 26, 1865, in Brown, "Correspondence of McRavens," 93.

19. *OR,* 8:450.

20. Entries for February 26–March 10, 1865, Canon Diary, WHS; entries for February 26–March 2, 1865, Henderson Diary, Manuscripts and Special Collections, New York State Library, Albany; entries for February 26–March 8, 1865, Dawes Diary, *CWTI* Collection, USAMHI; entries for February 26–March 9, 1865, Shelton Diary, Shelton Papers, 1861–1865, PM, NC.

21. *OR,* 8:210; entry for February 15, 1865, Albert Heffley Diary, in Boyer, *Civil War Diaries,* 89.

22. *OR,* 8:224, 234, 450, 454; entry for February 17, 1865, Keeler Diary, Keeler Family Papers, UM, BHL; entry for February 18, 1865, Hurst Diary, PSA.

23. Entries for February 20–March 7, 1865, Keeler Diary, Keeler Family Papers, UM, BHL; entries for February 20–March 5, 1865, Heffelfinger Diary, *CWTI* Collection, USAMHI.

24. Headquarters, Camp Parole, General Orders 16, March 10, 1865, Camp Parole, Near Annapolis, General Orders and Special Orders, RG 393, NA; *OR,* 8:435–36.

25. Entry for March 18, 1865, Umstead Diary, ANHS; entry for March 18, 1865, Ely Diary, Ely Papers, OHS; entry for March 18, 1865, Duff Diary, ANHS.

26. Entries for March 22, 27, 1865, Ames Diary, in Carlson, "Diary of Prison Life," 17; entries for March 23, 25, 26, 1865, Umstead Diary, ANHS; entries for March 22–23, 1865, Whitten Diary, LC; entries for March 22, 24, 1865, Ely Diary, Ely Papers, OHS.

27. Entry for March 25, 1864, Ely Diary, Ely Papers, OHS; entries for March 25–27, 1865, Umstead Diary, ANHS; entries for March 25–27, April 3–5, 1865, Knight Diary, Manuscripts Division, J. Willard Marriott Library, University of Utah, Salt Lake City; *OR,* 8:492–93.

28. *OR,* 8:284–85, 404–5; Bryant, *Cahaba Prison and the* Sultana *Disaster,* 111–13.

29. D. A. Johnston to Abbey E. Stafford, April 9, 1865, Abbey E. Stafford Letters, DU.

30. Entries for April 1, 9, 1865, Ely Diary, Ely Papers, OHS; entry for April 1, 2, 1865, Clarkson Diary, ANHS.

31. Entries for April 6, 16, 1865, Clarkson Diary, ANHS; entries for April 13, 18, 1865, Ely Diary, Ely Papers, OHS.

32. Entry for April 24, 1864, Clarkson Diary, ANHS.

33. Bryant, *Cahaba Prison and the* Sultana *Disaster,* 118–19, 128; entry for April 25, 1965, Clarkson Diary, ANHS.

34. Adam Russell Memoirs, WHS; Van Vlack Reminiscences, Van Vlack Family Papers, UM, BHL.

35. Entries for April 27–May 21, 1865, Clarkson Diary, ANHS.

36. *OR,* series 1, 48, pt. 1: 217; Bryant, *Cahaba Prison and the* Sultana *Disaster,* 137.

37. *OR,* 8:427, 436, 445.

38. Entries for April 4–8, 1865, Duff Diary, ANHS; entries for April 4–8, 1865, Whitten Diary, LC; *OR,* 8:465.

39. Entries for April 13, 17–19, 1865, Whitten Diary, LC; entries for April 13, 23, 1865, Duff Diary, ANHS; entries for April 11, 17–20, 1865, Knight Diary, Manuscripts Division, J. Willard Marriott Library, University of Utah, Salt Lake City; entries for April 11–13, 20–22, 1865, Ames Diary, in Carlson, "Diary of Prison Life," 18–19.

40. Entries for April 23–28, May 11–12, 1865, Duff Diary, ANHS; entries for April 24–28, 1865, Whitten Diary, LC; entries for April 25–29, May 29, 1865, Knight Diary, Manuscripts Division, J. Willard Marriott Library, University of Utah, Salt Lake City; entries for April 24–28, 1865, Ames Diary, in Carlson, "Diary of Prison Life," 19.

41. Entries for March 18, 19, 1865, Arthur E. Gilligan Diary, Briscoe Center for American History, University of Texas at Austin.

42. Entries for March 30, April 6, 11–15, 1865, Gilligan Diary, Briscoe Center for American History, University of Texas at Austin.

43. Entries for April 19, 23, May 13–15, 1865, Gilligan Diary, Briscoe Center for American History, University of Texas at Austin.

44. *OR,* 8:531; entries for May 17, 18, 1865, Gilligan Diary, Briscoe Center for American History, University of Texas at Austin.

45. Entries for May 23, 25, 28, June 9–August 1, 1865, Gilligan Diary, Briscoe Center for American History, University of Texas at Austin.

46. Futch, *History of Andersonville Prison,* 117–20; Patricia L. Faust, ed., *Historical Times Il-*

lustrated Encyclopedia of the Civil War (New York: Harper & Row, 1986), 837; Marvel, *Andersonville,* 243–47; *OR,* 8:785.

47. *OR,* 8:956–960.

48. Parker, *Richmond's Civil War Prisons,* 68; Samuel H. Root to wife, May 14, 1865, Samuel H. Root Letter, USAMHI; *OR,* 8:912.

49. Blakely, *General John H. Winder,* 202–3; *OR,* 8:819, 887–88.

Bibliography

Manuscript Sources

Abraham Lincoln Presidential Library, Springfield, IL
- James Buckley Diary
- William Culbertson Robinson Diary
- Nathan B. Webb Diary

Alabama Department of Archives and History, Montgomery
- Isaac Morgan Civil War Letter

Andersonville National Historic Site, Andersonville, GA
- John A. Baer Diary
- George Clarkson Diary
- Alonzo Tuttle Decker Diary
- Michael Dougherty Diary
- John Duff Diary
- Joseph B. Felton Diary
- Samuel L. Foust Diary
- Chester Townsend Hart Diary
- William T. Peabody Diary
- George M. Shearer Diary
- Henry H. Stone Diary
- Henry W. Tisdale Diary
- M. J. Umstead Diary
- Levi Whitaker Diary
- Oscar C. Wood Diary
- Amos Yeakle Diary

Boston Public Library, Rare Book Department
- William A. Noel Diary

Bowling Green State University, Bowling Green, OH, Center for Archival Collections
Samuel McClain Diary
Bradley University Library, Peoria, IL, Peoria Historical Society Collection
Edmund E. Ryan Diary
Central Michigan University, Mt. Pleasant, Clarke Historical Library
Sheldon Curtiss Diary
Thomas S. Montgomery Memoir
William D. Wilkins Diary
Chicago Historical Society
William Henry Powell Diary
Connecticut Historical Society, Hartford
Anonymous Diary (Eighteenth Connecticut Infantry)
Churchill-Woodford Family Papers
Hiram Eddy Papers
Samuel E. Grosvenor Diary
Robert Hale Kellogg Diary
Nehemiah Solon Diary
Henry G. Tracy Diary
Cornell University Library, Ithaca, NY, Division of Rare Books and Manuscript Collections
John S. Crocker Letters, in Frank S. Brockett Collection
Dartmouth College Library, Hanover, NH, Special Collections
Moses T. Anderson Diary
Delaware Public Archives, Dover
Bell Collection
Duke University, Durham, NC, Rare Book, Manuscript, and Special Collections Library
Frank T. Bennett Diary
Patience Everett Papers
George W. Grant Diary
Samuel Henderson Diary
George W. Kenney Papers
Abbey E. Stafford Letters
Isaiah H. White Papers
Eastern Washington University Library, Cheney, WA, Archives and Special Collections Department
Thomas L. Evans Papers
Emory University, Atlanta, Manuscript, Archives, and Rare Book Library
James Appleton Blackshear Diary
James Burton Diary
James Chesnut Letterbook, 1864–1865
John L. Hoster Diary
Filson Historical Society, Louisville, KY
George F. Gill Diary
Daniel B. Walker Letters

Gettysburg College, Gettysburg, PA, Musselman Library
Henry N. Bemis Diary
Historical Society of Pennsylvania, Philadelphia
William Seeley Diary
James E. Wenrick Diary
Kansas State Historical Society, Topeka
John Melvin Converse Diary
Library of Congress, Washington, DC
Breckrinridge-Long Papers
William M. Collin Diary
S. J. Gibson Diary
James Jenkins Gillette Papers
Bernard John Dowling Irwin Papers
Byron Parsons Diary
Revere Family Papers
John Whitten Diary
William D. Wilkins Diary
Library of Virginia, Richmond
George E. Albee Diary
William H. Harrison Letter
William S. Tippett Diary
Massachusetts Historical Society, Boston
John B. Gallison Diary
Higginson Family Papers
James M. Sampson Diary
Minnesota Historical Society Library, St. Paul
Ransom Chadwick Diary
David Kennedy Diary
James Woodbury Diary
Missouri Historical Society, St. Louis
William H. Haun Diary
James Edwin Love Papers
Madison Miller Diary
Elias Perry Letter
National Archives and Records Administration, Washington, DC
Record Group 109, War Department Collection of Confederate Records
Andersonville Prison, Georgia, Letters Sent, May 1864–March 1865
Letters and Orders Issued, Military Prison at Richmond, January 1862–December 1863
Letters Sent by Capt. C. Morfit, Assistant Quartermaster at Richmond, 1863–1865
Papers relating to Confederate Prison Camps and Other Places Where Federal Prisoners Were Confined during the Period 1861–1865
Schedule of Papers in the Archive Office Referring to the Exchange and Treatment of Prisoners in Southern Prisons

Record Group 249, Records of the Office of the Commissary General of Prisoners
Benton Barracks, St. Louis, Missouri, Abstracts and Copies of Orders, Letters, and Telegrams relating to Paroled and Exchanged Federal Prisoners of War
Camp Parole, Maryland, Letters and Telegrams Sent
Records of the Commissary General of Prisoners, Letters and Telegrams Sent
United States Paroled Forces, Columbus, Ohio, Correspondence relating to Imprisoned, Paroled, and Disabled Union Veterans
United States Paroled Forces, Columbus, Ohio, Journal of Costs of Arrest and Transportation of Paroled Federal Prisoners of War Who Failed to Return from Furloughs
Record Group 393, Part IV, Records of the United States Army, Continental Commands
Benton Barracks, St. Louis, Missouri, Headquarters, Paroled Men, General and Special Orders Issued and Received
Camp Banks, Alexandria, Virginia, Letters Received
Camp Banks, Alexandria, Virginia, Orders Issued
Camp Chase, Ohio, General Orders
Camp Lew Wallace, Columbus, Ohio, General and Special Orders Issued and Received
Camp Parole, Near Annapolis, General Orders and Special Orders
Headquarters, United States Paroled Forces, Columbus, Ohio, Letters Sent
United States Paroled Forces, Columbus, Ohio, General and Special Orders Issued and Received

Navarro College, Corsicana, TX, Pearce Museum
John A. Boudwin Papers, 1863–1864
Edwin T. Marsh Papers, 1863–1917
Thomas and Wilson N. Paxton Letters, 1861–1863
Henry Sauer Papers, 1866
Fred T. Shelton Papers, 1861–1865

New York Historical Society, New York
Simon Hulbert Diary

New York State Library, Albany, Manuscripts and Special Collections
Calvin A. Haynes Letters
Harvey Henderson Diary

Ohio Historical Society, Columbus
John C. Ely Diary, John C. Ely Papers
Nelson Purdum Diary
James W. Vance Papers
William T. Wilson Diary

Pennsylvania State Archives, Harrisburg
Templeton B. Hurst Diary
John A. Porter Diary

Rowan Public Library, Salisbury, NC
N. Alexander Letter
Patrick Henry Campbell Diary
R. C. Craven Letter
Henry H. Ladd Diary

Oscar D. Morhaus Diary
B. White Letter
South Carolina Historical Society, Charleston
Charles Kline Civil War Letters
Manigault Family Record
Ravenel Family Papers
Young Family Papers
State Archives of Florida, Tallahassee
John Pond Diary
State Historical Society of Iowa, Iowa City
James Bradd Diary
Charles Whipple Hadley Diary
Henry Mahler Diary
United States Army Military History Institute, Carlisle Barracks, PA
Civil War Miscellaneous Collection
Charles Wesley Belknap Diary
Jonathan Boynton Memoirs
Budd Walcer Letters
Arthur Wyman Diary
Civil War Times Illustrated Collection
Francis A. Dawes Diary
Nicholas De Graff Diary
Samuel Fulton Reminiscences
Charles Gardner Reminiscences
Joseph Heffelfinger Diary
George C. Parker Letters
Samuel H. Root Letter
Jonathan P. Stowe Diary
Benjamin Thompson Reminiscences
Harrisburg Civil War Roundtable Collection
Aaron E. Bachman Memoirs
Samuel M. Jackson Diary
University of Alabama, Tuscaloosa, W. S. Hoole Special Collections Library
Nathaniel Kenyon Diary
University of Georgia, Athens, Hargrett Library
Howell Cobb Papers
Cobb-Erwin-Lamar Papers
Williams Family Papers
University of Michigan, Ann Arbor
Bentley Historical Library
Francis Everett Hall Papers
John B. Kay Diary
Keeler Family Papers
Hiram F. Penland Diary

Jerome J. Robbins Diary
Ryder Family Papers
Schmalsriedt Family Papers
De Witt Spaulding Diary
Charles Van Riper Diary
Van Vlack Family Papers
William L. Clements Library, James S. Schoff Collection
William L. Aughinbaugh Diary
William L. Curry Letters and Journals
Daniel Hutchins Diary
Ziba Roberts Diary
Willard W. Wheeler Diary
University of Missouri, Columbia, Western Historical Manuscript Collection
Bergun H. Brown Papers, 1861–1872
University of North Carolina Library, Chapel Hill, Southern Historical Collection
Edward C. Anderson Diary
Louis R. Fortescue Diary
Charles Carroll Gray Diary
James Addison Lowry Letters
Mangum Family Papers
Julius Frederic Ramsdell Diary
Ira Russell Papers
Ira B. Sampson Diary
University of Texas at Austin, Briscoe Center for American History
Arthur E. Gilligan Diary
University of Texas at San Antonio Libraries, Special Collections
Anonymous Diary, R. H. Porter Civil War Collection
University of Utah, Salt Lake City, Manuscripts Division, J. Willard Marriott Library
Charles A. Knight Diary
University of Vermont Libraries, Burlington, Special Collections
Charles Blinn Diary
Bradford Sparrow Diary
Charles B. Stone Diary
University of Virginia Library, Charlottesville, Special Collections
George W. Hichborn Diary
Francis Trowbridge Sherman Diary
William Smith Diary
Thomas W. Springer Diary
Vermont Historical Society, Barre
Valentine G. Barney Letters
Daniel F. Colledge Diary
George R. Crosby Diary
Kendrick R. Howard Diary

Asa D. Mathews Diary
Edmund Pope Diary
Henry A. Smith Letters
Virginia Historical Society, Richmond
Morton Tower Memoirs
Virginia Polytechnic Institute and State University Library, Blacksburg, Special Collections
Samuel D. Foster Letter
Wisconsin Historical Society, Madison
Newell Burch Diary
Alfred D. Burdick Diary
James Canon Diary
Willis Peck Clarke Papers
Willard W. Felton Diary
Charles D. Grannis Reminiscences
George M. Hinkley Diary
John Edwin Holmes Diary
Elisha Rice Reed Diary
Nathaniel Rollins Diary
Adam Russell Memoirs
Horace Smith Diary
Henry Clay Taylor Papers
Jackson Thompson Diary
William L. Tritt Diary
Wisconsin Veterans Museum, Madison
Levi Minkler Diary
John Ogden Reminiscences
Yale University, New Haven, CT, Beinecke Rare Book and Manuscript Library
Francis Wilbur Goodyear Diary

Newspapers

(Salisbury, NC) *Carolina Watchman*
Charleston Courier
Charleston Mercury
Macon Telegraph
New York Herald
New York Times
Richmond Dispatch
Richmond Enquirer
Richmond Examiner
Richmond Sentinel
Richmond Whig
(Americus, GA) *Sumter Republican*

Published Primary Sources

Allison, Don, ed. *Hell on Belle Isle: Diary of a Civil War POW.* Bryan, OH: Faded Banner, 1997.

Armstrong, William M., ed. "Libby Prison: The Civil War Diary of Arthur G. Sedgwick." *Virginia Magazine of History and Biography* 71 (October 1963).

Bartlett, Louis, ed. "Captain T. W. Rathbone's 'Brief Diary of Imprisonment,' July 1–November 21, 1864." *Ohio History* 71 (January 1962).

Boaz, Thomas M., ed. *Libby Prison and Beyond: A Union Staff Officer in the East, 1862–1865.* Shippensburg, PA: Burd Street, 1999.

Boyer, Earl E., ed. *Civil War Diaries of Capt. Albert Heffley and Lt. Cyrus P. Heffley.* Apollo, PA: Clossen, 2000.

Breedon, James O. "Andersonville—A Southern Surgeon's Story." *Bulletin of the History of Medicine* 47, no. 4 (1973).

Brown, Louis A., ed. "The Correspondence of David Orlando McRaven and Amanda Nantz McRaven, 1864–1865." *North Carolina Historical Review* 26 (January 1949).

Carlson, Dorothy, ed. "A Diary of Prison Life in Southern Prisons." *Annals of Iowa* 40 (Summer 1969).

Coulter, E. Merton, ed. "From Spotsylvania Courthouse to Andersonville: A Diary of Darius Starr." *Georgia Historical Quarterly* 41 (June 1957).

Crisfield, C. M., ed. *William Dolphin's Civil War Diary, August 15, 1863 through April 14, 1864.* Ossining, NY: Ossining Historical Society, 1991.

Cryder, George R., and Stanley R. Miller, eds. *A View from the Ranks: The Civil War Diaries of Corporal Charles E. Smith.* Delaware, OH: Delaware County Historical Society, 1999.

Danker, Donald F., ed. "Imprisoned at Andersonville: The Diary of Albert Harry Shatzel, May 5, 1864–September 12, 1864." *Nebraska History* 38 (June 1957).

Davis, Roger, ed. "The Camp Ford Diary of J. B. Leake." *Chronicles of Smith County, Texas* 42 (2003).

Destler, C. M., ed. "A Vermonter in Andersonville: Diary of Charles Ross, 1864." *Vermont History* 25 (July 1957).

Downes, Ralph C., ed. "The Civil War Diary of Fernando E. Pomeroy." *Northwest Ohio Quarterly* 19 (July 1947).

Futch, Ovid, ed. "The Andersonville Diary of Sergeant J. M. Burdick." *Georgia Historical Quarterly* 45 (September 1961).

Hansen, Ann N., ed. "A Southern Odyssey: The Narrative of Abram Price." *Timeline* 6 (October–November 1989).

Harris, William C. *Prison-Life in the Tobacco Warehouse at Richmond. By a Ball's Bluff Prisoner.* Philadelphia: George W. Childs, 1862.

Helmreich, Paul C., ed. "The Diary of Charles G. Lee in Andersonville and Florence Prison Camps, 1864." *Connecticut Historical Society Bulletin* 41 (January 1976).

Heslin, James J., ed. "The Diary of a Union Soldier in Confederate Prisons." *New York Historical Society Quarterly* 41 (July 1957).

Jeffrey, William H. *Richmond Prisons, 1861–1862, Compiled from the Original Records Kept by the Confederate Government; Journals Kept by Union Prisoners of War, Together with the*

Name, Rank, Company, Regiment, and State of the Four Thousand Who Were Confined There. St. Johnsbury, VT: *Republican* Press, 1895.

Jennings, Warren A., ed. "Prisoner of the Confederacy: Diary of a Union Artilleryman." *West Virginia History* 36 (July 1975).

Marchman, Watt P., ed. "The Journal of Sgt. Wm. J. McKell." *Civil War History* 3 (September 1957).

McLaughlin, Florence C., ed. "Diary of Sailsbury [*sic*] Prison by James W. Eberhart." *Western Pennsylvania Historical Magazine* 56 (July 1973).

Moran, Frank E. "Colonel Rose's Tunnel at Libby Prison." *Century Magazine,* March 1888.

Niccum, Norman, ed. "Diary of Lieutenant Frank Hughes." *Indiana Magazine of History* 45 (September 1949).

Penfield, James A. *The 1863–1864 Diary of Captain James Penfield, 5th New York Volunteer Cavalry, Company H.* Ticondergoa, NY: Press of America, 1999.

Pollan, Howard O., ed. "The Camp Ford Diary of Captain William Fortunatus McKinney." *Chronicles of Smith County, Texas* 25 (Summer 1996).

Racine, Philip N., ed. "*Unspoiled Heart": The Journal of Charles Mattocks of the 17th Maine.* Knoxville: University of Tennessee Press, 1994.

Roe, Alfred S., ed. *The Melvin Memorial.* Cambridge, MA: Riverside, 1910.

Turino, Kenneth C., ed. *The Civil War Diary of Lieut. J. E. Hodgkins, 19th Massachusetts Volunteers, from August 11, 1862 to June 3, 1865.* Camden, ME: Picton, 1994.

Tusken, Roger, ed. "In the Bastile of the Rebels." *Journal of the Illinois State Historical Society* 56 (Summer 1963).

U.S. War Department. *The War of the Rebellion: A Compilation of the Official Records of the Union and Confederate Armies.* 128 vols. Washington, DC: Government Printing Office, 1880–1901.

Wallace, Lew. *Lew Wallace: An Autobiography.* 2 vols. New York: Harper & Brothers, 1906.

Wiley, Bell Irvin, ed. *Fourteen Hundred and 91 Days in the Confederate Army.* Wilmington, NC: Broadfoot, 1987.

Wilkeson, Frank. *Turned Inside Out: Recollections of a Private Soldier in the Army of the Potomac.* 1887. Reprint, Lincoln: University of Nebraska Press, 1997.

Secondary Sources

Bailey, Anne J. "A Texas Cavalry Raid: Reaction to Black Soldiers and Contrabands." *Civil War History* 35, no. 2 (1989).

Berry, Stephen, *House of Abraham: Lincoln and the Todds, a Family Divided by War.* Boston: Houghton Mifflin, 2007.

Blakely, Arch Frederic. *General John H. Winder, C.S.A.* Gainesville: University of Florida Press, 1990.

Bridges, Hal. *Lee's Maverick General: Daniel Harvey Hill.* New York: McGraw Hill, 1961.

Brown, Louis. *The Salisbury Prison: A Case Study of Confederate Military Prisons, 1861–1865.* Wendell, NC: Avera, 1980.

Bryant, William O. *Cahaba Prison and the* Sultana *Disaster.* Tuscaloosa: University of Alabama Press, 1990.

Byrne, Frank L., ed. "A General Behind Bars: Neal Dow in Libby Prison." In *Civil War Prisons,* edited by William B. Hesseltine. Kent, OH: Kent State University Press, 1962.

———. "Libby Prison: A Study in Emotions." *Journal of Southern History* 24, no. 4 (1958).

Cornish, Dudley Taylor. *The Sable Arm: Black Troops in the Union Army, 1861–1865.* Lawrence: University Press of Kansas, 1956.

Faust, Patricia L., ed. *Historical Times Illustrated Encyclopedia of the Civil War.* New York: Harper & Row, 1986.

Furgurson, Ernest B. *Ashes of Glory: Richmond at War.* New York: Alfred A. Knopf, 1996.

Futch, Ovid. *History of Andrsonville Prison.* Gainesville: University of Florida Press, 1968.

Hesseltine, William Best. *Civil War Prisons: A Study in War Psychology.* 1930. Reprint, Columbus: Ohio State University Press, 1998.

Klemm, Amy L. "A Shared Captivity: Inmates and Guards in the Texas Military Prison System, 1863–1865." MA thesis, University of Houston, 1997.

Levy, George. *To Die in Chicago: Confederate Prisoners at Camp Douglas, 1862–65.* Gretna, LA: Pelican, 1999.

Marvel, William. *Andersonville: The Last Depot.* Chapel Hill: University of North Carolina Press, 1994.

McPherson, James M. *The Negro's Civil War: How American Negroes Felt and Acted during the War for Union.* Urbana: University of Illinois Press, 1965.

Mitchell, Leon, Jr. "Camp Ford Confederate Military Prison." *Southwestern Historical Quarterly* 66 (July 1962).

———. "Prisoners of War in the Confederate Trans-Mississippi." MA thesis, University of Texas, 1961.

Paludan, Philip Shaw. *The Presidency of Abraham Lincoln.* Lawrence: University Press of Kansas, 1994.

Parker, Sandra V. *Richmond's Civil War Prisons.* Lynchburg, VA: H. E. Howard, 1990.

Pickenpaugh, Roger. *Camp Chase and the Evolution of Union Prison Policy.* Tuscaloosa: University of Alabama Press, 2007.

———. *Captives in Gray: The Civil War Prisons of the Union.* Tuscaloosa: University of Alabama Press, 2009.

Robertson, James I., Jr. "Houses of Horror: Danville's Civil War Prisons." *Virginia Magazine of History and Biography* 69 (July 1961).

Sanders, Charles W., Jr. *While in the Hands of the Enemy: Military Prisons of the Civil War.* Baton Rouge: Louisiana State University Press, 2005.

Speer, Lonnie. *Portals to Hell: Military Prisons of the Civil War.* Mechanicsburg, PA: Stackpole Books, 1997.

Thomas, Emory M. *The Confederate Nation: 1861–1865.* New York: Harper Colophon, 1979.

Thomas, Eugene Marvin, III. "Prisoner of War Exchange during the American Civil War." PhD diss., Auburn University, 1976.

Urwin, Gregory J. "'We Cannot Treat Negroes as Prisoners of War': Racial Atrocities and Reprisals in Civil War Arkansas." *Civil War History* 42, no. 3 (1996).

Westwood, Howard C. "Captive Black Union Soldiers in Charleston—What to Do?" *Civil War History* 28, no. 1 (1982).

Wiley, Bell Irvin. *The Life of Johnny Reb: The Common Soldier of the Confederacy.* Baton Rouge: Louisiana State University Press, 1987.

Index